# DATE DUE

| | | | |
|---|---|---|---|
| | | | |
| | | | |
| | | | |
| | | | |
| | | | |
| | | | |
| | | | |
| | | | |
| | | | |
| | | | |
| | | | |
| | | | |
| | | | |
| | | | |
| | | | |
| | | | |
| | | | |
| | | | |

DEMCO 38-296

# A HISTORY OF LAOS

# A HISTORY OF
# LAOS

## MARTIN STUART-FOX
*University of Queensland*

**CAMBRIDGE**
UNIVERSITY PRESS

ATE OF THE UNIVERSITY OF CAMBRIDGE
The Pitt Building, Trumpington Street, Cambridge CB2 1RP, United Kingdom

CAMBRIDGE UNIVERSITY PRESS
The Edinburgh Building, Cambridge CB2 2RU, United Kingdom
40 West 20th Street, New York, NY 10011–4211, USA
10 Stamford Road, Oakleigh, Melbourne 3166, Australia

First published 1997

Printed in Singapore by SNP Offset

Typeset in Palatino 9/11 pt

*National Library of Australia Cataloguing in Publication data*

Stuart-Fox, Martin, 1939– .
A history of Laos.
Bibliography.
Includes index.
ISBN 0 521 59746 3 (pbk.).
ISBN 0 521 59235 6.
1. Laos – History. 2. Laos – Politics and government.
I. Title.
959.4

*Library of Congress Cataloguing in Publication data*

Stuart-Fox, Martin, 1939–
A history of Laos / Martin Stuart-Fox.
p.    cm.
Includes bibliographical references and index.
ISBN 0-521-59235-6 (alk. paper). – ISBN 0-521-59746-3 (alk. paper)
1. Laos – History. I. Title.
DS555.5.S79  1997
959.4–dc21                                                                97–12091

*A catalogue record for this book is available from the British Library*

ISBN 0 521 59235 6 hardback
ISBN 0 521 59746 3 paperback

*For my parents-in-law*
*Maurice and Rose Cavalerie*
*former proprietors of the*
*Hotel Constellation, Viang Chan*

# CONTENTS

*List of Maps*                                   viii
*Acknowledgements*                                ix
*Chronology*                                       x
*Abbreviations*                                   xiv

  Introduction                                     1
1  The Kingdom of Lān Xāng                         6
2  French Laos, 1893–1945                         20
3  Independence and Unity, 1945–1957              59
4  Neutrality Subverted, 1958–1964               99
5  War and Revolution, 1964–1975                135
6  The Lao People's Democratic Republic          168

*Notes*                                          209
*Select Bibliography*                            232
*Index*                                          245

# MAPS

1  Lao People's Democratic Republic                                    xv
2  Mainland Southeast Asia: mid-16th to early 19th centuries           17
3  French Laos: road and rail links                                    48
4  Laos in the Second Indochina War                                   137

# ACKNOWLEDGEMENTS

Over the years of living in, visiting, and writing about Laos I have received friendship and assistance from many people. Many Lao officials have granted me formal interviews, and many more have talked to me about their country. Even now it is best that some remain anonymous. Among those I would particularly like to thank are Mayoury and Pheuiphanh Ngaosyvathn, Souneth Phothisane, Viliam Phraxayavong, Gar Yia (Gary) Lee, Somphou and Sourisane Oudomvilay, Nouansy Keohavong, Khamsing Khammanivong, Khamphuang and Khetsamouth Bouahom, and the late Claude Vincent, whose untimely death in the country he loved is deeply felt by his family and friends. Sīxana Sīsān and the late Phūmī Vongvichit gave me of their time and expressed interest in my work. My good friend Rod Bucknell advised me on transcription.

Anyone attempting to write a general history of a country is greatly in debt to previous scholars. While the historiography of Laos remains, like the country, underdeveloped, much important research has been, and continues to be, done in France, in the United States, in Australia, and not least in Laos itself. It would be impossible to acknowledge my intellectual debt to all from whom I have learnt much in my studies of Laos. But apart from Lao friends mentioned above, I would particularly like to thank McAlister Brown, David Chandler, Jean Deuve, Arthur Dommen, Amphay Doré, Grant Evans, Bernard Gay, Geoff Gunn, Pierre-Bernard Lafont, Ng Shui Meng, Christian Taillard, Bill Vistarini, and Joe Zasloff.

Of those responsible for bringing my sprawling manuscript to the stage of publication, I owe a debt of gratitude to commissioning editor Phillipa McGuinness and my copy editor Janet Mackenzie at Cambridge University Press for their interest and support. Adnan Moussalli kindly produced the maps, while Serena Bagley prepared the final manuscript. Finally, my heartfelt thanks to my wife, Elisabeth, who may at times have wondered if this project would ever see publication, but who always gave me her love and encouragement.

# CHRONOLOGY

| | |
|---|---|
| 1353 | Foundation by Fā Ngum of the Lao kingdom of Lān Xāng. |
| 1479 | Vietnamese invasion of Lān Xāng. |
| 1548 | Xētthāthirāt briefly unifies kingdoms of Lān Xāng and Lān Nā. |
| 1560 | Capital moved from Luang Phrabāng to Viang Chan. |
| 1563–75 | Series of Burmese invasions of Lān Xāng. |
| 1638–95 | Reign of Surinyavongsā. |
| 1641–42 | First Europeans to leave records arrive in Viang Chan. |
| 1707, 1713 | Division of Lān Xāng into three kingdoms of Luang Phrabāng, Viang Chan and Champāsak. |
| 1779 | All three Lao kingdoms reduced to tributaries of Siam. |
| 1826–28 | Chau Ānuvong's war of independence results in destruction of Viang Chan by Siam. |
| 1820–40 | Earliest Hmong migrations into Laos. |
| 1861 | French explorer Henri Mouhot arrives in Luang Phrabāng. |
| 1867 | French Mekong expedition maps river through Lao territories. |
| 1887 | Auguste Pavie, first French vice-consul, arrives in Luang Phrabāng (February). |
| 1893 | French seize Lao territories east of Mekong, ceded by Siam. (Treaty signed 3 October.) |
| 1899 | Administrative reorganization of Laos under Résident Supérieur. |
| 1901–07 | 'Holy Man's revolt' in southern Laos. |
| 1907 | Franco-Siamese treaty establishes present frontiers of Laos. |
| 1908–10 | Leu insurrection in northern Laos. |
| 1914–16 | Leu revolt in Luang Namthā, and Hô-Tai revolt in northeast. |
| 1919–22 | Hmong insurrection in northern Laos. |
| 1923 | First session of Indigenous Consultative Assembly (30 August). |
| 1934–36 | Revolt of Kommadam in the Bôlavēn region. |
| 1941 | Franco-Thai war leads to loss of Lao territories on the west bank of the Mekong. |
| 1945 | Japanese intern French (9 March). |
| | King forced to declare Lao independence (8 April). |
| | Japanese surrender (15 August). |
| | Prince Phetxarāt proclaims unity and independence of Laos (15 September). |
| | Lao Issara provisional government formed (12 October). |
| 1946 | French reoccupy Laos (March–April). |
| | Thailand returns Lao west-bank territories (November). |

| | |
|---|---|
| 1947 | Promulgation of Lao Constitution (11 May). |
| | Elections for first National Assembly (August). |
| 1949 | Suphānuvong breaks with Lao Issara (May). |
| | Laos 'independent' within French Union (19 July). |
| | Lao Issara government-in-exile dissolved (October). |
| 1950 | United States recognizes Laos as independent state (7 February). |
| | Pathēt Lao Resistance government formed (August). |
| 1951 | Suvanna Phūmā forms his first government (November). |
| 1953 | Vietminh invade Laos (April, December). |
| 1954 | French surrender at Dien Bien Phu (7 May). |
| | Signing of Geneva Agreements (20 July). |
| 1955 | Formation of Lao People's Party (22 March). |
| 1956 | Formation of Lao Patriotic Front (January). |
| | Second Suvanna Phūmā government (March). |
| | Negotiations with Pathēt Lao to form coalition government. |
| 1957 | Formation of First Coalition government (19 November). |
| 1958 | Supplementary elections (4 May) result in leftist gains. |
| | Formation of US-backed right-wing Committee for the Defence of the National Interest (10 June). |
| | Suspension of US aid forces resignation of Suvanna Phūmā (22 July). |
| | Formation of right-wing government (18 August). |
| 1959 | Forced integration of Pathēt Lao forces fails. |
| | Arrest of Pathēt Lao leaders in Viang Chan (27 July). |
| | Succession of King Savāngvatthanā (29 October). |
| | Attempted military *coup d'état* forces resignation of Phuy Xananikôn government (31 December). |
| 1960 | Rigged national elections won by rightists (24 April). |
| | Neutralist *coup d'état* of Captain Kônglae (8–9 August). |
| | Third Suvanna Phūmā government formed (16 August). |
| | Battle of Viang Chan (13–16 December). |
| 1961 | Neutralist–Pathēt Lao forces seize Plain of Jars (January). |
| | Kennedy administration announces US support for neutralization of Laos (23 March). |
| | Geneva Conference on Laos opens (16 May). |
| 1962 | Crushing rightist defeat at battle of Namthā (May). |
| | Formation of Second Coalition government (23 June). |
| | Conclusion of Geneva Conference on Laos (23 July). |
| 1963 | Assassination of Kinim Phonsēnā signals *de facto* collapse of Second Coalition (1 April). |
| 1964 | Second Congress of Lao Patriotic Front (6 April). |
| | Attempted rightist military *coup d'état* (19 April). |
| | Pathēt Lao drive Neutralists from Plain of Jars (May). |
| | US bombing of communist targets in Laos begins (May). |
| 1965 | Attempted rightist *putsch* foiled (31 January). |
| | Indochina People's Conference, Phnom Penh (February). |
| | Pathēt Lao forces named Lao People's Liberation Army (5 October). |

| 1966 | Political crisis leads to new elections (September) |
| 1968 | Combined forces of the North Vietnamese Army and the Lao People's Liberation Army take Nam Bāk, Phū Phā Thī (January). |
| | Third Congress of Lao Patriotic Front (25 October). |
| 1969 | Hmong 'Secret Army' forces take Plain of Jars (September). |
| 1970 | Combined forces of the North Vietnamese Army and the Lao People's Liberation Army retake Plain of Jars (February). |
| 1971 | South Vietnamese forces launch operation Lam Son 719 against Ho Chi Minh trail; heavily defeated (February). |
| 1972 | Elections for National Assembly (2 January). |
| | Second Congress of the Lao People's Revolutionary Party held secretly in Viang Xai (February). |
| 1972–73 | Negotiations on cease-fire and coalition government (October–February). |
| 1973 | Cease-fire comes into effect (21 February). |
| | Agreement on formation of Third Coalition (14 September). |
| 1974 | Third Coalition government takes office (5 April). National Political Consultative Committee adopts Eighteen-point Political Program (24 May). |
| 1975 | National Assembly dissolved by royal decree (13 April). |
| | Demonstrations force rightist leaders to flee (9 May). |
| | 'Liberation' of Viang Chan (23 August). |
| | Pathēt Lao hold local and provincial elections (November). |
| | Abdication of King Savāngvatthanā (1 December). |
| | Proclamation of Lao People's Democratic Republic (2 December). |
| 1976 | Lao People's Revolutionary Party embarks on socialist phase of revolution. |
| 1977 | Hmong uprising; former King imprisoned at Viang Xai (March). |
| | 25-year Treaty of Friendship and Cooperation signed with Vietnam (18 July). |
| 1978–80 | Interim Three-year Plan. |
| 1978 | Agricultural cooperativization program launched (May). |
| | Laos sides with Vietnam against China over Cambodia (July). |
| 1979 | Formation of Lao Front for National Construction (20 February). |
| | Suspension of agricultural cooperativization program (July). |
| | Seventh Resolution of Party Central Committee endorses new economic policy (December). |
| 1981–85 | First Five-year Plan |
| 1982 | Third Congress of the Lao People's Revolutionary Party (27–30 April). |
| 1984 | Suvanna Phūmā dies in Viang Chan, aged 82 (10 January). |
| | Border conflict with Thailand over three villages (June). |

| | |
|---|---|
| 1985 | First Lao–US search mission for soldiers missing in action (February).<br>First nationwide population census (1–7 March).<br>Celebrations mark tenth anniversary of LPDR (December). |
| 1986–90 | Second Five-year Plan. |
| 1986 | Fourth Congress of the Lao People's Revolutionary Party endorses New Economic Mechanism introducing market economic principles (13–15 November). |
| 1987–88 | New border conflict with Thailand (November–January). |
| 1988 | Foreign Ministry announces all Vietnamese troops withdrawn from Laos (23 November). |
| 1989 | First elections for Supreme People's Assembly (26 March). |
| 1990 | Visit of Chinese Premier Li Peng marks warming of relations with China (15–17 December). |
| 1991–95 | Medium-term Policy Framework replaces Third Five-year Plan. |
| 1991 | Fifth Congress of Lao People's Revolutionary Party elevates Kaisôn Phomvihān to presidency of the State and the Party (27–29 March).<br>Supreme People's Assembly endorses constitution (13 August). |
| 1992 | Kaisôn Phomvihān dies (21 November), replaced by Nūhak Phūmsavan as State President, and Khamtai Sīphandôn as prime minister and president of the Party.<br>Elections for renamed National Assembly (20 December). |
| 1993 | Further economic reforms and environmental protection law passed. |
| 1994 | First bridge spanning the Mekong opened (8 April). |
| 1996 | Sixth Congress of the Lao People's Revolutionary Party (18–20 March). |

# ABBREVIATIONS

| | |
|---|---|
| ASEAN | Association of Southeast Asian Nations |
| *BSEI* | *Bulletin de la Société des Etudes Indochinoises* |
| CDNI | Committee for the Defence of the National Interest |
| CIA | Central Intelligence Agency |
| DRV | Democratic Republic of (North) Vietnam |
| ECAFE | Economic Commission for Asia and the Far East |
| FBIS | Foreign Broadcasts Information Service |
| *FRUS* | *Foreign Relations of the United States* |
| ICP | Indochinese Communist Party |
| ICSC | International Commission for Supervision and Control |
| IMF | International Monetary Fund |
| LPDR | Lao People's Democratic Republic |
| LPF | Lao Patriotic Front |
| SEATO | South-East Asia Treaty Organization |
| UNDP | United Nations Development Program |
| USAID | United States Agency for International Development |

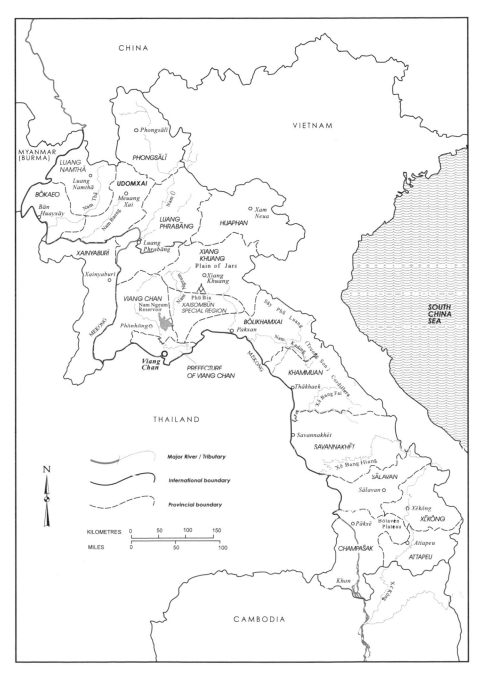

**Map 1** Lao People's Democratic Republic

# INTRODUCTION

Histories of nation states lie under something of a cloud in these post-modern times. Such histories have a narrative structure and centralizing rhetoric, and largely of necessity they focus on the activities of political elites; thus they legitimize the authority of those elites at the expense of repressed minorities – whether of gender, ethnicity, or religious or political belief – which alternative histories might go some way towards empowering.

Foreigners writing the histories of nation states not their own labour under an additional burden of criticism, for to their methodological assumptions are joined those, often unconscious, cultural presuppositions that so easily shade into 'orientalist' arrogance. That such histories are not designed primarily for readers from the nation written about does not in any way excuse unexamined assumptions; for they create the images by which readers 'see' the world. Moreover, their impact on indigenous historiography cannot be ignored.

Historians writing broad national histories at the end of the twentieth century must at least be reflectively aware of where they stand and what they anticipate their histories will achieve, and be prepared to reveal as much to their readers. Once written, of course, such histories become open to criticism from alternative perspectives; that is, they enter into the discourse of historiography conducted both within and across national borders. So let me try to put my case for writing the kind of history I have written about modern Laos, a history that to some may seem old-fashioned in terms of both its narrative structure and its political emphasis.

To begin with, the writing of Lao history is impoverished – in each of the sequential four phases into which Lao historiography naturally falls. The first of these phases comprised the chronicles of the early Lao kingdoms. These accounts of the unified Lao Kingdom of Lān Xāng and the successor kingdoms into which it divided (Luang Phrabāng, Viang Chan, Champāsak and Xiang Khuang) provided legitimation for a dynasty (and subsequently dynasties) of kings. The chronicles legitimized kings both by tracing their descent from Khun Bôrom, the mythical first ancestor of all the Tai peoples, and by exhibiting their karmic credentials as Buddhist monarchs whose merit, accumulated in both previous and present existences, gave them the right to rule. Though this historiography fulfilled its ideological purpose, the legitimation it provided allowed more powerful (Siamese) kings claiming the same descent, and presumably exhibiting greater merit, to reduce the Lao kingdoms to tributary status.

French imperialism transferred some parts only of the former

Kingdom of Lān Xāng from Siam (Thailand) to France. The French ascendancy produced the second phase of Lao historiography. Not surprisingly, the writing of this history, while acknowledging the earlier greatness of the Lao kingdom, portrayed the Lao as a people under threat, needing the continued protection of France simply to survive. As a historiography that legitimized French rule, it hardly empowered a nationalist movement to prepare to lead an independent Lao state. Moreover, it portrayed Siam as the arch-enemy and at the same time camouflaged the French intention to reduce Lao territories to the status of the mere hinterland of French Indochina, an intention whose principal beneficiaries would have been the Vietnamese.

Even so, the groundwork for a third phase, a nationalist Lao historiography, was being laid. Studies of the chronicles of Lān Xāng by Lao scholars (Prince Phetxarāt, Silā Vīravong) formed the basis for narrative histories, closely modelled on the chronicles, that glorified the earlier Lao kingdom and served as a foil to counter French assumptions. Both the second and the third phase, however, were equally partial: for if the French stressed the period of Lao division and Siamese domination, the elite Lao nationalists all but ignored those unfortunate two centuries. They linked the modern Kingdom of Laos that finally achieved independence from France in 1953 directly with the Kingdom of Lān Xāng.

This elite Lao nationalist historiography was deficient, moreover, in another sense, for its concentration on ethnic Lao political domination excluded all those upland ethnic minorities which together by then constituted almost half the total population. In other words, it was no longer adequate as a nationalist historiography, for it failed to draw together the ethnically diverse population that remained within modern Lao borders. The fourth phase of Lao historiography emerged from the Pathēt Lao movement that waged a thirty-year revolutionary struggle against the Royal Lao government. The Pathēt Lao constructed an alternative historiography based on an inclusive tradition of resistance to domination, whether of peasants to nobility, Lao to Thai, or minority groups to the imposition of French rule.

Once the revolutionary movement gained power in 1975 and established the Lao People's Democratic Republic, the challenge facing this historiography of revolutionary struggle was how to include the Kingdom of Lān Xāng, previously all but ignored, in a way that both glorified Lao achievement and included other ethnic groups. Yet before this challenge could be met, Lao Marxism (or what passed for it as official ideology) was itself in crisis as economic market forces again took precedence and the country opened up to foreign capital investment. By the 1990s, Marxism in Laos had given way to one-party authoritarianism, and a need was evident for a new Lao historiography.

The point about the three later phases of Lao historiography is that, unlike the chronicle phase, they remained undeveloped, each superseded by another responding to new circumstances. As a result Laos, among the countries of Southeast Asia, has the most poorly developed nationalist historiography to provide ideological support for construction of an inclusive national identity. This poses a considerable challenge for Lao historians, for arguably the fragile construct that is modern Laos requires firm support for a national identity from an inclusive and centralizing historiography. Such history must be written before it can be deconstructed in ways that are beginning to be evident in, for example, Thai historiography.

I see the historiography of Laos, therefore, as requiring *at this stage* a narrative that provides support for the existence of a nation state now internationally recognized as such. In this I believe I reflect the desires, beliefs and convictions of Lao people, not only in Laos but also among the refugee community outside the country. The history I have written is *not*, of course, for the people of Laos: that history can be written only by Lao historians. This history is written for those who view Laos from the outside, including the Westernized children of the Lao diaspora.

This history seeks to tell a number of stories. It endorses the Lao claim for the continuity of Lao history from the Kingdom of Lān Xāng to the Lao People's Democratic Republic (LPDR). In this it opposes those who would, in their new orientalist hubris, deconstruct that continuity ('Who are the Lao?') without ever considering the real political dilemmas facing the Lao nation state. It traces the struggle for independence and unity in the face of forces, both internal and external, making for division. And it recounts some of the attempts that have been made to grapple with the challenge of constructing a new nationalism appropriate to the nation state the Lao now possess. In doing this, I freely admit, my sympathies have been with the Lao against those who would subordinate, divide, or disempower them.

I begin with a brief outline of the rise and decline of the Kingdom of Lān Xāng, showing how it was weakened by shifts in population and trade and by internal division, yet arguing for the continuity of Lao history. In Chapter 2 my contention is that French failure to create a unified Laos which might make its way towards self-government and independence was due to a fundamental ambiguity in French policy over what to do with the Lao territories. For although Laos was administered as a separate entity, its future was seen as providing a hinterland for Vietnamese expansion and exploitation. Thus I argue that it was the Lao themselves, and Prince Phetxarāt in particular, who took the lead in reconstructing a unified and independent Lao state.

Independence and unity are the themes of Chapter 3, which determine its periodization and that of subsequent chapters. Thus it was not the external events of two international conferences at Geneva (1954 and 1962), nor internal *coups d'état* that marked off significant phases of post-independence Lao history, but those occasions when unity was either briefly re-established (1957), or irrevocably broke down (1964). But there is also a sub-text in this chapter, and that is the failure of the governing elite to construct an appropriately inclusive nationalism to reinforce Lao unity and independence, once established. Despite some notable exceptions (such as Suvanna Phūmā), far too many of the Lao political elite during the Royal Lao regime placed self-indulgence and self-interest above national considerations.

Chapter 4 begins to shift focus from Lao efforts to create an independent and unified nation state to those forces preventing them from doing so. As the disastrous results of and implications of intervention by the United States became apparent, a last attempt was made to re-establish the unity that had been lost – alas, too late. Laos was already being drawn into the maelstrom of the war in Vietnam, better referred to, since it spilled over into both Laos and Cambodia, as the Second Indochina War (following the First against the French). The sub-text here is the increasing disempowerment of the Lao elite – of the right by the United States, and the left by (North) Vietnam.

The impact of war is considered in Chapter 5. It was massive not only in terms of material damage in those areas most heavily bombed, but also in terms of social disruption as a quarter of the population became refugees in their own country. During these years, disempowerment of the Lao elite resulted in political frustration and growing corruption on the one hand, and on the other a resigned war-weariness that sought only an end to conflict on whatever terms. So was the way prepared for the Pathēt Lao accession to power.

Declaration of the Lao People's Democratic Republic restored the unity of the country, but at the expense of subservience to Vietnam. Independence was thus, in a sense, still partial. Only with the collapse of the Soviet Union, which had provided most of the financial support for the Lao regime, did the power configurations in mainland Southeast Asia shift sufficiently to permit the LPDR to open up relations with the states of the Association of Southeast Asian Nations (ASEAN) and the West. Thus the 1990s found Laos at last both unified and independent, but still with a fragile sense of national identity. The unity, like the independence, was still partial, for the Pathēt Lao victory, rather than healing the social divisions of war and ideology, instead had resulted in a new exodus of population.

Remarkable economic and social changes are already sweeping Southeast Asia. As in previous centuries, Laos again finds itself at the crossroads of important trade routes. But as the country opens up to foreign investment and modern technology, its very cultural, if not national, identity is once again threatened. Not the least of the challenges facing the multi-ethnic Lao people as the country is buffeted by the global forces of the twenty-first century will be construction of a historiography that can serve to reinforce an inclusive Lao identity. If this book contributes in any way to this end, it will have fulfilled at least part of its purpose.


## A NOTE ON TRANSCRIPTION AND SPELLING

Transcription of Lao names into roman script presents something of a problem, for the system worked out by French writers can be quite misleading for speakers of English. Since no officially endorsed system of transcription exists, this book uses a modified version of the one used by Peter Koret in his 1994 doctoral dissertation on Lao literature submitted to the University of London. I have preferred 'ch' to Koret's 'j' and have retained the French distinction between 'x' and 's' for different Lao letters, both of which, however, are pronounced as 's'. Other consonants are pronounced as in English. An 'h' following any consonant simply indicates that it is aspirated. Even though Pathēt Lao cultural tsar Phūmī Vongvichit decreed the elimination of 'r' from the Lao alphabet, I have retained it, on the urging of Lao friends, where it indicates Sanskrit or Pali derivation. Thus I have preferred 'Xainyaburī' to 'Xainyabulī', where '-burī' derives from '-pura' meaning 'town'.

Because words are transcribed as they sound, and certain Lao letters are pronounced differently depending on whether they occur in the initial or final position in a syllable, the same Lao letter may be transcribed in two or three ways. A case in point is the letter pronounced half-way between a 'v' and a 'w' at the beginning of a syllable. I have preferred 'v', as in *vat* (temple). But where the same letter represents a semi-vowel, I have transcribed it as 'u' when it occurs at the beginning of a glide (as in *Luang Phrabāng*), and 'o' where it occurs at the end of a syllable (to preserve the accepted spelling *Lao*).

Vowels in Lao are either short or long. Simple short vowels are pronounced as in about, pet, pit, pot, and put, while their long counterparts, marked by a bar over the letter, are pronounced as in father, dairy (the long 'e'), machine, story, and rule. The 'ô' in *Nakhôn* is pronounced approximately as the 'or' in corn. As for digraphs, the 'eu' in *Attapeu* is a sound which does not exist in English but is approximately the 'u' in fur; the 'ae' in *Nāpae* is approximately the 'a' in can; while the 'oe' in *Khamkoet* is the 'oe' in Goethe. Three glides are pronounced as follows: the 'ia' in *Viang* as the 'ia' in India; the 'eua' in *meuang* roughly as the 'eu' in masseur; and the 'ua' in *Luang* as the 'ua' in truant. Regarding the diphthongs, the 'ai' in *Khamtai* is pronounced as the 'ai' in aisle; and the 'au' in *chau* is the short 'ow' as in cow. Finally, although 'Lao' is pronounced and more properly written as 'Lāo', the long vowel in this combination has been left unmarked.

Applying this transcription alters some familiar spellings, but corrects pronunciation. Thus the French 'Vientiane' becomes 'Viang Chan', though 'Vientiane' is retained where it occurs on the title page of publications. I have, however, inconsistently retained 'Mekong' in preference to 'Maekhông', and 'Issara' rather than alternative possible spellings such as 'Itsala'. Where dialectical differences exist, as in *nam* (water, river) where the vowel can be either long or short, I have adopted the alternative as written in Lao. Finally, while most proper names are written as a single word (King Sīsavāngvong), I have retained Suvanna Phūmā in order to use the shortened form Suvanna. For the names of Lao authors of published works, I have retained the spelling used in the publication.

# CHAPTER 1

# THE KINGDOM OF LĀN XĀNG

The construction of Laos as a modern nation state dates only from 1945. Before then Laos was administered as a province of French Indochina, conceived more as a hinterland for Vietnamese expansion and French exploitation than as a political entity in its own right. But the independent Lao state constructed after 1945 comprised the territory established by treaty between France and Siam (Thailand) between the years 1893 and 1907. Thus any history of modern Laos must begin with the fifty years of French colonial rule. For the Lao themselves, however, their history is far more ancient, reaching back well before the mid-fourteenth century when the Kingdom of Lān Xāng was founded. For the Lao today, their right to self-determination and independence rests firmly on that early history, to which Lao historiography gives considerable prominence. The official *History of Laos* produced by a team of writers under the direction of the Lao People's Revolutionary Party consists of three volumes, though only the third at the time of writing had been published.[1] These cover the period before the founding of Lān Xāng, its rise and decline, and the period since 1893. Thus the communist regime is as anxious as was the previous Royal Lao government to establish that Laos has a long and glorious past and that a continuity exists between that past and the present Lao state.

Apart from archaeological excavations of prehistoric sites, especially in northeastern Thailand, the earliest sources for the history of the central Mekong basin come from Chinese dynastic records. These mention a people inhabiting southwestern China known as the Ai-Lao (Āy-Lao), the term used subsequently by the Vietnamese to refer to the Lao. But whether the Ai-Lao were ancestral to the Tai[2] peoples who eventually spread over much of mainland Southeast Asia, let alone the sub-group that became the Lao, seems extremely doubtful. The Chinese texts also name a number of small kingdoms apparently located in the middle Mekong region, though exactly where is disputed. What we do know from bringing together archaeological evidence, Chinese sources and, more doubtfully, references in later Lao texts is that in the second half of the first millennium of our common era (CE), small polities were beginning to form on the Khōrāt plateau of northeastern Thailand and along the middle Mekong. As 'men of prowess' built concentrations of political, economic and military power, they borrowed notions of legitimation from Indian religions (Hinduism and Buddhism).[3] Ritual centres of religious worship, closely associated with secular rule, provided ideological justification for the exercise of power, which fluctuated in accordance with the resources available to a ruler from trade, tribute, or military conscription.

To call such developments 'state formation' is to import European notions of administration over a defined territory that are inappropriate to describe these 'circles of power'. A preferable term is *mandala* which better captures both their segmentary structure (larger power centres extracting tribute from similarly organized smaller ones), and variability of power relationships.[4] In the middle Mekong basin such *mandalas* were established in the region of Champāsak (with its ritual centre at Vat Phū), Thākhaek (ritual centre Thāt Phanom), in the upper Xī valley (Meuang Fā Daet) and on the plain of Viang Chan. While the first appears to have been Khmer and Hindu, the other three were in all likelihood Mon and Buddhist in both culture and language. By the end of the twelfth century, all had been absorbed within the expanding Khmer empire.

In northern Laos, on the Plain of Jars and in the region of Luang Phrabāng, formation of early *mandalas* is shrouded in mystery and myth. A millennium earlier on the Plain of Jars a megalithic iron-age culture had flourished, characterized by standing slabs and vast stone jars.[5] But who the people of the jars were, and why the culture declined, remains a mystery. Nor do we know when the first *mandala* was established in the region of Luang Phrabāng. Legend tells how two brother hermits consolidated territories protected by snake kings, who were probably guardian spirits (protective *phī*); how the throne was offered to a sandalwood merchant from Viang Chan; and how the region was seized from a certain Khun (Lord of) Xua (as Luang Phrabāng was then called) by the first Lao ruler, Khun Lô. Who occupied the region before the arrival of the Lao, and who Khun Xua was, we can only speculate. It seems likely that these early inhabitants were ethnically and linguistically akin to the Austroasiatic-speaking peoples still found throughout the region, the Lawa (Lavā) of northern Thailand and Khamu of northern Laos, and possibly even descendants of the people of the jars.

In the version of the Lao chronicles known as the *Nithān Khun Bôrom* (The Story of Khun Bôrom) containing the origin myths of the Tai peoples, Khun Lô is the eldest son of Khun Bôrom, the original ancestor of all Tai. Different versions agree that Khun Bôrom was sent by the king of the *thaen* (celestial deities) to rule over the earthly realm. They also recount that life on earth was threatened by the growth of a gigantic vine. An elderly couple volunteered to chop it down, but were crushed to death when the vine fell. The vine bore two or three giant gourds, from inside which cries could be heard. Holes were made in the gourds using first a red-hot poker, then a knife. From the blackened holes came the *khā* (literally 'slaves', the pejorative term for those Austroasiatic-speaking minority tribes now known collectively as the Lao Thoeng, or 'Lao of the mountain slopes'); from the holes cut with a knife came the Tai – and in that order.[6]

These were the peoples over whom Khun Bôrom ruled. In time he sent his seven sons to found seven new kingdoms, from Burma (Shan state) to Vietnam (the Tai highlands), and from southern China to Laos, including both Luang Phrabāng and Xiang Khuang. As we would expect, no mention is made of the middle Mekong, which until the twelfth century was still dominated by non-Tai peoples. As historical sources, it would be easy to dismiss these myths as valueless. But myths preserve ancient folk memories of migration and displacement, as well as providing a sense of identity. The myth of Khun Bôrom and Khun Lô, founder of the first Lao dynasty of Luang Phrabāng, not only suggests how the Lao Lum (the Tai-speaking 'Lao of the valley floor') came to dominate the Lao Thoeng; it also provided, through annual repetition in performance and recital, an anchor in time for what it was to be Lao. This identity was regularly reinforced in the annual festivities associated with the Lao New Year. Royal rituals reiterating the relationship between Lao Lum and Lao Thoeng were performed right up to 1975 when the monarchy was abolished, while figures representing the old couple who had cut down the vine bearing the gourds still continue to be paraded each year through the streets of Luang Phrabāng.

Debate continues over the origins of the Tai peoples, but historical, linguistic and comparative anthropological evidence suggests that they originally occupied a region of southern China covering southeastern Yunnan and western Guangxi provinces. Their dispersal and migration was probably associated with the extension of Han Chinese control south as far as northern Vietnam during the last century BCE and the first centuries CE. Movement was slow as population increased slowly, but as early as the eighth or ninth century a small Tai principality (*meuang*) probably already existed in the region of Chiang Saen in the far north of Thailand. Tai peoples also moved into the high valleys of northwestern Vietnam, and it is possible that at about this time Meuang Thaeng (Dien Bien Phu) became a point from which further migration occurred. By the end of the first millennium, Tai peoples were evidently widely spread, from the Shan highlands across northern Thailand and into the upper Mekong basin, in a region between contending *mandalas* in southern China (Nanzhao) and mainland Southeast Asia (Mon and Khmer).

The pattern of Tai expansion is evident from the *Nithān Khun Bôrom*, as sons of local rulers (*chau meuang*) led their followers from one mountain valley to another. The linked settlements so formed were held together by common descent (as 'clan-based' *meuang*). Where riverine plains opened out, however, more extensive 'principality-like' *meuang* developed.[7] As Tai-Lao settlers spread south they left behind them the heavily forested mountains and steep, narrow valleys of northern Laos with their high rainfall and fast-flowing rivers for the broader plains of the middle Mekong basin. There they encountered the well-watered western slopes of the Sāy Phū Luang (Truong Son) cordillera separating Laos from Vietnam, and the sandier soils, more open forest and lower rainfall of the Khōrāt plateau.

Whereas the Mekong river once formed the axis of the Lao world, it now marks most of the country's western frontier with Thailand. Two sets of rapids, one between Luang Phrabāng and Viang Chan, the second near Savannakhēt, and the 13-kilometre-wide cataracts of Khôn on the Lao–Cambodian border, divide the river into three geographically distinct regions of population and political organization, each with its own historically defined identity. To the north, centre and south, strategically important high plateaux (respectively the Xiang Khuang plateau, known colloquially as the Plain of Jars, the Khammūan plateau and the Bôlavēn plateau) support higher concentrations of population. By the mid-thirteenth century, Tai-Lao were widely settled throughout the Mekong basin and the time was ripe for the next stage in their political evolution.

The second half of the thirteenth century was a time of great turmoil. The Mongol armies of Kubilai Khan overran the last independent kingdom in Yunnan in 1253, and pressed on south. Pagan, the capital of the Burmese *mandala*, was destroyed, and a Mongol army marched down the middle Mekong to invade Cambodia. By then, however, Khmer power was already on the wane. In its wake Tai rulers founded the first powerful Tai *mandalas* of Lān Nā, centred on Chiang Mai, and Sukhothai, further to the south. Both were tributary to the Mongol Chinese Yuan dynasty, and Mongol influence remained strong. In fact, it has been suggested that Mongol intervention may have been directly responsible for the rise of the first Lao *mandala* on the upper Mekong.[8]

The mid-fourteenth century saw the founding, within three years of each other, of two imperial *mandalas* which, together with Lān Nā, divided the Tai world between them over the next four centuries. These were the Tai-Siam *mandala* of Ayutthaya formed in 1351, later strengthened through its absorption of Sukhothai in 1438; and the Tai-Lao *mandala* of Lān Xāng with its capital at Xiang Dong Xiang Thong, as the Lao then called Luang Phrabāng.[9]

A Lao *meuang* of limited extent had existed at Xiang Dong Xiang Thong since the region had been seized by Lao warriors from its earlier, probably Khamu, inhabitants. The earliest recorded date in the Lao chronicles to which any credence can be attached is 1271. In that year a dynasty took power whose rulers bore the title 'Phrayā', a Pali term meaning 'He Who Upholds', suggesting strong Buddhist influence. Fā Ngum, founder of the imperial *mandala* of Lān Xāng, was a hereditary prince of the Phrayā dynasty.

Like many great founders of kingdoms, Fā Ngum's person became surrounded by legend. More space is devoted to his exploits in founding Lān Xāng in the Lao chronicles than to the next two centuries of Lao history. Briefly, he is said to have been exiled from Xiang Dong Xiang Thong for reasons that are unclear but are quite likely to have included an attempt to seize the throne, either by his father or himself. By one means or another he made his way to Cambodia. There at the court of Angkor he eventually obtained a Khmer princess, and an army with which he fought his way back to Xiang Dong Xiang Thong, forcing the scattered *meuang* along his invasion route to accept his suzerainty. He is also said to have put into place the administrative structures that held together the *mandala* of Lān Xāng over the next three and a half centuries, the frontiers of which were established through treaties with surrounding powers (Vietnam, Lān Nā, and Ayutthaya).

The *mandala* that Fā Ngum constructed is known in the chronicles as *meuang* Lao, for the term applies to both larger and smaller political entities. How far it extended is debatable, though it probably did not at first include the region of Champāsak. What held together the *meuang* of northern Laos in their narrow mountain valleys and the scattered *meuang* of the central Mekong were bonds, essentially feudal in nature, of loyalty and patronage. The mode of production was not, however, feudal in the European sense. Rather than serfs toiling for a lord, a free peasantry owed certain obligations at times of planting and harvest to work the land of the hereditary ruling family; to contribute on special, usually festive, occasions; and to fight when called upon.

Fā Ngum is also credited with introducing Buddhism into Laos, though this is manifestly incorrect. Discoveries at Luang Phrabāng make it certain that Buddhism was known well before the time of Fā Ngum, though his Khmer queen may well have introduced a new Theravāda school, the form of Buddhism now practised in Laos. As for organization and borders, the accounts of these attributed to Fā Ngum probably reflect expansion and accommodations arrived at over the century and a half separating Fā Ngum and Vixun, the king on whose instructions the earliest recension of the *Nithān Khun Bôrom* was composed (in 1503). For Lao historians, however, Fā Ngum remains a heroic figure of epic proportions, even though he was eventually exiled from his own kingdom.

Why this was so is something of a mystery. He is said to have offended the aristocratic families of Xiang Dong Xiang Thong by taking their wives and daughters as his concubines. In fact, the exile of Fā Ngum is far more likely to have resulted from a struggle between powerful court factions which probably pitted the old aristocracy against upstart newcomers, many of them foreigners (Khmer), who had arrived with the King. Two events in 1368 probably weakened the Khmer faction: the death of Fā Ngum's Khmer queen, and the overthrow of the Yuan dynasty in China by the Ming, especially if Fā Ngum's position rested in part on a Khmer–Lao tributary alliance with the Mongols. In any event, Fā Ngum's eldest son, Unheuan, succeeded to the throne, taking as his throne name Sāmsaenthai, literally 'Lord of 300,000 Tai', the number a census revealed could be called upon to fight in the King's armies.

Over the next century, the organization of the Lao *mandala*, and thus the pattern of Lao power, became established. So did Theravāda Buddhism, though not to the exclusion of the worship of powerful spirits (*phī*) associated particularly with regions (*meuang*) and striking landmarks. Society consisted of three classes – aristocracy, free peasantry, and slaves. Below these came the Lao Thoeng, the indigenous minorities also commonly referred to as slaves (*khā*). Free men became slaves because they were captured in war, were being punished for crimes committed, or because they were indebted. They were not badly treated, however, as early law codes indicate. By no means did Lān Xāng rest on anything that could be called a slave mode of production.

The wealth of the Lao court came from tribute, taxation and trade.

The *mandala* was loosely structured. Provided they paid a prescribed tribute and regularly presented themselves at court, and were prepared to contribute men and arms when called upon to do so, rulers or lords of constituent *meuang* (*chau meuang*) were virtually autonomous. Taxation was confined to the region of the capital, and usually took the form of delivery of goods, whether food or handicrafts produced by villages of artisans (pottery, silverwork, silk weaving and embroidery, etc.). Trade was in more valuable items, many of them forest products such as ivory, rhinoceros horn, aromatic benzoin and the sticklac from which lacquerware is made, but also including silk, iron and salt.

Probably not until the reign of Vixun (1501–20) did the various strands of the Lao Buddhist worldview come together to provide legitimation for kingship and the structure of Lao society, and the core ideas around which Lao culture came to cohere. For it was Vixun who both ordered what may until then have been in large part an oral tradition to be written down as the *Nithān Khun Bôrom*, and who brought the Phra Bāng, the sacred Buddha image which became the palladium of the kingdom, to Xiang Dong Xiang Thong. The essential elements of this worldview were two: belief in descent from a common ancestor, with the royal family representing the direct line from Khun Bôrom via Fā Ngum; and acceptance of Buddhism as a superior truth, especially the notions of *karma* leading to rebirth and the making of merit as central to Buddhist morality. The King ruled both by right of descent, and by right of his merit: he had accumulated the necessary merit in previous existences to be born a king and conspicuously continued to make great merit during his lifetime through generous gifts to the Buddhist monastic order (*Sangha*). The reciprocal relationship between monarch and *Sangha* was thus crucial, for the legitimation of the former depended on the teachings of the latter.

The shifting power relationships between neighbouring *mandalas* in mainland Southeast Asia left frontiers relatively fluid, for frontier *meuang* could always change allegiance under pressure. Frontiers were also fuzzy where new villages were bringing new land under cultivation. At any one time, however, the rough extent of *mandalas* was known, especially on established trade routes where merchants passed from one jurisdiction to another. Thus for Lān Xāng, while the frontier of settlement on the Khōrāt plateau was often hard to determine, points of contact down the Mekong with Cambodia and across the Petchabun range with Ayutthaya were precisely located. To the northeast and northwest, however, borders with Vietnam and Lān Nā shifted more easily. The Phuan principality of Xiang Khuang on the Plain of Jars and the Sipsông Chu Tai to the northeast, as well as the Sipsông Phan Nā to the northwest, were contested areas which at various times paid tribute to more than one of the powerful *mandalas* that sought to dominate them.

Warfare was endemic in mainland Southeast Asia, fought by large conscripted armies of foot soldiers and elephant corps. The very name Lān Xāng, A Million Elephants, stated a claim to military power. A clear distinction was made, however, between Tai *mandalas* sharing descent from Khun Bôrom, with whom agreements could be concluded, and peoples such as the Vietnamese and Burmese, who were recognized as sharing no common descent. Not surprisingly, the worst wars that racked Lān Xāng were the Vietnamese invasion of 1479, which took and sacked the Lao capital, and the series of Burmese invasions which shook the Tai world in the second half of the sixteenth century.

A weakness that Lān Xāng shared with other Theravāda Buddhist *mandalas* was that no strict rule of primogeniture applied in succession to the throne. As kings frequently had many sons, succession was often disputed and kingdoms weakened as a result. Lān Xāng was powerful when it had powerful kings who ruled for more than a few years. Unfortunately, however, two such kings died while still in their prime. Phōthisālarāt was an ardent Buddhist who set out to destroy all public worship of *phī*. He was killed when crushed by his falling elephant, soon after placing his son, Xētthāthirāt, on the throne of Lān Nā. Xētthā-thirāt thereupon returned to Lān Xāng, only to lose the throne of Lān Nā. Thus the only real chance of uniting these two kingdoms into a greater Lao state was lost.

It was during the reign of Xētthāthirāt that Burmese armies invaded the Tai world. Chiang Mai fell in 1558, and Lān Nā remained tributary to the Burmese for more than two centuries. The Lao response to the Burmese threat was to take defensive action. In 1560, Xētthāthirāt con-cluded a strategic alliance with Ayutthaya, and the same year ordered the Lao capital to be moved south to Viang Chan. It was a decision his father had probably already been contemplating, for the move made sense in terms of the changing demographic, economic and strategic balance in the region. As Lao settlers moved south down the Mekong to the region of Champāsak and onto the Khōrāt plateau, so too did the centre of gravity of Lao political power.

It probably took the best part of four years to build the new capital. In addition to a defensive perimeter, a new palace and Buddhist temples had to be constructed. The Vat Phra Kaeo was built to house the Emerald Buddha, along with a much enlarged Thāt Luang stupa on the site of a sacred shrine that legend ascribed to the great Indian king Aśoka. Xētthāthirāt played good religious politics by leaving the Phra Bāng in Xiang Dong Xiang Thong and renaming the city Luang Phrabāng. He also ordered construction there of Vat Xiang Thong, the most graceful remaining example of sixteenth-century northern Lao architecture.

The Burmese threat persisted, however. Ayutthaya fell in 1569, leav-ing only Lān Xāng to face the great Burmese conqueror Bayinnaung. Xētthāthirāt resorted to guerrilla warfare, and although the Burmese occupied Viang Chan, they were forced to withdraw for lack of supplies after a few months. Xētthāthirāt was at the height of his power when, the following year, he invaded Cambodia. But his army was heavily defeated, and the King mysteriously disappeared on his retreat north. Once again Lān Xāng was weakened by a series of succession disputes, leaving it prey to the Burmese.

Not until 1637, when Surinyavongsā won the throne, did the Lao *mandala* enter a time of peace and prosperity which continued throughout his long reign of fifty-seven years. It was during Surinyavongsā's rule that the first Europeans to leave records of their stay visited Viang Chan. The first to arrive was the Dutch merchant Gerritt van Wuysthoff, in the employ of the Dutch East India Company, closely followed by the Italian Jesuit missionary Giovanni-Maria Leria. While van Wuysthoff stayed for less than two months, Father Leria remained for five years, learning the language though never gaining permission to proselytize.

From the accounts of both men we gain a good idea of the greatness and glory of Lān Xāng at the apogee of its power. By this time the Lao had assimilated Siamese notions of kingship. Surinyavongsā was a remote and regal figure, secluded from his people in his vast and luxurious palace which Leria described as 'of a prodigious extent, and so large that one would take it for a town'.[10] There he was served by a retinue of officials and courtiers, and entertained by the music, dance and theatre that we are told flourished in the metropolitan Lao capital.

Both visitors remarked on the wealth of the kingdom, and van Wuysthoff in particular was interested in opportunities for trade. Both regretted, however, that so much of that wealth found its way to the Buddhist *Sangha*, for Viang Chan was a great centre of Buddhist studies. Monks, who came from as far afield as Cambodia and Burma, were, van Wuysthoff noted in wonder, 'more numerous than the soldiers of the Emperor of Germany'.[11] Leria, as might be expected, loathed the monks who refused to take his Christianity seriously, but he found the Lao in general 'very affable, accommodating, open to reason, and very respectful'.[12]

Both European visitors arrived in the 1640s, in the early part of Surinyavongsā's reign. No others arrived over the next nearly fifty years until his death in 1694 or 1695, by which time Laos was almost as remote and mysterious as Tibet. During this half-century, however, though the magnificence of Viang Chan may not have dimmed, the balance of power was swinging, slowly but surely, against the isolated inland *mandala* of Lān Xāng and in favour of neighbouring kingdoms enjoying access to the sea and to seaborne trade with European powers selling improved military technology. For the Lao, such trade was at best indirect, down the Mekong to Cambodia, or via Ayutthaya where the Siamese creamed off much of the profit.

Because Surinyavongsā in his stern old age had had his only son executed for adultery, on his death the kingdom was once again racked by a drawn-out succession dispute. This was more than usually destructive, however. Both Vietnamese and Siamese became involved and the outcome was to divide the kingdom, at first into two, and subsequently into three, separate principalities, each claiming the status of kingdom and the mantle of Lān Xāng. This so fatally weakened the Lao polity that Lao power never recovered. Within less than a century, all three kingdoms fell under the sway of a new and powerful Siamese *mandala*.

Less is known about the history of the Lao kingdoms in the eighteenth century than about Lān Xāng in the reign of Surinyavongsā.

No missionary or merchant, traveller or diplomat left any first-hand account, and the regional chronicles are meagre in the extreme. Indeed they tell us more about the making of royal merit through largesse to the *Sangha* and miraculous images believed to legitimate royal rule and protect the realm than they do about political events or foreign relations, let alone social change or the state of the economy.

In the 1760s a new Burmese dynasty again invaded the Tai world. Chiang Mai fell in 1763, Luang Phrabāng two years later, and Ayutthaya succumbed on 7 April 1767. This time the Siamese capital was put to the sack. Under the inspired leadership of a young military commander named Taksin, son of a Chinese father and Siamese mother, Siamese forces staged a remarkable recovery. Within a decade not only had the Burmese been driven from Lān Nā, but all three Lao kingdoms had submitted to Siamese suzerainty.

The Lao did not bow to superior Siamese might without a fight. Taksin used the execution of a Lao rebel who claimed to be a vassal of Siam as a pretext to invade first Champāsak and then Viang Chan. After a siege of four months, during which the Siamese were assisted by a Lao force from Luang Phrabāng, Viang Chan capitulated. King Siribunyasān managed to escape, but died the following year. The city was thoroughly looted. Its most sacred images, including the Emerald Buddha, were carried off to Bangkok, along with members of the royal family as hostages. Hundreds of Lao families were forcibly resettled on the Chaophraya plain north of the Siamese capital. Nor did Luang Phrabāng's perfidious assistance save it too from becoming a tributary *meuang*.

Siam, however, remained a Southeast Asian *mandala*, not a modern state. There was no centrally appointed administration. The larger principalities, such as the three Lao kingdoms and Chiang Mai, were entirely autonomous. Even smaller *meuang* on the Khōrāt plateau that progressively transferred their allegiance, under pressure, from Viang Chan to Bangkok, could collect their own taxes and enforce their own justice. Only three matters had to be referred to Bangkok for approval: permission to raise the necessary force to discipline a recalcitrant vassal; nomination of high officials to rule the *meuang*; and sentences of capital punishment. The only constraints on the Lao kingdoms were that the ruler and *uparāt* (vice-ruler) had to be endorsed by the Siamese court, and war could not be declared on a neighbouring kingdom. Viang Chan was not prevented, however, from reinforcing its own suzerainty over Xiang Khuang.

Rama I, founder of the Bangkok Chakri dynasty, took a lively interest in Lao affairs. Nanthasēn, eldest son of Siribunyasān, was permitted to return to Viang Chan to rule as a tributary of Siam. Some years later, some families that had been forcibly resettled were also allowed to return. Viang Chan was rebuilt and its population grew. In 1804 Ānuvong succeeded his two elder brothers on the throne of Viang Chan.

Ānuvong began his reign in a manner expected of any Buddhist king, by building a new palace and by demonstrating his superior merit by giving generously to the *Sangha*. New temples were built, including Vat Sisakēt, still a gem of later Lao architecture. Tributary relations were restored with the new Nguyen dynasty in Vietnam, yet so confident were the Siamese of Ānuvong's loyalty that they agreed to appoint his son as ruler of Champāsak.

Perhaps it was this that suggested to Ānuvong the possibility of reconstituting the Lao *mandala* of Lān Xāng independent of Siamese hegemony. Or perhaps it was growing irritation with what he saw as Siamese high-handedness. Considerable Lao resentment had been provoked by the Siamese decision to extend their policy of tattooing peasants and forcing them to perform corvée labour. Also Ānuvong had been insulted by the churlish treatment he had received when attending the funeral of Rama II in Bangkok. At any rate, upon his return to Viang Chan Ānuvong seems to have decided to throw off the Siamese yoke.

Ānuvong's strategy was simple: seize the entire Khōrāt plateau, repatriate and unite all Lao, and proclaim Lao independence with the support both of other tributary kingdoms, such as Luang Phrabāng and Chiang Mai, and of external allies, notably Vietnam.[13] By the end of 1826, he was ready to make his move. Four Lao armies, three from Viang Chan and one from Champāsak, thrust across the Khōrāt plateau as far as Khōrāt itself. Lao on the Chaophraya and the southern plateau were repatriated north, but with so many people to move, the process was slow. The Siamese had time to respond. Three armies were raised. Khōrāt was retaken, and the Lao were in retreat.

In retrospect, Ānuvong had miscalculated the situation. He had apparently believed that the new king, Rama III, would respond much more hesitantly than he did, because the Siamese would be too worried over British intentions (the British had just defeated the Burmese in the First Anglo-Burmese War) to pursue the Lao. But the Siamese court had already concluded a treaty with the British, which left them free to deal with the Lao. In doing so, not only could the Siamese recruit larger, better-equipped armies than the Lao, but they also had better intelligence.

The outcome was never in doubt. The Lao made their last stand south of Viang Chan in mid-May 1827, but to no avail. Ānuvong fled down the Mekong as Siamese forces entered the Lao capital. The city was put to the sack, its palaces and houses looted and burned, its population carried off for forcible resettlement. The following year, after Ānuvong briefly returned with a small force, Viang Chan was totally destroyed. The King was captured and died in cruel custody in Bangkok. Not only was the Kingdom of Viang Chan erased from the map: so too was any remaining shadow of the *mandala* of Lān Xāng.

Ānuvong's attempt to throw off Siamese hegemony has been viewed very differently in Thai (Siamese) and Lao historiography. What for the Thai was an unprovoked rebellion by an ungrateful vassal has been seen by the Lao as a just struggle for independence. These differing perceptions are not simply academic: they still haunt Thai–Lao relations, sharpened by the fact that far more ethnic Lao now live in Thailand than in Laos.[14]

The Vietnamese court in Hué was slow to support its Lao tributaries, but the forward policy pursued by the Siamese in the Lao territories and by the Vietnamese in Cambodia soon brought the two powers into conflict. Siamese–Vietnamese hostilities continued on and off from 1834 to 1847, terminated only by a political agreement jointly to exercise influence over Cambodia. Joint suzerainty also came to be exercised over the Plain of Jars, which the Vietnamese called Tran Ninh and the Lao, Meuang Phuan.

Lao resistance to Siamese hegemony was never entirely quelled. East of the Mekong, Lao regional elites called on Vietnamese assistance to defend their autonomy. The Siamese response was to depopulate these territories as far as possible, leaving a wasteland between themselves and the Vietnamese. Lao resettled on the Khōrāt plateau, however, kept alive an oral tradition of resistance to Siamese domination, while vigorously maintaining their uniquely Lao culture. Thus the *meuang* of the Khōrāt plateau continued to be identifiably Lao.

As early as the 1830s, new immigrants began driving their hardy mountain ponies into northwestern Laos. These were the Hmong, known pejoratively as Meo (Maeo) and Mien (Yao), grouped by the Lao government along with smaller Tibeto-Burman-speaking minorities under the rubric Lao Sūng, or 'Lao of the mountain tops'. They settled at higher altitudes than the Khamu, grew opium as a cash crop, worshipped their gods, obeyed their chiefs and shamans, and kept to themselves. In fact, Lao authorities were often unaware of their settlements until they came down to trade, when they were incorporated into the tributary structure of the Phuan *meuang*.

The mid-nineteenth century was the low point in Lao history. Lao *meuang* throughout the middle Mekong and the Khōrāt plateau were all tributary to Bangkok. Only Luang Phrabāng maintained a semblance of independence by paying tribute not only to Bangkok and Hué, but also to Beijing. In return, the Chinese bestowed on the ruler a seal denoting kingship. The sorry state of the country, especially east of the Mekong, was remarked upon by the first French explorers; the naturalist Henri Mouhot, who died near Luang Phrabāng in 1861, and members of the Lagrée–Garnier expedition exploring the Mekong.[15]

Yet despite a combination of Siamese exploitation and neglect, Lao communities managed to survive. Trade continued in slaves, gold, ivory, horn, skins and forest products. Beeswax, cardamom, ivory and silk were demanded by Siamese authorities as tribute, or tax in kind. But reluctance to comply often left Lao towns years late in their payment. Such were the forms of popular resistance.

Politically, however, the Lao *meuang* remained separate and divided. No attempt seems to have been made to create new political alliances, through marriage or other means. Each ruling family sought only to preserve its own little fiefdom. Only in Champāsak was some attempt made to reconstruct a larger *meuang* through establishing new dependent villages. When Siamese 'commissioners' (*khāluang*) began to assert more direct Siamese administration, the Lao *meuang* were in no state to resist.

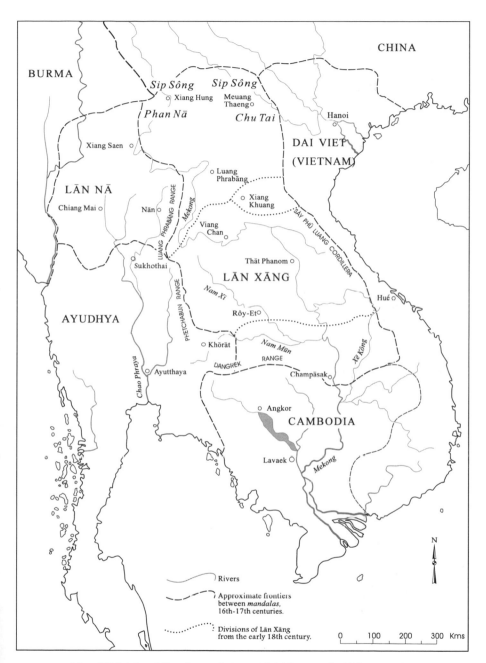

**Map 2** Mainland Southeast Asia: mid-16th to early 19th centuries

Had the Siamese King Chulalongkorn, Rama V, been able to introduce his reform program in the 1870s instead of twenty years later, it is arguable that even the Lao territories west of the Mekong might have effectively been incorporated into a modernizing Siamese state before the French were able to wrest them away in 1893. In the event, Siamese control was shaky enough to be disputed by an aggressive French imperialism determined to extend the boundaries of French Indochina.

What the French created, as we shall see, was a province which they called Laos. This left by far the majority of the ethnic Lao population under Siamese rule, and thus throws into question whether and in what sense the Laos thus created can claim continuity with the far more extensive Lao kingdom of Lān Xāng. For the Lao who remained in Laos, that has never been problematic. They trace their historical heritage back, quite unselfconsciously, to well before the time of Fā Ngum, and to suggest that there is some problem of continuity meets with incomprehension.

For non-Lao historians, especially those influenced by post-modernist concerns over constructions of identities and traditions and competing historiographies, the continuity of Lao history is less obvious. There is a hiatus of almost two centuries between the break-up of Lān Xāng and the reconstruction of French Laos. Moreover, while successor kingdoms explicitly claimed the mantle of Lān Xāng, for sixty-five years after 1828 the most convincing candidate making that claim ceased to exist. And when in 1893 a political entity called Laos was recreated, less than half the territory and a fraction of the population of the former kingdom of Lān Xāng were included. In fact, therefore, what the French created as a province of Indochina and the Lao elevated to an independent nation state in 1945 was a new entity which could only partially claim to be the lineal successor of the earlier Lao *mandala*.

My own sympathies in the debate lie with the Lao. Admittedly the Lao population of the Khōrāt plateau can make just as strong a claim that Lān Xāng is their historical heritage too, but that is a problem for Thai historiography. It cannot detract from the claim of the Lao of Laos. The future challenge for Lao historiography, and this is just as demanding, is to come to terms with its own alternative historical traditions, for the Lao chronicles present a picture from the perspective of the lowland Lao elite that marginalises not only Lao Thoeng and Lao Sūng, but also Lao Lum minorities, both lowland (Tai-Leu, Tai-Yuan) and upland (Tai-Dam, Tai-Daeng). In time, alternative historiographies drawing on alternative historical, mostly oral, traditions of minority groups will need to be written and incorporated into a more diverse and nuanced Lao historiography. But that lies in the future.

What is required first is to establish the continuity of Lao history, and that can only rest on social and cultural foundations. Specifically, as I have argued elsewhere,[16] it rests on the continuity of the Lao *meuang*. It matters not at all that the *meuang* as a sociopolitical entity is shared by other Tai peoples. What is important is the continuity of the *meuang* that are Lao; this is the sociocultural substrate which could serve, as circumstances permit, as the basis for political resurgence.

The peculiar structure of all Tai *mandalas* (Lān Xāng, Lān Nā, Ayutthaya) was both their weakness and their strength. Kingdoms could be expanded as power permitted through the simple addition as tributary units of segmentary *meuang* whose political structure reflected that of the *mandala* itself. *Meuang* did not necessarily have to share a common culture. Relations within the *mandala* drew on available sources of social power – political, military, economic and ideological. The extent of each *meuang* was a function of the sources of power at its disposal. As these increased, so the *meuang* could expand by absorbing smaller neighbouring *meuang*. Thus each *meuang* acted as a potential nucleus for political expansion.

For Theravāda Buddhists, however, whether or not the *meuang* expanded depended on the *karma* of its ruler. A *chau meuang* of great merit was a potential *cakkavattin*, or universal ruler. His *meuang* had the potential of becoming an imperial *mandala*. But for a *meuang* to become the nucleus of a Lao *mandala*, it had to be a Lao *meuang*. That meant it had to be culturally Lao, as defined by ideas (worldview, comprising both Buddhist and earlier mythical beliefs), behaviour (for example, performance of such ritual ceremonies as the *bāsī sūkhuan*), and material way of life (centred on the cultivation and consumption of glutinous rice). Whatever befell the Lao *meuang*, this cultural substrate remained, and an important dimension of that culture, broadly understood, was social and political – a social structure in which a hereditary elite was expected to rule; a political structure that allowed for the inclusion of segmentary units.

On the Lao *meuang*, therefore, rests the continuity of Lao history. The intervention of European powers, particularly France, created a new equation of power relations in mainland Southeast Asia that permitted Lao *meuang* to escape Siamese hegemony. It thus created conditions for the possible future re-establishment of Lao political power, even if this was not the French intention when France seized Lao territories. How a new territorial entity called Laos came to be formed, and how this was perceived by its French administrators, thus constitutes the first chapter in the history of modern Laos.

# CHAPTER 2

# FRENCH LAOS, 1893–1945

For half a century Laos was a colony of France. But from the time of conquest an ambiguity lay at the heart of the French presence in Laos. For while the French were responsible for the territorial reconstruction of the Lao state, they never saw it as a viable political entity that should exist in its own right. French interest in Laos was always in relation to somewhere else. The expedition of Doudart de Lagrée and Francis Garnier was undertaken to discover a 'river road' to China. The goal of Auguste Pavie and other French imperialists of the late nineteenth century was to extend French jurisdiction over as much of Siam as possible. Their real interest lay in the rich and populous territories west of the Mekong: Lao territories on the east bank which could be claimed in the name of Vietnam were annexed merely as a springboard, and to gain control of the river itself. For colonial governors of French Indo-china, the value of Laos was primarily as a resource-rich hinterland for Vietnamese settlement and French exploitation, neither of which took place either in sufficient numbers or with expenditure of sufficient capital to produce revenue enough to cover administrative costs. Once the series of ethnically based rebellions caused by initial disruption to traditional lifestyles had been quelled, French interest remained minimal, but for a brief flurry of investment in tin mining. Not until threatened with the loss of Laos, initially when enticed to become part of a greater pan-Thai state, and subsequently in claiming independence, did French policy encourage development of Laos as a political entity in its own right. In the meantime, the French found willing collaborators among the Lao elite, who demanded little in the way of political participation or reform. As a result Lao nationalism developed slowly and painfully, lacking both direction and commonality of purpose.

## FRENCH INTERVENTION

In the period following the humiliation of the Franco-Prussian war of 1870, French imperialists sought to rebuild national prestige through the pursuit of empire. The death of Francis Garnier in northern Vietnam (Tonkin) in December 1873 provided the opportunity to extend French influence through accreditation of a French Résident at the Vietnamese court in Hué, and the posting of French military garrisons at Haiphong and Hanoi. Civil unrest caused by Chinese irregular forces operating in northern Vietnam led the French in 1882 to reinforce their Hanoi garrison. The death of the French commander at the hands of these Hô (Chinese) irregulars, known as the Black Flags, and the parading of his head around the villages of the Red River delta, provoked an outcry in France and despatch of a French military expedition. The imperial government in Hué sued for peace, and in August 1883 a treaty was signed establishing a French protectorate over central and northern Vietnam. A subsequent treaty signed the following year guaranteed among other things that France would defend all Vietnamese territories. It was on the basis of these two treaties that French claims to those areas of Laos that had at one time or another been tributary to Vietnam were to be vigorously pursued.

In Bangkok, King Chulalongkorn and his court viewed these developments with understandable concern. In the same year that a French protectorate was extended over Vietnam, French explorers began systematically surveying Lao territories. French intentions to assert maximum territorial claims in the name of Vietnam became clear with the publication of a stream of reports, books, maps, and pamphlets urging imperial expansion in Indochina. The Siamese response was to attempt to thwart French designs by enforcing their own tenuous control over outlying regions, a move that met with disingenuous protests from the Quai d'Orsay.

Over the next few years, the European concept of a centrally administered territorial state, with clearly marked, agreed-upon boundaries, came into conflict with the Southeast Asian *mandala* model based on tributary relations with subsidiary centres.[1] In the process, the French exploited previously existing differences between Siamese and Vietnamese conceptions of what a tributary relationship entailed. Requests to enter into tributary relations by local Lao rulers (*chau meuang*) were for them practical means of counter-balancing opposing power centres in order to maximize local autonomy. While this was well understood by the Siamese, for the Vietnamese such requests were interpreted as a desire to share in the benefits of imperial order and benevolence. Tributary Lao principalities (*meuang*) were incorporated as administrative divisions in the imperial records, even when Vietnamese influence, let alone presence, was minimal. The court of Hué was well aware of the reality, but the records were a godsend to the French, seeking as they were to extend the narrow confines of their Indochinese territories as far west as possible.[2]

The key player in the extension of French jurisdiction over Laos was that indefatigable schemer in the cause of French imperialism, Auguste Pavie. At first glance, Pavie seems an unlikely protagonist in the struggle to promote French interests. Of below average height, he was described by a contemporary as 'thin and weak-looking', but he was a man endowed with intelligence, energy, courage, and 'a force of will without equal'.[3] By the time he was chosen for the sensitive position of French vice-consul in Luang Phrabāng, Pavie was a veteran of seventeen years spent in Cochinchina and Cambodia, during which time he travelled widely, recorded assiduously, and learned how to relate to those among whom he worked and lived. In addition to a gift for languages, Pavie took a genuine interest in the peoples he encountered, if only as prospective French subjects. For Siamese officials he developed an intense dislike, and he was single-minded, even ruthless, in his determination to get the better of them.

Pavie owed his appointment to a court where the French had no interests to protect but many to promote indirectly to Britain. When the British obtained permission to appoint a consul in Chiang Mai, the French took advantage of agreements assuring them equal privileges to name Pavie as consul in Luang Phrabāng. Negotiations for establishment of a joint Franco-Siamese border commission to determine the frontier between Luang Phrabāng and Tonkin proved inconclusive, and a provisional accord in May 1886 allowed only for a vice-consulate in Luang Phrabāng and regulated French commerce there. As the French themselves were well aware, however, such an agreement implicitly recognized Siamese suzerainty over Luang Phrabāng; hence French reluctance to ratify it.

Pavie did not arrive in Luang Phrabāng until February 1887. There he was politely received by the two Siamese commissioners (*khāluang*) appointed to oversee the affairs of the kingdom. A month later, the Siamese commander, Wai Woronat, returned with hostages from an expedition to pacify the Sipsông Chu Tai, and claim the region for Siam. Faced with Wai Woronat's confident assertion that the entire population, both Tai and Chinese (Hô) who had settled in northern Laos, now recognized Siamese suzerainty, Pavie could only acquiesce in the Siamese *fait accompli*. But fate was to play into Pavie's hands.

While exploring the Nam Ū, Pavie received word of an imminent attack by the White Tai chieftain, Khamhum (known to the Vietnamese as Deo Van Tri). Hurriedly returning to Luang Phrabāng, he discovered that Wai Woronat, despite being warned of impending trouble, had already departed with his hostages for Bangkok, leaving the city virtually defenceless. Fearing to give battle, the small Siamese garrison and their Lao auxiliaries fled, and Luang Phrabāng fell to Khamhum and his mixed force of some six hundred Hô and upland Tai warriors. The rescue of the aged king from his burning palace during the sack of the city, the exodus down river to Pāklāy with the wounded, Pavie's care for the sick king while piecing together the early history of Lān Xāng as recorded in the royal archives, and the appeal in gratitude by King Unkham for French protection in place of Siam, all these have entered the legend of Pavie's single-handed 'conquest of hearts' by which he freed what now constitutes the territory of Laos from Siamese domination.[4] But if Pavie was successful in pressing the cause of French protection for Luang Phrabāng with King Unkham, it was to be some years before this could be formalized and extended to the rest of the country – and then more as a result of gunboat diplomacy than the winning of hearts.

What Pavie did accomplish, through his explorations and negotiations of 1888, was the inclusion of the Sipsông Chu Thai within the borders of Tonkin. The Siamese still hoped, however, to retain the allegiance of Luang Phrabāng to which the two Siamese commissioners had returned. Meanwhile Pavie set his sights on other Lao territories in the region of Khammūan, east from the Mekong to the watershed of the Sāy Phū Luang (Truong Son) cordillera, an area that was to become the new arena of Franco-Siamese confrontation. Here he found the Siamese clearly in possession. Although a small French garrison took up residence at Nāpae, on the Lao side of the watershed, Pavie could do little but accept the Siamese presence. Possession of territory was not, however, in his view, any basis on which to demarcate the frontier between French Indochina and Siam.

Pavie's determination 'to make of Laos a French country'[5] was supported by the powerful *Parti Colonial* in the French parliament, which wanted to see the frontiers of Indochina extended to the Mekong and beyond. What was envisaged was eventual annexation of Siam, but the first step was to seize control of the east bank of the Mekong. This could be done, according to one submission to the Quai d'Orsay, by refusing to recognize Siamese sovereignty over east-bank Lao *meuang*, and then 'at the appropriate moment' appointing 'commissioners for the suppression of slavery who are intended in fact to become virtual *résidents*'.[6] Similar means were to be used to ensure that Luang Phrabāng became a French protectorate. In both areas, Siamese garrisons would have to be persuaded to withdraw.

It was time for a more aggressive French policy. On the pretext of refusing to negotiate frontier agreements without detailed local knowledge, Pavie embarked upon his second 'mission' to extend French influence in Laos. Three separate teams of surveyors and scientists set about mapping and exploring regions of southern and central Laos, while Pavie himself travelled north to the Sipsông Phan Nā. Upon completion of these explorations, 'commercial agents' were posted at four points on the Mekong between Stung Treng, now in northern Cambodia, and Luang Phrabāng to establish a French presence. A Siamese offer to discuss the increasingly tense situation was rejected by Pavie, who continued to urge more resolute French action.

This was soon forthcoming. The new Governor-General of Indochina was Jean de Lanessan, an outspoken proponent of the 'forward policy'. In February 1892 Pavie was appointed French Consul-General in Bangkok, with the rank of Minister and the task of negotiating the Siamese out of Laos. Both in the Chamber of Deputies and in the French Foreign Ministry, the conviction had been growing that possession of the Mekong – already referred to by the colonial lobby as 'our river' – was vital for the future economic exploitation of French Indochina. Despite its unnavigable rapids, the Mekong was believed to provide potential trade access into southern China. Every possible argument was advanced in support of French claims – the most important being France's right of inheritance of territories formerly tributary to Vietnam. Two arguments that cut both ways, and thus could rebound against the French case, were natural boundaries and ethnic affinities, or as Pavie put it 'limits and races'. He urged the Quai d'Orsay to reject not only Siamese pretensions to rule in the name of all Tai to the limits of Tai settlement, but also any suggestion that the Mekong be accepted as a frontier.[7] By failing to take Pavie's advice, and instead moving first to secure the Mekong as the boundary of French Indochina, France was to find itself not poised, as Pavie hoped, to claim all the former kingdom of Lān Xāng, and indeed Siam itself, but up against the reality of stubborn Siamese resistance and British power. The result was to truncate a future Lao state.

## BRITAIN, FRANCE, AND THE BOUNDARIES OF FRENCH LAOS

French expansion of Indochina never depended simply on getting the better of Siam. The government in Paris was always well aware of the need to take British interests into account. Early in 1892, France began sounding out British reaction to the extension of French influence to the Mekong. Where the middle Mekong was concerned, the Foreign Office had few reservations. All the British wanted was to preserve enough of Siam to act as an independent buffer between French Indochina and British Burma, and to ensure British commercial and political interests remained dominant in what remained. The upper, rather than the middle, Mekong was of more concern to Whitehall.

As it happened, developments in the region itself made the running, rather than negotiations in Europe. Under the prompting of foreign advisors, and in the erroneous belief that Britain would support Siam in any confrontation with France, the government in Bangkok refused at first to make concessions over territory east of the Mekong. Siamese administration was strengthened, and garrisons reinforced. Meanwhile minor incidents between Siamese officials and French 'commercial agents' began to multiply, and haughty French patience to wear thin. The Siamese were proving 'difficult'. The crisis came to a head when, in two separate incidents, three French merchants were expelled from the middle Mekong on the orders of Siamese governors at Khammūan and Nôngkhāy, and the French vice-consul in Luang Phrabāng, ill and disheartened, committed suicide on his way back to Saigon. The French were outraged, and Pavie seized the opportunity to demand compensation. While the Siamese procrastinated, Pavie increased French demands to include immediate Siamese evacuation of all east-bank military posts from Khammūan south, an area he now formally claimed for France on the questionable grounds that it had once 'belonged' to Vietnam. When the Siamese court rejected these demands, de Lanessan ordered three French military columns into the disputed area in order to assert French administrative control. For Pavie the first step had been taken in what he hoped would lead to imposition of a French protectorate not just east of the Mekong, but over all of 'Siamese Laos'.

More force was required, however, to ensure Siamese compliance. The pretext for further French demands was provided by Siamese resistance to the French advance. While the central column achieved the peaceful withdrawal of eight small Siamese garrisons to west of the

Mekong, the southern and northern columns both ran into resistance. In the south, Siamese troops laid siege to the French position on the island of Khong and captured a French officer. In the north, a surprise Siamese attack killed the French commander and all but three of his Vietnamese troops. Both incidents were seized upon by the colonial lobby in France to whip up anti-Siamese sentiment. The government in Paris demanded reparations. Meanwhile anger over the French action fuelled an anti-foreign backlash in Bangkok. Three British navy ships were sent to the mouth of the Chaophraya in case it became necessary to evacuate British nationals. The French immediately followed suit, but instead of remaining outside the bar as instructed, two French warships forced the issue by sailing upstream. On 12 July 1893 both ships were fired on by the fort at Pāknam guarding the river entrance. One was hit. Both returned fire, and sailed on to Bangkok, where they anchored with their guns trained on the royal palace. The colonial lobby called for immediate annexation of Siam, but more moderate counsel prevailed and the French ultimatum on 20 July demanded only recognition of French rights to all territory east of the Mekong and to all islands in the river; withdrawal of all Siamese garrisons; compensation for military incidents and punishment of those Siamese involved; and payment of an indemnity of two million francs.

Failure to enlist British support left the Siamese court with no option but to capitulate. On 3 October 1893, a treaty was signed incorporating the terms of the original ultimatum, together with additional provisions for a 25-kilometre-wide demilitarized zone the length of the west bank of the Mekong (where the Siamese had the right to maintain civil administration and the French to establish a consular and commercial presence). All former inhabitants of the east bank were free to return. French Laos was beginning to take shape.

Interest next focused on two areas the Khōrāt plateau and the region northwest of Luang Phrabāng. In both Paris and Saigon, possession of the east bank of the Mekong was seen as only the first stage in the expansion of French Indochina. Early administrators of the newly acquired east-bank territories were well aware that they had been left with 'a depopulated, devastated country'[8] while the richer, more populated Lao lands west of the Mekong remained in Siamese hands. Pressure continued, therefore, for France to extend its Indochinese empire to include all the Khōrāt plateau, and even the Chaophraya valley. Meanwhile in the north France claimed all areas formerly tributary to Luang Phrabāng, plus eight of the twelve *meuang* making up the Sipsông Phan Nā (even though these owed primary allegiance to China or Burma). Only a small part of this territory, the province of Luang Namthā and part of Phongsālī, was subsequently gained by France under the terms of a treaty signed with China in June 1895.

To complicate matters further, British claims to the Shan state of Keng Tung included a tributary *meuang* east of the Mekong, Meuang Sing, which was also claimed by France under the terms of its 1893 treaty with Siam. British policy at this time was to minimize the possibility of conflict with France in Southeast Asia by maintaining Siam as a buffer state between the British Indian and French Indochinese empires. The British wanted therefore to cede a strip of territory on the upper Mekong to either China or Siam. The French, however, were determined to annex Meuang Sing and thus gain control of the Mekong. A joint commission despatched to the region could not agree on boundaries, and the situation threatened to bring Anglo-French rivalries in Southeast Asia to flashpoint – especially after Meuang Sing was temporarily occupied by a force of British Gurkhas. Both sides, however, preferred to avoid war.

Throughout the tedious negotiations that followed, the French government adamantly opposed any suggestion that France might contribute territory east of the Mekong to some putative buffer zone. In the end it was the British who backed down. Britain accepted the thalweg (the line joining the deepest points) of the Mekong as the frontier between the British Shan states and French upper Laos, in return for French acceptance of a neutral and independent Siam. Meuang Sing was handed over to France, but the Anglo-French agreement signed in London in January 1896 only preserved Siamese independence within the central Chaophraya basin. No mention was made of other areas, so by implication each power was free to pursue its interests elsewhere – Britain on the Malay peninsula and France in the Mekong basin, including western Cambodia and the Khōrāt plateau.

Over the next few years the French attempted to extend their Lao territories through pressure and negotiation. But already the government in Paris was beginning to lose interest. The opportunity to make a *casus belli* of an incident in 1902, when Siamese troops moved into the demilitarized zone along the Mekong to crush a popular rebellion, was not exploited – much to the disgust of French officials in Indochina. 'We would have been able,' wrote Lucien de Reinach, 'purely and simply, with the necessary military effort, to annex to Cambodia the provinces seized by Siam, and to reunite to our Laos all the country comprising the basin of the right [west] bank of the Mekong. Our situation in Indochina would then have been consolidated and our colony formed within its natural limits.'[9] Instead, all the French got in February 1904 were two extensions of territory west of the Mekong (Xainyaburī and part of Champāsak). France still retained a foothold in the 25-kilometre zone on the central Mekong through commercial 'establishments' at Nôngkhāy, Mukdāhān, Khemmarāt and four other sites.

Two months later signature of the *Entente Cordiale* between Britain and France recognized their respective zones of influence in those parts of Siam beyond the Chaophraya basin, while renouncing any intention by either to annex Siamese territory. This did not, however, prevent France from concluding one further treaty with Siam (in 1907) ceding western Cambodian territories to France, or Britain (in 1909) obtaining from Siam four northern Malay states, both in return for limitations to extraterritorial privileges. The 1907 treaty affected the boundaries of French Laos only marginally, with loss of a small southern extension of Xainyaburī province down to Dānxāy.

Further boundary changes were made subsequently in both the

northeast and southeast, as a result of French decisions on intra-
Indochinese administrative divisions. Of these, the more notable were
the transference of Huaphan (part in 1893 and the remainder ten years
later), and Xiang Khuang (in 1895) from Tonkin to Laos, and of Stung
Treng from Laos to Cambodia (in 1904); and the inclusion of parts of the
Central Highlands west of the watershed in southern Vietnam rather
than Laos (in 1904 and 1905).[10] These changes, while to some extent
recognizing historic allegiances and relationships, were more for
reasons of administrative convenience. They left the upland Tai of the
Sipsông Chu Tai and certain tribal minorities of the Central Highlands
under Vietnamese administration and created a Lao minority in
northeastern Cambodia.

More significant than the division of tribal minorities in the east,
however, was the division of ethnic Lao to the west. By accepting the
Mekong as the frontier of French Laos, the Lao were divided into two
unequal populations. The Siamese depopulation policy of earlier years
had concentrated a majority of Tai-Lao and many Tai-Phuan west of the
Mekong, mostly on the Khōrāt plateau. East of the Mekong a sparse
population remained, amounting to hardly one-fifth of all Lao previously under Siamese jurisdiction and barely half the total population
of French Laos, the rest being made up of various tribal minorities.[11] The
failure of France to press for creation of a Lao state including all the
middle Mekong basin was not due to ignorance of either the history or
ethnology of the region. The Mission Pavie had done its work well.
Once the French had claimed the east bank of the Mekong as territory
formerly tributary to Vietnam, they could as well have used the same
argument to claim the Khōrāt plateau as formerly part of the kingdom
of Viang Chan. This was what several French officials urged at the time,
in order to avoid 'deplorable consequences'.[12]

It is a common error in looking back upon the past to believe that
events that transpired could not have been otherwise. Yet at each point
in the game played between Britain and France in mainland Southeast
Asia, alternative choices and decisions could have been made. Had they
been, the map of the region might today have been very different. Had
France seized all of Siam, the state of Laos would not now exist.
Alternatively, under some pretext France might have occupied the
Khōrāt plateau. Had such a move been successful, no matter what
French intentions might have been at the time, this would effectively
have reconstructed the kingdom of Lān Xāng.

French failure to press for further territorial gains in those crucial
years between the treaties of 1893 and 1904 was due to two considerations that dominated French thinking at the time, almost as much in
Hanoi and Saigon as in Paris. The first had to do with French perceptions of power relations as they existed in mainland Southeast Asia,
the other with power relations in Europe. Britain figured in both. The
French saw only three powers in mainland Southeast Asia – Britain in
Burma, France in Vietnam, and Siam. Both Cambodia, and even more
so Laos, were mere extensions of French Vietnam. The Vietnamese were
seen as an active, expansionist people whose historic destiny, now

inherited by France, was to extend their control over weaker, less 'fit' (for this was the age of Social Darwinism) neighbouring peoples.[13] In French eyes, the Lao and Cambodians had had their day. Their kingdoms were in decline. Few at the time seriously believed either could form the core of a viable modern state. For the French, therefore, Indochina constituted a single entity comprising five parts;[14] not three territories which would eventually become three independent nations. Once the Mekong was accepted as the border between Indochina and northeastern Siam, the east-bank Lao territories were consistently thought of not so much as a separate centre of population and power, but rather as an extension of French Indochina, to be exploited for the benefit and greater glory of France.

The principal French concern, however, was not with Britain as the aggressive occupying power in Burma and dominant competitor for foreign influence in Siam, but with Britain as exercising the balance of power in Europe – the Britain which France came to see over these years leading up to the signing of the *Entente Cordiale* as potential ally rather than potential foe. This was the second, European, factor. By 1902, whatever the view promoted by French officials in Saigon or Bangkok, the French Foreign Ministry was making it clear to the British Foreign Office that France had no intention of actually annexing even those areas of Siam where, by agreement, the French were free to extend their influence. The Khōrāt plateau, the British were assured, would remain under Siamese control. Thus the great majority of all Lao continued to be ruled from Bangkok, for France had no intention of, indeed by then no interest in, recreating a greater Lao state.

French Laos, within its eventual borders, covered an area of 236,800 square kilometres, or about half the area of metropolitan France. It shared a mountainous frontier with Vietnam to the east of 1957 kilometres and China to the north of 416 kilometres. The Mekong formed the Lao border with the Shan state of Burma for a distance of 230 kilometres, as it did for most of the frontier with Siam (920 out of a total of 1730 kilometres). In the south, Laos shared a 492-kilometre border with Cambodia.[15] Its population was ethnically mixed and sparsely settled. Most were illiterate subsistence farmers, who produced little that was valuable by way of trade. Indeed as time went on, despite widespread belief that this *must* be a land of rich resources, if only they could be developed, there must have been those who wondered what France was doing in Laos.

What is evident in looking back over these years is that, despite the hopes of some French officials of reconstructing a greater Lao state, the territorial limits of the French colony and eventual independent state of Laos were the result of a series of historical accidents, the products of changing patterns of British, French and Siamese competition and compromise. Neither during its formation, nor during the half-century that Laos was administered by France, did its future viability as an independent political entity enter the calculations of French authorities. French Laos was never regarded as a resuscitated Lao state to be led towards independence free of threat from both Thai and Vietnamese.

Rather it was regarded as a province of Indochina, a mere hinterland to Vietnam, an area whose economic potential awaited exploitation through the investment of French capital and the introduction of Vietnamese labour.

## THE FRENCH ADMINISTRATION

The Franco-Siamese treaty of 1893 transferred a vast and varied region to French administration which the tireless Pavie, as France's first Commissioner-General for Laos, promptly took in hand. At the time, French Laos consisted of a number of distinct territories. In the north was the Kingdom of Luang Phrabāng: not the entire kingdom, for that had extended over both banks of the Mekong and Xainyaburī then still remained in Siamese hands, but yet an integral political entity administered by a ruler whom the French could guarantee to protect. Central Laos had no such cohesion. It consisted of a series of small regional *meuang* previously owning allegiance, either directly or indirectly, to the courts of Bangkok and/or Hué, neither of which had evinced much interest in territories east of the Mekong. This region was the responsibility of a provisional military administration by French officers commanding Vietnamese troops. It was an omen of French intentions.

A more anomalous situation prevailed in the south. There a descendant of the kings of Champāsak still exercised authority as a tributary of Siam. But since Champāsak, unlike Luang Phrabāng, was situated on the west bank, it remained after 1893 in Siamese hands. The French were thereby precluded from imposing a protectorate similar to that in Luang Phrabāng. Only the east-bank Champāsak territories fell under direct French administration. Not until the treaty of 1904 were some of the kingdom's west-bank territories ceded to France, including the royal capital. While most of the royal family took refuge in Bangkok, the resident prince, Chau Nyūy, elected to stay. The French were not then prepared to reconstitute the Kingdom of Champāsak, but the superior status of Chau Nyūy was recognized by naming him governor of Champāsak province with its new capital (after 1908) at Pākxē.[16]

The distinction that existed between the protectorate exercised over the Kingdom of Luang Phrabāng and direct administration of the rest of Laos as a colonial possession left unresolved the legal status of the whole as a constituent territory of French Indochina. In April 1917 France confirmed the 'special protectorate' status of Luang Phrabāng, but the matter was raised again prior to the Colonial Exhibition of 1930. The French Legislative Council then decided that Luang Phrabāng was not after all a protectorate, that agreements signed with the King carried no more than administrative force, and that the whole of Laos was therefore a French colony.[17] In response to objections from King Sīsavāngvong, this ruling was reversed by the Minister for Colonies in an exchange of letters with the King in December 1931 and February 1932. Thereafter Luang Phrabāng was accepted as having the status of

a French protectorate, even though its relationship to the rest of the
country remained unclear. Never did the French permit the King to
become even a figurehead symbol of unity for all of Laos. That unity
was proclaimed by the Lao Issara, the Free Lao movement that grew up
during World War II, not by the French. Not until negotiation of the
Franco-Lao *modus vivendi* of August 1946 did French authorities
acquiesce to extension of the jurisdiction of the King of Luang Phrabāng
to become King of Laos.

Initially the Lao territories were divided into three regions administered from Vietnam. In 1895 the country was divided into two regions
– Upper Laos to the north of Khammūan and Lower Laos from
Khammūan south – each administered by a 'Commandant Supérieur'
(resident respectively at Luang Phrabāng and Khong). Not until four
years later was Laos constituted as a single administrative entity, with
its own Résident Supérieur, based first at Savannakhēt and the
following year at Viang Chan. The change came as part of the political
and financial reorganization of Indochina ordered by Governor-General
Paul Doumer. Effectively this established a division of responsibilities
between the federal administration of Indochina and the administrations of its five constituent parts. Federal responsibilities included
security, customs, communications and large-scale public works, financed by indirect taxation (excise, tariffs, and the monopolies of alcohol,
salt and opium), while regional administrations handled such matters
as education, health, and justice, financed by direct taxes (notably the
capitation tax and administrative charges).

For Laos the change was beneficial, not least because administrative
costs were subsidized from the general budget. The new capital of
Viang Chan was centrally situated and enjoyed better communications
both with Luang Phrabāng and Bangkok. Moreover, the move had
symbolic significance: France restored the former Lao capital that the
Siamese had destroyed. At the local level, each of the eleven provinces
plus the Kingdom of Luang Phrabāng into which Laos was eventually
divided for administrative purposes became the responsibility of a
French Résident (or Commissioner in the case of Luang Phrabāng),
supported by a civilian official charged with financial and administrative affairs and a military commander of the provincial contingent
of the Garde Indigène.

Administration was direct, except in the case of Luang Phrabāng,
which lost Phongsālī in 1916 (constituted as Military Territory V) and
gained part of Huaphan in 1933. In Luang Phrabāng, King Sīsavāngvong, who had succeeded his father in 1904, presided over the administration. It was headed by the *uparāt* (at the time Chau Bunkhong, who
held office from 1888 to 1920), and the *rāxavong* and *rāxabut*, ministers of
the right and left, both princes of the ruling house bearing the
hereditary title *Thao*. Below them came three senior officials with the
rank of *Phrayā*; together with three others they comprised the Hôsanām
Luang, the supreme administrative council. All senior officials were
drawn from the nobility. Justice was administered by seven traditional judges. A corps of royal pages looked after the palace and court

ceremonial, while a separate category of officials was responsible for policing. The kingdom was divided into several *khuaeng* (still initially known as *meuang*) each presided over by a leading member of the local nobility, the *chau khuaeng*, assisted by three other hereditary officials.

Elsewhere the French Résident was responsible for everything from dispensing justice to taxation and public works. Law and order were maintained by the Garde Indigène, a unit of which was posted in each provincial capital under the command of a French officer; it was composed at first mainly of Vietnamese, but with more Lao recruits over time.[18] At first numbering only a minimal staff, the administration of larger and more populous provinces came to include an assistant résident, an agent of the Sûreté Général de l'Indochine (the colonial secret police), a paymaster, postmaster, school-teacher, and doctor. Representatives of other services were added as the need arose. Upper- and middle-level clerks were mostly Vietnamese, with Lao employed at the lower level as translators, junior clerks, cleaners, and 'coolies'. Each province was divided into districts (*meuang*, or *khong* in mountainous minority areas, presided over by an appointed *chau meuang*, or *nāy khong*), and each district into cantons (*tāsaeng*) grouping a number of villages (*bān*), each with its *nāy bān* or *phô bān* (village chief).

Even in directly administered provinces, the number of French officials was so small (three or four only in the smaller, more remote provinces) that French rule was effectively indirect. This was most evident in the administration of the Lao Thoeng and Lao Sūng minorities. For example, in the celebrated case of the Lamet, a small group inhabiting part of Haut Mékong province, the French created a separate Lamet *meuang* and appointed Lamet village chiefs. The *meuang* was administered by Tai-Leu tax collectors under the direction of a Tai-Lao *chau meuang*, who in turn reported to a provincial administration staffed in large part by Vietnamese.[19] The ethnic hierarchy thus formalized was administratively convenient. Its benefit for the French administration was that resentment over corruption, extortion, or burdensome corvée and taxation tended to focus on the next higher level, rather than on the French themselves, and could be diffused simply by rearranging the hierarchy. Traditional relationships were, however, thereby undermined and new ethnic antagonisms fostered whose implications spilled over into the post-colonial period.

The early French administrators, both military and civilian, set out to bring orderly, enlightened French rule to what most considered the ignorant and benighted peoples of Laos. Villages were counted, censuses taken, headmen appointed. Two matters concerned the French in particular, besides law and order: abolition of slavery, and taxation. The former lent moral weight to France's 'civilizing mission'; the latter covered its costs. Despite Siamese decrees, slave raiding continued and trafficking was widespread. Swift action was taken after 1893 to eliminate all trade in slaves. What French officials took to be the virtual slavery of certain Lao Thoeng tribes traditionally required to serve Lao masters was also abolished, and an enquiry conducted with a view to eliminating debt slavery.

Taxation was an even more pressing problem, if the administration of the new colony was to pay for itself. Prior to 1893, both Lao Lum and Lao Thoeng in southern Laos paid a head tax to the Siamese Commissioner at Champāsak, either in cash or in kind. This was collected by the local Lao nobility, who also demanded traditional levies in kind and labour as needed. At first French taxes were levied at similar rates, payable in cash or kind, with the customary exemptions for the sick, Buddhist monks, officials, and (former) slaves. Corvée for public works, unpopular from the start, was fixed at ten days per annum for both Lao Lum and Lao Thoeng, though this could be avoided through an additional cash payment. As the Lao nobility continued to collect traditional taxes, the tax burden was, in fact, greater. As of 1896 taxation was increased, payable only in cash, and a distinction drawn between Lao Lum on the one hand and Lao Thoeng and Lao Sūng on the other. While the former had their head tax doubled, the latter were expected to perform more corvée labour. Additional charges were progressively introduced and increased. With the extension of the alcohol monopoly to Laos, each household had to pay an alcohol consumption tax (later doubled) whether or not they consumed any alcohol. Other monopolies were also extended to Laos, notably opium and salt. Payment was demanded for services, such as issuing travel papers and registration of firearms, and duties were charged on any merchandise and livestock exported to Siam. Initially there was no tax on land, though one was eventually introduced in 1935. Vietnamese paid double head tax with no corvée, while Chinese paid five times the Lao head tax, plus an additional charge if they owned a shop. While in absolute terms taxes may not have seemed excessive, they had a regressive cumulative effect, given the very low income levels prevailing, and this imposed a considerable and often excessive burden on the poorest levels of society.[20]

The need to increase taxation, and the distinction made between Lao Lum on the one hand and Lao Thoeng and Lao Sūng on the other, reflected both the difficulties encountered by the French in meeting the costs of administration, and their ambitions for development of the colony. By 1910 direct taxation contributed just over one-third to a total budget of some 900,000 *piastres*, a threefold increase in locally raised revenue since 1896. Indirect taxes amounted to a little more than 160,000 *piastres*.[21] The shortfall was made up by a direct grant from the federal budget for Indochina. Despite the need for increased expenditure on basic infrastructure, this subvention was steadily reduced. As a result, despite increased revenue, the budget for Laos grew by only 12.5 per cent between 1896 and 1911.[22] It was obvious that, if Laos was to pay its way, either the tax base would have to be increased through increasing population; or natural resources would have to be exploited. As a short-term measure to increase revenue, Lao Lum were urged to redeem their period of corvée in the form of cash. Another means was to encourage the sale of opium, the most profitable government monopoly in Indochina.

The principal effect of the new system of taxation imposed by the

French was to strengthen and centralize administrative control and to force a change from a predominantly barter economy to one based increasingly on money as the means of exchange. Apart from exceptional cases, taxes had to be paid in cash, which meant that families were forced to undertake production of commodities with a market value which could be sold to meet tax demands. The effects of this were less disruptive in Laos than in other parts of French Indochina, however, because the Lao Lum peasantry enjoyed relatively egalitarian access to abundant land, and could often simply grow a little more rice, while the Lao Sūng and Lao Thoeng could sell opium or forest products. Thus no impoverished landless rural proletariat developed in Laos as it did in Vietnam.

Far more unpopular than the head tax was the corvée that had to be performed by every male between the ages of eighteen and forty-five at times the administration designated. Traditional labour demands were for specific purposes – to build a house, to prepare for a ceremony. All Lao considered forced labour to be demeaning, especially in road gangs under the direction of arrogant officials. Sometimes insensitivity to local conditions extended to demanding corvée at times when crops had to be sown or harvested, or forest products collected. Those who had the means would redeem their corvée, though this was discouraged on the part of Lao Thoeng, whose labour was required to build roads in sparsely populated mountainous regions. Additional demands were often made in the form of porterage and requisitions, giving rise to a growing reservoir of resentment.

By the turn of the century, the French had reason to be proud of their initial labours in Laos. An administration, though skeletal, had been established. The capture and sale of slaves had been outlawed, and conditions imposed which would lead to the elimination of debt slavery. Increasingly the Lao Thoeng tribes to the east of the Bôlavēn plateau were being brought under French administrative control. Taxes were being collected, and labour performed to develop the infrastructure of colonial control – housing, offices, barracks, prisons, roads. Catholicism had gained a small foothold, and a few French *colons* had taken up land. The Lao, it would seem, had passively accepted French imperialism, though just what lay in store for them was unclear.

## THE LAO RESPONSE

Though many Lao at first seemed ready to welcome the French as liberators from the exactions of the Siamese, others were more suspicious. It was not long, however, before new administrative measures began to have an impact on the structure of traditional Lao society – by favouring some social groups at the expense of others, by undermining traditional economic relationships, or by setting one ethnic group against another. Resistance to an often intrusive and insensitive French military presence was widespread, taking either active or passive forms depending on local circumstances. The new system of taxes and charges was widely unpopular. So too was forced labour. That these did not lead to an exodus of population across the Mekong was in large part because the Siamese too had increased taxation and tightened their administrative hold on the Khōrāt plateau in the face of French territorial ambitions. On both banks of the Mekong, new administrative structures undermined, and eventually destroyed, traditional tributary and trading relationships, and threatened the status of those who profited from them. In both areas a distant central government began exercising new and intrusive measures of control that curtailed traditional freedoms of the Lao population – to manage their own affairs, to trade with whomsoever they pleased, to own slaves. Progressively local leaders came to depend for their positions not on recognized hereditary rights but on appointment as civil servants by French or Siamese officials, in whose hands power now lay. These administrative changes and increased taxation occurred at a time when alternative sources of wealth had been lost or reduced. In the north the principal source of wealth affected was opium: in the south, slaves. In both regions discontent eventually led to open revolt.

The earliest forms of resistance to these disruptive changes were passive – refusal to accept French regulations or to cooperate with French officials, avoidance or minimization of tax by deliberately understating population (by as much as 35 per cent according to some estimates), or in a few cases migration elsewhere.[23] Though there was some unrest in the north in 1895 in Huaphan province, the first serious violent opposition came in the same year in southern Laos. The so-called 'Holy Man's revolt' drew on traditional millenarian beliefs to mobilize resentment against both French and Siamese authorities. But whereas the Siamese were quick to suppress the insurrection west of the Mekong, the French were less successful. It took until 1910 to restore French authority throughout the Bôlavēn region. Even so, one rebel group held out in the mountains to the east for another twenty-five years.[24]

The revolt seems to have been provoked by the methods used by the French Commissioner at Sālavan in attempting to 'pacify' Lao Thoeng tribes – that is, to convince them to pay taxes and perform corvée labour. Fearful that a self-proclaimed 'holy man' (or phū mī bun, meaning 'he who has merit') was gaining too much influence, the Commissioner burned a pagoda erected to honour him. This only fanned the flames of the movement. In April 1901, the Commissioner and his guards were attacked by several hundred Lao Thoeng armed with flintlock rifles, an incident which served to signal a general uprising. The leader of the revolt was Bak Mī, known to his followers as Ong Kaeo, a Lao Thoeng of the Ālāk tribe and former monk who claimed to possess supernatural powers. Within weeks, unrest had spread throughout much of the southern Lao highlands. By June increasing numbers of Lao Lum were joining the movement, including members of the nobility, and it began to attract adherents west of the Mekong.[25] Within six months one Frenchman and more than a hundred members of the Garde Indigène had been killed, massive damage had been done to property and crops, and almost the entire Bôlavèn region was in the hands of the insurgents.

Both the messianic and millenarial character of this revolt have been remarked upon by scholars. Ong Kaeo proclaimed himself *Chau Sadet* or Great King – a title which associated earthly power with the messianism of the future Buddha Metteya – and called for the elimination of the French from Laos. In popular Buddhist belief, Metteya will be born on earth at an appointed time 'to save humankind from sin'. His reign will be one of righteousness and plenty, when all will live in accordance with the Buddhist *Dhamma*. Even if the *phū mī bun* was not himself Metteya, he was for his followers endowed with magical powers, and possessed the merit to become either a great religious or a great military leader (*cakkavattin*). Either way, the *phū mī bun* offered the prospect of a golden age to replace the misery of the present.

As a proclaimed *phū mī bun*, Ong Kaeo attracted a number of able lieutenants. They included Ong Man, who led the revolt on the Siamese side of the Mekong, and Ong Kommadam, a Lao Thoeng of the Nya Heun tribe, each of whom recruited and led his own band of insurgents. Meanwhile a certain Phô Kaduat, also claiming to be a *phū mī bun*, gained a separate following among the Lao Lum of Savannakhèt. By early 1902, the rebellion reached its peak. In March Ong Man seized and sacked the town of Khemmarāt in the demilitarized strip west of the Mekong, and began marching on Ubon. The Siamese rushed in military reinforcements and fought a series of engagements with Ong Man's followers: more than three hundred rebels were killed and four hundred captured.[26] Ong Man escaped and rejoined Ong Kaeo.

The French authorities in both Viang Chan and Hanoi followed these events with rising alarm, concerned both for the security of the 25-kilometre demilitarized zone, and that its status should be preserved. But local French officials had more pressing problems to contend with. On 21 April 1902, a chanting force more than two thousand strong, mostly Lao Lum, attacked two posts guarding the approaches to Savannakhèt, both of which had been reinforced by a detachment of the Garde Indigène. Apparently in the belief that they were invulnerable and that bullets would turn into frangipani flowers, traditional offerings to the Buddha, Ong Kaeo's followers mounted three suicidal attacks, only to be shot down. About one hundred and fifty were killed, and many more wounded.[27]

Following this massacre, French repression was swift. Four contingents of the Garde Indigène converged on the region west of Savannakhèt. Leaders implicated in the revolt were shot and villages burned. By August, resistance was at an end. Phô Kaduat fell back on Xēpōn, but was a hunted man. He was killed the following year. Ong Kaeo, other leaders and small bands of Lao Thoeng insurgents meanwhile withdrew to strongholds in the mountains southeast of the Xē Kông river to the east of the Bôlavèn. For the next two years, the French pursued their pacification of southern Laos, but the peace imposed was deceptive, for the rebels still enjoyed widespread support. Three of the four traditional chiefs of the Nya Heun tribe, for example, remained with the insurgents.[28]

In November 1905, a rebel band under the command of Ong Kommadam massacred thirty-nine Lāven tribesmen, and the newly appointed French Commissioner of Sālavan, J.-J. Dauplay, determined to put an end to the rebellion. This was easier said than done, and not until October 1907 were Ong Kaeo and most of his followers forced to surrender. Only Kommadam and his band still remained defiant in the mountains of Attapeu. From there he issued a set of political demands: replacement of Lao Lum *chau meuang* by a Lao Thoeng chief for the Bôlavēn; the plateau to be reserved for the Lao Thoeng alone; and reduction (though not the complete elimination) of taxes.[29]

Dauplay hoped that the surrender of Ong Kaeo would discredit him in the eyes of his followers. Over the next three years, far from losing prestige, Ong Kaeo maintained his reputation as a *phū mī bun*. By then Dauplay had had enough of 'this brute of a Kha Alak' whose very existence constituted a standing affront to French authority.[30] On 11 November 1910, Ong Kaeo was arrested. Early next morning he was bayoneted to death by a guard while allegedly trying to escape. Two days later Dauplay attended a meeting with Kommadam to negotiate surrender terms. Both sides were searched for weapons, but Dauplay, knowing that his head would not be touched, had hidden a revolver under his hat. This he drew and fired at Kommadam from point-blank range. Though wounded, both Kommadam and his brother escaped. A furious Dauplay burned the rebels' village and displayed Ong Kaeo's head for all to see. Three of his lieutenants were condemned to death and guillotined. Others were sent to serve long sentences on the prison island of Poulo Condore, off the coast of Vietnam.

Kommadam survived his wounds, later to resume his implacable struggle, but for the authorities at the time, the death of Ong Kaeo put an end to the *phū mī bun* revolt. The area was declared pacified, even though Kommadam was still at large. When corvée demands and taxes were increased in 1914, the administration was careful to place more of the burden on the Lao Lum rather than the Lao Thoeng.[31] In 1924, Kommadam again began secretly to make his presence felt, sending his emissaries throughout the region to contact tribal groups. A year later he wrote to the French authorities calling for a unified administration for all Lao Thoeng tribes, and respect for their customary rights. The French refused to respond. As Résident Supérieur Jules Bosc stated in his instructions to the Résident of Sālavan: 'The absolute preservation of our prestige is the overriding question.'[32] In the early 1930s, Kommadam again began attracting followers in the build-up to the final phase of his sustained defiance of French authority. By that time, as we shall see, his revolt merged with new forms of opposition to French rule to fuel the revolutionary independence movement in Laos.

In the north too resentment against French rule boiled over into insurrection. As on the Bôlavēn, the underlying reasons were again disruption of traditional power structures and relationships, interference with traditional trade patterns and other means of generating wealth, increased burdens of taxation, and onerous and demeaning corvée labour. These were particularly felt by those at the bottom of the social and ethnic hierarchy. The Lao Lum elite were better off. At the level of the *meuang*, the French made a virtue of retaining local administration intact – as both Vietnamese and Siamese had done before them. Only at the province level was a French administration superimposed. For the provincial Lao nobility this merely substituted a new hegemony for the hated Siamese, one better able to protect them and less likely to make arbitrary exactions. Taxes had to be paid, but then so had tribute to the Siamese. The prestige and standing of the provincial nobility thus remained intact. Whatever demands the French made by way of taxes could be passed on to those they administered. A basis for collaboration thus existed that provided the foundation for French rule in Laos.

Nor did the Lao Lum peasantry suffer unduly. Taxes might be levied individually, but they were often paid communally at reduced rates as village chiefs deliberately underquoted the number of inhabitants. Besides, nature was abundant and population density low. Also the lowland Lao were more likely to benefit from new opportunities for trade, from improved communications, from better security, and later by way of health care, education, and agricultural and veterinary programs. This was much less likely where the Lao Thoeng, and in the north Lao Sūng, were concerned. In their case lowland Lao administrators gouged the maximum in the form of taxation and corvée; additional demands, particularly for porterage, were more likely to be made; and they gained far less than the lowland Lao by way of benefits.

The first serious outbreak of unrest in the north came in Phongsālī, in one of the two Tai-Leu cantons previously forming part of the Sipsông Phan Nā (the other being Meuang Sing). The imposition of artificial borders between Laos and China had divided the ancient Leu polity and created political instability in the parts annexed to Laos. For the Leu chiefs, their former tributary relationship with a distant China had weighed much less heavily than did the direct administration progressively introduced by the French. Effectively the French presence undermined the traditional authority of the Leu chiefs (whose position in their own fiefs was as independent princes rather than dependent regional Lao nobility), while at the same time reducing economic and social relations with the Chinese portions of the Sipsông Phan Nā. Over a period of almost ten years relations between Vannaphūm, the local Leu hereditary chief, and the French gradually deteriorated to the point where the French Commissioner in March 1908 personally attempted to engineer his arrest. Vannaphūm escaped and the Leu rose in revolt. It was two years before the French were able to restore their authority. Vannaphūm was finally captured, only to be killed when his followers attempted to free him.[33]

Four years later it was the turn of the Leu of Meuang Sing. French administration of the region was only fully established in 1904. Meuang Sing had been ruled by hereditary Tai-Leu princes with the title of *Chau*

*Fā*. While the old Chau Fā had acquiesced in the French takeover, his son Ong Kham who succeeded him on his death in 1907 deeply resented the French presence and the limitations this imposed on his own powers and prerogatives. By December 1914 relations had reached their nadir. Chau Fā Ong Kham fled to the Chinese Sipsông Phan Nā where he raised the flag of revolt, and for the next two years Leu guerrilla bands mounted a hit-and-run war against the French. Three military expeditions were necessary to re-establish French authority. Meuang Sing was reduced from a principality to a *meuang* under direct French administration.

The outbreak of fighting in Meuang Sing coincided with an anti-French uprising further east. Both were probably influenced by the instability in southern China following the republican revolution of 1911 that overthrew the Qing dynasty. In November 1914 a force of some forty Chinese, supported by an equal number of hill Tai, attacked and overran the French administrative garrison at Xam Neua, killing the French Résident and seizing arms, opium and cash. The town was retaken a month later, but the revolt spread swiftly into northwestern Vietnam and Phongsālī. Leu, upland Tai and even Khamu (though not the Hmong) joined the Chinese-led rebellion. By February 1915 most of northeastern Laos was in rebel hands. Two companies of French troops sent to restore order were forced to withdraw. In November 1915 a major military expedition was mounted from Tonkin, comprising 160 French and 2500 colonial troops divided into two columns, with 800 pack animals carrying supplies, ammunition and artillery pieces.[34] In six weeks of fighting the two columns succeeded in dispersing rebel forces and driving them north across the Chinese border. Phongsālī was placed under military administration, and the following March became Military Territory V, extending the four already established in the north of Vietnam along the border with China.

The anti-French nature of this rebellion was made very clear in the proclamations posted by its Chinese leadership. The causes of the revolt lay not in the loss of powers or prerogatives, but in the disruption to the lucrative opium trade made illegal by the imposition of the opium monopoly. Local Chinese (Hô) in northern Laos had traditionally acted as agents for opium merchants arriving from southern China with their caravans of pack mules. Local producers, mainly the Hmong, could consume their own product but were supposed to sell their excess to the *Régie d'Opium*, the French-run monopoly. Production of opium in Laos was not encouraged, however, since it was considered to be of poor quality. Chinese agents, supposedly acting as middlemen for the *Régie*, were in fact continuing to sell at better prices to Chinese smugglers. When harsh fines began to be levied on those discovered with illegal opium in their possession, not only Chinese merchants, but also Lao officials in their pay, lost a major source of income.

Tai partisans who joined the revolt did so for other reasons. They neither produced nor traded in opium. Rather they blamed the French for the burden of taxation, which had been added to those demanded by the traditional Tai chieftains of the Sipsông Chu Tai. It was not the chiefs, but the poorest elements of the upland Tai population who had little to lose who responded to Chinese promises to create a more just administrative order.

Somewhat surprisingly, the only part the Hmong played in the events of 1914–16 was on the French side. Yet within less than three years the Hmong too rose in revolt. The origins of what became known as the Pāchai rebellion, or the 'madman's revolt', lay in brutal suppression of a Hmong uprising in southern China in 1918, which resulted in an exodus of Hmong into northern Vietnam and Laos. Hmong agitation in these regions increased, especially as the uprising took on an 'anti-mandarin' complexion aimed as much against upland Tai chiefs as against Chinese. In northern Vietnam, there was deep Hmong resentment against the Tai chiefs whose agents collected inflated taxes nominally on behalf of the French. These feelings came to a head at the end of October 1918, when hundreds of armed Hmong attacked Tai villages in the vicinity of Dien Bien Phu.

The leader of the revolt was a Hmong shaman named Pāchai, described by the French as a sorcerer and a madman because of his messianic promise to establish an independent Hmong kingdom. In response to the re-establishment of French authority in northwestern Vietnam, Pāchai and his followers withdrew into Laos. There the seeds of revolt were sown during the first half of 1919, and by October they had flowered into a general uprising taking in most of northeastern Laos. The targets, apart from the French, were Lao rather than Tai. Telegraph lines were cut, villages burned, and inhabitants forced to flee. Khamu villagers were reduced to virtual slavery, carrying supplies and building defence works for the Hmong insurgents. Not all Hmong, however, joined the revolt. Some traditional chiefs were reluctant to surrender their authority to Pāchai. From September 1919 to April 1920, the French military mounted large-scale operations against the rebels. Throughout 1920 more and more Hmong made their submissions to French authorities as the Garde Indigène pursued its systematic pacification of the area. Ringleaders were summarily executed, weapons surrendered, and reparations imposed for damage inflicted. By March 1921 the revolt was over. Pāchai and two or three faithful retainers fled to the mountains, where they were finally ambushed and killed by Lao Thoeng in November 1922.[35]

By that time French rule had been restored. A commissioned report identified the principal cause as inter-ethnic tension created by the structure of colonial administration. Taxation was burdensome. Collection of taxes from Hmong villages was in the hands of Phuan and Tai officials. Amounts collected were up to three times the official rate, as tax collectors exacted traditional tribute to Phuan chiefs in addition to French-imposed taxes. Such abuses were directly addressed by the announcement in April 1920 that henceforth the Hmong 'would no longer depend on any other race' but would administer themselves through the election of Hmong chiefs who would be responsible for collecting taxes from their own people.[36]

Until then Hmong clan leaders, known as *kiatong*, had been

answerable to Lao provincial authorities. After the Bāchai rebellion, *kiatong* were appointed as *tāsaeng* (canton or district) chiefs, the most important of which was the *tāsaeng* of Nônghaet on the Lao–Vietnamese frontier. To this strategic position was appointed Lôbliayao, *kiatong* of the powerful Lô clan. His secretary was his son-in-law Līfung, of the Lī clan. In 1938, the French authorities replaced Lôbliayao's eldest son with Līfung as chief of Nônghaet, much to the anger of the Lôbliayao family: they considered the loss of the position a slur on their honour. When Līfung died the following year, elections were held between Faidāng, Lôbliayao's second son, and Līfung's eldest son, Tūbī, the first Hmong to have completed high school. Tūbī won, but incurred the bitter and lasting resentment of the Lô clan and so gave rise to a feud that thereafter divided the Hmong community, with tragic repercussions for the post-colonial history of Laos.[37]

More scholarly attention has been given to these anti-colonial revolts than to most other aspects of French colonialism in Laos. What all had in common was their opposition to changes introduced through new administrative controls and increased taxes, which threatened traditional interests, relationships, lifestyles and economies. All were reactions to the disruptions caused by the initial intrusion of French imperialism. In the *phū mī bun* and Pāchai rebellions, strong messianic elements were present. Resistance took forms sanctioned by traditional worldviews. Both the Lao Thoeng of the Bôlavēn and the Hmong fought for more than independence from both French and Lao. Both also sought to maintain a way of life that closed out the new forces of the modern world. They looked backwards, in other words, to discover the shape of the future.

At the time, the French dismissed these rebellions as disturbances brought about by the irrational superstitions of primitive peoples. Their suppression was essential to restore order and authority. It was a position that met with some sympathy from the Lao elite, apart from those few actually involved. For most Lao, rebel Lao Thoeng and Hmong were but 'slaves' and 'savages'. Not surprisingly, accounts of the uprisings were relegated to insignificance in the historiography of colonialism and ignored by its elite collaborators, who thus could conveniently overlook the fact that relatively few lowland Lao took up arms against their French colonizers.[38]

These rebellions have also been seen, however, in another light – as heroic resistance to French colonialism and as forerunners to the later radical nationalist movements of the Lao Issara and Pathēt Lao. From a Western perspective, to interpret them as 'proto-nationalist' forms of political struggle, let alone to discover in these revolts the origins of modern Lao revolutionary nationalism, can only be condemned as anachronistic. Even after 1945 little sense of 'nation' or 'nationalism' existed in Laos inclusive of the minority groups who principally rose in rebellion. But for Pathēt Lao historiography as this developed in the 1950s, such an interpretation served an important political end. The central involvement of both Lao Thoeng and Lao Sūng minorities in these uprisings, far from being an embarrassment, served to include them in the revolutionary movement. Their leaders were remembered as national heroes of the anti-colonial struggle. Thus the significance of these revolts for subsequent Lao history lies primarily in the way they have figured in nationalist discourse to draw marginalized ethnic groups into an 'imagined community' able to unify all the 'multi-ethnic' Lao people.[39]

## THE FRENCH IN LAOS

French attitudes to Laos were fundamentally ambiguous, due in large part to the tensions that existed between the levels at which policy was decided. While some French officials who served in Laos viewed their assignment as an unfortunate hiatus in their career before appointment elsewhere, many developed a warm affection for the country and its people. Not a few took Lao wives, married in ceremonies that conveniently were not officially recognized under French civil law. Their disposition towards their charges was for the most part benign and paternalistic. But Laos was a part of French Indochina, for the future of which policy decisions were made in Hanoi and Paris. Within Laos, French policy might be formulated in ways beneficial to the Lao; but from the perspective of Hanoi, policy had to benefit Indochina as a whole, and in Indochina, French and Vietnamese interests took precedence over Lao.

Virginia Thompson, an acute observer of Indochina in the late 1930s, remarked of Laos that it was the country where the French were happiest:

> For the rare Frenchman who sees in the Lao a silly, lazy, and naive people, there are hundreds who are charmed by their gentle affability and their aesthetic appearance ... The effect which the French have had upon the Laotian people is as yet – perhaps because the economic exploitation is so dilatory there – very slight in comparison with the influence Laos has had upon the French ... For the European wearied with Western greed and strife, Laos seems to be the answer to all his problems ... Laos is in itself a passive reproach to the futility of Europe's bustling activity and soul-searchings ... The Laotians ... render lip-service to European superiority, because it is too much trouble to be impolite, but the Laotians do not believe in it. Nor does the European for long who lives in their amiable midst. Europe is well lost to gain a Laotian soul.[40]

The French who made Laos their home or their career regarded the Lao with a mixture of affection and exasperation. French attitudes were shaped by Pavie's 'conquest of hearts'. The Lao were naïve, charming, indolent and childlike, with little incentive to do much more than enjoy themselves. They were gentle, hospitable, submissive and respectful, and had 'all the qualities of a good subject of whom one should not ask too much'.[41] The image of Laos and the Lao in France was constructed through a romantic haze that combined equal measures of sex and sentiment. It was Lao courtship ritual in which young men and women exchanged sexually allusive verses that titillated French travellers. In the half-dozen French novels set in Laos, love is the central theme. Laos was a land where the simple pleasures of life and the exotic charms of its women – 'adorable, soft and playful' – exerted an attraction that was both sensuous and timeless.[42]

That Lao women raised children and performed much of the physical labour of field and home struck no chords in the French imagination. Moreover, there was always a negative side to the orientalized image the French constructed of the Lao, women and men alike. In French eyes the Lao were credulous, mendicant, and incapable of either initiative or hard work.[43] As a consequence, therefore, the French believed they could never depend on the Lao either to administer the country effectively, or to develop its resources in the best interests of France. For that they turned to the Vietnamese, who from the beginning staffed much of the middle level of the French administration.

The European presence always remained slight. By 1910 only some two hundred Frenchmen administered the entire country. Though this figure slowly increased after World War I, there were never many more than a thousand Europeans in French Laos, something over half of whom were there in an official capacity. They administered a Lao population that increased from an estimated 600,000 in 1910 to 819,000 by 1921, and 1,038,000 by 1936.[44] More important, however, than any increase in the Lao population was French policy to encourage Chinese and Vietnamese traders and artisans to settle in the urban centres, where they quickly outnumbered the Lao themselves.

By 1920, after two decades of unrest brought about by the imposition of French administrative control, the country was at peace. To be sure, Kommadam was still unsubdued in the mountains of the southeast, but it would be five years before he would make his presence felt again. World War I was over and France had emerged victorious, still a great if diminished power. The jewels of her empire were North Africa and Indochina. In Laos an administration was in place and functioning as well as could be expected, as was a new judicial system. Rudimentary services providing health care, education, and agricultural and veterinary advice were slowly being expanded as communications improved. Hopes were held for steady, if not rapid, economic development.

In October 1920 the administration felt secure enough to introduce the first political reforms. Provincial advisory councils were established in directly administered provinces, comprising the *chau meuang* and two other nominees from each district. Members were appointed; deliberations were confidential; and recommendations were not binding. Three years later, Laos was the last of the five territories of Indochina to establish an Indigenous Consultative Assembly to advise the Résident Supérieur. Members of the Assembly were elected on a limited franchise, restricted to appointees of provincial advisory councils plus those who had reached higher grades in the indigenous civil service or who possessed the requisite level of education. It was, therefore, representative only of the Lao elite. At the same time, a Mixed Chamber of Commerce and Agriculture, in which French interests predominated, advised the Résident Supérieur on economic and commercial matters.

As the Résident Supérieur, Jules Bosc, reminded delegates at the opening session of the Indigenous Consultative Assembly on 30 August 1923, this was the first time since the division of Lān Xāng in the early eighteenth century that representatives of all of Laos had met together to deliberate on the future of their country.[45] But the Lao elite were never allowed to forget their dependency on France, and political reform went no further. Forms of representative government that encouraged nationalism in the 1930s in Burma and the Philippines were never introduced in French Indochina, where the French were more interested in keeping the lid on nationalist sentiment.

In Laos, the educated elite was small enough and dependent enough to be convinced by French arguments that the primary need was for modernization under French direction, not political representation. But modernization was slow. It took thirty years for a definitive legal system to be put in place. Not until 10 July 1928 did French authorities establish a Practical School of Law and Administration to train Lao civil servants. Until then most administration at the province level had been carried out by Vietnamese (except in Luang Phrabāng where an indigenous Lao administration functioned at the regional level of *chau khuaeng*), while at the district level Lao *chau meuang* brought nothing but their own experience to the job at hand.

French failure to provide adequate training for Lao officials reflected the inadequacy of education in general. Not until 1905 did education figure as a specific item in the budget for Laos. Expenditure on education was minimized through retention of traditional pagoda schools supposedly to teach literacy in Lao at the primary level, but often providing little more than rote instruction in Buddhist doctrine and morality. Primary schools offering instruction in French were established only in a few provincial capitals. Though labelled Franco-Lao, they were mainly patronized by the expatriate Vietnamese community. By 1907 there were still only four French teachers in all of Laos.[46] Over the next twenty years the number of such schools slowly increased to cater for the growing urban population in the larger centres, though not until 1917 were six full years of primary education available in French.

Not until 1921 was the first and only junior secondary school, the Collège Pavie, established in Viang Chan. To complete their secondary studies in preparation for university, Lao students had to go to Hanoi. In 1923 a technical training school was opened in Viang Chan to train bricklayers and carpenters, while in 1928 the first Pali school was established as a branch of the Buddhist Institute in Phnom Penh to deepen knowledge of Buddhism in the Lao *Sangha*. By 1930, there were eighty-two schools staffed by 208 teachers, 21 of them French, teaching 6500 students.[47] Thereafter, education suffered severe budgetary cuts during the depression years. By the end of the decade fewer than one in twenty school-age children were attending school. Enrolment for the full four years at the Collège Pavie was still only 120, 17 of whom were girls, but fewer than half Lao.[48] Few secondary graduates advanced to the tertiary level, and in 1939 only seven Lao students were attending tertiary institutions in Vietnam. Not until the early 1940s did education receive any greater priority.

If the French record in education was unimpressive, the record in health was mixed. Health services were at first confined to provision of medical care for Europeans, who were particularly prone to tropical diseases. By 1910 there were only five French doctors in all of Laos. But expenditure on health did slowly increase. By 1930 there were six hospitals, fifty-five dispensaries and two leprosaria staffed by twelve French and twelve auxiliary 'Indochinese doctors' with four years of medical studies. Eight years later, however, partly as a result of the financial crisis of the mid-1930s, these numbers had declined. Only in Viang Chan was there a hospital of any size. Medical facilities served primarily the French community and urban areas, where ethnic Lao usually formed a minority. As a result, little appreciable improvement was registered in the health of the general population (in terms of increase in life expectancy, reduction of infant mortality, or reduction of the incidence of diseases such as malaria or tuberculosis), despite vaccination against childhood diseases.

More funds were available to ensure internal security and collect revenue: both were matters of greater importance for the French administration. The Garde Indigène continued to have a substantial Vietnamese component. In fact as late as 1937, 46 per cent of all senior indigenous positions in the federally controlled administrative services in Laos, which included the military, were still held by non-Lao (almost all by Vietnamese).[49] Policing was the responsibility of the Gendarmerie, concentrated mainly in the urban centres. Prisons were established not only in major towns, but also in provincial centres such as Phongsālī, Xiang Khuang and Attapeu. Taxes, charges and tariffs were efficiently collected. By contrast, not until 1926 was an agricultural extension service established.

Other major areas of expenditure designed to maintain French control were public works, and posts and telegraphs, both of which continued to draw upon corvée labour to improve navigation on the Mekong, construct roads and erect telegraph lines. Much effort went into building comfortable accommodation and offices for French officials. Set in gardens bright with bougainvillea and frangipani, the yellow stucco villas and administrative buildings clustered near the Mekong in Viang Chan and other riverside towns were characteristically French colonial in style. Most of the commercial centre was Chinese-owned, but there was a *Circle Sportif* on the river, and all the proper conventions of polite French society were scrupulously observed. Neat roads with names like Quai Pavie and rue Maréchal Foch bisected the downtown area, only to peter out within a couple of kilometres in either direction. Thus did spatial configuration symbolize and reinforce relations of social power: beyond the French core and its Chinese and Vietnamese extension lay the Lao periphery, its village communities virtually untouched by the French presence.

In two areas, however, French initiatives did provide some stimulus to Lao nationalist sentiment. These were the restoration and preservation of ancient monuments, and scholarly research into Lao history and literature. In Viang Chan the Thāt Luang and Vat Phra Kaeo were restored with the assistance of the École Française d'Extrême-Orient. Archaeological excavations were undertaken at Vat Phū, the ancient Khmer sanctuary in Champāsak province, and at Xāy Fông, the Khmer garrison town just south of Viang Chan. Other research was undertaken by a series of French scholars into Lao history, literature, art and architecture. The Lao writing system was standardized. Spelling was made largely phonetic, as most letters indicating only Pali derivations (still retained in Thai) were dropped. Lao Buddhism was reformed and temples renovated. In 1931 an independent Lao Buddhist Institute was established where courses in Pali were taught. This led to establishment of a College of Pali in Viang Chan in 1937.

The importance of these developments lay in the impetus they gave to a resurgence of interest in Lao classical history and culture. The leading Lao figure behind this revival was Prince Phetxarāt Rattanavongsā, second son of the *uparāt* Bunkhong. A graduate of the elite École Coloniale in Paris, Phetxarāt had also spent a year at Oxford. On his return to Laos, he had joined the colonial administration in the office of the Résident Supérieur in Viang Chan. His subsequent appointment in 1923 to the position of Indigenous Inspector of Political and Administrative Affairs provided him with just the wider stage he needed on which to pursue his ambitions for himself and his country. A rare American visitor who met Phetxarāt soon after his appointment was impressed by his dignified manner – 'His sensitive features, crowned with a high, thin forehead, were given a certain distinction by a carefully clipped moustache'[50] – and by his knowledge of and interest in the history of his country.

Phetxarāt's first priority as Indigenous Inspector was to increase the number of Lao serving in the bureaucracy at the expense of the Vietnamese, through improving opportunities for the training and promotion of Lao civil servants. He opposed unrestricted Vietnamese migration, and was determined to retain a separate Lao identity within 'Indochina'.[51] Just as important as his political views were his cultural pursuits. With Phetxarāt's encouragement, his private secretary, Silā Vīravong, undertook the collection of Lao texts for the library at Vat Chan where he taught Pali. His literary and historical research, both in Laos and in the National Library in Bangkok, resulted in the rediscovery of classical Lao manuscripts carried off during earlier invasions, a number of which were later edited and published.[52]

These historical, literary and cultural studies and the discussions to which they gave rise provided an early stimulus to elite Lao nationalism, thus laying the groundwork for the more overtly nationalist movements of the 1940s. As elsewhere, this cultural nationalism received no official encouragement, though it did benefit, as in Cambodia, from the activities of French scholars associated with the Buddhist Institute. The colonial historiography taught to the Lao elite in French-language schools stressed not the greatness of Lān Xāng, but the protective role of France in freeing Laos from Siamese domination. By implication, therefore, only a continuing French presence could guarantee a continuing Lao identity. Given such a deeply emotive basis for collaboration, it is little wonder that elite nationalism was slow to flower in Laos, or that initially it defined itself more in opposition to the Vietnamese presence than to the French.

## THE DILEMMA OF DEVELOPMENT

Nowhere is the ambiguity present in French policy towards Laos more apparent than in approaches to economic development. The major problem that continuously exercised French officials in Laos was how to achieve the *mise en valeur* of their new possession. Only if the country's resources could be exploited in economically profitable ways would Laos be of value to France and be in a position to finance its own administration and further development. Early explorers and travellers had written of the country's natural resources and potential for economic development in such glowing terms that it was almost universally believed that Laos was little short of a new El Dorado. The realization soon dawned, however, that these exaggerated expectations had little foundation. Hopes of concentrating substantial trade from throughout the Khōrāt plateau in French hands proved illusory. The pattern of trade from the larger Mekong river towns on the west bank was too well established via Khōrāt to Bangkok to divert down the Mekong to Saigon. Even on the east bank most commerce was in the hands of Chinese merchants who exported their cardamom, sticklac and benzoin, hides and skins, ivory and antlers, to business houses in Bangkok. Nor did Laos prove to be a profitable market for French goods, for the same Chinese merchants imported cheap British and German manufactured products by the same route. Attention thus turned to the problem of economic development, to be brought about by two means: increased population and improved access. Laos would need more people, and would have to be 'unblocked' in the direction of Vietnam before its wealth could be exploited.[53]

Right from the beginning, the French had been eager to increase population. Families who had been forcibly settled west of the Mekong were encouraged to return to their former villages. Siamese repression and the protection offered by the French presence did convince a substantial number of west-bank Lao to cross the river. But the problem was not simply a matter of numbers of people, in the French view: it was a question of whether they would work. Here the French had serious doubts. The Lao might have numerous fine qualities, but the work ethic was not one. Even those early administrators like de Reinach who knew the country and its people better than most, and had developed a deep affection for the Lao, conceded that, though 'it would be unjust to maintain that the inhabitants were incapable of initiative and hard work', if a labour force was needed to develop the country 'it seems difficult to be able to count on the Lao'.[54]

So if the Lao were not sufficiently industrious to undertake the rapid economic development of the colony, who would do the job? While some believed that European settlement would be possible at higher altitudes on the Plain of Jars, if not on the Bôlavēn plateau, others were equally convinced that Laos was not a country for European migration. Europeans could direct and supervise, but the hard manual labour would have to be done by 'Asiatics'. French capital could be invested to establish plantations, or raise herds and flocks on large concessions, but only with the assistance of imported labour. Chinese coolies were rejected, so the obvious choice was to bring in Vietnamese. As early as 1880, even before France had extended its 'protection' over Annam and Tonkin, this was already the solution favoured by the explorer Jules Harmand. He wrote:

> we can count on the Annamites, when they will be our subjects, to colonize to our profit a large part of the valley of the great Indo-Chinese river [Mekong] where they will rapidly supplant the débris of decrepit races which inhabit it. By ourselves, we cannot attempt any enterprise in this country, so rich but so unproductive due to the fault of its actual possessors. It is necessary first that the Laotians be eliminated, not by violent means, but by the natural effect of competition and the supremacy of the most fit.[55]

Since by one calculation, however, the population of Laos would need to triple in order to generate sufficient revenue to cover costs of administration,[56] massive migration would be required. And for that to occur, access across the Sāy Phū Luang (Truong Son) cordillera would have to be greatly improved.

Natural access to Laos has always historically been via the Khōrāt plateau to the Gulf of Thailand. Access from the east is far more difficult, over a series of high passes. In the north, the passes from Laos to the upper reaches of the Black river and the upper Ca river valley rise to over 1000 metres. Further south, the Nāpae and Mu Gia passes are more accessible. The only other means of access between Laos and Vietnam was down the Mekong, at first the only route by which the French communicated with their Lao possessions. The first priority, therefore, was to clear a channel for navigation. Major obstructions still remained, however – the rapids at Khemmarāt and the falls of Khôn – which prevented the use of larger vessels. A 7-kilometre railway was constructed to circumvent the latter, but added greatly to transhipment costs. Large subsidies had to be paid to the French riverboat company Messageries Fluviales to maintain a minimal service linking Viang Chan with Phnom Penh and Saigon.

The obvious alternative to river transport was access by road. A grandiose network of national routes was planned for all of Indochina. Constructed at great cost in time and labour, these were to 'unblock' Laos by linking the Mekong towns to coastal Vietnam. A major north–south highway would run from Saigon to Kratié in Cambodia, follow

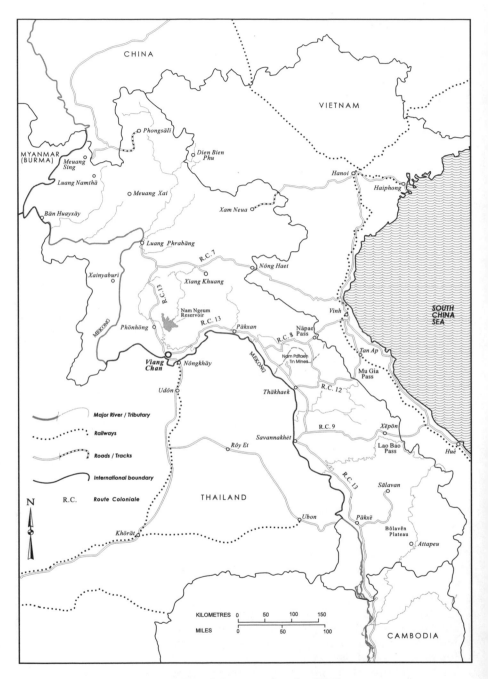

**Map 3** French Laos: road and rail links

the Mekong to Viang Chan, and thence north to Luang Phrabāng. This was national Route 13, the Saigon–Thākhaek stretch of which was completed (for dry season traffic only) by 1930, but whose final section from Viang Chan to Luang Phrabāng was constructed only between 1941 and 1944. Three trafficable roads eventually crossed the Sāy Phū Luang cordillera: Route 12 from Thākhaek via the Mu Gia pass northeast to Vinh, the first open for regular transport; Route 9 from Savannakhēt via Xēpōn and the Lao Bao pass to Quang Tri (open by 1930); and Route 7 from Luang Phrabāng to Xiang Khuang and southeast to Vinh (open 1937). Route 6, linking Xam Neua to the Lai Chau–Hanoi road, Route 8 from Thākhaek through the Nāpae pass to Vinh, and Route 19 from Phongsālī to Dien Bien Phu were little more than tracks of slight economic significance. Forced labour to construct not only these, but also local roads, was bitterly resented, and in some cases whole villages decamped to avoid the corvée.

With construction of Route 12, goods could reach Savannakhēt from Saigon in three days by road, compared to twelve by boat up the Mekong, and so undercut the price per tonne. Even so, potential for transportation by road of bulk produce, whether agricultural or mineral, was limited. The only hope of really 'unblocking' Laos, it was all but universally concluded, was to construct a railway from the coast of Vietnam to the Mekong. River shipping on the central navigable reaches of the Mekong would bring produce to a river port where it would be loaded onto wagons and transported to one of the Vietnamese ports, either Danang or Vinh. Apart from a visionary suggestion for a railway from Saigon to Yunnan following the Mekong valley,[57] the first serious study of the possibility of constructing a railway into Laos was undertaken under the governor-generalship of Paul Doumer. Surveys were carried out to determine the best route and likely cost, but other lines had priority, especially as a Vietnam–Laos line would not at first be commercially viable.

World War I slowed railway construction in Indochina, but in 1921 a new program was drawn up coordinating road and rail networks. Funds were short, however, and little materialized. What galvanized the French later in the decade were the exploitation of tin deposits in the vicinity of Thākhaek, and the rail construction program undertaken in Siam. The Siamese northeastern railway reached Ubon in 1928, and another branch was planned to Nôngkhāy, opposite Viang Chan. Despite the depression, therefore, a new grand plan was drawn up in 1931, with priority given to a 187-kilometre line from Tan Ap in Vietnam through a tunnel under the Mu Gia pass to Thākhaek. The line was due for completion by 1936, and was to be funded by French capital. By 1933 the first 17.5 kilometres had been constructed west from Tan Ap and opened to traffic. A 40-kilometre aerial cable was then built to link the railhead to Nāpae across the Mu Gia pass to supply construction gangs. This continued to carry merchandise from Vietnam and tin concentrates on the return leg until 1945, but the railway itself was never constructed.

A rail link from Laos to Vietnam was for French colonial officials the single means by which all the economic problems of Laos would be solved. Despite the cost and numerous delays, it was an article of faith that a railway would eventually be built, and would have the desired economic impact. It would bring migrants in and take produce out, enabling Laos at last to fulfil its 'natural' role as the resource-rich hinterland of French Indochina. Without the railway, economic development was slow. Not until the early 1920s did exaggerated reports of the colony's great mineral wealth lead to a rush of capital investment. New companies were floated on the Paris Bourse to exploit mining concessions in the Nam Pātaen basin, though some were little more than exercises in fraud and speculation. By 1929, before the bubble burst, total paper value in Lao tin shares amounted to an extraordinary 1106 million francs.[58] Yet in the 1930s only two companies produced just over 1000 tons annually. The benefit to Laos was negligible, however, as profits were repatriated to France, and the 2000 workers were almost all Vietnamese. Other companies turned their attention to forestry and agriculture. Some 12,000 to 15,000 trunks of teak were cut annually in northern Laos to be floated downstream to Saigon when the river was high, an amount small enough to do little damage to the environment. More profitable were forest products such as wax, resin, medicinal plants, perfumed woods, and particularly sticklac and benzoin, production of which by 1936 stood at 100 and 40 tonnes respectively.[59]

Plantation agriculture hardly developed in Laos, with the partial exception of coffee in Haut Mékong and on the Bôlavēn plateau, where an extensive area of land was cleared. Total production reached around 200 tonnes by the late 1930s, half for export. Rubber was tried, but only experimentally, despite its success in Vietnam and Cambodia. Several textile crops, including cotton, jute, kapok and silk, were locally produced, with small quantities finding their way to Siam. The principal Lao agricultural exports, however, were cardamom from the Bôlavēn and, unofficially, opium from Xiang Khuang. Opium production figures are hopelessly inaccurate for Laos, since there was always a massive 'leakage' through smuggling. Not until the early 1940s was local opium production officially encouraged to meet the needs of the opium monopoly (when imported Indian opium was no longer available due to the outbreak of war).

Throughout the half-century of French administration, the vast majority of the population – Lao Lum, Lao Thoeng and Lao Sūng – remained subsistence farmers growing little more than the essentials necessary for survival – and to pay their tax. This 'natural economy' was entirely dependent on climate, as irrigation was minimal. Total annual production of glutinous rice fluctuated from a maximum of just over 500,000 tonnes in 1923 to an average of less than 300,000 tonnes during the 1930s, providing consumption of approximately one kilogram per person per day.[60] Shortages of rice were made up by maize, an introduced crop grown mainly in upland swiddens, and various root vegetables (sweet potato, cassava), because transport was inadequate to supply areas of need from areas of plenty. Minimum attention was given to increasing either yields or area under cultivation. Exportation of rice amounted to no more than 3000 tonnes annually from Champāsak to Siam. So low was production in 1936 that the export of Lao rice was banned entirely. Thus few Lao farmers produced any commercial crop for export.

The depression of the 1930s caused commodity prices to collapse and severely strained the Lao budget. Tax receipts, especially cash payments in lieu of corvée, fell, as did the subvention paid to Laos from the general budget for Indochina. The administration responded by tightening tax collection, increasing the rate for redemption of corvée, and limiting expenditure. By 1937 the crisis was over, revenues had increased, and the grant from the general budget was up slightly (though not to earlier levels).

One effect of tightening revenue collection was to provoke renewed unrest among the Lao Thoeng of the Bôlavēn. Kommadam, active again, urged villagers not to pay their taxes, much to the anger of French officials. In September 1936 a military operation by the Garde Indigène into the mountains east of the plateau finally brought Kommadam's rebellion to an end. Kommadam himself was killed and two of his sons captured. A second revolt by Lao Thoeng followers of a sorcerer known as Sambran, the 'White Python', spilled over into Laos from the southern Vietnamese highlands; it was finally quelled only in 1939. In both cases, dissatisfaction over tax and corvée demands fuelled rebellions that again took the form of millenarian religious movements. The financial crisis and social unrest together eventually led to reform of the taxation system in 1940, with personal tax determined according to five levels of income.[61]

The budgetary problems of the 1930s again focused the attention of French officials on the problem of how to make Laos 'pay'. Immigration was still the favoured means, and by 1943 the Vietnamese population had increased to almost 40,000. In major Lao cities Vietnamese formed a majority of the population and enjoyed the right to elect their own leaders.[62] By then, 53 per cent of the population of Viang Chan were Vietnamese. In Thākhaek the figure was 85 per cent; in Pākxē 62 per cent. Only in Luang Phrabāng was the population predominantly Lao. More than 4000 Chinese, grouped into 'congregations' according to dialect and area of origin, controlled much of the commerce of the country. The children of the more successful attended French schools and intermarried with the Lao aristocracy. But French policy was for even more Vietnamese migration. As late as 1945 an ambitious plan was drawn up massively to increase Vietnamese settlement in three key areas: on the Viang Chan plain, in the region of Savannakhēt, and on the Bôlavēn plateau.[63] The plan was discarded only after the Japanese interregnum had irrevocably changed the political destiny of French Indochina. Had it gone ahead, the Lao might well have lost control over their own country.

Here lay the real ambiguity in French policy towards Laos. On the one hand, the need to obtain the collaboration of the Lao elite required the French to portray themselves as protectors of a separate entity, French Laos, which they were altruistically assisting to modernize; on the other, they were intent on implementing a policy of economic exploitation that in the long term would have subordinated Lao interests to those of French Indochina as a whole, to the benefit, ultimately, of the Vietnamese. Only the accident of war resolved this ambiguity in favour of the Lao.

## THE STIRRINGS OF NATIONALISM

A few figures are enough to suggest one reason why modern nationalist sentiment was slow to take root in Laos. Throughout the 1930s only fifty-two Lao graduated from the Collège Pavie (middle school), just over half the number of Vietnamese,[64] and even fewer Lao completed their secondary education at high schools in Vietnam. Those who did, or who went on to university in France, constituted a minute educated, mainly aristocratic, elite who owed their social status to the presence of France. By 1937, despite the best efforts of Prince Phetxarāt, only 54 per cent of 286 positions in the upper and middle levels of the French administration in Laos (not including Luang Phrabāng) were held by Lao.[65] Resentment among civil servants was directed against the Vietnamese, however, rather than against the French. As for the rest of the population, some 90 per cent of lowland Lao remained subsistence peasant farmers; even in the few towns there was virtually no Lao working class; and next to nothing had been provided by way of education for either the Lao Sūng or Lao Thoeng. Opportunities were minimal, therefore, for raising the political consciousness of the Lao population through either education or inter-ethnic contact.

As we have seen, the 1930s saw the first stirrings of Lao cultural nationalism. This was not, by its nature, a popular movement with mass appeal. Rather it was confined to a tiny, culturally active group who made little attempt to pursue political goals. Consensus at the time on the need for continued collaboration with France as the only means of modernizing the country was all but universal. It was in the interests of the Lao elite to preserve their own social power by becoming agents in this process.

The only political movement active in Laos in the 1930s that sought a popular following was the Indochinese Communist Party (ICP). It was founded in Hong Kong on 3 February 1930 by a veteran Vietnamese agent for the Communist International (the Comintern), Nguyen Ai Quoc, better known by his later pseudonym as Ho Chi Minh. Despite the fact that its early membership was exclusively Vietnamese, the ICP was so named specifically to include both Cambodia and Laos. Early attempts by the Party to establish an underground organization were overtaken by the peasant uprisings of September 1930 in north central Vietnam, suppression of which led to decimation of the Party leadership. Refugees and unemployed from the region moved into Laos, either to look for work or on their way to seek asylum in Siam. From there most of the early communist activity in Laos was organized. To maintain surveillance of Vietnamese communities in central and southern Laos and across the Mekong, the Sûreté, the French secret police, increased its presence in all the major Lao Mekong towns. In 1931 the Sûreté successfully uncovered several ICP cells while investigating sabotage at the tin mines in the Nam Pātaen basin, and arrested their members.[66]

By October of the following year, the ICP was beginning to rebuild. Cells were established in Viang Chan, in the tin mines, and at Thākhaek. Activities included organization of various associations and unions among Vietnamese residents and workers, and publication of a clandestine bimonthly Vietnamese-language news-sheet. Direction and support came from the Committee Responsible for Indochina, then located in northeastern Siam. In November 1933 a meeting of delegates of Party organizations in Laos was held near Nakhôn Phanom, at which a resolution was adopted to step up indoctrination among the Lao community. By mid-1934 this had borne fruit with the recruitment in Viang Chan, according to Sûreté records, of the first two Lao members of the Party.[67] In September 1934, progress was apparently judged sufficiently encouraging by a conference of Party representatives meeting at Udôn in Siam to warrant establishment of a Regional Committee for Laos. The only Lao member of this committee was a civil servant from Savannakhēt by the name of Khamsaen, since honoured as the first Lao communist.

The effectiveness of the Regional Committee was quickly reduced, however, by further arrests in late 1934 and early 1935. Indeed by 1936 the entire Party structure in Laos was all but destroyed. Relief from repression came in the form of election of the Popular Front government in France in May of that year. Until the outbreak of war in Europe, when the communist party was banned, the ICP was able to organize among workers more openly. In Laos the Party had begun clandestine publication of a Lao language periodical in addition to its Vietnamese news-sheet, and some communist material was translated into Lao. There was little Party activity, however, except for agitation for improved wages and conditions among tin miners. Lao interest in communism remained minimal, as communism in Laos during the 1930s remained overwhelmingly a Vietnamese phenomenon. Successive reports from the Résident Supérieur to the Governor-General in Hanoi could with some justification claim that the population of Laos remained both tranquil and loyal to France. Only later did Marxism make any important contribution to the development of Lao nationalism.

Marxism in Laos had little ideological appeal, and suffered from its association with an organization dominated by Vietnamese. In fact it was fear of neighbours on both sides that led even cultural nationalists to view France more as a protecting than as an occupying power. The ambitions of the Vietnamese to make of Indochina 'a single country that Vietnamese blood will have fertilized by galvanizing its dynamism and power of action'[68] was apparent particularly among Vietnamese resident in Laos. This was worrying enough, but even more so were the ambitions of the new military government which took power in

Bangkok in December 1938 under prime minister Phibunsongkhram. The following year the name of the country was changed from Siam, the kingdom of the Tai-Siam of the central Chaophraya plains, to Thailand, with its implicit claim to include all Tai-speaking peoples. In Laos, the new pan-Thaiïsm of Bangkok was viewed with misgivings as threatening the very existence of Laos as a separate political entity. Between the Thai threat and Vietnamese expansionism there might seem little to choose (other than French protection), but both had the effect of stimulating a (defensive) Lao nationalist response.

The French, as protectors of Laos, had tended to be complacent in their relations with Siam, for these had been generally amicable. War in Europe and an ultra-nationalist government in Bangkok destroyed such complacency. Despite agreeing in June 1940 to a non-aggression pact initiated by the French, Thailand took advantage of France's capitulation in Europe to pursue irredentist demands for a return of territories ceded to France in 1904 and 1907. Intensive pan-Thai propaganda promising to free Laos from French colonial domination was followed by Thai attacks on Lao territory in December (on Xainyaburī and Champāsak, west of the Mekong). The principal conflict was, however, fought in Cambodia (where French troops were forced to retreat) and at sea (resulting in a French victory). Japan, which already had forced French acquiescence to the stationing of Japanese troops in Indochina, then stepped in to impose a cease-fire and settlement. The Treaty of Tokyo, signed on 9 May 1941, surrendered much of western and a strip of northern Cambodia to Thailand, along with the Lao west-bank territories of Champāsak and Xainyaburī. The worst Lao fears were thus realized. Even France had proved unable to defend the territory of Laos from its avaricious neighbours. French subservience to Japan after the outbreak of the Pacific War in December 1941 only confirmed France's reduced power status, and forced the Lao elite to consider their own position.

The loss of territory was particularly felt in Luang Phrabāng, which was deprived of its valuable west-bank royal teak reserves. In an agreement signed in August 1941, the French attempted to compensate the King by extending his rule to include all of northern Laos south to Viang Chan, while formalizing the status of the kingdom as a French protectorate. This went some way towards soothing royal sensitivities, but it did nothing to alleviate deeper Lao fears. The quaint feudal Kingdom of Luang Phrabāng was hardly a match for the rapidly modernizing Thai state, even after the King's Council was expanded to accommodate Prince Phetxarāt as prime minister and given the form of a cabinet.[69] Moreover, Laos still lacked a single identity. South and north, Champāsak and Luang Phrabāng, were mutually antagonistic; while Viang Chan was essentially a French and Vietnamese city.

Together these circumstances gave rise to the first overtly nationalist movement in Laos, known as the Movement for National Renovation, designed primarily to counter the pan-Thai appeal of Bangkok. Official French support for the movement came from Admiral Jean Decoux, wartime Governor-General of Indochina, though the real impetus came from the French Director of Public Education in Viang Chan, Charles Rochet, and a small group of young, educated Lao led by Nyūy Aphai and Katāy Don Sasorit.[70] The Renovation Movement was primarily cultural. It lauded Lao literature, theatre, music and dance and resuscitated Lao history as means of stimulating a sense of Lao identity and pride. Even so, its success was regarded with great misgivings by French officials, especially after an amateurish coup attempt by young activists was foiled in July 1940. (Ringleaders crossed the Mekong where they formed the semi-secret Lao Pen Lao movement – Laos for the Lao – with support of local Thai officials.)

The mouthpiece of the Renovation Movement was the journal *Lao Nyai* (Great Laos), first published in January 1941. Of its ten pages of articles, poems, short stories and news items, eight were in Lao and two in French. New French and Lao publications (*Le Nouveau Laos, Tin Lao*) followed. A national anthem was chosen (*Xāt Lao*) and the Lao flag honoured. Committees and associations were organized both in Viang Chan and the provinces to encourage cultural pursuits and bring together youth and women. A School of Lao Arts was established at Khong in the south, where pan-Thai propaganda had been more effective than further north. Sport was particularly encouraged because sporting organizations provided opportunities for indoctrination, anti-Thai and pro-French. Much of this movement was Pétainist in inspiration. It deliberately emphasized the role of the family (all Lao were instructed to choose a family name), physical development, discipline and loyalty. Politically it encouraged a pan-Lao response to Thai propaganda and envisaged, in Decoux's words, grouping all Lao, 'provisionally' divided between Laos and Thailand, under the folds of the French flag.[71] It was a goal as anachronistic as it was contradictory. A genuine Lao nationalist movement could hardly affirm continued colonial subjugation to France, particularly if it sought to include the Lao of northeastern Thailand.

A minor event in 1944 illustrated this contradiction. When Rochet encouraged the writing of Lao using the Roman alphabet, he was vigorously opposed by Phetxarāt, who was well aware of its political implications and the threat it posed to the historical identity of Laos and the Buddhist roots of Lao civilization. The idea was dropped, but Phetxarāt's victory gave notice that Lao nationalism was coming of age, that it was outgrowing French influence. Pan-Lao it might pretend to be, but not pro-French.

Though many French officials in Laos viewed the Renovation Movement askance, it did benefit from official encouragement. Lao provincial governors were raised to the rank of *chau khuaeng*. The School of Law and Administration was reorganized in order to speed up replacement of Vietnamese by Lao in the public service. Education received renewed emphasis, with more new schools being constructed between 1940 and 1945, many in rural areas, than had been built between 1893 and 1940. Road construction was stepped up, and social and agricultural services improved. In 1943, the first purely Lao military units were formed – two companies of Chasseurs Laotiens. To pay for these projects, the subvention from the general Indochinese budget was raised; this was only reasonable in view of the fact that an increasing proportion of its revenue was coming from sale of Lao opium. As the war precluded importing opium, the monopoly turned to the Hmong to supply Indochina's 100,000 addicts. Hmong taxes were raised, but made payable in raw opium at prices high enough to minimize smuggling and encourage production. Control over opium reinforced the dominance of the clan of Tūbī Līfung, but the silver flooding into the highlands increased corruption as everyone who could scrambled to profit from the bonanza.[72]

As the Lao nationalist movement began, however slowly, to develop a momentum of its own, French sponsorship became increasingly irrelevant. For young activists, the goal was no longer the negative one of warding off Thai and Vietnamese with the help of France, but the positive one of national independence. The catalyst for this change came with the Japanese ultimatum and *coup de force* of 9 March 1945. The effect of this, in the long term if not immediately, was to destroy what remained of the illusion of French might, and to open the way for more sweeping nationalist demands.

Until February 1945, when a Japanese detachment moved onto the Plain of Jars, the Japanese presence in Laos was limited to a few agents of the *Kempetai* (Japanese Military Police) whose job it was to gather military intelligence on the French administration. With the liberation of France in 1944, the Japanese not unreasonably suspected that the pro-Vichy government of Indochina under Admiral Decoux would be replaced by one owing allegiance to General Charles de Gaulle and his Free French. The Japanese military presence was increased, and planning finalized for Operation Meigo Sakusan, the Japanese pre-emptive strike against French forces in Indochina. When the Japanese made their move, French resistance was minimal. Only in northern Vietnam, where a sizeable French force conducted a fighting retreat into China, and in Laos, where small units were able to take to the maquis before the Japanese arrived, did French troops escape the Japanese net. Viang Chan was seized by a Japanese force crossing from Thailand on the night of 9–10 March, but the Japanese did not reach Luang Phrabāng until 5 April, thus giving Free French officers ample time to organize their retreat. Elsewhere the few French officers and NCOs of the Garde Indigène took to the jungle. Crown Prince Savāngvatthanā called upon all Lao in the name of the King to oppose the Japanese and give every assistance to the French, and many Lao fought bravely for the French resistance – even though the offer of an 'Indochina Federation' within a 'French Union' offered by General de Gaulle's Provisional Government was hardly very attractive.[73]

As in other parts of Southeast Asia, some nationalist leaders were prepared to cooperate with the Japanese in the hope of furthering their goal of independence and, in the case of Laos, opposing Vietnamese ambitions. The most prominent such leader in Laos was Prince Phetxarāt, who was annoyed at the Crown Prince's impulsive commitment to France.[74] As it was, the King was forced under Japanese pressure to declare Lao independence from France on 8 April 1945. Phetxarāt's preparedness to work with the Japanese led to his confirmation as prime minister of Luang Phrabāng, though he was unable to convince the Japanese to unify the country. Phetxarāt exercised his authority to further reduce Vietnamese influence in both the administration and the economy. More Lao were appointed in place of Vietnamese in the civil service, while some Vietnamese merchants were expelled from Luang Phrabāng and Viang Chan. Vietnamese resistance was tenacious, however, and in towns such as Thākhaek and Savannakhēt, Vietnamese residents formed armed units. Their strongly anti-French sentiments gained them the support of local Japanese garrisons, and deep suspicion on the part of the Lao. In Xiang Khuang an attempt by local Vietnamese to declare the province part of Vietnam was thwarted, though similar hopes were entertained by the Vietnamese of Savanna-khēt.[75] Despite attempts by both the Japanese 'Supreme Counsellor' in Viang Chan and Phetxarāt's government to maintain a semblance of effective administration, it was a time of disruption, with new movements beginning to compete for political power.

The best-organized and most important of these wartime organizations was undoubtedly the Viet Nam Doc Lap Dong Minh (League for the Independence of Vietnam), or Vietminh. This had been formed in May 1941 by the ICP as a broad anti-Japanese and anti-French front while the ICP itself went underground. It was envisaged that similar fronts would take up the struggle in Laos and Cambodia under ICP direction. These took longer to organize, and in both countries national-ist organizations developed which owed little or nothing to Marxism, and were almost as anti-Vietnamese as they were anti-French. In Laos the first such organizations were the closely linked Lao Sērī (Free Laos) and Lao Pen Lao.

The Lao Sērī was formed in 1944 as an offshoot of its Thai equivalent. It was primarily an anti-Japanese underground resistance movement, but dedicated to getting rid not only of the Japanese, but also the French. It was under Thai control and based in northeastern Thailand, though its target field of operations was French Laos. Both Thai and Lao groups gained assistance from a United States organization, the Office of Strategic Services, forerunner of the CIA (Central Intelligence Agency). Young Lao nationalist recruits were trained in northeastern Thailand to be ready to seize power in Laos upon the defeat of Japan. Their commander was Un Xananikôn, scion of an influential family from Viang Chan.[76] Though the Lao Sērī were strongly anti-Vietnamese, they were distrusted by the Thai, who feared creation of a 'Greater Laos' incorporating both French Laos and the northeastern Lao-populated provinces of Thailand. With the Japanese surrender, ringleaders formed the secret Lao Pen Lao and prepared to join with other nationalist groups to oppose the return of the French.

The movement which eventually embraced all anti-French Lao nationalists was the Lao Issara, or Free Lao. Though this was the name taken by the independent government established following the Japan-ese surrender, the roots of the movement go back to the earliest stirrings of Lao nationalism in the 1930s. The Lao Issara included not only those who collaborated with the Japanese in the cause of Lao independence, but also those who threw in their lot with the Thai, and young Lao animated by the examples of both Vietnamese and Japanese nationalism.[77] While some older nationalists, Phetxarāt in particular, saw the Japanese occupation as an occasion to seize the political initiative, most were youthful patriots excited by the changes around them. Many had already been influenced by the National Renovation Movement, some by events in Vietnam. The Japanese occupation, brief as it was, acted as the catalyst for cultural nationalism to take on a political dimension. While a few more perceptive French officials recognized the extent of this change – that 'the Japanese *coup de force* … [had] caused the disappearance of a world none will see again'[78] – most did not. Many believed that, with the Japanese surrender in August 1945, France could simply pick up the pieces and return to the *status quo ante* of the previous March. But by the time French forces finally completed the reconquest of Laos, more than a year had passed, and Lao patriots had shed blood in the name of independence. It was to be seven more years before the French bowed to the inevitable and finally recognized Laos as a fully independent state.

# CHAPTER 3

# INDEPENDENCE AND UNITY, 1945–1957

Laos, like the rest of Indochina, was caught up late in the maelstrom of World War II. Just thirteen and a half months elapsed between the Japanese seizure of power in March 1945 and French reoccupation of Viang Chan at the end of April 1946. Yet it was a year that altered forever the relationship between colonizers and colonized. The triumphal return of French forces could not disguise their defeat at the hands of the Japanese, any more than their deferential welcome back by King Sīsavāngvong masked the deepening divisions in Lao society over the future of the country. Formation of the Lao Issara (Free Lao) marked the rapid maturity of Lao nationalism as a political force with which the French would thenceforth have to contend. Partial independence offered under various guises proved insufficient to satisfy Lao demands. The Convention of 1949 providing a quasi-independence for Laos within the French Union did no more than mark a phase in the struggle for full independence, finally achieved under the compulsion of events in Vietnam in October 1953.

With the outbreak of the First Indochina War at the end of 1946, Laos again found itself drawn into a wider conflict, which would set Lao against Lao. In the process, the Pathet Lao developed its own form of radical nationalism at odds with that of the Royal Lao government, a nationalism based not on an elite Lao tradition of royal legitimation and aristocratic patronage, but on more broadly inclusive participation in forms of popular resistance. Dependency on external powers, however, undermined the claims of both these contending nationalisms, and divided the country. The *de facto* division of Laos under the terms of the Geneva Agreements of 1954 took three years of patient negotiation to overcome. The territorial unity achieved under the First Coalition government promised to provide the basis on which to construct a modern nation state. It was a unity, however, that was destined not to last.

## THE LAO ISSARA

The Japanese surrender on 15 August 1945 was as much a surprise to the people of Laos as the *coup de force* of 9 March had been. Under the terms of the Potsdam Agreement, Chinese forces were to receive the Japanese surrender in Indochina north of the sixteenth parallel, and the British to the south. No role was envisaged for the Free French, though

US President Harry Truman had notified General de Gaulle that the United States would not, after all, oppose eventual restitution of French jurisdiction over Indochina. In Laos, however, unlike other places in Indochina where French resistance forces had been eliminated, the French were in a position to play some part in the surrender process. Thanks to the support of Lao partisans, five resistance groups (divided into twenty-six sub-groups comprising some 200 French and 300 Lao) held out in jungle hideouts throughout the Japanese occupation, supplied by air from India.[1] Two days after the Japanese surrender, these resistance forces received radioed orders to occupy the major urban centres in Laos and restore French administration of the country.

The French presence in Laos not only complicated the surrender process, but also prejudiced Lao nationalist attempts to assert independence. The continued presence of French resistance groups during the Japanese occupation divided the Lao elite into those who were prepared, if not to cooperate with the Japanese, then at least to take advantage of their presence to further the cause of Lao independence; and those who preferred the former colonial regime to the Japanese and looked forward to its return. The brevity of the Japanese occupation and the continuing existence of an alternative focus of loyalty in the form of the French resistance made it difficult for the nationalist movement in Laos even to develop an effective organization.

Laos in 1945 was deeply divided, rent by regional antagonism and personal rivalry. Lao society was still strongly hierarchical, for French policy had been to preserve the prerogatives of the traditional aristocracy, not only in Luang Phrabāng and Champāsak but also through appointment to office in directly administered provinces. Political culture was still regional, centred on the *meuang*. Powerful families wielded political influence through extended clans held together by marital and patronage relationships. No 'imagined national community' bound together even all lowland Lao, let alone the ethnic minorities.

It is hardly surprising, therefore, that the initial Lao response to the end of the war was hesitant and indecisive. No nation-wide nationalist organization existed like the Vietminh in Vietnam able swiftly to take advantage of the power vacuum produced by the Japanese surrender. In northern Laos, a French presence was quickly re-established in several centres almost immediately following the Japanese surrender. King Sīsavāngvong welcomed the arrival of Colonel Hans Imfeld, the officer appointed French Commissioner *ad interim* in Laos, with the assurance that his declaration of independence under Japanese duress was null and void. In the south, Prince Bunūm, scion of the former ruling family of Champāsak and the most influential figure in southern Laos, had joined forces with the French resistance. By mid-September, thanks to British mediation and the collaboration of the southern Lao elite, the French had returned to Pākxē. From there, six months later, French forces launched their military reoccupation of Laos.

Only in central Laos were pro-independence nationalists able to hold their own, and then only with the support of armed local Vietnamese, and some encouragement from members of the clandestine US Office of

Strategic Services, forerunner of the CIA. On 27 August, Phetxarāt took control of Viang Chan from the Japanese, and refused to reinstate the former French Résident Supérieur. A small force of French guerrillas which tried to enter the city was met by a noisy crowd of armed, mainly Vietnamese, demonstrators and forced to withdraw. The previously interned French civilian population was meanwhile evacuated to Thailand. Further south, Un Xananikôn crossed over from Thailand with a contingent of his Lao militia to seize control of Savannakhēt and Thākhaek from both Japanese and Vietnamese.

The loose coalition that came together in late August and early September 1945 as the Lao Issara included those who had compromised themselves in the eyes of the French by cooperating with the Japanese, whether from nationalist or less exalted motives; former supporters of the National Renovation Movement and its youth wing; former members of the Lao Sērī and the semi-secret Lao Pen Lao association; and anyone else who had been influenced by the intense nationalism of the Japanese and the anti-colonialism of the Vietminh.

The recognized leader of this motley coalition was Prince Phetxarāt Rattanavongsā, who since 1941 had been prime minister of the government of Luang Phrabāng, and *uparāt* (or viceroy) of the kingdom. Phetxarāt's background and position of power made him an imposing figure, both respected and feared, believed by the more credulous to possess supernatural powers. The French, while recognizing his abilities, distrusted him for what they considered to be his intransigent nationalism. Jealousy of Phetxarāt's high profile and suspicion of his evident ambition to lead an independent Laos, however, only reinforced the traditional rivalry which existed between the royal family and that of the *uparāt* in Luang Phrabāng, and the personal antagonism between Phetxarāt and Crown Prince Sāvangvatthanā. Moreover, if the Crown Prince suspected Phetxarāt of harbouring monarchical ambitions, Bunūm suspected his political intentions. Their combined opposition to Phetxarāt's *de facto* assumption of power goes some way towards explaining the difficulties encountered by the Lao Issara in its attempts to prevent re-establishment of the French protectorate.

Differences between Phetxarāt and the King on the future of the country were evident by the end of August. In a telegram to all province chiefs, Phetxarāt reaffirmed his contention that the failure of France to defend Laos from the Japanese had rendered all Franco-Lao treaties and agreements null and void.[2] Lao independence remained in force. On 2 September, Phetxarāt sought royal endorsement of his actions, and called upon the King to declare the unity of the country. In reply, the King informed his prime minister that he had already formally abrogated his declaration of independence and had returned Laos to the protection of France. Phetxarāt's response on 15 September was defiantly to proclaim the unification of Luang Phrabāng with the southern provinces on his own authority, thereby creating the state of Laos as an independent nation.[3]

Phetxarāt must have been encouraged in his course of action by what had happened in Vietnam. There Ho Chi Minh had proclaimed national independence, Emperor Bao Dai had abdicated, and a government of the Democratic Republic of Vietnam had been formed. Urged on by Vietminh activists, the Vietnamese community in Laos strongly endorsed these developments, and mobilized to prevent a French return anywhere in Indochina. In the towns of Viang Chan, Thākhaek and Savannakhēt, Vietnamese formed a majority of the population. Their paramilitary groups were well organized and well armed, thanks to the Japanese. Their virulent hatred of the French made them natural, if unpredictable, allies of the Lao Issara, in the short term at least. In the longer term most Lao nationalists regarded any substantial Vietnamese presence in Laos as a threat to Lao independence.

What tipped the balance in favour of the Lao Issara in northern and central Laos against both the French and the Vietnamese was the arrival in September of elements of the Nationalist Chinese 93rd Division. Nominally, they were there to accept the surrender of Japanese forces (all of whom hastily moved south of the sixteenth parallel to surrender to the British); in reality, they were there to occupy the country for the purpose of plunder. The Chinese refused to allow any official, or even semi-official, role for the French. In Luang Phrabāng the small French force was disarmed. In Viang Chan, Phetxarāt welcomed the Chinese in the name of the Lao Issara. Both Thākhaek and Savannakhēt were held by small Lao Issara, and larger Vietnamese, contingents in uneasy alliance with the Chinese. Only in the south did Sālavan and Pākxē remain in French hands.

Disagreement between the King in Luang Phrabāng (still advised by Commissioner Imfeld) and Phetxarāt in Viang Chan (urged on by more radical nationalists) over the status and future of the country eventually came to a head in October. Believing that the King was no longer a free agent, Phetxarāt appealed to the Allies to recognize Lao independence, but without result. On French advice, including a personal telegram from de Gaulle promising to recognize his sovereignty over the whole of Laos,[4] the King then dismissed Phetxarāt both as prime minister and *uparāt*. A 'People's Committee' promptly met in Viang Chan, reiterated the country's independence, promulgated a provisional constitution, and appointed a provisional government of Pathēt Lao ('The Land of the Lao'). Since elections could hardly be held, a 45-member provisional National Assembly was coopted by the provisional government. All this the King declared illegal, and he summoned Phetxarāt to Luang Phrabāng. But Phetxarāt refused to go, and on 20 October the provisional National Assembly passed a resolution deposing the King. The conflict was joined.

Formation of a Lao Issara government had been under discussion for some time. The King's dismissal of Phetxarāt was but the catalyst that brought it into being. The government not only brought together leaders of the various nationalist groups, it also marked the political debut of many of the principal players who would figure in the drama of the next three decades of Lao history, the so-called 'thirty-year struggle' that eventually led to formation of the Lao People's Democratic Republic in December 1975.

Most prominent among these players were eventually Phetxarāt's younger brother, Prince Suvanna Phūmā, and his youngest half-brother Prince Suphānuvong. Both were the products of privileged circumstances. The favoured sons of the second most influential family in Laos after the royal family itself, both had received the best of French education. Both graduated as engineers from elite French institutions. Despite their social rank and qualifications, both had experienced on returning to Indochina the slights of French colonial prejudice. There their similarities ended. Where Suvanna was measured, moderate, even phlegmatic, Suphānuvong was energetic, headstrong and ambitious. While Suvanna married a Frenchwoman and always retained an affection for France, Suphānuvong's wife was Vietnamese, a supporter of the Vietminh who consistently encouraged her husband's radical nationalist aspirations. Perhaps it was indicative of differences in character that at first Suvanna was not included in the provisional Lao Issara government, while Suphānuvong, even in his absence, was given the portfolio of public works and communications.

The prime minister and Minister for Foreign Affairs in the new government was Khammao Vilai, former *chao khuaeng* of Viang Chan and close confidant of Phetxarāt. Other members included Phetxarāt's nephew, Prince Somsanit Vongkotrattana (interior and justice); two leaders of the Lao Sērī and Lao Pen Lao, Un Xananikôn (Economy) and Major Sing Rattanasamai (Defence); and two of the principal figures in the National Renovation Movement, Katāy Don Sasorit (Finance), ambitious and intelligent, and the scholarly Nyūy Aphai (Education). The first problems facing the new government were to secure its finances and extend its writ as far as possible. One of the few available sources of revenue, opium, was declared a government monopoly, though most of the harvest was subsequently seized by the Chinese. Export of other products had either been entirely disrupted by the war (tin), or was beyond government control (teak, forest products, rice). Some financial support came from the Vietnamese community, and from Thai sources, but it was insufficient to run a government.

Suphānuvong did not arrive in Viang Chan to join the new Lao Issara government until the end of October. He had been in Vietnam when the Japanese surrendered. The week following the Vietnamese declaration of independence found him in Hanoi making contact with Ho Chi Minh, assuring the Vietminh of Lao support for their independence struggle, and exhorting his comrades in the Lao Issara movement by means of lengthy telegrams. Early in October he crossed into Laos, accompanied by a twelve-member Vietminh escort wearing Lao uniforms. The little party arrived in Savannakhēt on 7 October to a tumultuous welcome from the Vietnamese community and a rather cooler one from Un Xananikôn and his Lao Sērī supporters. Among those already working for the military administration that Un had established under his chief-of-staff Phūmī Nôsavan were Kaisôn Phomvihān and Nūhak Phumsavan, later to become the two most powerful figures in the Lao communist movement.[5]

Though Un had been appointed by Phetxarāt as the Lao Issara's

Commissioner for the five southern provinces, he deferred to Suphānuvong in agreeing to serve as his deputy in both a 'Committee for Lao Independence' and an 'Army for the Liberation and Defence of Laos'. Each military service – personnel, armament, intelligence, etc. – was headed by a Lao, with one of Suphānuvong's Vietminh officers as 'adviser'.[6] It was a pattern that was to become well established in the Lao communist movement. After extending his military organization to Thākhaek, Suphānuvong left for Viang Chan, where by the end of October he had obtained not only formal government approval for his actions, but also changes to the government. As Commander-in-Chief of the Army for the Defence and Liberation of Laos, Suphānuvong wanted the defence ministry in preference to his allotted portfolio. Phetxarāt refused to replace Major Sing Rattanasamai, himself the commander of a motley Lao–Thai force, but in a conciliatory move, Suphānuvong was appointed Minister for Foreign Affairs, and Suvanna Phūmā was brought into the cabinet as Minister for Public Works.

Suphānuvong's ability to get his own way derived from his assertive character and social standing; moreover, of the Lao Issara leaders he alone enjoyed full support from the Vietminh. Alliance with the Vietminh was almost entirely his doing. Under his direction a Military Convention was drawn up and endorsed by the government, which both formalized the presence of Vietnamese military units in Laos and opened the way for further cooperation between Vietminh and Lao Issara armed forces. A joint Lao–Viet 'General Staff' was organized to coordinate the activities of the two armies, while the military intelligence service was placed under Vietnamese direction.[7]

The first priority for the Lao Issara government was to enforce its jurisdiction. On 13 November, partly to impress the Chinese, the government declared martial law. A military expedition under the command of Major Sing was despatched to retake Xiang Khuang and Xam Neua. By the end of November, the French had been forced to withdraw from all administrative centres in northern Laos. The only exception was Luang Phrabāng, but even there a popular demonstration had already forced the King to submit to a Lao Issara administration and prevented him from having any contact with Colonel Imfeld. By early December, therefore, the Lao Issara had the illusion of ruling all of central and northern Laos. French property had been nationalized, and what French forces remained had either been disarmed or forced to return to the jungle as hunted outlaws. But independence rested on the doubtful basis of the Chinese army of occupation and alliance with the Vietminh, each of which had its own interests to pursue in which the Lao Issara figured only marginally.

The problems facing the new government were immense. The administration was in a shambles, civil servants had not been paid, and the treasury was empty. The government could not even meet the cost of its own defence and legitimation. Arms could not be purchased, nor propaganda printed to counter the pro-French bias in everything from school texts to radio broadcasts from French-controlled areas. Nor did the government have the means to seek international support beyond its immediate neighbours.

By the end of January 1946, it was obvious that the French had no intention of negotiating the independence of Laos with the Lao Issara. French hopes of splitting Phetxarāt and the moderates from pro-Vietminh elements had been abandoned, for fear that any such move would alienate the King and southerners suspicious of Phetxarāt and his ambitions.[8] By then the British had left Indochina to France and negotiations were already under way for the withdrawal of the Chinese army of occupation. France's intention to reoccupy Laos was signalled by the recapture of Xiang Khuang at the end of January, with the assistance of Lao and Hmong partisans. Throughout February, French forces reinforced their position in southern Laos, recruiting and training Lao auxiliary units. The Lao Issara, bankrupt and ill-equipped, could only await the inevitable French return.

Two events opened the way for the French reconquest of Laos: the *modus vivendi* agreed between Ho Chi Minh and the French government on 6 March, which prolonged the suspension of hostilities in Vietnam and left the Lao Issara exposed; and agreement on the withdrawal of Chinese forces. Lao Issara and Vietnamese paramilitary forces abandoned Savannakhēt, but at Thākhaek a defiant Suphānuvong commanding combined Lao–Viet forces determined to make a stand. The French assault came on 21 March, backed by armoured cars, artillery and aircraft against the lightly armed Lao and Vietnamese. Within a few hours it was all over. The defenders suffered more than a thousand casualties, many of them civilians shot and drowned as they attempted to cross the Mekong to Thailand. Suphānuvong was himself badly wounded when an aircraft strafed his boat, but Un Xananikôn escaped to lead three hundred survivors north to Viang Chan, via Thailand. Franco-Lao casualties were nineteen dead and twenty wounded,[9] but in revenge the Vietnamese quarter of the town was systematically destroyed.

In the month remaining to the provisional government, attention shifted from the military to the political front, as negotiations resumed between the government and the court in Luang Phrabāng to resolve constitutional, if not political, differences. The result was a compromise which saw King Sīsavāngvong reluctantly accept reinstatement as constitutional monarch in return for legitimation of the Lao Issara government and constitution. While Phetxarāt and his ministers attended the ceremonial endorsement of this compromise in Luang Phrabāng, Viang Chan was in turmoil awaiting the imminent arrival of the French. Only the presence of a Chinese garrison had prevented a French attack. When the Chinese commander announced he would withdraw his forces, the decision was taken to evacuate the city. Viang Chan was reoccupied by French troops on 24 April, and Luang Phrabāng in mid-May. The entire Lao Issara government, along with some two thousand of its principal supporters and their families, crossed into Thailand. The first flowering of Lao nationalism had met with ignominious defeat. Thousands of Vietnamese also fled, virtually depopulating the Mekong towns.[10] The King declared his 'gratitude, fidelity and affection' for France, and appointed Prince Kindāvong, yet

another younger half-brother of Phetxarāt, as provisional prime minister (of the royal territories of Luang Phrabāng) until a new governmental structure could be put in place.

## THE KINGDOM OF LAOS

Once the reconquest was complete, the French set about reconstituting
their administration. By this time there was recognition that a new
constitutional framework would be required, one that French authorities hoped would, by permitting a degree of self-government to a
collaborationist elite, preserve the French Union. A Franco-Lao joint
commission met in July. Its report formed the basis for a provisional
*modus vivendi* signed on 27 August 1946, formally endorsing the unity of
Laos as a constitutional monarchy within the French Union. A secret
protocol guaranteed Prince Bunūm na Champāsak the position of
Inspector-General of the kingdom for life, in return for renunciation of
his claim to the throne of a separate principality of Champāsak. Several
additional conventions covered specific matters, including finance,
military cooperation and public works.[11] The Garde Indigène was
replaced by a Lao National Guard and a Lao gendarmerie (police force).
Their roles were not only to protect the frontiers of the state and
maintain internal law and order respectively, but also to 'educate the
nation' by providing moral, civic, military and technical training.[12] Only
a limited devolution of power took place, however, and France
remained responsible not only for defence and foreign relations, but
also for a variety of other matters, from customs and postal services to
meteorology and mines. The Lao government was responsible only for
such services as public works, agriculture, health and education. In fact
the former administrative structures of the Indochinese Federation
remained essentially in place. The Résident Supérieur became French
Commissioner to Laos, and provincial councillors replaced the prewar
*résidents* in each of the twelve provinces. Councillors were also
appointed to oversee the functioning of each ministry responsible for
other than federal services. Real power thus rested not with the prime
minister but with the French Commissioner, who had the right to veto
even royal decrees. Not surprisingly the agreement was roundly
condemned by the Lao Issara.

Slowly, however, the new Kingdom of Laos began to take shape. In
November 1946 at the Washington Conference, Thailand was obliged
to return all the territories it had acquired in 1941. Meanwhile preparations went ahead to convene a Constituent Assembly. Elections
on the basis of universal male suffrage were held in December for
forty-four deputies, who met for their inaugural session on 15 March
1947. From that date, while the Assembly deliberated the constitution, government was exercised by a provisional cabinet under the
leadership of Prince Suvannarāt, yet another younger half-brother of
Phetxarāt. After much debate, a constitution was eventually adopted
and duly promulgated. This confirmed the status of the Kingdom of

Laos as a unified 'autonomous state' within the French Union, and established a basis for continued French assistance 'on the path to civic, moral and material progress'.[13] Provision was made for a unicameral National Assembly elected by universal suffrage for a period of four years. A twelve-member King's Council was to act as a High Court and house of review of legislation. In August elections were held for thirty-five deputies to the National Assembly; at its first sitting in November, it endorsed Suvannarāt as prime minister, together with his six cabinet colleagues comprising the first Royal Lao government.

All were members of the Lao elite, the class to which the French intended power should devolve. As such they shared a French education and aristocratic pride in their own social standing. Many could trace their ancestry to collateral lines of the royal families of Luang Phrabāng, Vieng Chan or Champāsak, and their regional links were important to them. Privilege and position they took as their due. Their families through patronage and influence formed the nuclei of extended clans of related and dependent families. Yet their numbers were small. Fewer than twenty families were politically powerful, out of an elite comprising perhaps two hundred.[14]

Cabinet membership was carefully balanced to include representation of the most powerful families and clans of the north, centre, and south of the country, for politics centred on personalities, not parties.[15] Because the families represented were to dominate Lao politics for the next two decades, it is worth examining this first ministry. Phetxarāt's brothers (Suvannarāt as prime minister, Kindāvong as Minister of State) represented Luang Phrabāng. Ku Aphai (Education and Health) and Leuam Insīxiangmai (Finance) were from Khong and Savannakhēt respectively, both suspicious of political dominance by Luang Phrabāng. Of the other three ministers, Ūthong Suvannavong (Interior and Defence) was the powerful representative of the leading family of Viang Chan. Like Ku Aphai, he was deeply conservative and pro-French. The other two ministers were younger, more ambitious men, for whom politics was an arena in which to perform, and which offered a means to personal power and wealth. Together Bong Suvannavong (Economy) and Ku Vôravong (Justice, Religion, Social Action and Public Works) formed the first officially-recognized political party, the Lao National Union with its own roneoed news-sheet, *Lao Mai* (New Laos). Bong belonged to a collateral branch of the influential Suvannavong clan and had been active in the Renovation Movement before falling out with the Lao Issara. Ku Vôravong, originally from Savannakhēt, was determined to build a following of his own in the capital. Both used the National Assembly as a forum from which to criticize the existing political order. For the Lao National Union, the *modus vivendi* was merely the first step in the complete devolution of power from French to Lao.

Another powerful Viang Chan clan with political ambitions was the Xananikôns. Their leader was Phuy Xananikôn, the first president of the National Assembly. The Xananikôn clan had managed to increase its power at the expense of the more patrician Suvannavongs, in part through intermarriage with the Aphais; but the family was divided, with two brothers in Viang Chan and two more with the Lao Issara. While the Suvannavongs tended to step back from the contest, much of the infighting on the political right in Viang Chan over the following years reflected a continuing struggle for power between the Xananikôns and their allies, and the Vôravong clan which counted Phūmī Nôsavan and the Chunlamanī family among influential members.

The struggle for power and perquisites of office between influential clans became endemic in Lao politics over the next three decades, particularly on the political right. As Laos was increasingly drawn into the Cold War, families competed for access to the increasing amounts of financial and material aid, mainly from the United States, that poured into the country. During this period personal, clan and regional interests in obtaining a share of this largesse tended to be pursued in preference to, indeed often to the virtual exclusion of, national welfare. Central government was weakened by the refusal of powerful families to implement measures they considered inimical to their own interests. In fact, the involvement of leading families in politics seemed primarily to ensure that their own interests were protected and that rival clans were not advantaged.

Elite clanism and regionalism had the effect of retarding development of a sense of Lao national identity and consciousness. Yet nation-building was the overriding need for a country so ethnically and regionally divided. Assumptions of ethnic and cultural superiority were implicit in the terms *khā* (slave) applied to the Lao Thoeng, and *maeo* (savage) applied to the Hmong by the lowland Lao; they translated into, at best, government indifference and, at worst, discrimination. Little or nothing was done to mobilize ethnic minorities by creating a national political culture in which they could participate, or by drawing them into the national economy. Nor did the powerful families evince much concern for the vast majority of Lao Lum who were subsistence village farmers. Government expenditure and government services were concentrated overwhelmingly in the large towns, the capitals of the larger and more populated provinces that constituted the power bases of the principal clans. Nevertheless, failure to develop a strong sense of Lao national unity during these crucial early years was not entirely due to the lack of vision of clan leaders. In part it was also the fault of the French, and in part it was due to the failure of the monarchy to become a supra-political focus of Lao nationalism.

The French had made no attempt before 1940 to prepare the Lao to take responsibility for the political direction of their own country, largely because they had never thought of Laos as a national entity in its own right. Even in 1946 the French still regarded Laos as an integral part of their Indochinese empire. The outbreak of the First Indochina War in December of that year, after negotiations between the Vietminh and the French government broke down, served notice that the French, unlike the British in Burma or the Americans in the Philippines, were determined to hold on to their empire in Indochina. The changes that were introduced as a result of the Franco-Lao *modus vivendi* were thus largely cosmetic. In 1946 France had no intention of giving Laos genuine independence. Negotiation, much less compromise, with the Lao Issara was ruled out. Despite the façade of constitutional self-government, French control continued to be almost as total as before the war.

The French did, however, make some effort to make amends for past neglect. Particular attention was given to education. New primary schools were constructed. The Collège Pavie was upgraded to a lycée (senior high school) in time for the 1947 school year, while junior high schools were opened at Pākxē, Luang Phrabāng and Savannakhēt. Fully 17 per cent of the national budget was devoted to education. 'The Lao school will forge the soul of modern Laos, it will be the cement of national unity', proclaimed one government publication, which at least recognized the challenge ahead.[16] The best students and those with influential family connections were sent to pursue higher studies in Vietnam and France. Health services were also improved, and new hospitals and dispensaries built, despite a shortage of qualified health professionals to staff them. A major effort went into teaching hygiene and prophylactic measures. Since local revenue was quite inadequate, almost the entire program was financed by French aid.

The task was immense, however, made more difficult by the inadequate basis laid in the pre-war years. The lack of properly trained civil servants to administer a country with poor communications and more than 11,000 villages was particularly pressing. Only 400 civil servants and 700 technical cadres were initially available throughout the entire country, and many of those had received minimal instruction.[17] Training was conducted 'on the job', and both the fledgling army and the police were called upon to help perform a nation-building role for which they were hardly equipped.

The continued presence of the French, however, allowed Lao politicians to concentrate on their own, rather than their nation's, interests. The only man who might have served as a symbol of Lao national identity was the King. But Sīsavāngvong, by then 'elderly, vacillating, and encumbered with 15 wives',[18] was an old man who looked to France to preserve his throne, and who left most decisions to his son, the thoroughly pro-French Savāngvatthanā. The King could have served as the symbol of Lao unity only if he had moved his palace to Viang Chan, the administrative and political capital of the country, and travelled far more widely among his subjects. But this significant opportunity was lost. By remaining in Luang Phrabāng, the King did nothing to overcome the regionalism that thrived on the distrust and jealousy between Luang Phrabāng and Champāsak. The royal family remained identified with their royal capital, not merely above, but entirely removed from, political life in Viang Chan. This left Viang Chan itself to become the principal prize for whichever clan won the new game for control of political patronage.

By mid-1949, the French position in Indochina had weakened. France had signally failed to obtain the swift victory expected against the Vietminh, and was under pressure from the United States to make concessions to nationalist groups. In Laos, government leaders were acutely aware of criticism by the exiled Lao Issara that they were nothing more than French lackeys, and increasingly sensitive to French paternalism.[19] In July 1949, a General Convention signed between France and Laos went some way towards granting Laos greater independence. The Lao government gained control over what previously had been Federal Indochinese services, except for monetary policy and customs, where Indochina-wide agreements still prevailed. Sovereignty also remained limited with respect to defence, foreign affairs and justice. French Union forces were permitted freedom of movement throughout Lao territory 'for the common defence of the states of Indo-China', and France retained the right to recruit Lao into 'mixed Franco-Laotian units' under French command.[20] While Laos could apply for separate membership of the United Nations, foreign policy was to be closely coordinated with that of the French Union, and French nationals continued to enjoy extraterritorial legal rights. As even Bunūm admitted, independence within the French Union still presented 'a duality of contradictory appearance',[21] but for as long as the war against the Vietminh continued, francophile Lao believed they still needed French protection.

If the provisions of the General Convention could hardly be said to grant Laos full independence, they did represent a considerable advance over the *modus vivendi* of 1946. In September 1949 an amended constitution making appropriate revisions was promulgated. More significantly, the qualified independence given to Laos under the terms of the General Convention was considered sufficient by moderates within the Lao Issara to warrant their return from exile to take part in the political process. Radical members, by contrast, who had already split with the Lao Issara leadership in Bangkok, entered instead into alliance with the Vietminh.

## EXILE AND RESISTANCE

When the Lao Issara government and their followers fled their country in April 1946, they were determined to carry on the struggle against the French. Though this was a period of political instability in Thailand, they received a sympathetic welcome from Thai authorities. Pridi Phanomyong, former Regent and leader of the underground anti-Japanese Thai Sērī (Free Thai) movement during the war years, remained the dominant political figure, and Pridi had no love for French imperialism. Lao Issara guerrillas made full use of Thai territory. Only when several joint Lao Issara–Vietminh attacks provoked hot French pursuit across the Mekong, resulting in an exchange of angry accusations between Thailand and France, did Americans from the Office of Strategic Services advise Issara leaders to distance themselves from the border.[22] While the government-in-exile based itself in Bangkok, with Thai blessing and financial support, guerrilla units continued their harassment of the French. A centre of resistance was established in the Mukdāhān area, opposite Savannakhēt, with a training camp near Sākon Nakhôn.

Lao Issara military operations in Thailand were organized into three sectors. The north was responsible for operations into Luang Namthā, Xainyaburī and Luang Phrabāng provinces; the centre covered an arc from Viang Chan to Savannakhēt; the south directed resistance in the region of the Bôlavēn plateau.[23] In all three areas, military leaders who would eventually find themselves on opposite sides of the political divide fought together against the French. Communications were difficult, and units often operated without central direction. Support came from local Thai, particularly former members of the disbanded Thai Sērī, but much of the organizational support was provided by Vietnamese members of the Indochinese Communist Party.[24] Both joint Lao Issara–Vietminh units and separate Vietminh units operated out of northeast Thailand until prevented from doing so by Thai authorities.

Phetxarāt accepted titular leadership of the Lao Issara government-in-exile, with Khammao as prime minister, and Suvanna Phūmā effectively his deputy. Suphānuvong retained the Foreign Affairs portfolio while continuing to act as military commander-in-chief. Subsequently he was also handed the Defence portfolio. Katāy added Propaganda to Finance, while Education lapsed. The government-in-exile devoted itself to publicizing its cause, denouncing the French, and lobbying foreign representatives. Contacts with the United States were disappointing, however, and with French contacts and go-betweens quite unproductive. Less dedicated supporters progressively gave up the struggle and filtered back into Laos. Others came to believe the only hope of getting rid of the French was through armed alliance with the Vietminh.

Suphānuvong resumed contact with the Vietminh in July 1946 when he made his way to Hanoi. At the time, while Ho Chi Minh was in France, an uneasy truce prevailed between the French and the Vietminh. Operations continued, however, against the Lao Issara. Following reoccupation of Savannakhēt and Thākhaek, French forces had driven Lao Issara and Vietminh elements east into the mountainous border areas. When Lao Issara guerrillas were forced to retreat across the frontier into Vietnam, Vietminh cadres provided them with training and logistical support.

In northern Laos, French forces did not reoccupy the last Issara stronghold at Bān Huayxāy until 23 September 1946, after which guerrilla activity was directed from the Thai bank of the Mekong. In the northeast, in Xam Neua and Phongsālī, the situation was more confused. Xam Neua had been reoccupied in April, Phongsālī in mid-June, but military activity continued. French forces benefited from support from Hmong partisans led by Tūbī Līfung; other Hmong, loyal to the Lô clan under the command of Tūbī's bitter rival Faidāng Lôbliayao, entered into alliance with the Vietminh. Convinced of the vital importance of continued Vietminh support for the Lao Issara armed struggle, Suphānuvong returned to Thailand to re-inspire his forces there.

Meanwhile, in Vinh in September 1946, a number of Lao resistance leaders came together under Vietminh auspices to form the Committee for Lao Resistance in the East, to complement the western theatre of Lao Issara operations based in Thailand. From its inauguration the committee, through its chairman Nūhak Phumsavan, was under the secret direction of the Indochinese Communist Party. Also attending the founding meeting were Kaisôn Phomvihān, responsible for liaison with the Vietminh, Faidāng Lôbliayao, appointed to command the Xiang Khuang–Xam Neua sector, and Ō Anurak, commander of Issara forces in the Xēpōn sector. Further south Sīthon Kommadam, who had been freed from prison in Phongsālī by the Japanese, had returned to mount his own resistance in the Bôlavēn region.

Communication between the two foci of resistance was via runners to Thailand and telegraph to Bangkok. The government-in-exile was notified of the formation of the Committee for Lao Resistance in the East, to which it gave approval. Activity in the eastern theatre was galvanized in December 1946 by the outbreak of the First Indochina War. Suphānuvong, active as ever, crossed into Laos to find out for himself how Lao guerrilla units were faring. There he gave his blessing to creation of joint Lao Issara–Vietminh units to operate in the border regions.[25] Guerrilla activity was sporadic, however. Weapons and ammunition were in short supply and finance was always a problem. Thai support continued, however, and in September 1947 Bangkok backed formation of a 'League of Southeast Asia' bringing together radical nationalists from Indonesia, Malaya and Burma, as well as the countries of Indochina. Suphānuvong was elected Secretary-General.

Less than two months later, a military *coup d'état* returned former dictator Phibunsongkhram to power in Thailand; it marked a shift to the right in Thai politics. The change of government coincided with growing anti-communism in the United States with the onset of the Cold War, and soon led to improved relations between Thailand and France. The Lao resistance was faced with the alternative of either ceasing all military activity on Thai soil, or of transferring operations to the eastern theatre along the Lao–Vietnam border. For Suphānuvong and his most committed followers, the choice was obvious. Ever closer military cooperation with the Vietminh was now essential, as he had argued all along. For others the choice was more difficult. Many were deeply suspicious of Vietnamese intentions towards Laos, feared the communism of the Vietminh, and were reluctant to leave the relative comfort of Thailand. As military activity tapered off, morale fell, and French envoys began to target likely returnees with offers of amnesty and employment.

Meanwhile dissension arose between committed communists (Nūhak, Kaisôn) trusted and supported by the Vietminh, and Issara commanders from Thailand who considered themselves superior in military rank and social status, and wished to retain some independence of action. For the ICP, however, Laos was part of a single field of operations against the French which it was determined to direct. Issara commanders were frozen out as the Party threw its support behind those it could trust. January 1949 is the official date given for the formation in southeastern Laos of the *Rāxavong* brigade, the first unit of what was eventually to become the Lao People's Liberation Army.[26] Its commander was Kaisôn Phomvihān, a trusted agent of the ICP who had undergone training at the Vietminh Military Academy, and who was subsequently to be named Secretary-General of the Lao People's Revolutionary Party. Further south, Khamtai Sīphandôn had joined Sīthon Kommadam in the Bôlavēn region. In the far north, Suphānu-vong and Phūmī Vongvichit were active in Luang Namthā, while Faidāng and his Hmong kept up the pressure in Huaphan and Xiang Khuang. All were receiving substantial Vietminh assistance in the form of cadres, equipment and training.

By March 1949 internal differences in the Lao Issara came to a head over Suphānuvong's high-handed refusal to be accountable to the Issara government for his military activities and financial expenditure. Concern had been growing for some time over the prince's relations with the Vietminh. Personal antagonisms were also acrimonious, espe-cially between Suphānuvong and Katāy, the Lao Issara's most effective propagandist (whose tracts appeared in English under the pen-name of William Rabbit).[27] The Issara government-in-exile was acutely aware of the changed political environment following the Thai military coup, and had publicly dissociated itself from Suphānuvong's actions in inviting not only the Vietminh, but also Kuomintang Chinese deserters and Burmese volunteers to cross into Laos to fight the French.

Suphānuvong's response was to submit an angry letter of resignation to Phetxarāt. In it he defended his decisions and actions, and ridiculed those who remained in Bangkok as children or old women in whom he had no confidence and for whom he had no respect. A subsequent exchange of letters in May between Suphānuvong and Katāy sealed the rift with a catalogue of mutual criticism and personal vilification. For Katāy, Suphānuvong was arrogant and devious, a man who refused to subordinate himself to collective policy, who had acted as a 'small god', and who had failed in his responsibilities both as commander-in-chief of the Lao Issara armed forces (in not organizing a Lao general staff), and as a minister (in not accounting for the financial assistance he had received from the Vietnamese). For Suphānuvong, Katāy's criticisms revealed how hopelessly out of touch Issara ministers in Bangkok had become. The resistance was organized in haste, motivated through personal encouragement, armed and financed by whatever means were available. Rough accounts had been kept but there was no time to write them up neatly. Such formalities were secondary to the struggle itself, which had to be waged by every possible means, through utilizing whatever foreign assistance was available. Only his own efforts in obtaining financial support from the Vietminh, Suphānuvong some-what ingenuously claimed, had sustained the resistance movement in eastern Laos. As for the Issara government-in-exile, it was 'purely fictiti-ous and nominal'. His own position, by contrast, was as a represent-ative of the 'resistance population' whose cause he actively espoused.[28]

In point of fact, in February 1949 Suphānuvong had already formed a political front, the Lao People's Progressive Organization, in his own area of operations in northern Laos that was not subject to the Lao Issara. For this, and for his high-handed disregard for Issara directives, he was relieved of both his ministries. Following his definitive break with the Lao Issara, Suphānuvong announced formation of a 'Resistance Committee' to bring together representatives of all resistance forces. Resistance fighters were thus faced with a conflict of loyalties: either continue to accept the leadership of the Lao Issara government in Bangkok, with Phetxarāt still its nominal head; or throw in their lot with Suphānuvong and the Vietminh.

The choice was made even more stark when in October, in response to the Franco-Lao Convention of July, a decision was taken by the remaining ministers of the government-in-exile to decree its dissolution on the grounds that the degree of independence obtained by the Kingdom of Laos satisfied the original demands of the Lao Issara movement. Led by Khammao, Suvanna Phūmā and Katāy, most of the moderate membership of the Lao Issara accepted a negotiated amnesty and returned to Laos. Only Phetxarāt remained in Bangkok, proud and bitter at the refusal of the King to restore his title of *uparāt*, and equivocal over the political divisions that had occurred.

The split in the Lao Issara marked the failure of the movement to provide unified leadership of the nationalist struggle. In the end, differences became too great between those espousing alternative means of achieving what all wanted: complete independence. These differences were exemplified by the positions of the three brothers whose force of character had vitalized the movement. Suvanna Phūmā, in touch with events in Laos, recognized the extent to which nationalist sentiment had gained ground, even among those who had initially welcomed the return of the French. Negotiation, he believed, could win what an ineffective insurgency was patently unable to achieve. Suphānuvong, adamant in his refusal to compromise, drew another lesson: there was no alternative but to rely on the Vietminh. Only by forcibly expelling the French, he believed, could Indochina free itself of its colonial past and achieve genuine independence and freedom. The small but dedicated band he led into alliance with the Vietminh formed the hardened core of the communist movement.

Phetxarāt, older and less impetuous than his brothers, took a longer-term view which rejected both compromise with the French and reliance on the Vietminh. He looked to a Laos neutral in the developing Cold War, playing neighbour against neighbour while keeping all at arm's length.[29] Ironically, it was this vision of Lao nationalism that Suvanna attempted to implement once independence from France had been achieved in 1953; and the Lao People's Democratic Republic too eventually came to embrace it as Lao dependency on Vietnam diminished in the late 1980s.

## TOWARDS INDEPENDENCE

The Laos to which Lao Issara leaders returned after their exile was already a different place from the country they had left three and a half years before. Issara guerrilla activity had not prevented a functioning administration from being put into place. In the towns, commerce was firmly in the hands of the Chinese, studiedly neutral in the Franco-Vietminh conflict. But as over 80 per cent of the Vietnamese population had left,[30] new openings had become available for employment of Lao with even a modicum of education in a variety of government services – public works, industry, agriculture, forestry, education, health – even if recruitment depended more often on nepotism or regional loyalties than on qualifications or ability. As families had moved into the towns from surrounding villages to take advantage of these opportunities, or to seek education for their children, the towns themselves had both expanded and become increasingly Lao.[31]

Upon their return, Lao Issara political leaders immediately took part in negotiations on the formal transfer of powers to the Royal Lao government, which was signed on 6 February 1950. Of the powers retained by France, the more significant allowed for continuing extra-territoriality in the administration of justice, and control over internal security (the secret police). Among the most important documents was a military convention providing for formation of a national Lao army. A French military training mission was established, and conscription introduced. External defence was made the responsibility of a Permanent Franco-Lao Committee, while the French Union Army on Lao soil remained under French command.

A sense of urgency attached to these negotiations. In October 1949, Mao Zedong had proclaimed the People's Republic of China. In response to an appeal by Ho Chi Minh, China officially recognized the Democratic Republic of Vietnam on 18 January 1950. The Soviet Union followed suit a week later. This opened the way for international communist assistance to the Vietminh, thus significantly altering the balance of advantage in Indochina. The United States, meanwhile, had been urging more substantial concessions on the part of the French towards genuine independence for the peoples of Indochina. The day following signature of the transfer of powers, both the United States and Britain recognized the independence of Laos, though neither established an embassy in Viang Chan. Their lead was followed by several European and Latin American states. Newly independent Asian nations generally withheld recognition on the grounds that Lao independence was still not complete, as no agreement with a foreign country could be concluded without endorsement by the High Council of the French Union. Only Thailand exchanged ambassadors. The country's international status was progressively enhanced over the next two years through membership of several United Nations agencies, and associate membership of the Economic Commission for Asia and the Far East (ECAFE). A Lao seat in the UN was vetoed by the Soviet Union, however, and Laos had to wait until December 1955 before being admitted to the General Assembly.

But if international recognition accorded Laos the external trappings of a nation state, the internal task of nation-building still remained. The return of the moderate Lao Issara entirely altered the complexion of internal Lao politics. To the clan rivalries and division between southerners and northerners was added the division between former Lao

Issara, who saw themselves as true nationalists, and those who had supported the French against them. The returnees formed their own political party, the National Progressive Party, to maintain their solidarity and to press for their political goals. In response, Phuy Xananikôn formed the Independent Party, grouping most of those who had opposed the Lao Issara. Neither was a party in the Western sense, but rather groups of politicians owing loyalty to influential leaders.

In the cause of national unity the Bunūm government resigned, claiming, prematurely, that it had achieved both independence and national reconciliation. The new government formed in February 1950, led by Phuy Xananikôn, included five Independent and two Progressive ministers – Khammao Vilai (Justice and Health) and Suvanna Phūmā (Planning and Public Works). Other portfolios were again distributed between powerful clans. The principal task facing the new government was to build on the start that had already been made in putting in place the administrative structures of a modern state. A shortage of trained and qualified personnel enabled the administration to absorb Issara returnees without difficulty. The problem was how to pay them. France warned it would halve the subsidy it had previously provided to cover the budget deficit. The government suggested a series of new taxes which the National Assembly was reluctant to enact. Political tensions also surfaced in respect to the army. Issara refusal to accept a commander-in-chief who had fought against them eventually led to appointment of a compromise civilian candidate, Sunthôn Pathammavong, rapidly elevated to the rank of colonel. In November 1950, with some reservations with regard to the dominant position of Vietnam, Laos signed the Pau Convention establishing inter-Indochinese agencies to control those services not transferred to individual states, notably customs and currency.

Although Laos itself was peaceful except for a few incidents in border areas, the region was progressively being drawn into the Cold War. With the outbreak of fighting in Korea in June 1950, the United States accepted France's contention that the war in Indochina formed part of the broader struggle to contain communist expansion in Asia. In response to a French request, President Truman approved the first grant of US military assistance for the war in Indochina, though he ran into strong French resistance in attempting to channel the aid directly to the three Associated States. Eventually an agreement was signed for US economic, but not military, assistance to be supplied directly to the Royal Lao government.[32]

Elections to the National Assembly in August 1951 resulted in a victory for the National Progressive Party over its Independent rival, though not to the extent of gaining an absolute parliamentary majority. When Phuy Xananikôn resigned, Suvanna Phūmā was called upon to form his first government. His first priority was to obtain the transfer of all services still under French control to the jurisdiction of the Lao government, thereby achieving the complete independence he believed essential for the reconciliation of all Lao. Progressively services were transferred. The police were placed under Lao control, and the justice system revamped. The following year a national customs service was established, and the national treasury became entirely responsible for drawing up the Lao budget, the financing of which remained the government's most pressing problem.

During the early 1950s further progress was made in areas such as education, health, agriculture and public works. More schools were built and, despite a new teacher training school in Viang Chan, the demand for teachers outstripped supply. Health services were developed, and agricultural extension encouraged. In both areas priority was given to training personnel and publishing and disseminating information. Public works included construction of government buildings (National Assembly building, central post office, etc.) and roads. A national five-year economic development plan was drawn up to run from 1952 to 1957.

Yet all the activity, the excitement even, of building a new state was confined to a very small section of the population, and affected institutions rather than attitudes. Politics was a game played by a few leading families, and the changes wrought were limited for the most part to urban areas. Most of the rural population remained untouched, especially in the highlands where virtually nothing was done to give the ethnic minorities any role in the new Lao state. No attempt was made to mobilize the population in the cause of nation-building. Lao nationalism thus remained an elite phenomenon. Political parties remained coalitions of influential families with no popular base, whose major role was to promote clan interests. Deputies performed no useful responsible service to those who elected them, merely enjoying the perquisites of office, particularly foreign travel. The government thus encouraged little sense of civic duty or public trust. The attitudes engendered permeated not only the political culture, but also the administration and bureaucracy. As a French adviser to the Lao government later remembered: 'There was too much corruption, too many favours and unfair promotions, too much supremacy of personal over national interests. There was a deficiency in the formation of both leaders and civil servants.'[33] Politics continued to be a game of grab for the powerful few, conducted in the language of colonial domination. The news-sheets of political parties sought no wider, national readership; nor did they discuss matters of national significance in a language accessible to village levels of literacy and comprehension.

Only Buddhism and history provided possibilities for a broadly cohesive nationalism, though both were limited almost exclusively to the Lao Lum. The modern kingdom adopted the full name of the ancient empire of Lān Xāng: Kingdom of a Million Elephants and the White Parasol. Flag and anthem too reinforced historical continuity as the basis for national identity. Yet the symbols of nationalism in Laos – king, country and religion, national flag and national anthem – failed to take on the kind of mystique they enjoyed in Thailand, imbued with the power of animating the life of the nation. Nationalism did provide some stimulus for historical research and for art and literature. Artists favoured subjects such as Buddhist temples, monks, and young girls in traditional costume, while a Literary Committee (later the Royal Academy) and the Institute of Buddhist Studies actively publicized Lao history and culture. But no-one in Laos performed the charismatic role of Sihanouk in Cambodia or Sukarno in Indonesia. The King remained a remote figure, unknown to most rural Lao,[34] let alone the mountain minorities, while Phetxarāt sulked in Bangkok. Yet the need to develop a sense of national cohesion was arguably greater in Laos than anywhere else in Southeast Asia, and in the years from 1946 to 1953 valuable opportunities were lost to build a spirit of Lao national unity capable of transcending narrow regional, ethnic, clan, and family loyalties.[35] Not surprisingly, those given no national part to play responded to promises of a radically different kind for a state that would sweep away all privilege and division.

## THE PATHĒT LAO AND THE VIETMINH

Following the dissolution of the Lao Issara, Suphānuvong again made his way to Vietnam to meet with Vietminh leaders. There he was advised to convene a Congress of People's Representatives with a view to creating a Lao revolutionary movement, complete with front organization, resistance government and liberation army, along lines already established in Vietnam and Cambodia. All three revolutionary movements would work together in close coordination with the single goal of finally expelling the French from Indochina.

Invitations were issued to combatants and eventually more than one hundred delegates met from 13 to 15 August 1950. The Congress established a Free Laos Front (Naeo Lao Issara) with vice-presidents representing the three broad divisions of the Lao population, and with a Central Committee of fifteen members presided over by Suphānuvong. The congress also endorsed a 'Resistance government' of the Pathēt Lao – the name by which the revolutionary movement became known. The government comprised a group of men who would, in twenty-five years' time, lead the revolutionary movement in Laos to victory. Suphānuvong was named president and Minister for Foreign Affairs. The Interior Minister was Phūmī Vongvichit, the tall, intellectual former governor of Huaphan province. Suk Vongsak, a minor prince of the royal family of Luang Phrabāng, was given the portfolios of Education and Propaganda, while Sīthon Kommadam and Faidāng Lôbliayao were included as ministers without portfolio, whose task it was to mobilize their respective ethnic communities. The remaining portfolios went to lesser-known but already more influential figures within the Lao communist movement: Kaisôn Phomvihān (Defence), and Nūhak Phumsavan (Economy and Finance). Kaisôn, the son of a Vietnamese father and a Lao mother,[36] had studied law in Hanoi, where he had been recruited into the ICP. A trader who had driven trucks between Laos and Vietnam, Nūhak too had joined the ICP. Both men were from Savannakhēt; both had excellent contacts with, and were trusted by, the Vietminh.

The congress issued a manifesto and a twelve-point political program which set the agenda for the revolutionary movement. After vowing 'to fight the French colonialists and their lackeys, the Lao traitors to the Fatherland' and 'to establish an entirely independent and unified Laos', the program called for formation of a national coalition government, the first mention of what subsequently became a consistent Pathēt Lao demand.[37] Significantly, the congress pledged itself to bring about equality between different nationalities, and to eliminate the corvée labour demands so detested by the upland minorities. Great emphasis was placed on joining with the peoples of Vietnam and Cambodia in a common liberation struggle.

The political program and composition of delegates attending this first Congress of People's Representatives, together with the location and circumstances of its calling, effectively established not only the leadership and revolutionary strategy of the Pathēt Lao movement over the next quarter of a century, but also the nature and extent of its dependency on the Vietnamese for ideological, organizational and logistical support. The congress brought together representatives of three elements in the leadership of the Pathēt Lao. The first comprised members of the ICP and/or the Committee for Lao Resistance in the East, men generally of humble origin recruited as a result of contact, through birth, marriage or business interests with the Vietminh. The most important in this group were Kaisôn and Nūhak, but others included Khamtai Sīphandôn and Phūn Sīpasoet. The second strand in the leadership of the movement was made up of revolutionary activist members of the traditional Lao elite, notably Suphānuvong, Phūmī Vongvichit, and Suk Vongsak. The third strand comprised traditional chiefs of the more important ethnic minorities, Faidāng for the Hmong and Sīthon for the southern Lao Thoeng. Together these three elements formed what turned out to be a remarkably stable revolutionary leadership, both of the Pathēt Lao, and after 1975 of the Lao People's Democratic Republic.

In Laos, as in Vietnam, the revolutionary movement was dependent on ethnic minorities in establishing base areas. But whereas in Vietnam the Vietminh also drew on a well-developed support network among lowland Vietnamese communities, the Pathēt Lao had little opportunity to mobilize lowland Lao. By the time the Pathēt Lao was organized as a revolutionary movement, a decade after the Vietminh, the Royal Lao government was firmly in control of the major lowland Lao areas of population. The Pathēt Lao movement was thus forced to rely to an even greater extent than the Vietminh on minority groups and external support.[38]

From its very inception, therefore, the Pathēt Lao was obliged to develop an effective minorities (nationalities) policy, and to consider questions which the Royal Lao government short-sightedly ignored concerning national identity and unity. Lao nationalism as developed by the Pathēt Lao was radically egalitarian with respect to ethnic minorities. In contrast to the communists in China and Vietnam, the Pathēt Lao refused to establish separate autonomous areas where minorities would be able to exercise a degree of self-government. Instead, minority cadres were offered an opportunity to play a part in the national political arena – by supporting the revolutionary struggle and rising within the army and/or the Party. The Pathēt Lao drew heavily on the history of ethnic insurrection to construct an inclusive tradition of revolutionary nationalism. All who had opposed French colonialism were heroes of a revolutionary struggle for Lao freedom from subjection and oppression that had never been subdued. All who continued to fight the French were true Lao patriots, whatever their ethnicity, and their contribution to the Pathēt Lao movement would be recognized and rewarded. The proof was the leadership role that had been given to Faidāng and Sīthon. Never before had any Lao Thoeng or Lao Sūng leader been accorded full ministerial rank. Never before had ethnic equality been proclaimed as a national political goal. Over the next five years, the promises the Pathēt Lao assiduously spread through its propaganda had time to take root among a substantial proportion of these populations.

The Pathēt Lao attempt to seize the nationalist initiative was much less successful in appealing to ethnic Lao than to highland minorities: for most Lao, alliance with the Vietminh carried with it the threat of Vietnamese domination. With some reason, Lao suspicions of Vietnamese intentions were deep and abiding. Attitudes towards the Chinese, by contrast, were always more positive.[39] More traditional Royal Lao governments were able to retain the support of ethnic Lao by playing on fear of Vietnam, and appealing to lowland Lao cultural values and to a history of Lao superiority harking back to the powerful kingdom of Lān Xāng. Only when these began to wear thin during the Second Indochina War, and war-weariness set in, did the Pathēt Lao begin to build significant support among ethnic Lao.

The Free Laos Front joined up with the resistance fronts of Cambodia and Vietnam in March 1951 to form a common 'Alliance Front' of all three countries; meanwhile, the nature of the First Indochina War was changing from a colonial conflict pitting the French against the Vietminh and their allies to a subsidiary theatre in the American-inspired containment of communism. Establishment of the People's Republic of China and the outbreak of war in Korea enabled the French to portray their colonial war in Indochina as part of the defence of the 'Free World' against the tide of communism in Asia. As US military assistance increased (still primarily through the back door of Marshall Plan aid to France), so too did Chinese military assistance to the Vietminh. As a consequence, the scale and intensity of fighting in Indochina escalated markedly.

From 11 to 19 February 1951, the ICP held its Second Congress to consider the changed situation. Despite declaring its own dissolution in November 1945, the Party had continued to function as a clandestine organization controlling and directing the Vietminh, and had continued to recruit new members. During this period, especially between 1949 and 1951, a number of prominent Pathēt Lao leaders were recruited into the Party.[40] At this congress the decision was taken, however, to replace the ICP by three separate parties, even though Vietnamese direction of the overall resistance struggle was to continue. As a secret document assured Vietnamese cadres: 'the Vietnamese Party reserves the right to supervise the activities of its brother parties in Cambodia and Laos'.[41] Moreover, the program of the Vietnam Workers' Party (Dang Lao Dong), as the Vietnamese Communist Party was then called, provided for formation of a 'federation of the states of Viet-Nam, Laos and Cambodia, if the three peoples so desire'.[42]

Whereas the Vietnam Workers' Party was formed in March 1951, and the Khmer People's Revolutionary Party a month later, the Lao People's Party (Phak Paxāxon Lao) was not officially founded until 22 March 1955, well after Laos had achieved full independence and the Geneva Agreements had brought the First Indochina War to an end.[43] During the intervening four years, former ICP members under the direction of Kaisôn Phomvihān are said to have constituted a Committee for the Organization of the Party, whose task it was to recruit and provide ideological training for prospective Lao party members.[44] This process was carried out under the close supervision of the Vietnamese Workers' Party, but it is not clear whether former Lao members of the ICP actually transferred their membership in the meantime to it.[45] The widely dispersed pockets of Pathēt Lao resistance made it difficult to organize the Lao Party. Coordination was managed by the 'inter-zone' committees of the Alliance Front of the three Indochinese resistance movements under the direction of the Lao section of the Office for Cambodian and Lao Affairs of the Vietnamese Workers' Party. While Pathēt Lao representatives served on these 'inter-zone' committees, all were under Vietnamese control.

Organization of the Lao party went hand in hand with recruitment for and organization of the Lao People's Liberation Army, and the steady extension of Pathēt Lao propaganda and influence. The methods applied were similar to those of the Vietminh. In fact the period of preparation of the Lao revolutionary movement from 1951 to 1953 recapitulated the organizational phase of the Vietminh from 1941 to 1945. Pathēt Lao cadres would move into remote villages along the Laos–Vietnam frontier, or in mountainous areas, organize meetings, form committees (of farmers, women, youth), help build schools and dispensaries, teach literacy and hygiene, encourage self-help projects, suggest improved methods of developing agriculture, and recruit for and organize village self-defence units. Performances, festivals and meetings were occasions for communicating not Marxism, or even socialism, but a message promising freedom and progress, new services and new opportunities, and above all a revolutionary nationalism free of ethnic or cultural prejudices. As villages were won over, expanding guerrilla base areas, so they were lost to the Lao government. French patrols met with sullen silence, a refusal to provide food supplies, an absence of young men.[46] Base areas close to the Vietnamese frontier received assistance from the Vietminh to establish political training centres, hospitals, and arms workshops. Elsewhere activity took the form of propaganda by lightly armed teams, ambushes of food supplies *en route* to remote military garrisons, and attacks on army patrols. With the war in Vietnam the focus of French military operations, the Pathēt Lao concentrated on establishing the organizational basis for its own ongoing guerrilla struggle.

## 'INVASION' AND 'INDEPENDENCE'

In the latter part of 1952, Vietminh armies swept through the Tai highlands of northwestern Vietnam (the Sipsông Chu Tai), thus positioning themselves the length of the border with the Lao provinces of Phongsālī and Huaphan. Early in 1953 Pathēt Lao and Vietminh agents gathered intelligence and prepared food and supply caches along an arc from Dien Bien Phu west into Phongsālī and down the valley of the Nam Ū. The fledgling Royal Lao Army, under French operational command, was ordered to pull back from exposed border posts in anticipation of a major assault. In April, General Vo Nguyen Giap's forces struck deep into Laos on two fronts – one division along the prepared northern route, two more directly into Huaphan, which was garrisoned by three Lao battalions. In the north only one Lao battalion of the French Union Army at Meuang Khua stood in the way of a rapid Vietminh advance towards Luang Phrabāng. Its orders were to hold out long enough for reinforcements to be flown into the royal capital, which the King had resolutely refused to leave. The Lao post held out for thirty-six days: there were three survivors.[47]

The garrison at Xam Neua meanwhile was ordered to make a fighting retreat to the Plain of Jars, the principal French defensive position in northern Laos. Ambushed repeatedly and burdened with their wounded, of the 2400 men who left Xam Neua just over 200 reached safety two weeks later.[48] By then reinforcements had reached the Plain of Jars. Xiang Khuang was overrun, but was retaken in a Franco-Lao counter-attack. By the end of May any threat to Viang Chan had subsided. Meanwhile after coming within 30 kilometres of Luang Phrabāng, Vietminh forces withdrew, apparently because supply lines were over-extended and supplies were running low.

In Viang Chan panic briefly seized the population. Some families crossed into Thailand, others fled south. The Psychological Warfare Service did its best to counter the more alarmist rumours. In Luang Phrabāng, by contrast, all was calm, for a highly respected clairvoyant blind monk, Phra Sāthôn, had revealed at the height of the defensive preparations that the Vietnamese would not enter the city. The building of fortifications gave way to a festival of thanksgiving, much to French amazement.[49] The example of the King in refusing to leave was widely praised. Patriotic fervour swept the country. What gratitude Lao felt to the French was tempered, however, by anger over a unilateral French decision in May to devalue the *piastre*. Massive inflation ensued, doubling prices over the next six months, and throwing government finances into disarray. As the cost of the war escalated, the government brought two opposition members into a 'Cabinet of Sacred Union' and decreed a 'general mobilization'.

Despite withdrawal of the Vietminh, much of northeastern Laos remained firmly in Pathēt Lao hands. In April 1953 Suphānuvong formally established his 'Resistance government' at Xam Neua, Pathēt Lao headquarters for what was by then an extensive 'liberated zone'. Organization was thorough, thanks to Vietnamese support and advice. 'People's Military and Administrative Committees' were established at every level from village to province (which the Pathēt Lao called *khēt*). Everyone was assigned a role in the resistance struggle – in village defence, production, health, education. Recruitment into the army was at three levels – village militia, regional forces, and regular army units which could be called upon to fight anywhere in the country. Everyone had to join an appropriate organization, even monks. People were also obliged to attend 'seminars' at which the political line of the Pathēt Lao was repeatedly explained, and participants encouraged to conduct public self-criticism.

By establishing an extensive 'liberated zone' in Xam Neua and Phongsālī under protection of the Vietminh, the offensive of April 1953 effectively divided Laos both administratively and politically. For the first time since its formation, the Pathēt Lao possessed a consolidated territory to govern. The Royal Lao government vehemently denounced these developments. For the government the offensive was a Vietnamese invasion, and the Pathēt Lao were but Vietnamese puppets. For the Pathēt Lao, the invasion had been a joint operation 'in co-ordination with volunteer Vietnamese troops'.[50] Neither version was accurate. The offensive of 1953 was a tactical episode in the First Indochina War between France and the Vietminh, a conflict from which the Lao could no more insulate themselves in 1953 than they could a decade later from the Second Indochina War between the Democratic Republic of (North) Vietnam and the United States.

By mid-1953 the French position in Indochina was coming under increasing military and political pressure. Close to half a million troops under French command were mostly tied down in static defence roles, while the Vietminh were free to concentrate forces on specific targets. There was widespread recognition that France could not win the war: all that was possible was a military stalemate leading to a negotiated settlement of the conflict. In July 1953 an armistice was signed in Korea, further increasing French domestic political pressure for an end to the war. In Cambodia, Sihanouk had embarked on his one-man 'crusade for independence'. The final phase in the struggle to force the French out of Indochina had begun.

In France itself, another of its periodic political crises led to formation in June of a new government which promptly declared its intention to 'perfect' the independence of the three Indochinese states by transferring all residual French powers in the areas of justice, finance and military affairs. Negotiations with the Royal Lao government were smoothly concluded and led to the signing by King Sīsavāngvong on 22 October 1953 of a Treaty of Friendship and Association with France which, in return for independence, reaffirmed Lao membership of the French Union. The French Commissioner in Viang Chan was replaced

by a High Representative, while remaining French civil servants became advisers to the Lao who replaced them. Under the terms of the
Military Convention accompanying the treaty, the Lao government
agreed to permit the free circulation on Lao territory of French troops in
order 'to guarantee the defence of the frontiers of Laos, in collaboration
with the Lao Army' (Article 4). Moreover, responsibility for planning
the defence of Laos still rested with France (Article 7).

France's obligation to defend Laos led directly to the humiliating
French defeat in Indochina. The French Commander, General Henri
Navarre, well aware that he lacked the means to guarantee the defence
of Laos, nevertheless hoped to discourage a repeat Vietminh invasion
similar to that of April 1953 by garrisoning the remote mountain valley
of Dien Bien Phu (known to the Lao as Meuang Thaeng). French
forces were parachuted in with few misgivings during November and
December 1953 to await the set-piece battle they were convinced they
would win.

The attack, when it came on 20 December, was aimed elsewhere.
Within four days, a Vietminh thrust into central Laos cut the country in
half and briefly captured Thākhaek. By early January the Vietminh had
driven south to threaten the major French military base at Xēnō, 30
kilometres east of Savannakhēt. Meanwhile in the north a Vietminh
force again advanced down the Nam Ū to threaten Luang Phrabāng,
only to withdraw after having again sucked in more vital French reinforcements. By then General Giap's principal target was clear. Surrounded from the beginning of March, under constant artillery
bombardment and supplied only from the air, the garrison at Dien Bien
Phu was finally forced to surrender on 7 May 1954.

Throughout the siege, and indeed right up to the cease-fire of
6 August, Pathēt Lao forces, often reinforced by Vietminh units, kept up
their military activity. They were aided by the progressive breakdown
of local administration, especially in remote areas, as unconcerned
officials at the province level pursued their own personal interests.
Royal Lao Army counter-attacks succeeded in recapturing some district
centres in the south, but the Vietminh incursions left behind them 'a
strong Pathēt Lao presence among all the ethnic minorities of central
and southern Laos',[51] most of whom had become increasingly disillusioned over government neglect. In the north, Phongsālī was lost to
the Pathēt Lao, along with areas of northeastern Luang Phrabāng
province, as both sides fought to gain on the ground advantages that
could influence the negotiations already under way in Geneva.

## THE GENEVA CONFERENCE AND ITS AFTERMATH

An international conference to seek an end to the First Indochina War
might have been held earlier had it not been for misplaced confidence
on the part of the French military command, and the readiness of the
United States to continue funding up to three-quarters of the cost of the
war. By February 1954, however, under increasing popular pressure
from the growing peace movement in France, the French government

at last determined to seek a negotiated settlement. Indochina was added to the agenda of the conference due to meet in Geneva to discuss the problem of Korea. Delegates met for the opening session on 8 May, the day after the garrison at Dien Bien Phu surrendered. The timing of the Vietminh victory could not have been better.

The Royal Lao delegation was led by Foreign Minister Phuy Xananikôn, who joined his counterparts from Cambodia, Ho Chi Minh's Democratic Republic of Vietnam, the French-supported Government of Vietnam, France, Britain, China, the Soviet Union and the United States. The DRV delegation was led by Pham Van Dong; it included two representatives of the Khmer resistance movement and two more, including Nūhak Phumsavan, representing the Pathēt Lao.

Vietnamese attempts to gain separate representation for both the Khmer and Lao 'resistance governments', a move supported by the Soviet Union, were rejected. In his own speech to the conference, Phuy Xananikôn poured scorn on the pretensions of the Pathēt Lao and the claims of its leader: 'Prince Suphānuvong ... has no mandate from Laos ... It would be almost comic to recognize him as representing anybody.'[52] Laos was already independent, Phuy argued, and any military activity was due solely to the presence of foreign Vietminh forces. The situation in Laos, Phuy maintained, was entirely different from that in Vietnam 'because withdrawal of the foreign invading troops would mean *de facto* the cessation of hostilities', for the so-called 'Lao Resistance government' had been 'fabricated lock, stock and barrel by the foreign invaders'.[53] It was a theme to be heard again over the years, as inaccurate as it was misleading.

The conference dragged on through May and June, and it was only through the intervention of Chinese Foreign Minister Zhou Enlai that a compromise agreement was finally reached. The Pathēt Lao succeeded in gaining *de facto* recognition, not as an alternative government administering part of the country, but as a guerrilla movement whose combatants needed to be assembled and demobilized. Thus while Vietnam was divided by a demilitarized zone into two separate political entities, and Cambodia remained intact, in Laos the two northeastern provinces of Phongsālī and Huaphan (referred to throughout the conference as Xam Neua), connected by a narrow corridor along the Vietnamese border, were set aside for the temporary regroupment of Pathēt Lao forces. Which forces, exactly, was never spelled out, but they clearly did not include the village militias so essential to Pathēt Lao control at the local level.

The Agreement on the Cessation of Hostilities in Laos was signed on 20 July 1954 by the Commander-in-Chief of French Union forces on behalf of the Royal Lao Army and by the Vietminh vice-minister for defence on behalf of the Pathēt Lao, which seemed appropriate for a proxy war. Under the terms of the agreement, belligerent forces were to disengage and assemble in assigned areas. Foreign forces were to withdraw from the country, with the exception of a French Military Mission not exceeding 1500 men to train the Royal Lao Army, and a garrison not exceeding 3500 men to maintain two French bases. Both exceptions were included at the request of the Royal Lao government, though neither figure was ever reached. The introduction of armaments and munitions was prohibited except for 'categories specified as necessary for the defence of Laos' (Article 9).

On the following day, Phuy Xananikôn made two declarations on behalf of the Royal Lao government which formed part of the Final Declaration of the conference. The government declared it would never pursue a policy of aggression, nor permit its territory to be used by another power for aggressive purposes. Nor would Laos join any military alliance 'not in conformity with the principles of the Charter of the United Nations or with the principles of the agreement on the cessation of hostilities'. The second document guaranteed political rights for all Lao citizens. Special administrative measures in Huaphan and Phongsālī provinces would protect the interests of those 'who did not support the Royal forces during hostilities'.[54]

An International Commission for Supervision and Control (ICSC), consisting of India as chair, Canada and Poland, was set up to monitor the terms of the agreement, in particular the cease-fire, disengagement of forces, and withdrawal of foreign troops. Both sides were to facilitate ICSC inspections and investigations. The commission was to remain in place until the political provisions of the agreement had also been complied with. These entailed holding general elections 'in the course of the year 1955, by secret ballot and in conditions of respect for fundamental freedoms'.[55] The commission was to report to the joint co-chairs of the conference, Britain and the Soviet Union.

The outcome of the Geneva Conference constituted a clear political gain for the Pathēt Lao. By being allotted regroupment areas, it had won a degree of recognition not accorded its Cambodian counterpart. Further concessions for the Pathēt Lao were not forthcoming, but this hardly mattered. The two provinces provided it with an internationally recognized base area from which to wage political struggle and within which to gain valuable administrative experience. As military regroupment areas, both provinces remained under the *de jure* authority of the Royal Lao government. However, the location of both provinces allowed direct contact between the Pathēt Lao and their Vietnamese patrons; and the provisions of the Geneva Agreements were sufficiently vague to permit legal procrastination for as long as it was in the interests of the movement to maintain a separate administrative identity.

Political fallout from the Geneva Conference was evident as early as May 1954, when demonstrations were organized by rightist politicians in Viang Chan and Luang Phrabāng protesting against any Pathēt Lao participation. Their political opponents (the Progressives led by Katāy Don Sasorith, and Bong Suvannavong's Lao Union Party) took the contrary position, arguing that the Pathēt Lao could not be excluded from any eventual political settlement. These political differences, as ever in Laos, were further complicated by personal antagonism, clan rivalry, and foreign interference, but they were not enough to prevent a joint commission of the Royal Lao government and the Pathēt Lao from meeting to implement the armistice agreement. It was as much as anything the slow progress of these negotiations that led to further political friction.

Dissatisfaction over the Geneva Agreements, insofar as they concerned Laos, focused on two matters – concessions made to the Pathēt Lao, and the continuing advisory role given to the French. Unfairly accused both of selling out Laos and of being pro-French, Phuy Xananikôn as the Lao representative in Geneva and leader of the conservative bloc of deputies in the National Assembly became the target for a concerted campaign of vilification in the opposition press. According to French sources, criticism of Phuy was linked to a plot by former members of the Lao Pen Lao to mount a military *coup d'état* to replace the government of Suvanna Phūmā by one led by Prince Phetxarāt, then still in self-imposed exile in Thailand.[56] After two attempts in June to provoke an uprising among troops at the Viang Chan garrison at Chīnāymō had failed, a contract was taken out on Phuy's life. The assassination was to be carried out by a band of Lao outlaws led by an escaped criminal operating from Thailand.

Phuy returned from Geneva in August, but it was not until 18 September that three members of the gang slipped across the Mekong, evaded police surveillance, and made their assassination attempt while Phuy was holding a dinner at his house. Phuy himself was only slightly wounded by a grenade, but one of his guests, Ku Vôravong, the Minister for Defence, was shot and killed. That the attempt on Phuy's life and the death of Ku were part of a plot to destabilize the government became evident in the days that followed, as several other government ministers received death threats.

The government was plunged into crisis. Though the actual assassins managed to cross back into Thailand, forty suspects were arrested, the most prominent being Bong Suvannavong. Ultimate responsibility for the affair was unclear, though investigations by the police uncovered some murky connections with Thai police and politicians. Ku Vôravong had been a fervent supporter of Prime Minister Suvanna Phuma's policy of negotiating a settlement with the Pathēt Lao. His death, though accidental, brought down Suvanna's government. It then took six weeks of political horse-trading before Katāy was able to form a government with Phuy as his deputy and portfolios divided between their followers. Even so, the assassination continued to haunt Lao politics. Despite a lack of evidence, the Vôravong clan accused their political rivals, the Xananikôns, of having planned the whole incident. Suspicions festered because of reluctance, not least on the part of Katāy, to mount an impartial investigation. As a result, clan antagonism generated by the assassination continued to have repercussions for years to come. More importantly, it distracted attention from the primary challenge facing Lao politicians – how to reconstruct a unified national state.

The cease-fire in Laos had come into effect on 6 August 1954, policed to the limited extent possible by the ICSC. The commission's first interim report was issued in January 1955, detailing developments to the end of the year – regroupment of Pathēt Lao forces in Phongsālī and

Huaphan and withdrawal of French troops and Vietnamese 'People's Volunteers'. As it proved physically impossible actually to verify that all the latter had left, the commission had no alternative but to accept a declaration to that effect by the Vietnamese high command.[57] Meanwhile intensive Pathēt Lao propaganda throughout other areas under their control resulted in between ten and fifteen thousand young recruits making their way to the two Pathēt Lao provinces. Other Pathēt Lao agents went underground. The Vietminh command post for Laos, known as Doan (Group) 100, was withdrawn to Bān Nāmaeo, a border village not far from Pathēt Lao headquarters. Its staff of about three hundred (two-thirds military, one-third political) continued to advise, train and equip the Pathēt Lao.[58]

Nominal fulfilment of the military provisions of the Geneva Agreements opened the way for political negotiations to re-establish national unity. Suvanna and Suphānuvong met for preliminary discussions, and the Pathēt Lao recognized the Royal Lao government's *de jure* authority over Xam Neua and Phongsālī. Hopes for rapid agreement foundered, however, when Suvanna was replaced as prime minister by Katāy. Even though Katāy continued negotiations, between himself and Suphānuvong there were not only acute ideological differences, but also deep personal antagonism and distrust dating back to their years in the Lao Issara. While Suphānuvong looked to Vietnam for international support, Katāy looked to Thailand, and increasingly to the United States. Agreement not to commit hostile acts against each other left the core of differences between the two sides untouched.

A principal problem concerned the interim administration of the two Pathēt Lao provinces. The Pathēt Lao argued that both provinces in their entirety should be under its control, and that consequently former French Union 'Special Commandos', mostly Hmong, should withdraw from the areas they still held. The Royal Lao government maintained that existing areas of control should be respected, as there was plenty of room for Pathēt Lao forces to regroup. Armed clashes continued to occur, however, and by April 1955 negotiations had reached a political stalemate. The government informed the ICSC that the Pathēt Lao 'consider themselves still under the authority of the Vietminh High Command, and as having conquered the provinces of Phongsālī and Xam Neua [Huaphan]'.[59] The Pathēt Lao responded by accusing the government of conspiring with the United States.

Essentially, disagreement was over timing. The government insisted that the first priority was to re-establish the Royal Lao government's administration of the two provinces so that elections could be held under the existing electoral law. The political status of the Pathēt Lao could be sorted out afterwards. The Pathēt Lao wanted an overall political agreement to be hammered out first, which would guarantee them political rights, modify the electoral law to provide universal suffrage, and permit joint supervision of elections. Talks in Viang Chan in July, postponement of the August elections, and more talks in Rangoon in October all failed to resolve the deadlock.

On 25 December the government went ahead with elections as

required by the Geneva Agreements in ten of the twelve provinces. These the Pathēt Lao denounced as illegal, though they did have the unforeseen effect of forcing Katāy's government to resign after it was unable to obtain two-thirds majority support in the new Assembly. This was despite the fact that the National Progressive Party increased its seats to nineteen out of the thirty-nine contested.[60] Katāy's blunt intransigence had failed to resolve the political stand-off or bring peace to the country, and not only neutralist left members of the Assembly opposed him: so too did the conservative right. In the end, it was left to Suvanna Phūmā to form a government, by promising to make his 'preoccupation number one, the settlement of the Pathēt Lao problem'.[61]

The task facing Suvanna was even more difficult, however, than it had been in 1954. The ICSC had failed to act decisively; the Pathēt Lao had become more intransigent; and foreign pressures on both sides had hardened. Yet an increasing number of Lao recognized with Suvanna the need for a political solution if the task of nation-building was to proceed. As it was, opposition to an eventual settlement came more from outside powers than from Suvanna's political opponents. Neither Thailand nor, more significantly, the United States wanted to see a central government in Laos which included the Pathēt Lao, and the Americans were prepared to do everything in their power to prevent it happening, even if this meant sabotaging Lao attempts to bring about national reconciliation.

## AMERICAN INVOLVEMENT

The United States was deeply unhappy over the outcome of the Geneva Conference. US Secretary of State, John Foster Dulles, had insisted that any settlement should meet certain conditions, namely ensuring the viability of stable non-communist regimes and preventing the spread of communism.[62] Because in his view the Final Declaration did not do this, the United States refused to endorse it. Instead it 'took note' of the agreements reached, and said it would 'refrain from the threat or the use of force' to disturb them, provided other countries did likewise. Presumably, therefore, the United States was prepared 'to respect the sovereignty, the independence, the unity and the territorial integrity of the above-mentioned [three Indochinese] States, and to refrain from any interference in their internal affairs' (Article 12 of the Final Declaration). President Dwight D. Eisenhower warned, however, that the United States 'has not itself been party to or bound by the decisions taken by the Conference'.[63]

The Eisenhower administration considered the Geneva Agreements to be a sell-out to international communism, whose aggressive, expansionist nature was taken for granted. Accordingly, American priorities following the conference were to strengthen anti-communist governments in the three 'dominoes' under most immediate threat – Laos, Cambodia, and the Republic of [South] Vietnam – and to shore up the anti-communist position throughout Southeast Asia by means of a collective security pact. The South-East Asia Treaty Organization (SEATO) was formed in Manila in September 1954. As a neutral country, Laos was precluded from membership. It was nevertheless designated a 'Protocol state', that is, a state where communist aggression might endanger the security of a signatory state, namely Thailand. As such, Laos fell under the 'umbrella' of SEATO.

US economic and military assistance to Laos was not, however, linked to its SEATO commitments. What SEATO did was to signal US intentions with respect to Indochina. How these intentions applied to Laos was spelled out by Dulles on his return from the inaugural SEATO Council meeting in Bangkok in February 1955. SEATO, Dulles noted, offered protection to the Lao government from external communist aggression in the event the government should decide to suppress 'Communists within',[64] and US pressure was subsequently brought to bear on the Lao government to do just that.

In August 1955, the US legation was raised to an embassy, and military assistance to the Royal Lao government expanded rapidly. Reluctance by the Joint Chiefs of Staff to recommend funding even a small army in Laos for purposes of internal security was overcome by political considerations. By the time the SEATO Council met for its inaugural session, a US Operations Mission was operating in Viang Chan, and the United States was financing a large proportion of the government's expenditure, including the entire cost of the Royal Lao Army and the police. The size of the army was set at 23,500, later increased to 25,000.[65] By the end of 1955, a Programs Evaluation Office had been attached to the US Operations Mission, functioning virtually as a Military Assistance Advisory Group. It was staffed entirely by military personnel, either retired or on secondment to maintain the fiction that they were civilians. Under the terms of the Geneva Agreements, tactical training of the Lao army was the responsibility of the French Military Mission, but it was a responsibility which the Americans believed the French were not taking sufficiently seriously. Apart from the 'civilian' Programs Evaluation Office, the United States got around the Geneva Agreements by training selected army officers in Thailand, by equipping and training a greatly expanded police force, and by laying the foundation for a substantial CIA presence.[66] Also active was the US Information Agency, which was responsible for anti-communist propaganda. This took the form of subsidized publications (of limited value in a country where the illiteracy rate was estimated at 85 per cent) and radio broadcasts (ownership of transistor radios was still only four sets per thousand people, but increasing).[67] Films and performances by traditional folk singers tended to be more effective as means of communication, though too often American material was poorly adapted to Lao requirements.

US assistance to the Royal Lao government took the form of direct cash grants, commodity imports to soak up some of the cash and control inflation, and assistance for specified economic projects. Most went to pay for the army: 84 per cent of all cash-grants went to pay military salaries and for local procurement.[68] And of the project aid, most was spent on road building, transport and communications, all of direct military value. As of 1955, the United States financed the entire cost of the Royal Lao Army, at a time when the DRV provided the only source of military assistance to Pathēt Lao fighting units. Laos thus became the only country in the world at the time where the armed forces on both sides of a civil conflict were entirely financed by foreign powers.

The extent of US financial support for the army and government, growing CIA involvement, and the dawning realization among those Lao in a position to do so that considerable fortunes could be made from American largesse, all won the US increasing support for its anti-communist cause. It did not take long for more venal Lao officials to appreciate that to profess anti-communism made one a friend of the Americans, and that America's friends would be rewarded. Within three years the US aid program in Laos became an example of mis-management and corruption, the extent of which was finally revealed in Congressional hearings in 1959. Apart from embezzlement, the principal forms of corruption were through manipulation of the exchange rate when importing commodities, and false staffing levels in the army and civil service. For every 35 *kip* deposited in the govern-ment's counterpart fund, one dollar's worth of import credit could be obtained, at a time when the black-market rate for the dollar was 110 *kip*.[69] If an inflated pro forma invoice was used to obtain a loan, extra dollars could be sold on the black market. Imported goods were sold back into Thailand, or simply diverted *en route* to Laos, with the differ-ence between official and free-market values constituting a substantial profit margin. By 1958, Lao imports were running at sixteen times the figure for 1949, an extraordinary increase, even allowing for inflation.[70]

US officials in the Operations Mission responsible for endorsing monthly withdrawals to pay military and civilian salaries had few means of verifying whether the soldiers and civil servants being paid really existed, or whether full salaries were paid to those who did. Army commanders in particular could easily claim for a few hundred non-existent extra troops. Moreover, the average cost of maintaining one Lao soldier was put at around $1000 per year, the highest in Asia.[71] Only a fraction of this went on salaries; the rest was for upkeep, the cost calculations for which were determined by senior officers.

Despite the abuses, no member of the Lao elite was ever indicted for corruption, and the 'deluge of dollars' continued. Over the period from 1955 to 1963, US foreign assistance to an estimated two and a half million Lao amounted to $192.30 per capita, the highest for any country in Southeast Asia, including South Vietnam. By contrast, Thais received $31 per capita over the period from 1946 to 1963, while Indonesians received $8.80.[72] Far from this amount being fairly spread throughout the population, however, between 1953 and 1959 only 7 per cent of project aid to Laos, a mere $1.3 million, was spent on agriculture, as against $184 million on military support[73] – this in a country where over 90 per cent of the population were peasant farmers. If the cost of military equipment and secret expenditure by the CIA on both its own behalf and that of the US Department of Defense were to be included, the imbalance would be even more striking.

American aid in such quantities not only required a growing body of American officials to disburse it, but also attracted a growing number of foreigners – Thai, Chinese, Indians and assorted Europeans – to share the economic bonanza. By the late 1950s, there were as many as 40,000 Chinese in Laos, still organized as under the French into self-administering 'congregations' (Swatow, Cantonese and Hakka in Viang Chan). Many married Lao wives or went into business with Lao families. By contrast, the Vietnamese population was half as numerous. Caucasians numbered around 6000, including 500 Americans, almost all present in some official capacity.[74] Most of the other Europeans were French, including teachers and military personnel. With the rapid increase in the expatriate population, accommodation was at a premium and there was a growing need for new administrative buildings. Viang Chan boasted only one French-run and two Chinese hotels. Entertainment was limited to French or Chinese movies, the frequent festivals at Viang Chan's many temples, or the few bars that were already doubling as brothels. It would be another five years before American popular culture made any considerable impact. In the meantime, widening ripples of corruption did spread some of the wealth. As consumption became more conspicuous, more motor bikes and cars appeared on the roads. Even so, they drove slowly. The pace of life remained tranquil, the pace of work measured.

US involvement in Laos after 1954 altered the balance of political forces. By increasing both the size and independence of the Royal Lao Army, the US positioned it to interfere directly in the political process. At the same time, US financial assistance to the Lao government effectively reinforced the clan patronage structure of Lao politics. Leading families maintained their social standing by becoming the principal beneficiaries of US aid. Thus the accumulation of wealth took precedence for the Lao elite over the responsible exercise of political power for the national good. Moreover, as real power increasingly lay with the US Embassy and USAID mission, the American presence fostered a dependent neo-colonial mentality which easily repudiated responsibility for political decision-making. As paymaster, the United States was able to influence political thinking to the point of creating its own clientele among conservative politicians. In this it was ably assisted by the Thai. Katāy was only one among many whose political allegiance shifted to the right at US and Thai urging.

The United States and Thailand were not, however, the only external sources of political advice. The French too remained active. Not only were they responsible for training the Royal Lao Army, as opposed to equipping and paying for it, but a number of French advisers were attached to key Lao ministries, including the office of the prime minister. A French economic and technical aid mission was established in August 1953. French-funded projects included road and bridge works, schools and hospitals. French doctors, engineers, technicians, and especially the 130 French teachers at the Lycée de Viang Chan, ensured continued French influence.[75]

The French view of Laos tended to be more realistic, less ideologically motivated, than the American. From bitter experience the French knew well that Laos could never defend itself against external communist aggression, and therefore they advised political accommodation with the Pathēt Lao in the context of a neutral foreign policy. Thus might Laos revert to becoming a buffer state, protected not by its proclaimed neutrality but because it posed no threat to any neighbouring country. Such a position would satisfy the Chinese, as Beijing's principal concern was to prevent the use of Lao territory by the United States.

The DRV had rather different priorities, the most important of which was to reunite Vietnam under a communist government. As it became obvious that the nation-wide elections envisaged for 1956 under the terms of the Geneva Agreements would not be held, Hanoi determined to resort to other means. Relations from then on with both Viang Chan and Phnom Penh depended on whether their policies facilitated or obstructed this overriding (North) Vietnamese goal. For the United States, by contrast, reunification of Vietnam as a communist state was to be prevented at any cost, so Lao neutrality was adamantly opposed. Americans and French in Laos thus found themselves proffering opposing advice, as relations between the two communities became increasingly strained.

## THE FIRST COALITION: UNITY RESTORED

Suvanna Phūmā shared the French conviction that the only real security for Laos lay in a flexible neutrality. The internal threat posed by the Pathēt Lao would be neutralized by entering into diplomatic relations with all neighbouring states. Joint declarations of friendship had already been signed with China, India, and the DRV, and the country's neutralist credentials had been reaffirmed at the Asian–African conference at Bandung, Indonesia, in April 1955. Suvanna's views were not, however, based simply on French advice. Like that of his brother Phetxarāt, Suvanna's position took as its foundation a historical perspective derived from centuries of necessary accommodation with powerful neighbours, a conviction that if left to themselves the Lao could work out their own affairs, and a belief that he, Suvanna, could always come to an acceptable agreement with his half-brother, Suphānuvong, whom he refused to think of as a communist.[76]

Not until August 1956, however, did the two brothers meet again. By then just over two years had passed since the final declaration at Geneva, a period made full use of by the Pathēt Lao to expand its organization both militarily and politically. Under the direction of Kaisôn Phomvihān, the strength of the Pathēt Lao armed forces had approximately doubled to comprise some fifteen regular battalions plus support units.[77] Chinese and Vietnamese weapons and equipment continued to be supplied via Doan 100, the DRV's liaison command for Laos, while advanced training for officers and political cadres was provided in schools in the DRV. On the political side, the activities of the

Committee for the Organization of the Party bore fruit with the establishment in March 1955 of the secret Lao People's Party (Phak Paxāxon Lao). According to later accounts, only twenty-five 'eminent delegates ... veteran members of the Indochinese Communist Party' attended the inaugural congress, representing a total membership of about three hundred.[78] A seven-member Politburo was elected, with Kaisôn as Secretary-General. The Party then organized a broad national front, the Lao Patriotic Front (LPF, Naeo Lao Hak Xāt) to replace the Free Laos Front. Member organizations included associations of youth, women, farmers, and ethnic minorities, along with 'patriotic' Buddhists and trade unions representing the virtually non-existent proletariat.

The LPF held its inaugural congress in January 1956. Suphānuvong was elected president with Sīthon Kommadam, Faidāng Lôbliayao, Kaisôn Phomvihān, and Nūhak Phumsavan as vice-presidents. A twelve-point political program was adopted; it called for, among other things, the unity of all Lao without distinction in support of the Geneva Agreements, opposition to American imperialism, commitment to democratic liberties and universal suffrage, and the 'complete equality of all inhabitants of Laos'. It also called for establishment of diplomatic relations with neighbouring states, and continued relations with France.[79] These developments were accompanied by a sustained propaganda effort, focusing particularly on the 'intransigence' of the Royal Lao government and the growing US presence.

The Pathēt Lao also declared its readiness to continue negotiations. An exchange of letters led to a first series of meetings between delegations led by Suvanna and Suphānuvong in Viang Chan in August 1956. Two declarations resulted, the thrust of which was that the two Pathēt Lao provinces would be reintegrated into the Royal Lao administration and Pathēt Lao armed forces into the Royal Lao Army in return for the holding of 'supplementary elections', formation of a Government of National Union and guarantees for the security, rights and freedoms of all citizens.[80] In a speech immediately following these agreements, Suvanna again emphasized what he saw as the 'categorical national imperative: to bring about the definitive unity and full independence of the Kingdom through the reconciliation of all Lao'.[81] The 'great democracies' had nothing to fear from such reconciliation, in Suvanna's estimation, as integration of Pathēt Lao cadres into the structure of government was the best way to neutralize the movement.

This was not the view of the United States. Obsessed by the Cold War and sceptical of Lao capacity to manage their own affairs, US policy-makers in Washington were horrified by the turn of events. All they could see in the 1956 agreements was a further threatened expansion of international communism. Better to isolate the Pathēt Lao in Huaphan and Phongsālī through military means than risk the 'virus' spreading throughout the whole country by legalizing the LPF. Neutralism was immoral in the view of Secretary of State Dulles, and coalition government with communists was anathema, for it would lead inevitably to a communist coup, as in Czechoslovakia.[82] In Washington's view, Suvanna was at best naïve, at worst a crypto-communist.

Suvanna's decision to visit Beijing and Hanoi in August 1956 was the last straw for the United States, even though he had patiently explained the purpose of his visit to two powerful neighbouring states with which Laos had no formal diplomatic relations as essential in order 'to create the best climate possible for talks with the Pathēt Lao'.[83] His visit laid the basis for acceptance by both China and North Vietnam of a Lao policy of strict neutrality and good-neighbourliness. Diplomatic relations were not entered into with either state, however, and offers of aid were politely refused. All that Suvanna pledged was that Laos would oppose US military interference and refuse to permit US military bases to be established on Lao territory, both of which had already been undertaken at Geneva.[84]

Over the following months the United States did all in its power to prevent a reconciliation in Laos. Ambassador J. Graham Parsons testified later before a US Congressional Committee that he had 'struggled for sixteen months to prevent a coalition'.[85] Apart from official warnings, the CIA worked hard, in fierce competition with the French Deuxième Bureau, to influence elite Lao opinion. In the midst of all this intrigue, Suvanna stood firm. Minor changes were made to the constitution in preparation for formation of the new government, and three more agreements were drawn up – on implementation of a cease-fire; on the need for a foreign policy of peace and neutrality through establishment of diplomatic relations with and acceptance of aid from all countries of goodwill; and on measures to guarantee the safety and civil rights of former Pathēt Lao. A further meeting between Suvanna and Suphānuvong in December led to agreement on formation of a coalition government *before* supplementary elections, and legalization of the LPF as a political party. With agreement two months later on a new electoral law, all was ready for supplementary elections.

In the meantime Prince Phetxarāt, still in self-imposed exile in Thailand, had been officially invited to return home. This he declined to do until an agreement had been concluded between the government and Pathēt Lao, negotiations on which he offered to chair. Restoration of his title and rank of *uparāt*, and the agreement between Suvanna and Suphānuvong fulfilled Phetxarāt's preconditions, and in March 1957, his pride intact, he returned to Laos after more than a decade in exile. Though his support for integration of the Pathēt Lao and a policy of neutrality undoubtedly reinforced popular acceptance of the settlement reached, the elderly prince played no public political role after his return. He died on 15 October 1959, just two weeks before the King he had so resolutely opposed. If anyone can be called the Father of Lao Independence, it must surely be he.

In the meantime, Suvanna was encountering difficulties. Despite a reluctant declaration of support for his policies from the United States, Britain and France,[86] his policy of accommodation with the Pathēt Lao was attacked in the National Assembly on the grounds that reintegration of the two Pathēt Lao provinces and armed forces should precede formation of a coalition government, not follow it. On this point a motion was finally lost by the government, which Suvanna interpreted as a vote of no confidence. On 30 May he resigned, precipitating a political crisis lasting two months. The US Embassy could hardly conceal its satisfaction.

Though Katāy was the preferred candidate of the United States, he failed by one vote to obtain the support of the National Assembly; so it was left to Suvanna once again to form a new government. In a dignified and statesmanlike speech to the National Assembly, Suvanna promised immediate resumption of negotiations with the Pathēt Lao, inauguration of five-year economic planning, and reduction of the armed forces to assist in balancing the budget.[87] It was not what the United States wanted to hear. Negotiations with the Pathēt Lao nevertheless resumed, leading to the so-called Viang Chan Agreements – ten separate documents. They included notably a joint communiqué by Suvanna and Suphānuvong establishing a coalition government; an agreement between political delegations re-establishing the Royal Lao administration in Phongsālī and Huaphan; and an agreement between military delegations on integration of 1500 (out of an estimated 6000) Pathēt Lao officers and men into the Royal Lao Army, the remainder to be demobilized.

On 18 November, Suphānuvong formally remitted to Crown Prince Savāngvatthanā, representing the King, the two provinces of Huaphan and Phongsālī, and the civilian cadres, armed forces and military equipment of the Pathēt Lao. The next day the National Assembly unanimously approved formation of a Provisional Government of National Union to include two Pathēt Lao ministers – Suphānuvong as Minister for Planning, Reconstruction and Urbanization, and Phūmī Vongvichit as Minister for Religion and Fine Arts – in a cabinet of fourteen. The ICSC notified the Geneva co-chairs Britain and the Soviet Union of these developments, which it viewed in a positive light. Even the United States limited its reaction to disapproval, and did not immediately carry through its threatened termination of aid.

Suvanna's achievement had been considerable. It had taken twelve years since Phetxarāt had declared the unity and independence of Laos finally to gain independence from France and reunify the country. Against strong US opposition, reunification had been achieved in the context of the Cold War in a country strategically situated on the frontiers of China and North Vietnam, largely through the vision, courage and perseverance of one man. For a moment the outlook was bright, symbolized politically by the unanimous endorsement of the Provisional Government by the National Assembly, and economically by an international agreement under the auspices of the Economic Commission for Asia and the Far East (ECAFE) to pursue the cooperative development of the lower Mekong basin.

Success in achieving unification was, however, illusory in the sense that it masked more fundamental problems. The first priority for Laos in 1945 had been to forge a nation state, to construct out of the regions and ethnicities into which the country was divided a sense of community and common identity that would be uniquely Lao. But the task of nation-building was handicapped by divisions within the Lao elite in terms both of regional and personal antipathies and of opposing conceptions of nationalism. The politics of self-interest clothed itself in the rhetoric of the struggle for independence at the expense of national vision. And when independence finally was achieved, a new political priority intervened. Thereafter, buffeted by foreign intervention, the politics of national reunification too easily concealed the more urgent politics of national construction.

For the Lao political elite (and politics throughout this period remained an elite game), it was all too easy to believe that decisions made on a day-to-day basis in Viang Chan were what determined the future of the country. Yet it was in the countryside that foundations for new loyalties and new political structures were being laid, structures that threatened to replace the traditional social hierarchies of blood relationship, patronage and ethnicity by political participation in and devotion to a revolutionary movement. In the process, however, a new division was being created, centred on class and ideology that in the longer term would set back the process of nation-building just as disastrously as earlier failures had done.

The unity that was achieved in 1957 came despite, not because of, the politicking in Viang Chan. Ironically, that it was achieved at all was due to the power and prestige of one family, that of the former *uparāt* of Luang Phrabāng, of which the absent Phetxarāt remained non-titular head. Phetxarāt's presence hovered unseen over the negotiations between his younger brothers. His vision of a unified and neutral Laos was essentially theirs, despite their differences. Agreement on reunification was thus largely an agreement within the family, which is why Suvanna felt so convinced he could bring it about. But the very political dominance of a single family elicited both jealousy and suspicion, not only on the part of other powerful families in Champāsak and Viang Chan, but also from the royal family which, through the activities of Crown Prince Savāngvatthanā, was increasingly becoming embroiled in, rather than standing above, politics. With the French backing Suvanna, his opponents sought alternative support from the US Embassy. For the United States, however, while unity was acceptable, neutrality was not. In the context of the Cold War, US interests took precedence over the interests of Laos. The French, given that they were no longer committed to Indochina, could take a more detached view of what was best for Laos. The Americans saw Laos only in its role as a pawn in their global opposition to communism.

Tragically for Laos, therefore, the country's neutrality, the need for which Suvanna so clearly recognized, was from the beginning problematic. As the monsoon clouds heralding the Second Indochina War gathered over Vietnam, Laos was unable to maintain either its independence or its unity, let alone neutrality – those three essential prerequisites for national construction. Yet the achievement stood. Under the influence of Suvanna's statesmanlike vision, party leaders had convinced their fractious followers to put aside their political differences and personal antagonisms for just long enough to pursue a national goal. The result was a triumph for Lao good sense. But Laos stood on the fault line of the Cold War. Regrettably, the First Coalition government offered a hope that was to remain unfulfilled. All that was left from its collapse was a model which later compromises, forged under even less auspicious circumstances, attempted unsuccessfully to emulate.

# 4

# NEUTRALITY SUBVERTED, 1958–1964

Despite high hopes and expectations, by mid-1958 the First Coalition government had collapsed, principally because of US machinations. Even so, Pathēt Lao leaders stayed on in Viang Chan, attempting to function as a legal political party, until arrested a year later. Civil conflict resumed. As the United States built up the Royal Lao Army, Pathēt Lao and DRV forces 'liberated' large areas. A new *de facto* division was thus imposed upon the country. In 1960, a military *coup d'état* overthrew the pro-American rightist government, in the vain hope of re-establishing Lao unity and neutrality. The only result, however, was to plunge the country more deeply than ever into civil war. As the crisis deepened, threatening to involve outside forces, a reversal of US policy opened the way for new Geneva Agreements and a Second Coalition government. But as Laos was ineluctably drawn into the Second Indochina War, the neutralist centre of Lao politics came under unrelenting pressure from both right and left: neither internally nor externally was neutrality any longer a viable option. Once again division and distrust prevented the urgent task of nation-building, as the competing nationalisms of the Royal Lao government and the Pathēt Lao both became ever more compromised by their deepening dependency on foreign powers.

## COLLAPSE OF THE FIRST COALITION GOVERNMENT

In the first flush of national reconciliation, hopes for peace and neutrality ran high. Suphānuvong and Phūmī Vongvichit performed as model ministers, industrious and efficient by comparison with the more casual attitudes of most of their cabinet colleagues. In January 1958 the Royal Lao Army reoccupied both Huaphan and Phongsālī without incident, and Pathēt Lao civil servants were integrated into the administration of the Royal Lao government. Problems arose on the military front, however, over the proportion of officers to men among the 1500 Pathēt Lao troops to be integrated into the Royal Lao Army. Thus though the two battalions were reassigned, south of Luang Phrabāng and on the Plain of Jars, neither was incorporated into the command structure of the Royal Lao Army. Though almost 5000 weapons were surrendered to the government, key well-equipped units withdrew into Vietnam under the direction of Pathēt Lao military commander Kaisôn Phomvihān – in effect, a reserve force to be called upon if and when needed. Clearly it would take time for the coalition government internally to break down mutual suspicion and distrust, and to convince external backers, both the United States and the DRV, that unity and neutrality were not inimical to their own national interests.

To convince a sceptical US administration, Suvanna visited Washington, where he pointed out that geography alone dictated that Laos could not 'place itself deliberately in the anti-Chinese camp'.[1] Nor, he maintained, would Marxism succeed in establishing itself in Buddhist Laos where there existed neither an industrial proletariat, nor an agrarian problem. What was essential was that US assistance to his government should continue, something even Suphānuvong accepted and approved.[2] The government wanted all aid given without strings attached. Had US aid been limited, like that of the Colombo Plan, to a few useful projects, this might have been possible; but in the climate of the Cold War, the United States wanted more return from what had become a substantial annual investment. Aid was seen as a powerful weapon in the anti-communist arsenal, and yet the high levels, per capita, of aid to Laos had not prevented what the United States considered to be significant communist gains. The aid program itself thus came under closer scrutiny.

In the three years from 1955 to 1958, the United States had given Laos over $120 million, about four times the amount France had expended over the preceding eight years.[3] The effect had been to create an artificial urban economy based on conspicuous consumption by a few wealthy families of politicians, military officers and businessmen. Large houses, American cars and lavish parties, not to mention holidays and education abroad, characterized the lifestyle of this small, self-centred elite. Viang Chan in particular took on a misleading air of prosperity, for little was spent on improvement of urban infrastructure, and industry remained on a small scale. The average $30 million a year paid to maintain the unnecessarily large Royal Lao Army could not but stimulate inflation in a subsistence economy in which per capita income was a mere $50 per annum. As a result, the urban cost of living doubled between 1953 and 1958.[4] As the wealthy appropriated greater amounts of American largesse, corruption became endemic and moral standards declined.[5] Meanwhile minimal expenditure was directed towards improving conditions of living for the vast majority of rural Lao, especially the upland minorities.

Any modest progress in social welfare was confined mainly to the urban areas. Since 1951, the first three years of primary education had been compulsory, yet many of the poorer and more remote villages were still without either school or teacher. In all, only about one-third of an estimated 300,000 eligible children were actually enrolled, of which only one-fifth completed the full six years of primary schooling, and only 7500 went on to the secondary level, two-thirds of them in private schools.[6] Though more teachers were being trained, these figures were disappointing. Health and hygiene were other priority areas suffering from a shortage of trained personnel. The country still had no medical training school, though one was planned. As an interim measure, three hospitals with American funds and Filipino staff were established under the Operation Brotherhood program. While administrative and legal systems were in place, many laws had been carried over from the 1930s and required updating. As for the economy, subsistence agriculture still employed most of the population. Industry was rudimentary, and the transportation and communications network quite inadequate. The total number of vehicles on Lao roads had increased fifty-fold in a decade (from 100 to 5000),[7] but these were overwhelmingly concentrated in the Mekong towns, and served only to accentuate the growing gap between rural and urban, poor and rich.

The effects of the US aid program provided ample ammunition for critics of the government. As a legal political party, the Lao Patriotic Front was free to pursue its own political agenda by condemning the policies of its opponents. Far from assisting the non-communist parties, US aid became something of a political liability. In recognition of the shortcomings of the aid program, in the run-up to the supplementary elections scheduled for 4 May, the US Embassy mounted a $3 million crash program, dubbed Operation Booster Shot, designed to bring the benefits of aid to the countryside in support of government candidates. To some extent this was effective, but its very success demonstrated deficiencies, both of commission and of omission, that the LPF was quick to seize upon. US involvement was portrayed as direct foreign interference in Lao affairs; this charge was all the easier to sustain since the US Agency for International Development (USAID) had created what virtually amounted to a parallel administration, comprising not only American aid workers and Lao employees, but also 'third-country nationals', mainly Filipinos. In part this was designed to minimize corruption, in part to circumvent Suphānuvong's Ministry of Planning and Reconstruction. At American urging, the army too had become involved in civic action, both to improve its image and to by-pass the government. But the sudden injection of aid to rural areas was also taken as proof that previous assistance had been diverted into the pockets of corrupt officials. American intervention and accompanying corruption thus became the central issues of the election campaign.

As the elections approached, the LPF made effective use of its political cadres. Phūmī Vongvichit, as Minister for Religion and Fine Arts, sent sympathetic monks and troupes of traditional singers and musicians to spread the LPF message. In the rural areas in particular the Pathēt Lao propaganda produced electoral dividends. For years cadres had worked to gain support in remote villages through means tested and found effective in both China and Vietnam. Rarely if ever were such villages visited by government officials who, if they came, would requisition food and lodging, and demand porterage to the next village. Pathēt Lao cadres arrived and stayed, working with the people to meet their needs, assisting construction of a village school or well, choosing the most receptive recruits to train and carry on the work of persuasion and propaganda. Ethnic minorities for the first time found themselves courted rather than exploited, their skills prized, their grievances recognized. Moreover, some of their most respected traditional leaders – Sīthon, Faidāng – were already high-ranking leaders in the LPF: it was only natural their followers should vote for the Front.

The Pathēt Lao campaign was aided by two small but vocal parties on the left. Both were led by men bitter over the monopolization of political office (and the perquisites accompanying it) by the powerful political families of Luang Phrabāng (represented by Suvanna Phūmā), Viang Chan (the Xananikôns), and central and southern Laos (Leuam Insīxiangmai, Bunūm, Katāy). The Democratic Party (still a vehicle for Vôravong ambitions), though anti-communist, joined in criticism of the government out of hatred of the Xananikôns. Further left, Bong Suvannavong maintained his anti-government crusade in concert with the newly formed Santhiphāp Pen Kāng (Party of Peace through Neutrality) of Kinim Phonsēnā. Despite strong US encouragement, political antagonism on the right prevented the Progressives of Suvanna and Katāy from agreeing with Phuy Xananikôn's Independents on a common slate of candidates. A so-called National Front was formed, but no-one could agree on who would represent it. By contrast, Santhiphāp and the LPF agreed not to stand candidates against each other.

Despite some claimed irregularities, the elections of May 1958 were remarkably free and fair. Only in Attapeu, where Kaisôn Phomvihān was the LPF candidate, was concerted intimidation used.[8] Out of twenty-one seats contested, the LPF won nine, Santhiphāp four, and rightist and independent candidates the remaining eight. Suphānuvong won the highest popular vote of any candidate, and was elected President of the National Assembly when it convened. Overall, however, left-wing candidates gained only about one-third of the popular vote, and would have won far fewer seats in first-past-the-post voting had their opponents not been divided.

The election had more far-reaching effects than the actual results warranted. Few bothered to analyse voting patterns or learn from them. Right-wing factionalism and indiscipline were major problems. In Viang Chan province, for example, no fewer than seven candidates representing different Progressive and Independent factions stood against Suphānuvong, not to mention two non-party independents. Some candidates demanded substantial payment to withdraw. The LPF was not only far more disciplined, but it was also more politically sophisticated and better organized and was the only party reaching down to the village level. Both the Progressive and Independent parties were little more than elitist groupings around powerful clan leaders who dispensed patronage in return for political support. The LPF had also been cleverer in its choice of candidates – a woman in Luang Phrabāng because women were voting for the first time;[9] a Lao Thoeng leader (Sīthon Kommadam) in the Bôlavēn area with a Lao Thoeng majority population; and men of known probity, like Suphānuvong and Phūmī Vongvichit in better-educated electorates. LPF political propaganda concentrated on criticism of the government. Corruption and the scandalous misuse of US aid were continually highlighted, themes often reiterated by Buddhist monks in the name of traditional Lao morality. The LPF called for 'one vote to the right, one vote to the left to prevent war', especially in provinces where the left was weak, and many responded out of a desire for peace. Even troops of the Royal Lao Army voted for the LPF, especially in remote garrisons which had not been paid because of the corruption of senior officers.

The shock election result had the effect of bringing Progressives and Independents together in an arranged marriage of convenience, the Rally of the Lao People (Lao Huam Lao), to replace the non-existent National Front. Its program was anti-communist and in favour of foreign investment. It was, however, little more than 'an assemblage of clans grouped around Katāy, Suvanna Phūmā and Phuy Xananikôn, subdivided themselves into family or regional coalitions',[10] with no rural organization. In the 59-member Assembly, its numbers, less those deputies assigned ministerial portfolios, were insufficient to ensure the two-thirds vote necessary to endorse a centre-right government. The left, however, could count on only sixteen votes, not enough to block it. The balance of power was held by independents and three members of the Democratic Party. The country clearly faced a period of political instability.

More significant as a response to the LPF victory than the parliamentary manoeuvring was the formation in June of the Committee for the Defence of the National Interest (CDNI). Promoted by the US,[11] this was an extra-parliamentary grouping of younger, better-educated public servants, diplomats, and army officers, strongly anti-communist and highly critical of the opening to the left that Suvanna had engineered. Members were critical too, for public consumption, of the clan-based politicking that passed for politics, and of the pervasive corruption that accompanied it. Though it claimed not to be a political party, the CDNI immediately began lobbying for inclusion of some of its members in government, stressing the 'rejuvenation' this would bring about. In this they had the support of both the Crown Prince and the CIA, but met concerted opposition from elected deputies who fancied themselves for ministerial appointment.

After the elections, Suvanna notified the ICSC that the Royal Lao government considered the terms of the Geneva Agreements to have been fulfilled. The ICSC, its task completed, agreed to adjourn *sine die*.[12] Over the next two months, however, Suvanna came under increasing pressure. National reconciliation was a fine ideal, so long as it did not threaten the position and privileges of the Lao elite. Deputies were much more susceptible to American 'persuasion' by July 1958 than they had been before the LPF's electoral success. It was not too difficult in the circumstances to engineer a political crisis that would destroy the fragile consensus on which Suvanna's coalition had been constructed.

The crisis when it came was financial, and behind it lay the United States. For some time the United States had been demanding currency reform as a means of curtailing profiteering from the aid program. Many of the worst abuses derived from the artificially high value of the *kip*.[13] Throughout 1957 the Lao government had opposed devaluation for fear it would lead to further inflation and reduce the level of dollar aid. By mid-1958, devaluation had become inevitable. Aid had been temporarily suspended in February to force the government's hand, but negotiations had been postponed until after the elections. When they resumed, Suvanna was still reluctant to devalue for fear this would lose him political support as he tried to form a government. In June the United States withheld payment of the monthly aid disbursement, and refused to sell dollars to the Lao National Bank. Suspension of aid and the financial crisis this precipitated convinced wavering deputies that Suvanna did not enjoy US backing, and was enough to tip the balance against him.[14] It was left to Phuy Xananikôn to form a markedly more right-wing government, whose first priority, Phuy announced, was to oppose communism. No Pathēt Lao ministers were included. Suvanna's policy of national reconciliation and neutrality was at an end, effectively sabotaged by the United States.

The First Coalition government had lasted eight months. Had Suvanna been able to form a government, even excluding the radical left (LPF and Santhiphāp), he would at least have continued to exercise a moderating influence and remained a symbol of national reconciliation in whom the Pathēt Lao could place some trust. His rejection marked the end not only of such hopes, but also of any opportunity to build a more inclusive political culture in which the radical left could take part. Just as significantly, collapse of the First Coalition marked both a victory for the United States, and a shift in power from the Lao National Assembly to the US Embassy. At the time, Suvanna contained his anger and disappointment. Only later did he express his resentment over the way he had been treated.

The First Coalition government was the last occasion when neutrality remained an option for Laos. The Soviet Union, as co-chair of the Geneva Conference, favoured Lao neutrality. So too did the Chinese, who linked it directly with the neutrality of Cambodia.[15] While the attitude of the DRV was a different matter, there are strong indications that it too was prepared to accept a neutral Laos, and would have continued to support a coalition government. Hanoi certainly voiced strong protests over its termination. The fact that the Vietnamese Workers' Party had already decided, at a Political Bureau meeting in June 1956, to prepare for armed struggle in the south does not imply that it was equally determined to pursue a similar policy in Laos. In Cambodia, the DRV respected its agreement with Sihanouk not to support an internal insurgency providing Cambodia remained 'neutral' to the point of at first ignoring and subsequently facilitating the movement of arms and personnel into South Vietnam. The discreet infiltration of cadres through a neutral Laos was far preferable from Hanoi's point of view to having to contest control of those areas with the United States. As it was, not until September 1959, more than a year after destruction of the First Coalition, did the DRV activate a new support group (Doan 959) to arm and supply a renewed Pathēt Lao insurgency.[16] By then civil war had resumed, as Laos was inexorably drawn into the burgeoning confrontation between the United States and North Vietnam.

## THE SHIFT TO THE RIGHT

The government that Phuy Xananikôn presented to the Assembly in August included four civilian members of the CDNI but no serving army officers. That US influence had been instrumental in the CDNI gaining political power without the bother of election to public office was a lesson not lost on ambitious young officers of the Royal Lao Army where US influence was even stronger. One of the new government's first acts was to devalue the *kip*, thus opening the way for a resumption of US aid. Preparations were made for a new five-year development plan to run from 1960 to 1964. Only perfunctory moves were made to limit corruption, a matter about which the CDNI in office lost most of its reforming zeal.

The extent to which the new government was prepared to tilt right was demonstrated by Phuy's announcement that Laos would 'coexist with the Free World only'.[17] Diplomatic relations were established with the Republic of (South) Vietnam and Taiwan, but not with the Soviet Union or China, both powers that had played pivotal roles at Geneva. Internally, anyone suspected of being a 'sympathizer' or 'long-time fellow traveller' of the Pathēt Lao was purged from government service.[18] A new secret intelligence organization, the National Documentation Centre, was established to report directly to the prime minister, while a Civic Action Commission worked closely with the army to counter Pathēt Lao propaganda in rural areas. The CDNI pressed for passage of a law outlawing communism, though this was finally withdrawn on the advice of the Western powers. Yet the government was deeply divided. Deputies of the Rally of the Lao People under the leadership of Katāy resented the presence of the upstarts of the CDNI. As the political infighting continued, rumours spread of the possibility of a *coup d'état* by the army.

At this point an incident occurred that distracted attention from the developing political crisis. On 15 December 1958, a Lao patrol was fired upon in a disputed area close to the demilitarized zone between North and South Vietnam.[19] This remote mountain valley was of considerable strategic importance for the DRV, since it provided an infiltration route around the western end of the demilitarized zone for communist cadres moving south. The DRV immediately protested against Lao intrusion into its territory and despatched 'a battalion-sized force' into the disputed area. In response to this incident, and to fabricated reports of more North Vietnamese troop concentrations on the Lao border,[20] Phuy Xananikôn demanded and received emergency powers to govern for a period of one year without recourse to the Assembly – a move which effectively eliminated any parliamentary forum for the LPF. Since endorsement by the Assembly was no longer necessary, one of Phuy's first acts was to reshuffle his cabinet, dropping three members of his own Rally of the Lao People in favour of three serving army officers, including Colonel Phūmī Nôsavan, all of whom were members of the CDNI. Their appointment was a triumph for extra-parliamentary forces (including the US Embassy), and a corresponding defeat for democratic processes. The CDNI and the army had succeeded in gaining substantial political representation, though at the expense of national reconciliation. Lao politics were further factionalized. Henceforth any pretence of the CDNI to project itself as a popular movement for better government was forgotten, and it became simply another pressure group serving the ambitions of its leaders.

The change of government had two immediate effects: to increase US influence within the Royal Lao government; and to intensify the anti-communist campaign conducted against the LPF. Both involved the army, which increasingly became the arbiter of political decision-making. American advisers, both civilian and military in civilian garb, were by this time operating with 'a lack of discretion' that undermined their own position,[21] for many Lao felt increasing disquiet over the growing US presence. Repression of the LPF by the army and police was intensified. Numerous arrests were made, and the Pathēt Lao accused the army of conducting a veritable campaign of intimidation and assassination in the rural areas, especially in Phongsālī.[22] Hundreds of Pathēt Lao cadres fled across the border into the DRV.

As if repudiation of the spirit, if not the letter, of the Viang Chan Agreements were not provocation enough, Phuy Xananikôn announced in February that since the Royal Lao government had fulfilled all its obligations under the Geneva Agreements, limits on acceptance of foreign military aid would no longer apply, an interpretation promptly endorsed by the United States, but denounced by both the DRV and China. The Soviet Union suggested the ICSC should resume its work in Laos, but Britain demurred and the matter lapsed. Taken in conjunction with Phuy's earlier statements, it must have seemed to both Hanoi and Beijing that the Lao government was repudiating any remaining com-mitment not only to neutrality, but to the Geneva Agreements as well. If Laos were to become a US 'base', nothing at all would have been gained by the communist powers at Geneva. What is surprising in the light of what both China and the DRV obviously considered to be a deteriorat-ing situation was the comparative restraint both countries showed.

Emboldened by its own bravado, the government set out to destroy the LPF as a political force. In March its newspaper, Lao Hak Xāt, was banned. Phuy's emergency powers had already denied the LPF its parliamentary forum. In the countryside the carrot of rural aid won some support for the government, even as the army continued to root out and arrest Pathēt Lao cadres in what a Rand Corporation study described as 'a stepped-up, methodical purge of [LPF] adherents and supporters'.[23] Yet the LPF was reluctant to break entirely with the government, for it still enjoyed certain advantages in continuing to function as a legal organization. Though its operations were increas-ingly constricted, the LPF still exercised some influence in the public service, in the Buddhist Sangha, and among the few industrial workers in Viang Chan. Abolition of what little remained of the Viang Chan Agreements would have eliminated any support base the LPF still enjoyed among the urban lowland Lao population in the approaching National Assembly elections. LPF cadres, led by Suphānuvong, stayed on in Viang Chan, though increasingly isolated, as their political opponents lurched ever further right into the eager arms of the United States.

Once the Royal Lao Army had gained control of the Ministry of Defence, it operated virtually independently of the government. Phūmī Nôsavan had emerged as the army strongman the Americans were seeking. Colonel Hugh Toye, former British military attaché in Laos who knew Phūmī well, remarked on his open smile, persuasive manner, and ability to get things done, all characteristics that endeared him to the United States.

> His voice was deceptively soft, his speech disarming, but in fact he was as ruthless as his appearance suggested. When among his own people, there was an air of muted violence about the man, a scarcely hidden enjoyment of power over people, a hint of conscious physical restraint. He was hated and feared, and his orders were obeyed.[24]

Under Phūmī's command, the military stepped up its repression against the LPF. Attempts by Phuy to rein in the army were without effect, even though it was recognized that its methods were deeply resented by the rural population. As the LPF was forced underground for its survival, the army simply measured success by the apparent reduction of LPF activity in the countryside, and informed its American patrons accordingly.

Buoyed up by a false belief in the army's efficacy, the Ministry of Defence decided to settle accounts with the Pathēt Lao by eliminating its last remaining units. Under the terms of the Viang Chan Agreements, two Pathēt Lao battalions of 750 men each were to be integrated into the Royal Lao Army. Negotiations had dragged on over the complement of officers to be included. Finally the government gave in to Pathēt Lao demands it had been steadfastly resisting for inclusion of 105 officers. The intention was to disarm both battalions, break them up as integral units, and weed out Pathēt Lao officers later by requiring them to pass examinations commensurate with their rank. By then, however, whatever trust had been built up as a result of the Viang Chan Agreements had been destroyed by the government's evident intention to eliminate the LPF 'once and for all'. The two battalions refused integration. Under pressure from the army, Suphānuvong and three other senior Pathēt Lao officials in Viang Chan were placed under house arrest, and both units were issued an ultimatum: accept integration or be forcibly disarmed. The First Battalion near Luang Phrabāng submitted, but the Second on the Plain of Jars slipped through the ring of three surrounding battalions of the Royal Lao Army to make its escape.[25] All the government could do was declare the absconding battalion to be in rebellion.

As part of its anti-communist campaign, the government also moved to eliminate Pathēt Lao influence in the Buddhist *Sangha*. In May 1959, the organizational autonomy of the *Sangha* was limited by royal ordinance. Appointment to all positions at each level in the *Sangha* administration henceforth required endorsement by government officials at the next higher level (village, district, province). Candidates for higher monastic office required cabinet approval. Even copies of correspondence between different levels of the *Sangha* had to be sent to the appropriate level of government. Such heavy-handed interference was resented, as were attempts to use the *Sangha* in support of government programs, and invitations to anti-communist monks of the Thammanyut sect from Thailand to take up residence in Laos. Politicization of the *Sangha* by both the Pathēt Lao and the Royal Lao government had already undermined its moral authority and standing. Many younger monks, often from rural backgrounds, still remained receptive to Pathēt Lao propaganda, however, and critical both of government policy (not least towards the *Sangha* itself) and of what they considered to be the corrosive effect of American popular culture.[26]

By succumbing to pressure from the army and the CDNI, the Phuy Xananikôn government precipitated what was the only logical outcome of its policies – a return to civil war. In the days immediately following the Pathēt Lao Second Battalion's dramatic escape, the government attempted to save the deteriorating situation by belatedly limiting the influence of the army and the CDNI. But it was too late. On the right, Phūmī Nôsavan and his generals had tasted power. On the left, the decision had been taken to return to armed struggle, a decision that came hard on the heels of a similar one taken by the Vietnam Workers' Party to throw all the resources of the DRV behind the insurgency in South Vietnam. Neutrality and national reconciliation were at an end. On both sides of the political spectrum, those who favoured confrontation over compromise seized the initiative. The time of testing had come: on one side stood the Royal Lao Army, soon increased to 29,000 men, and its American advisers; and on the other less than one-quarter as many Pathēt Lao guerrillas, supplied and advised by North Vietnam.[27] The first skirmishes indicated the shape of things to come.

In mid-July, in the middle of the rainy season when reinforcement of remote mountain garrisons by road or air was all but impossible, the Pathēt Lao began to re-establish its base area in Huaphan. Within a fortnight the mud-walled military posts of the Royal Lao Army in much of the north and northeast of the province had one after another been overrun by Pathēt Lao guerrillas. Large Pathēt Lao concentrations were not needed. Units of the Royal Lao Army felt exposed and their small garrisons were only too ready to retreat to safer surroundings, leaving the people they were supposed to protect to welcome, or submit to, the Pathēt Lao.

The government responded by imprisoning Suphānuvong and fourteen other LPF representatives in Viang Chan, leaving leadership of the revolutionary movement firmly in the hands of Kaisôn Phomvihān.[28] The government hurriedly assembled reinforcements, declared a state of emergency in northern Laos, and accused North Vietnam of being behind the Pathēt Lao 'rebel offensive',[29] a charge denied by Hanoi, which promptly called for reactivation of the ICSC. This the Royal Lao government rejected, and it appealed directly to the United Nations. Relations were strengthened with both Thailand and South Vietnam. In the first half of August, most of the Pathēt Lao First Battalion melted back into the jungle, and another rash of small-scale attacks was reported against outposts of the Royal Lao Army.

Appeals to the United Nations for an emergency UN force to protect the country from 'invasion' sent the international community into a flurry of diplomatic activity.[30] A UN fact-finding mission was despatched to investigate government accusations of DRV involvement, but found no evidence during its four-week stay. Subsequent appeals to the United Nations were met with disbelief. Meanwhile, insurgents gained control of extensive areas. Only a few larger government posts remained in Huaphan, where the countryside was again in the hands of the Pathēt Lao. Fighting had also spread to Phongsālī and parts of Xiang Khuang and Luang Phrabāng provinces. In the south, where military action against Lao Thoeng supporters of the Pathēt Lao had been particularly repressive, Sīthon Kommadam and his followers reactivated their insurgency. Arms caches were reopened, base areas re-established, and attacks carried out on outposts and communications routes of the Royal Lao Army. In the north Faidāng brought perhaps one-third of the Hmong into the Pathēt Lao camp, and many hill Tai joined the insurgency, reinforced by their ethnic cousins from north-western Vietnam.

The outbreak of fighting in 1959 thus took on a significant ethnic dimension. The Royal Lao Army was overwhelmingly Lao Lum, its officers sharing ethnic Lao disdain for Lao Thoeng and Lao Sūng, and even for the hill Tai. Far from recruiting minority youths after 1957, the army had punished them for favouring the Pathēt Lao. Nothing was done to improve living conditions for the mountain peoples – only 8 per cent of US aid had been spent on schools, clinics, roads and other development projects, and of that virtually none in the highlands.[31] When the call came from their leaders to return to the maquis in the mountains they knew so well, former guerrillas responded with alacrity, only too happy to drive out the hated lowland troops who requisitioned scarce food supplies and abused local women. Significantly, therefore, the breakdown of the First Coalition deprived the Royal Lao regime of the opportunity to pursue policies aimed at building an ethnically inclusive nationalism. This was left to the Pathēt Lao, whose nationalist credentials appealed not only to the ethnic minorities, but also began to attract those lowland Lao who objected to the growing American presence.[32]

In October, the deaths of both Prince Phetxarāt and King Sīsavāng-vong signalled the passing of a generation. The King was succeeded by his somewhat remote and taciturn son, Savāngvatthanā, a man who in Phetxarāt's view was incompetent, reactionary, and unpopular. If this was a harsh judgment, the new King was hardly a charismatic figure, and made no secret of his premonition that he would be the last of his line to rule. A physically imposing man, he was as pro-French as he was anti-communist, but was convinced that only the United States could guarantee Lao security. His grasp of politics, however, was never as sure as Suvanna's, and faced with his first political test he proved to be both devious and naïve.

On 24 December, on the patently false pretext that a Pathēt Lao attack on Viang Chan was imminent, Phūmī Nôsavan deployed troops throughout the city. The prime minister's house was surrounded, and pressure exerted on him to resign. The King was torn between his preference for the CDNI's tough anti-communism and his respect for parliamentary procedures. As the stand-off continued, royal support for the prime minister began to waver and Phuy resigned. The army thereupon seized the radio station and other government buildings, and instructed senior civil servants to take orders only from the army high command. Phūmī Nôsavan's creeping *coup d'état* was all but complete. It remained only for the King to appoint a military government.

At this point opposition, both external and internal, began to mount. Western ambassadors made it known to the King, who had given tacit support to the CDNI, that they were opposed to a military government. When Prince Bunūm also voiced objections to a military dictatorship, Phūmī felt his position crumbling. He notified the King that the army 'having achieved its task of reestablishing legality' looked forward to the appointment of a civilian government.[33] The King thanked the army, thereby absolving Phūmī of any blame for his attempted coup, and appointed a caretaker government to hold new elections. It was a typically Lao solution, reminiscent of the compromise that gave royal recognition to the Lao Issara government in 1946, though as before the monarchy suffered some loss of prestige. Not so Phūmī Nôsavan, who despite his backdown retained his position as Minister for Defence. Moreover, the army and the CDNI still wielded sufficient power to determine the outcome of the forthcoming elections.

Remembering the 1958 electoral results, the US Embassy again urged formation of a single National Front combining the Rally of the Lao People and the CDNI. So deep was the ill-feeling between the two groups, however, that this proved impossible. In order to reduce the opportunities for opposition candidates (LPF and Santhiphāp) to benefit from divisions on the right, a new electoral law was enacted making it far more difficult for left-wing candidates even to stand, much less get elected. Finance for the elections from both the United States and Thailand went almost entirely to the CDNI, whose candidates benefited from overt military and police support. Independent and opposition candidates were bribed to withdraw, allowing the CDNI to run unopposed in eleven seats. The only other unopposed seat was in Luang Phrabāng, where the popularity of Suvanna Phūmā was such that all other candidates (including the CDNI) withdrew from the contest. LPF leaders imprisoned in Viang Chan were prevented from standing at all.[34]

The LPF Central Committee denounced this 'comedy of an election' as a travesty of the Viang Chan Agreements, and appealed without success to the co-chairs of the Geneva Conference, Britain and the Soviet Union, to intervene. For the Pathēt Lao, these events merely confirmed their propaganda claim that the *de facto* dictatorship of the CDNI was turning the country into an American colony. The political message of the Pathēt Lao stressed national reconciliation, strict adherence to the Geneva Agreements, a policy of neutrality, and an end to foreign interference in the form of American, Filipino and Thai military advisers and technicians. All Lao could live together in harmony if only the Americans would leave. It was a message that struck a chord among civil servants disgusted by the venality and corruption of leading politicians and generals, among monks concerned over the deterioration in traditional values and morality, and among junior officers sent to fight a civil war under miserable conditions by men who seldom left the luxury of their expensive villas and air-conditioned offices.

Political propaganda was, however, only one side of Pathēt Lao strategy. The other was armed struggle, often in response to 'mopping up' operations by the Royal Lao Army, and political organization of 'liberated' areas. From his command post close to the Lao–Vietnamese border, Kaisôn continued to direct military operations; by early 1960 these had spread to most provinces with the exception of Luang Namthā and Xainyaburī. By that time some 20 per cent of the population spread over almost half the country was no longer under government control.[35] Even where government authority remained in place, in the form of a military post, district office, school and health clinic, actual control was often limited to a 20-kilometre radius. Beyond that it was merely nominal. In this no-man's land, ambushes, attacks on transport, mines and booby traps maintained a level of insecurity behind which armed Pathēt Lao propaganda teams pursued their single-minded tasks of political indoctrination and revolutionary organization. About this struggle for the hearts and minds of rural Lao, the political generals in Viang Chan knew little and cared less.

The elections on 24 April were as blatantly rigged as the opposition had feared – 'the model of fraud and dishonesty'.[36] Counting became a farce as votes for CDNI candidates exceeded the total number of enrolled voters, and opposition candidates in electorates that had returned left-wing members two years previously were limited to a handful of votes. For example, in Xam Neua province, almost entirely controlled by the Pathēt Lao, the LPF candidate received thirteen votes as against 6508 for his CDNI opponent.[37] Of the fifty-nine seats, CDNI-backed candidates gained thirty-four, the Rally of the Lao People seventeen, and independents eight. No candidate from the left-wing opposition parties won a seat. The CDNI deputies constituted themselves as a political party, the Paxā Sangkhom, or Social Democratic Party, which formed the majority of the new government.

Prince Somsanit Vongkotrattana, the new prime minister, was little more than an affable front-man for the real power-brokers in the new government: Phūmī Nôsavan as Minister for Defence and Khamphan Panyā of the CDNI as Minister for Foreign Affairs. Both men were determined to keep Laos closely allied with the United States and Thailand, the sources of their financial and political support. Both were committed to pursuing a strongly anti-communist domestic policy, including the public trial of Suphānuvong and his imprisoned associates. Two weeks before the government was formed, however, all fifteen Pathēt Lao leaders, together with those of their guards whom they had won over to their cause, made a dramatic, well-planned escape from prison and disappeared into the jungle. Four months and 500 kilometres later they turned up at Pathēt Lao headquarters in Xam Neua, an epic march that has since taken on legendary proportions.

Phūmī's political victory and Suphānuvong's escape set the stage for the next crisis in Lao politics. Systematic sabotage of any remaining hope for an internationally neutral Laos left no alternative but resumption of civil war. It was a prospect that not all Lao welcomed, particularly not those who would be called upon to fight. The stages leading up to the hopeless situation that faced the country in mid-1960 might not have been evident to those responsible for bringing it about – the political right, the army high command, the CDNI, and their American and Thai patrons – but they certainly had been to others – Suvanna's followers within the Rally of the Lao People, the moderate left, the French, and rather surprisingly, even some within the army itself.

## THE *COUP D'ÉTAT* OF AUGUST 1960 AND ITS AFTERMATH

On the morning of 8 August 1960, almost the entire Royal Lao government flew to Luang Phrabāng to consult the King over the elaborate arrangements necessary for the state funeral of King Sīsavāngvong. For anyone planning a military *coup d'état*, it was a perfect moment to move. In the early hours of 9 August, troops of the Second Paratroop Battalion swiftly seized control of Viang Chan. Their commanding officer was a 26-year-old captain by the name of Kônglae.

Small of stature, but already a veteran soldier who enjoyed the unquestioning loyalty of his elite unit, Kônglae was of mixed Lao Lum–Lao Thoeng parentage. He was unpretentious and politically naïve, but possessed of an independent mind, a ready smile, and a simple and direct mode of address which struck an immediate chord in many of his compatriots. At a public rally following his coup he called for an end to 'Lao fighting Lao', the overthrow of those who 'made their harvest on the backs of the people', a return to genuine neutrality ('If we sit in a boat, we must sit in the middle'), and an end to foreign interference in Lao affairs.

> What leads us to carry out this revolution is our desire to stop the bloody civil war; eliminate grasping public servants, carry out inquiries on military commanders and officials whose property amounts to much more than their monthly salaries can afford, and chase away foreign armed forces as soon as possible ... [38]

The coup came as a complete surprise to Lao of all political persuasions, not to mention their various foreign backers. While it engendered enormous enthusiasm among the mass of the people, particularly students in Viang Chan, others were more cautious. The political fall-out was immediate. On 13 August, as a noisy crowd and numbers of paratroopers waited impatiently outside the Assembly building, the forty-one out of fifty-nine deputies present agreed prudently and

unanimously to withdraw their confidence in the Somsanit government, and called upon the King to appoint Suvanna Phūmā, Kônglae's
personal choice, as prime minister.

General Phūmī took the coup as a personal affront by forces he had
believed loyal to himself, and as Minister for Defence was determined
to crush it. Armed with authorization from the Somsanit government
before it resigned, he first assured himself of American and Thai support before flying to his home town of Savannakhēt, headquarters of
Military Region III of the Royal Lao Army. There he declared martial
law, and with US and Thai assistance set about marshalling forces
opposed to the coup. Under Phūmī's direction, most members of the
Somsanit cabinet joined twenty-one Assembly deputies in forming a
Counter-*Coup d'état* Committee. Leaflets were dropped over Viang
Chan denouncing the coup leaders, and 'Radio Savannakhēt' began
broadcasting a steady stream of anti-coup propaganda over its
American-supplied transmitter. The scene seemed set for civil war,
unless a face-saving political solution could be found.

Upon receiving word of the Assembly's vote of no confidence in his
government, Prince Somsanit had agreed to resign and the King had
commissioned Suvanna to form a government. Members duly took the
traditional oath of office at Vat Sīsakhēt in Viang Chan, though formal
investiture by the King was prevented by Phūmī's unilateral declaration of martial law. To this government Kônglae handed over power,
declaring his *coup d'état* at an end. Despite its neutral complexion,
however, this was not a government acceptable to the political right.
Apart from Suvanna, its most prominent member was Kinim Phonsēnā,
named to the Interior Ministry. Kinim, leader of the Santhiphāp party,
an intelligent but humourless man of Sino-Lao ancestry, had lost his
seat in the April elections, and become a close adviser to Kônglae. He
was heartily loathed by the right, and Suvanna knew that if civil war
was to be averted, a coalition government would have to be formed
comprising both neutralists and rightists. After negotiations with General Phūmī, Suvanna put together a new government with the general
as Minister for the Interior and Kinim demoted to the Information
Ministry. A last flurry of opposition to Phūmī's inclusion on the part of
Kônglae was overcome, and the crisis appeared to have been averted.

At this point the plan began to unravel. According to Hugh Toye, as
Phūmī was about to board the aircraft that was to fly the government to
Viang Chan for formal investiture, he was handed a message that had
'come through American channels' warning him of a planned assassination attempt at the ceremony.[39] Phūmī flew instead to Savannakhēt
where, assured of unofficial US and Thai backing, he reactivated his
Counter-*Coup d'état* Committee. Within days this was transformed into
a Revolutionary Committee under the leadership of Prince Bunūm, in
effect a rebel organization seeking the overthrow of what was by then
the legally constituted government of Laos.

Officially the United States took a neutral position in response to
Kônglae's coup and its aftermath. The new US ambassador, Winthrop
G. Brown, was sympathetic to Suvanna's attempts to defuse the crisis,

as were both the French and the British.[40] Brown recommended support for the new government. Even the CIA chief of station initially concurred. Opposition came from the Pentagon, urged on by both South Vietnam and Thailand, which placed its own total trade embargo on Viang Chan.[41] Opinion within the CIA swung to Phūmī, and soon massive supplies of arms and ammunition were being flown into Savannakhēt from Thailand by Air America planes on contract to the CIA – even though by then the United States had officially declared its support for Suvanna's government.

From its re-established base areas in northern Laos, the Pathēt Lao observed these developments with keen interest. Suphānuvong, still *en route* after his dramatic escape from prison, promptly despatched an agent to make contact with Kônglae. On 24 August, a new Pathēt Lao radio station broadcast the movement's support for Suvanna, promising cooperation in the quest for national reconciliation. As conditions, the Pathēt Lao called for a cease-fire, release of political prisoners, dismissal of rightist ministers, and a strictly neutral foreign policy welcoming diplomatic relations with and accepting aid from all countries. Only after the United States refused to assist in overcoming the Thai blockade did Suvanna formally invite the Pathēt Lao to send a delegation to Viang Chan to begin talks. Meanwhile, Pathēt Lao radio announced that the guerrillas would avoid conflict with neutralist forces in what amounted to a *de facto* alliance against the right. In a move denounced by General Phūmī as a new invasion, Pathēt Lao guerrillas strengthened their military positions in Phongsālī, Huaphan and Khammūan provinces.

The division between the neutralist military command loyal to Suvanna and Phūmī's rightist forces in Savannakhēt forced army garrisons to choose sides. In an initial engagement between opposing forces, two companies of Kônglae's paratroopers routed two of Phūmī's battalions advancing from Pākxan, and pursued them south across the Nām Kading. In Phongsālī, Colonel Khamuan Bubphā tried to avoid any commitment, while the Xam Neua garrison commander declared for Savannakhēt. Hugh Toye recounts that when Kônglae dropped a few paratroopers near Xam Neua to win over the town for Suvanna, the whole 1500-strong garrison fled, only to be ambushed and disarmed by Pathēt Lao guerrillas on their retreat to the Plain of Jars.[42]

The US diplomatic response to these unsettling events was to attempt to put pressure on Suvanna. Requests for food and fuel to alleviate shortages resulting from the Thai blockade were ignored. Military supplies were no longer reaching Kônglae's forces, while the monthly cash-grant to pay government and military salaries was suspended for September. A mission was meanwhile despatched from Washington to warn Suvanna of mounting US displeasure, especially over resumption of negotiations with the Pathēt Lao. Chosen to lead the US delegation was J. Graham Parsons, Assistant Secretary of State for Far Eastern Affairs, who, as ambassador to Viang Chan three years earlier, had done everything in his power to prevent formation of the First Coalition government. Given the feelings of antipathy and distrust Parsons and

Suvanna had for each other (Suvanna was later to describe Parsons as 'the most nefarious and reprehensible of men'),[43] prospects were not auspicious. Nor was the timing well chosen. Suvanna opened negotiations with Pathēt Lao representatives the day before Parsons arrived, while the first Soviet ambassador to Laos flew into Viang Chan to an enthusiastic welcome the day Parsons left for Luang Phrabāng to see the King. Suvanna refused either to break off negotiations with the Pathēt Lao, or to accept Parsons's suggestion that the seat of government be transferred to Luang Phrabāng. As for Phūmī Nôsavan, Suvanna did not consider it was up to him to instigate negotiations with a declared rebel. It was left to Ambassador Brown to salvage a 'gentlemen's agreement' with Suvanna that enabled resumption of payment of the monthly cash subsidy to the government in return for permission for US military aid to be delivered to Savannakhēt – on condition it was used against Pathēt Lao, not neutralist, forces. The proviso meant nothing. Following Parsons's visit, the Soviet Union declared its willingness to provide assistance to the legally constituted Lao government; and in Washington, 'State and Defense agreed that Suvanna must go'.[44]

The means of his going was to be General Phūmī. Besides massive military assistance, the United States supplied Phūmī with logistic and technical aid and paid for his entire force. Clandestine radio stations urged neutralist officers to defect, while rightist agents made much of US support for Phūmī, and the growing isolation of Suvanna. By mid-November the balance of forces had shifted decisively in favour of Savannakhēt. Four out of five military regions and three out of five officers of general rank declared for Phūmī. Suvanna was forced to rely increasingly on the Pathēt Lao, whose own position was strengthened immeasurably by this *de facto* alliance. Not only was Huaphan firmly in Pathēt Lao hands: Pathēt Lao 'administrative committees', a kind of parallel village administration which progressively usurped power from the elected village chief, were rapidly established throughout much of Xiang Khuang and parts of other northern provinces. Following the defection of the garrison of Luang Phrabāng to Phūmī, Suvanna flew to Xam Neua where he joined with Suphanuvong to issue a last appeal – to the King not to favour the rebels, to the people to support the government, and to foreign powers to cease interfering in Lao affairs.[45] Pathēt Lao agreement to form a tripartite coalition government – including the right, but excluding Bunūm and Phūmī Nôsavan from the cabinet – was transmitted to Savannakhēt in the hope of averting the looming civil war.

All was to no avail. With the end of the rainy season, and with CIA and Thai support, Phūmī had reinforced his front line on the Nām Kading. US-supplied artillery and heavy mortars opened up on Kônglac's lightly armed paratroopers. Led by US Special Forces officers, Phūmī's troops drove into Pākxan. News of the advance shocked Viang Chan. Left-wing demonstrators, surreptitiously encouraged by Kinim Phonsēnā, took to the streets. More than two weeks passed, however, before the battle for Viang Chan was joined, during which

time the United States gave Suvanna false assurances that no further
military assistance would be provided to General Phūmī, and an
emergency Soviet airlift of supplies from Hanoi to Viang Chan got
under way at Suvanna's request.

Thereafter events moved quickly. As Phūmī's forces closed on Viang
Chan from two directions – from Pākxan along Route 13, and through
northeast Thailand to Nôngkhāy – the majority of Assembly deputies
deserted Suvanna, and it was only a matter of time before they withdrew confidence in his government.[46] All Suvanna's attempts to avert
civil conflict had come to nothing. On 9 December, Suvanna and most of
his ministers left Viang Chan for voluntary exile in Cambodia, except
Kinim who flew to Hanoi to appeal for Soviet military assistance. The
Russians responded by flying in three 105-millimetre howitzers and
three heavy mortars, along with a supply of ammunition, hardly a
match for Phūmī's armament.

Two days later, thirty-eight deputies met in Savannakhēt to pass their
expected motion of no confidence in the government. The King thereupon dismissed Suvanna's government and called upon Prince Bunūm
to form a provisional administration – which was promptly recognized
by Thailand and the United States. Without awaiting instructions from
the new government, General Phūmī launched his attack on Viang
Chan on 13 December. The outcome was never in doubt. Even so, it
took rightist forces three days to seize the city. Outgunned and outnumbered, Kônglae's troops staged an orderly withdrawal north, but
not before fighting had resulted in hundreds of casualties and caused
considerable damage. As the citizens of Viang Chan cowered in their
homes, the opposing forces mounted artillery and mortar duels across
the city. In the chaotic street battles, as both sides were reluctant to shed
Lao blood, soldiers tended to fire high, which did little to protect
civilians in their wooden, palm-thatched houses. In the Hotel Constellation, the international press corps sat out the battle unscathed, but
as many as 500 people lost their lives.[47]

The political effect of the Battle of Viang Chan was to force Kônglae's
neutralists into the waiting arms of the Pathēt Lao, thus greatly enhanc-
ing the international profile of the communist movement in Laos. Yet
this was portrayed by the right as a defeat for communism. Over the
next three months the 'defeated' forces, both neutralist and Pathēt Lao,
consolidated their hold over most of northern and eastern Laos, beginning with the Plain of Jars. Rightist campaigns conducted early in 1961
failed to regain any lost ground.

If the Battle of Viang Chan gained nothing militarily, it was even less
decisive in settling the political crisis. The semblance of legality which
the government of Bunūm could claim might have been enough to
ensure it Western recognition, but was hardly sufficient to convince the
communist bloc, which continued to recognize the government of
Suvanna Phūmā. Suvanna himself, after some hesitation, decided he
was still prime minister. He remained, however, in Phnom Penh,
graciously granting interviews to a stream of visiting journalists to
whom he castigated the short-sightedness and stupidity of American

policy and endorsed Prince Sihanouk's proposal to convene a new Geneva conference to re-establish at least the nominal neutrality of Laos. It was an option more thoughtful observers, even in the United States, were prepared to consider.

Meanwhile the Plain of Jars, in the ideal strategic situation to receive Soviet and Chinese military supplies by both air and road via North Vietnam, was rapidly becoming an armed camp.[48] Both Moscow and Hanoi could claim to be responding to requests from the legitimate government of Laos, whose Supreme Military Council, nominally presided over by Kônglae, commanded both neutralist and Pathēt Lao forces. In Viang Chan the United States matched the Soviet airlift of weapons and ammunition and the influx of North Vietnamese military advisers with its own military build-up. The fledgling Lao Air Force was equipped with T-6 trainer aircraft, while 400 US Special Forces advisers were assigned to rightist units in the form of White Star Mobile Training Teams.[49]

Two components of this military escalation were of particular significance for later developments in the civil war. On the Pathēt Lao side, Soviet weapons and North Vietnamese advisers enabled guerrilla forces to be organized as regular units capable of combating the similarly constituted right-wing army. The more or less defined 'front line' that subsequently separated the Pathēt Lao zone of control from that of the Royal Lao government owed much to this development. More significant, at least for the Lao Sūng communities of Xiang Khuang and Huaphan, was the improvised beginning of what became known as the 'Secret Army' (Armée clandestine), an independently organized Hmong guerrilla force trained, equipped and paid for by the CIA. Under the French, Hmong villagers had been armed as an auto-defence militia, which had continued to resist the Pathēt Lao. When the arrival of Kônglae's paratroopers sent the Lao army garrison on the Plain of Jars fleeing south, the Hmong commander of the town of Xiang Khuang, Colonel Vang Pao, ordered the prearranged evacuation of 200 Hmong villages to prevent the population falling under Pathēt Lao control. Seventy thousand men, women and children trekked deeper into the mountains south of the Plain of Jars where, supplied by American air drops, they formed the population base from which Hmong irregular forces were recruited to fight what became a thirteen-year-long 'secret war' against the Pathēt Lao.

In retrospect, the 1960 coup and ensuing political crisis can be seen as a last desperate bid to re-establish the ideological consensus that had briefly existed three years before. But, driven by American anti-communism, political polarization had gone too far. All the coup achieved was to create a third political grouping that was never cohesive enough to resist being torn between left and right. The impact of the coup was not so much to exacerbate political instability, which was already considerable, as to create the illusion of a solution to it. But an illusion it was, for the hopes centred on the Second Coalition government came to nothing. The *de facto* divison of the country was never overcome, and neutrality proved impossible to achieve. The 1960 coup thus marked no significant turning point in Lao history – just a dwindling hope that the country might escape civil conflict. All that the coup did, paradoxically, was to provide an opportunity for the United States to extricate itself from an increasingly alarming situation, for the prospect of US forces fighting a war against communist-backed guerrillas in Laos was not one that a new administration in Washington looked upon with any enthusiasm.

## THE GENEVA AGREEMENTS OF 1962: FORMATION OF THE SECOND COALITION GOVERNMENT

The first four months of 1961 were a time to take stock, both internally among the Lao factions, and externally in the capitals of the world. The balance of power had changed dramatically in the year between the military intervention of December 1959 and the Battle of Viang Chan a year later. Judged by any criteria, the role of the CDNI and the army had been disastrous. Compounding the ineptitude of the Phuy Xananikôn government, not only had its thirst for power and flagrant electoral corruption provoked the coup of Kônglae, but it had then aggravated the crisis by refusing to agree to a compromise political settlement. By choosing, under American pressure, to adopt the military option in order to shore up its own political position, it had in fact undermined it, for the neutralists were left with no alternative but alliance with the Pathēt Lao. The bitterness Suvanna felt was understandable.

The first task of the Bunūm government was to enforce its control over the organs of administration and security. Priority tasks included reorganization of the armed forces, establishment of the National Directorate for Coordination bringing together civil, military and pol-itical police under the single command of Phūmī's faithful lieutenant, Captain Sīhō Lānphutthakun, and the systematic purging of all civil servants suspected of harbouring pro-neutralist sympathies. The cool reception Phūmī had received from the people of Viang Chan con-vinced him that it was wise at first to return by helicopter each evening to sleep at a Thai military base. He was determined, however, to root out his enemies.

On the Plain of Jars, Kônglae and Kinim Phonsēnā moved quickly to cement their alliance with the Pathēt Lao. Agreement was reached to co-ordinate operations by and supplies to the two armies, which remained under their separate respective command structures. The neutralist government re-established itself at Khang Khai on the Plain of Jars, under the direction of Kinim and with the assistance of those civil servants and students who had joined Kônglae's retreat from Viang Chan. Suvanna remained in Phnom Penh. Not until late February did he fly to Khang Khai to be greeted by Suphānuvong and other Pathēt Lao leaders.

In world capitals attention centred on the best means of defusing what threatened to become a serious international crisis. As early as September 1960, Prince Sihanouk had broached the idea of an inter-national conference, a suggestion he renewed the following January when it was endorsed by France, the Soviet Union and China. India and Britain favoured reactivation of the International Commission for Supervision and Control. The problem was: to which government would the ICSC be accredited, Bunūm's or Suvanna's? The British suggestion to the Soviet Union as co-chair of the 1954 Geneva Conference that a mission be despatched to the King met with the objection that the King was not empowered under the Lao constitution with executive authority, and that in any case he was 'a prisoner of the rebels'.[50]

Nowhere was reassessment more agonizing than in Washington. The failure of the military option in Laos had also been a failure of US policy. The initial US reaction to Phūmī's success in recapturing Viang Chan had been one of self-congratulation. But for the military option to have been effective, neutralist and communist forces would have had to be swiftly routed. Not only did this not occur, but over the next four months the Royal Lao Army proceeded to demonstrate both the incompetence of its leadership and its reluctance to fight. As it became apparent that a military victory was out of the question, support hardened in Washington, among members of the incoming administration of President John F. Kennedy, for a political solution involving the neutralization of Laos.

Offensive operations by both neutralist and Pathēt Lao forces in March led the United States to place Marines on Okinawa on alert and despatch elements of the Seventh Fleet to the Gulf of Thailand. At a press conference two days later, however, President Kennedy announced a significant change in policy towards Laos. The United States, Kennedy said, 'strongly and unreservedly' supported a 'neutral and independent Laos', and he called for 'constructive negotiation' among concerned nations in order to ensure its 'genuine neutrality'.[51] In case the overture was rejected, however, secret military preparations were under way. Whole units at a time of Lao army troops began training in Thailand, while Thai military advisers with false Lao identity papers worked in Laos. The CIA presence in Laos was also increased: its assignment was to work mainly with the Hmong, though separate operations also began in southern Laos.

The Soviet response to Kennedy's initiative was conciliatory. If the United States saw Laos as the strategic 'cork in the bottle' in Southeast Asia, for the Soviets it was much less important.[52] Soviet involvement in Laos had more to do with competition with China in support of revolutionary clients than with challenging the United States. Even as the US military presence increased, Moscow's reaction remained muted. But while the Soviet Union agreed to join Britain in calling for a cease-fire prior to an international conference, China, North Vietnam and the Pathēt Lao were reluctant to surrender the military advantage. It required considerable Soviet pressure, and visits by both Suvanna and Suphānuvong to Beijing and Hanoi, to win over the Chinese and Vietnamese, before moves to neutralize Laos through international agreement could gain momentum.

On 24 April the co-chairs of the 1954 Geneva Conference, Britain and the Soviet Union, jointly issued invitations to twelve other countries –

Laos and its six neighboring states, the three members of the ICSC, France and the United States – to attend 'an International Conference on the Laotian question', to be convened following an agreed cease-fire. In Laos, however, fighting continued. As lavish cremation rites were finally held for the late King Sīsavāngvong, neutralist and Pathēt Lao forces mounted a last-minute offensive. Hmong bases came under attack while the last strategic garrison, Xēpōn, in Savannakhēt province, fell to Pathēt Lao assault the day before the cease-fire came into effect, leaving two-thirds of the country in Pathēt Lao and neutralist hands on the eve of the Geneva meeting.

The conference in Geneva finally convened on 16 May 1961, after an ICSC team sent to Laos had verified that the cease-fire was holding. All three Lao factions were represented. The first tripartite meeting between military delegations of the factions had taken place five days earlier at the village of Bān Nāmôn, just south of Vang Viang, where the front line had temporarily stabilized. The Bān Nāmôn talks created the precedent for seating the Pathēt Lao and neutralists as separate delegations at Geneva, despite objections from the Bunūm government and the United States. Progress at Geneva was slow, primarily because of disagreement between the three Lao factions. Just how determined, however, were the United States and the Soviet Union to remove Laos as a source of East–West tension was evident at the summit meeting of President Kennedy and Premier Nikita Khrushchev in Vienna at the beginning of June. In their joint statement, both leaders 'reaffirmed their support of a neutral and independent Laos under a government chosen by the Laotians themselves, and of international agreements for ensuring that neutrality and independence. In this connection they have recognized the importance of an effective cease-fire.'[53]

It was one thing, however, for the superpowers to agree on the need for a neutral and independent Laos, and quite another for either regional powers (North Vietnam and Thailand) or the Lao factions themselves to create the necessary conditions. Both the principal regional powers had to be convinced to cooperate. North Vietnam was understandably reluctant to recommend a cease-fire when Pathēt Lao forces, reinforced by significant numbers of Vietnamese 'volunteers', were proving militarily superior to rightist forces and could operate under the umbrella of their alliance with the neutralist army and government. Thailand feared that any agreement would only endorse communist gains and thereby threaten Thai security. The Thai at first refused to send a delegation to Geneva at all, and only turned up for the eighth session after bowing to intense US pressure.

As for the three Lao factions, hopeful signs of compromise at Bān Nāmôn on formation of a new tripartite coalition government evaporated within a few days, as renewed fighting broke out around the Hmong stronghold of Phādong, just south of the Plain of Jars, and no agreement was forthcoming over the role of the ICSC in monitoring what was obviously a flagrant cease-fire violation. Not until Phādong had been abandoned by Vang Pao did the Pathēt Lao give permission for an ICSC team to verify that no fighting was going on. To show its displeasure over the fall of Phādong, the US delegation boycotted the Geneva conference for a week. More significantly, the decision was taken to build up the Hmong 'secret army', a task 'not asked for and not particularly welcome' that was entrusted to the CIA.[54]

On the political front, some progress was made. Thanks to the patient efforts of Prince Sihanouk, the three Lao princes met at Zurich towards the end of June, where they agreed in principle to form a new Provisional Government of National Union in which all three factions would be represented. A delegation of this government was to represent Laos at the Geneva Conference. There was no agreement, however, on the composition of the new government. At this point the process stalled. A meeting in Phnom Penh in August achieved nothing. Both sides meanwhile built up their armed forces with generous military assistance from their respective backers.

What is evident from a reading of US foreign policy documents on Laos for this period is the extent to which events in Laos were seen in Washington in the reinforcing perspective of the Cold War and the need to preserve the pro-American dictatorships of Ngo Dinh Diem in South Vietnam and Sarit Thanarat in Thailand.[55] Lao neutrality could contribute to this end only if it could be adequately policed. Early indications that the ICSC would again be ineffective led the United States to formulate a number of contingency plans for military intervention. One such plan involved cooperation with America's SEATO allies; another envisaged occupying the Mekong valley and southern Laos with the assistance of South Vietnamese and Thai forces, leaving the north of the country to the Pathēt Lao. As the US Joint Chiefs of Staff recognized, problems of terrain and logistics would have been formidable, but it is interesting to speculate that, had the Geneva talks collapsed and this option been taken, the commitment of US forces in the Second Indo-china War might have been primarily in Laos rather than Vietnam, with possibly a very different outcome.[56] But intervention was only to be in response to a renewed communist offensive. In the meantime, rightist forces were increased and their training and weaponry improved.

For the United States, Laos was a pawn on the chessboard of Southeast Asian security, to be manipulated as required. But what is equally evident is how recalcitrant both allies and dependants could be – on both sides. For Phūmī, the change of American policy was a betrayal, both of himself and his country, and, American 'puppet' though he was, he refused for as long as possible to comply with American demands. As the Kennedy administration – particularly Assistant Secretary of State for Far Eastern Affairs, W. Averell Harriman — became convinced that Suvanna Phūmā was the key to Lao neutrality, and US political support shifted to Suvanna,[57] Phūmī became increasingly obdurate. Even after Harriman had gained the agreement of King Savāngva-tthanā, and rejected all his reservations and pretexts, Phūmī still doggedly opposed formation of a Second Coalition government headed by Suvanna.

As negotiations dragged on, international patience began to wear thin. Both US and Soviet pressure was necessary before the three princes agreed to meet in Geneva in January 1962. There the Pathēt Lao formula of equal representation in government for itself and the right, with Suvanna's neutralists holding a majority of portfolios, was finally accepted, though not who should get the key ministries of defence and the interior. American insistence that both should go to the neutralists had little effect, and American annoyance was evident. Given the possibility of renewed fighting, the United States was reluctant to withdraw either military or economic aid. Eventually, however, Kennedy saw no alternative and both were temporarily suspended.

As if in response, Phūmī announced that Laos was being invaded by North Vietnamese, Soviet and Chinese forces, a claim that met with universal scepticism. Wolf had been cried too often before. Further political manoeuvres were no more successful. On 24 March Harriman met with Phūmī in the presence of Marshal Sarit, the Thai dictator and a distant relative of Phūmī's, at Nôngkhāy, on the Thai bank just downstream from Viang Chan. Yet even this last attempt to coerce Phūmī was unsuccessful. Only diminishing finances (Phūmī turned to opium to fund the army)[58] and a further crushing defeat of rightist forces eventually forced his compliance.

The battle of Namthā had been looming for some time. The town, capital of Luang Namthā province, is situated only about 30 kilometres south of the Chinese border. Late in 1961, a series of skirmishes occurred during which both sides violated the cease-fire. Phūmī's response to what he described as Pathēt Lao 'provocation' was massively to reinforce Namthā, against the advice of his US advisers. The Pathēt Lao responded with a force build-up of its own. More rightist reinforcements were parachuted in, and by mid-April Phūmī's forces numbered 5000 and skirmishing was continuous. By early May, Namthā was effectively isolated, with resupply only possible by air. The similarities with Dien Bien Phu were ominous. As the defence perimeter came under fire, defending forces were demoralized by exaggerated claims of Vietnamese and Chinese involvement broadcast from Viang Chan. When the US Special Forces team attached to the garrison was evacuated, the defence simply collapsed. Three thousand of its defenders fled south to Bān Huayxāy on the Mekong: the remainder surrendered.[59] As a flood of Lao troops crossed to the safety of Thailand, Bān Huayxāy itself was abandoned, its civilian population sheepishly returning a few days later when it was discovered there were no Pathēt Lao in the vicinity. Namthā, however, remained in Pathēt Lao hands, eventually to be connected to the Chinese-built road network in northern Laos.

The American response to the Namthā débâcle was twofold. Although no communist forces were known to be closer than 50 kilometres to the Thai border, President Kennedy again ordered the Seventh Fleet into the Gulf of Thailand, moved 1000 American troops already in Thailand for SEATO exercises to Udôn, and ordered deployment of another 4000. These moves were primarily to reassure the Thai. At the same time, the United States privately acknowledged Phūmī's provocation, and assured the Soviet Union that Washington still wanted to see a neutralist coalition in Laos, provided there was a proper cease-fire. Within a fortnight this again seemed to be holding. But the United States had lost all confidence in Phūmī. With no cards left to play, and fearful he would be replaced by another general (which the Americans were prepared to do),[60] Phūmī signalled to Suvanna his readiness for renewed talks on the formation of a coalition government.

Negotiations between the three princes resumed early in June on the Plain of Jars, resulting in agreement within five days on a Provisional Government of National Union comprising eleven neutralists, four rightists and four Pathēt Lao (two full ministers and two deputy ministers, or secretaries of state). Suvanna, in addition to being prime minister, took on the Defence Ministry. Bunūm announced his retirement from politics, leaving the way open for General Phūmī to become one of two deputy prime ministers and Minister for Finance. The other deputy prime minister was Prince Suphānuvong, who also took on the Economics portfolio. Phūmī Vongvichit for the Pathēt Lao was assigned Information, Propaganda and Tourism, while key neutralists included Pheng Phongsavan as Minister for the Interior, and Kinim Phonsēnā as Foreign Minister. The new government was duly sworn in on 23 June. Its first decisions were to announce a new cease-fire, name a delegation to leave for Geneva, and establish diplomatic relations with both the DRV and the People's Republic of China.

On 2 July participating member states reassembled at Geneva, with Kinim leading the Lao delegation. Three weeks later the final agreements were signed, comprising a declaration on the neutrality of Laos, plus a protocol of nineteen articles spelling out the means by which that neutrality was to be ensured. The declaration incorporated the text of a statement by the Royal Lao government committing the kingdom to follow the five principles of peaceful coexistence, not to enter into or recognize the protection of any military alliance (including SEATO), and not to permit any foreign interference in its internal affairs. All foreign troops and military personnel were to be withdrawn. Aid, providing no strings were attached, could be received from any country. All participating countries signing the agreements pledged themselves to respect these conditions, and to refrain from resorting to any 'measure which might impair the peace of the Kingdom of Laos', from introducing foreign troops into Laos or establishing any military base, from using Lao territory to interfere in the internal affairs of another country, and from using any territory for interference in the internal affairs of Laos. The attached protocol stipulated procedures for withdrawal of foreign troops within seventy-five days, transfer of the former French military base at Xēnō to Lao jurisdiction, and release of all captured military or civilian personnel (including a number of Americans in Pathēt Lao hands), and spelled out the (weakened) role of the reactivated ICSC.

From the Lao point of view, what was significant about the 1962 Agreements was what they did *not* say. No time-limits were set for any of the tasks set out in the Zurich joint communiqué, the only Lao political document referred to in the Agreements. In that communiqué, priority was given to formation of the Provisional Government of

National Union and elections for the National Assembly according to the electoral law approved in 1957. During the 'transitional period', however, until a 'definitive government' could be formed following elections, 'the administrative organs set up during the hostilities [would] be provisionally left in being'. In other words, the country would remain divided into separate administrative zones. Superficially this resembled the situation in 1954, but then the balance of forces internally had been much less favourable to the Pathēt Lao – and still it had taken more than three years to achieve national unity. In 1962, reintegration of the two administrative zones was far less likely since the Pathēt Lao and the right were much more evenly matched. Moreover, despite the apparent victory of the neutralist centre, both in achieving the neutralization of Laos and in obtaining eleven out of nineteen cabinet posts, its position had been seriously weakened. Attitudes had hardened on both the left and the right, each of which could still draw upon the powerful support of international patrons. Only France and Cambodia, in a global and regional context respectively, provided weak backing for the neutralists.

Nevertheless the Government of National Union got off to a brave start. Suvanna obtained promises of substantial aid on visits to the United States, France and Japan. Under the supervision of the ICSC, some foreign troops at least left the country,[61] and prisoners were exchanged. Tripartite administrative and military commissions were set up to examine formation of both a single administration and a unified army composed equally of troops of all three factions. The first priority was to assure the authority of government ministers in their respective functions. Suvanna moved slowly, attempting to ensure support from both left and right for each decision. Yet such was the suspicion that by then characterized Lao politics, such the determination of opposing foreign powers to have their own way, that all of Suvanna's persuasion proved inadequate. But then no-one, it is safe to say in the context of the Cold War, could have steered the troika of Lao political factions in the same direction after 1962. Possibly the only opportunity to do so had been lost four years earlier.

Though agreement on the neutrality of Laos may have been significant as an exercise in international diplomacy, its value in bringing peace and neutrality to the country itself was rather more problematical. Sihanouk, despite his pivotal role in bringing the conference about, as early as August 1961 expressed his doubts as to whether genuine neutrality was any longer an option for Laos. Those who signed the Geneva Agreements did so out of very different motives. Already Lao territory was being used for the infiltration of agents and supplies from North to South Vietnam, a vital route which authorities in Hanoi had no intention of closing off just because Laos had been neutralized. The only neutrality Hanoi was prepared to accept was the kind that operated in Cambodia, where a secret agreement permitted the use of Cambodian territory by communist forces in return for recognition of Cambodia's borders.

As for the United States, neutralization of Laos was initially the means of defusing a potentially dangerous Cold War confrontation in a part of the world where Washington was unwilling to commit substantial forces. As negotiations wore on, however, the United States became increasingly concerned over what was happening in South Vietnam. In December 1961, the State Department had marshalled its evidence for substantial infiltration through Laos.[62] As Hugh Toye remarked: 'It was basic to [US] acceptance of the Geneva Agreement of 1962 that this traffic should be stopped.'[63] But that could only happen if the neutrality of Laos were universally respected. What seems surprising in retrospect is that US policy-makers ever believed that Soviet pressure could prevent, or at least limit, the movement of communist cadres into South Vietnam. Only a genuine neutrality would have been in the interests of the United States. What emerged instead was a compromise, a 'tacit understanding', to use US General Maxwell Taylor's phrase,[64] that Laos would not become a primary theatre of war, and that the real struggle was to be waged in Vietnam.

This 'tacit understanding' had the advantage of enabling the United States to keep control of the Mekong valley, deemed essential for the security of Thailand, without having to commit ground forces in Laos. But it left Laos divided north–south, and did nothing to close off infiltration routes from North to South Vietnam. As McGeorge Bundy, President Kennedy's Special Assistant for National Security Affairs, had warned as early as April 1961: 'A "neutral" Laos may prove to be fatal very soon for South Vietnam.'[65] The only way South Vietnam could have been protected would have been by dividing Laos east–west somewhere about Thākhaek, an alternative given some consideration, but rejected as requiring too great a commitment of US troops. That the 'tacit understanding' might still serve US interests was based on two miscalculations, one strategic, the other logistical. First, in terms of American Cold War logic, monolithic international communism was manipulated in Asia principally by Beijing, and it was supposedly just as interested in subverting Thailand as South Vietnam: all the dominoes were equally targeted. In fact, Hanoi was much more influential than Washington believed in setting the revolutionary agenda, and the first priority was to reunify Vietnam. Thailand was of marginal interest, though some assistance was subsequently given to promoting insurgency in the Thai northeast. Second, to accept that the struggle would be waged in Vietnam could only be based on a belief that the United States would have some advantage there. And that belief in turn rested on a conviction that the rate of infiltration from North to South Vietnam would not escalate uncontrollably. In 1962, though, a US strategic analyst could perhaps be forgiven for not foreseeing the eventual extent of the Ho Chi Minh trail, or the impossibility of staunching the flow down it of men and arms.

From the Lao perspective there was little anyone could do to avoid the gathering cataclysm. The very weakness of Laos made the preservation of neutrality impossible, no matter how many embassies of opposing Cold War antagonists maintained cordial relations with the Royal Lao government in Viang Chan. Moreover, given its strategic position in relation to the antagonistic regimes in North and South Vietnam, even the most determinedly neutralist government in Laos could do little to enforce its proclaimed neutrality. But if Vietnamese use of Lao territory was strategically essential, it was just as essential for the United States to attempt to stop it. For neither side, therefore, was there any advantage in strict observance of the Geneva Agreements. The only question was how best to subvert Lao neutrality without appearing to do so; that is, without making it too obvious that Lao leaders on both sides were being manipulated in the interests of outside powers.

## POLITICAL POLARIZATION: NEUTRALITY SUBVERTED

As soon as it became clear after the battle for Viang Chan that the neutralists intended to maintain a separate political and military identity, they became the target for both left and right, both of which hoped to benefit from their eventual elimination. Until the signing of the Geneva Agreements, the strength of the antagonism existing between neutralists and rightists was enough to prevent any co-operation. By early 1962, by contrast, tensions were already evident between neutralists and Pathēt Lao, despite efforts by leaders on both sides to prevent misunderstandings.

In order to strengthen the political organization of the neutralists, Suvanna had founded in September 1961 the Lao Pen Kāng (Neutral Laos) party, with himself as President and Kônglae and Pheng Phongsavan as vice-presidents. There existed, however, two other neutralist political parties: the Santhiphāp Pen Kāng (Peace through Neutrality) party of Kinim Phonsēnā, with a past history of close co-operation with the Pathēt Lao dating from the supplementary elections of 1958; and the Mittaphāp (Friendship) Party formed by left-wing students in support of the goals of the 1960 coup. Though neither was Marxist, in many respects their political platforms differed little from that of the Lao Patriotic Front, which they saw as their natural ally. The neutralists were thus divided among themselves, making fissiparous pressures that much more likely to succeed.

Return of neutralist civil servants and officers to Viang Chan in mid-1962 to take part in government exposed them to political pressure not only from former rightist comrades, but also from the US Embassy which hoped to see a common front formed between the two non-communist factions. For his part, Phūmī ordered the National Directorate for Coordination (the police and security apparatus) both to target neutralist troops to win them over to the right, and to prevent the neutralist parties from functioning freely in areas under right-wing control. Much the same tactics were used by the Pathēt Lao. Neutralists were subjected to continuous propaganda, while being prevented from extending their own organization into areas under Pathēt Lao control. They were thus able to exercise administration only of areas in possession of their own forces.

Suvanna, to whom the National Assembly had voted plenary powers in October, was well aware of the pressures the neutralists were under. Jean Deuve, a close adviser, summed up Suvanna's thinking:

> He estimated it would take two years, through developing little by little the influence of each ministry in each zone, by technical decisions, in the areas of health, post and telecommunications, etcetera; through multiplying personal contacts with civil servants and officers; and through bringing the King into the game. It was necessary to proceed by very small steps, and to resolve all misunderstandings. Once the military merger was achieved – that was the key to success – the neutralist party would have to win the elections by attracting as many adherents as possible from each wing, right and left.[66]

It was a vain hope. Although in November an agreement was signed to create a tripartite army of 30,000 men, one-third from each faction, and a tripartite police force of 6000, no concrete measures were taken to demobilize or disarm additional forces, or to limit the powers of the ubiquitous Coordination. Rightists remained in control of their own area, as did the Pathēt Lao of theirs. As a result, the neutralists were confined to an intermediate zone, subjected to pressures from both sides.

Within the neutralist faction, differences arose over the role of the United States in continuing to supply Hmong irregular forces in Huaphan and Xiang Khuang provinces,[67] and the continued presence of Vietnamese advisers with the Pathēt Lao. But it was the resupply of neutralist forces themselves that caused a division within the movement. The problem had come about as a result of two developments. With the signature of the Geneva Agreements, the Soviet airlift had been terminated. While the Pathēt Lao continued to receive weapons and supplies from the Vietnamese, these were secretly provided and no longer shared with the neutralists. Nor were rightist forces any more ready to make supplies available. In desperation, after turning down previous offers, Suvanna accepted US deliveries of food, spare parts and communications equipment to neutralist forces. The move was denounced by the Pathēt Lao, who called for an end to the activities of Air America.

Differences among the neutralists over whether or not US aid should be accepted were thereafter skilfully exploited by the Pathēt Lao. The principal target for criticism was Colonel Ketsanā Vongsuvan, Kônglae's chief of staff, and principal architect of the resupply agreement. On 27 November 1962 an Air America transport plane was shot down as it came in to land on the Plain of Jars. The anti-aircraft unit responsible was under the command of neutralist Colonel Deuan Sunnarāt, an ambitious officer who had been critical of Kônglae's decision to accept US aid. When Colonel Ketsanā attempted to arrest those responsible, he was prevented by the Pathēt Lao. Thereafter he was a marked man. On 12 February 1963 – the day after King Savāngvatthanā, accompanied by Suvanna Phūmā and Foreign Minister Kinim Phonsēnā, left on a nine-nation tour to shore up international support for Lao neutrality – Ketsanā was assassinated. Kônglae responded by arresting suspects and forbidding access to neutralist-held areas by either Pathēt Lao cadres or troops under the command of Colonel Deuan. By mid-March, the split within neutralist ranks was definitive. Deuan threw in his lot with the Pathēt Lao, who assisted in consolidating his leadership of the 'Patriotic Neutralists'. So the die was cast. There would be no territorial reunification as in 1957, no attempt at integrating opposing forces.

On 1 April, the day after his return to Laos from accompanying the royal tour, Kinim too was assassinated by one of his own guards, apparently in revenge for the death of Ketsanā. The political repercussions were even more serious than those which followed the killing of Ku Vôravong. Recriminations were immediate. The subsequent murder of the neutralist police chief in Viang Chan by rightist military assassins[68] convinced Pathēt Lao ministers that their own lives were in danger. Both Suphānuvong and Phūmī Vongvichit left for Khang Khai. Though their ministries were held open for them in order to preserve the facade of the Provisional Government of National Union, the Second Coalition had effectively broken down. It had lasted nine months. The Americans blamed Pathēt Lao 'intransigence' and Suvanna's 'indecisive leadership',[69] but the causes went deeper. Not the Lao on either side, but the struggle for supremacy in Indochina between (North) Vietnam and the United States was responsible for the collapse of the Second Coalition.

One immediate effect was that fighting broke out between Kônglae's forces on the Plain of Jars and troops under the command of Colonel Deuan aided by the Pathēt Lao. Badly outnumbered, Kônglae's men were forced to retreat to a defensive perimeter confined to the western third of the Plain of Jars. Khang Khai, Xiang Khuang town, and the vital Plain of Jars airfield were all abandoned to the Pathēt Lao. Efforts by the ICSC (hamstrung by Polish intransigence), by the British and Soviet ambassadors representing the Geneva co-chairs, and by Suvanna Phūmā all failed to bring an end to the conflict. Suvanna's request for a permanent ICSC presence on the Plain of Jars was rejected by the Pathēt Lao, but a 'temporary' presence was allowed to continue. Each side blamed the other for the crisis.

Both the Pathēt Lao and the right took advantage of the division within neutralist ranks to reinforce their own positions. As the Pathēt Lao strengthened its defences around Khang Khai, the right parachuted reinforcements to Hmong outposts to the south of the Plain of Jars. Meanwhile in central and southern Laos, exposed neutralist garrisons withdrew, leaving large areas in Pathēt Lao hands. General Phūmī seized control of the former neutralist region of Thāthōm, 80 kilometres north of Pākxan, and occupied the former French military base at Xēnō. Pressure increased on both the dissident 'Patriotic Neutralists' of Colonel Deuan and those loyal to Kônglae to merge their identities with, respectively, the Pathēt Lao and the right. Though both resisted their political demise, both eventually succumbed for the same reason – total dependency for all military and food supplies on their respective allies. Unfortunately 'the neutralists had to beg, and begging could only lead to subjection'.[70] As DRV convoys trucked in weapons and supplies for the Pathēt Lao, the United States increased its own deliveries. Arms and ammunition as well as food and spare parts began to be supplied to Kônglae, who had been deprived of promised Soviet military assistance since the previous October.

The elimination of the neutralists as a significant military and political force progressed apace during the latter part of 1963, despite Suvanna's warning that 'only a very strong centralist party can prevent Laos from becoming Marxist', and that to weaken the neutralists would be 'stupidity'.[71] Both North Vietnam and the United States interfered directly in Lao affairs, in contravention of the Geneva Agreements. North Vietnamese units took over defence of the eastern border areas, through which ran the network of infiltration routes from North to South Vietnam making up the Ho Chi Minh trail. As Pathēt Lao agents bought up or requisitioned rice to supply increased numbers of Vietnamese troops working on or moving down the trail, a rice shortage resulted in southern Lao provinces. At the same time the United States stepped up its 'secret war' in the north. Supplies were by then being airdropped to over 15,000 Hmong guerrillas, grouped in 'special guerrilla units', and ten times that number of civilian refugees, most of them Hmong.[72] In addition to Hmong 'secret bases' in Xiang Khuang and Xam Neua, notably Vang Pao's headquarters at Lông Chaeng, guerrilla groups were established in Namthā province using Hmong, Mien and increasingly Khamu recruits reinforced by Thai and Nationalist Chinese mercenaries supplied from a Thai base west of Bān Huayxāy.[73] As of 1964, guerrilla units were also organized in the south to operate against the Ho Chi Minh trail, entirely independent of the command structure of the Royal Lao Army.[74]

As US military involvement in Laos once again expanded, General Phūmī became more brazen in his exercise of power. Once Suphānuvong and Phūmī Vongvichit had fled Viang Chan, leaving only two deputy ministers with a skeleton staff, and a handful of guards to maintain liaison, Phūmī devised what became known as the 'Special Office' to coordinate activities in various ministries and ensure that all important decisions were made by himself. The real source of his power, however, remained the Coordination, which maintained a climate of fear and tension in Viang Chan directed primarily against neutralist officers and civil servants. When Suvanna left Laos to attend the UN General Assembly in September 1963, numbers of neutralists sent their families out of the city, or left themselves for fear of Sīhō's police. All attempts to neutralize Viang Chan and Luang Phrabāng were blocked by Phūmī. Early in December, the rightist assassination of the commander of Suvanna's personal guard convinced more neutralists, including two left-leaning deputy ministers, to flee the capital.

By the end of 1963 the Second Coalition had irrevocably broken down and civil war had resumed. Neutrality had proved an impossible hope, as Laos was drawn ineluctably into the struggle in Vietnam. General Phūmī had resumed his position as strongman of the right, and Viang Chan was at the mercy of the Coordination. Corruption was once again rife, as military officers and politicians alike seized every opportunity to enrich themselves. Prostitution and gambling flourished (Phūmī opened a casino in the capital; Bunūm, not to be outdone, opened another in Pākxē), and Viang Chan boasted the world's largest legal opium den, housed in a converted theatre. US aid was flowing freely to the rightist armed forces, and increasing numbers of US personnel with military skills were at work not only in the office of the military attaché, but also in USAID and Air America, both of which acted as fronts for agents of the CIA. USAID in particular expanded rapidly to the point where its parallel administration included counterparts for virtually every government ministry and department, a structure that could only be described as neo-colonial.

As USAID increasingly functioned as a parallel administration, so it increasingly undermined the relationship between the Lao government and those it governed. For, as Christian Taillard has pointed out, the bond between governing and governed, or between centralized state and decentralized local power, rested traditionally on the payment of tribute and the reciprocal obligations that entailed. Failure to impose and collect a land tax, and the one-way flow of US development aid, freed rural communities of any obligation towards the central government and any expectation in return. But elimination of the responsibilities of rural communities to contribute to the state only weakened state authority. And as the gap separating rich from poor, and urban from rural lifestyles grew, the peasant response towards state officials became one not of envy, but indifference. By contrast, in villages under Pathēt Lao control the parallel hierarchy established by the LPF mobilized peasants, through membership of village associations and contributions of rice, in support of national goals proclaimed by leaders to whom they felt themselves closely bound in a common struggle.[75]

The economic impact of the American presence was reflected in rising prices and inflation. In part this resulted, however, from government failure to increase revenue. To tax the peasants, it was argued, would send them into the arms of the Pathēt Lao, and the elite had no intention of taxing themselves. So, to cover its perennial budget deficit, the government had resorted to printing money: the amount in circulation increased sevenfold between 1960 and 1965. At American urging, the *kip* was devalued to 240 to the US dollar, and a Foreign Exchange Operations Fund was established to stabilize the currency by financing the trade and current account deficits. (By 1964, imports were running at around thirty times the value of exports, while domestic revenue covered about one-fifth of expenditure.) The fund did little to encourage investment, however, for Chinese entrepreneurs kept their reserves in dollars and gold, not *kip*. By the mid-1960s, Chinese businessmen, many with Lao 'sleeping partners', had established some two hundred incorporated companies and more than three hundred small businesses in Viang Chan alone, where almost all this activity was located.[76] Yet an urban working class was slow to develop, for most enterprises employed few workers. Even in the vicinity of Viang Chan a majority of residents continued to earn much of their income from agriculture, for apart from its administrative centre the city was still little more than a collection of villages. As the war resumed, a growing number of refugees fled the fighting. Many were settled in new villages, but others made their way to the Mekong towns, adding to unemployment and swelling the urban population.

Yet Viang Chan in the early 1960s was a pleasant enough place to live, combining measured Lao charm with something of the feel of a frontier town. Yellow stucco villas of the French period were joined by others of brick and concrete built by the *nouveau riche* to rent to foreigners. Following his recapture of Viang Chan, Phūmī ordered the Avenue Lān Xāng widened and a vast 'victory monument', modelled on the Arc de Triomphe in Paris and popularly known as 'Phūmī's Folly', constructed opposite the National Assembly building. New morning and evening markets followed, and the Hotel Lān Xāng on the bank of the Mekong looking across to Thailand. But along with the new construction, religious as well as secular, went open drains and unsurfaced roads. Girlie bars and nightclubs catered for certain appetites; some fine restaurants for others. Lured by possible employment or cheap drugs, a trickle of Western backpackers arrived from Bangkok. A number stayed, drawn by the ambience of shady temples and a way of life whose pace was both gracious and relaxed. Those with an interest in politics could even visit the Pathēt Lao in their villa next to the morning market. For the more adventurous, some travel outside Viang Chan was still possible.

Increased wealth expended by growing numbers of foreigners not only raised urban living standards, but also provided a boost for Lao arts and crafts. While artists painted mainly traditional themes in a style insipid enough to appeal to foreign taste, fine arts, particularly wood-carving, weaving and silverwork, flourished. The finest weaving and embroidery were reserved for the *sin*, the traditional dress of Lao women, whose lavish borders revealed intricate and abstract designs in silk and fine gold thread. Also sought after were the large silver *repoussé* bowls in which women carried their offerings to the *vat*, and upon which Lao craftsmen lavished hundreds of hours of devoted labour.

On the political front, by early 1964 relations between rightist and neutralist forces could almost be described as cosy, much to American satisfaction. Reorganization of the neutralist command structure ordered by Suvanna had been completed, as had the re-equipping of neutralist forces with American weapons. Occasional disquiet expressed by some neutralists over their loss of independent identity was ignored. Even so, rightist–neutralist military cooperation was more effective in some areas than in others. The rout of their joint forces east of Thākhaek in January caused panic in the city, but the Pathēt Lao kept their distance. South of the Plain of Jars, Vang Pao's Hmong guerrillas mounted a series of small-scale attacks that gave notice of the shape of fighting to come. Relations were also strengthened between the Lao and South Vietnamese armies, permitting South Vietnamese 'liaison teams' to operate in southern Laos.

This drift of affairs was roundly denounced by the Pathēt Lao, who demanded that Luang Phrabāng be demilitarized and placed under control of a tripartite security force as a venue where the Provisional Government of National Union could meet free from the malicious attentions of the Coordination. Suvanna flew to Xam Neua to discuss the Pathēt Lao plan, then obtained the agreement of the King to the neutralization of the royal capital. But he still needed General Phūmī's assent, and Phūmī found his own position increasingly threatened by those jealous of his power. The Namthā fiasco and the death of Marshal Sarit had resulted in a loss of both US and Thai support. Sensing his political vulnerability, the powerful Xananikôn family accused Phūmī of not being sufficiently tough over the presence of North Vietnamese troops in Laos, and began scheming to bring about his downfall.

In early April, as skirmishing continued in several parts of the country, Suvanna flew to Beijing and Hanoi to obtain Chinese and Vietnamese support for dissociating Laos from the war in Vietnam. On his return he met with Suphānuvong and Phūmi at the neutralist military headquarters on the western edge of the Plain of Jars. There Suphānuvong insisted on the immediate neutralization of Luang Phrabāng as the venue for reforming the coalition government. Phūmi demurred, and the talks broke down.[77] On the evening of 18 April on his return to Viang Chan, Suvanna, tired and discouraged, announced his intention to resign as prime minister. Before dawn next morning, the airport, radio station and government buildings were occupied by Coordination police under the command of Police General Sīhō Lānphutthakun and troops loyal to General Kupasit Aphai, commander of the Viang Chan garrison. Those neutralists who failed to gain asylum in an embassy or with the ICSC were arrested and taken to the Coordination headquarters at Phōnkheng. Among them was the prime minister.

The next morning Radio Viang Chan announced that a 'Revolutionary Committee' had seized power. 'Realizing that the Government of National Union could do nothing, the Committee has taken the responsibility of assuming the maintenance of order in order to resolve the problems for the people', a radio announcement stated.[78] All government ministers, including General Phūmī, were dismissed. Army generals took over the various ministries. Further announcements during the day claimed that neutralists and rightists had unified their armed forces, and that Suvanna had surrendered all his powers to the Revolutionary Committee. Both claims were false. Behind the scenes, opposition to the coup was being coordinated by the diplomatic community.

The ambassadors of Britain and the Soviet Union, the United States, France and Australia, in a remarkable display of unanimity, refused any contact with the Revolutionary Committee, announced the severance of all aid to Laos, and declared their support for Suvanna Phūmā. The coup was violently denounced by the Pathēt Lao. By late afternoon, when official condemnation of the coup by the United States was known in Viang Chan, Suvanna was released. The following day Suvanna, Phūmī and the two coup leaders flew to Luang Phrabāng, where the King made known his displeasure. They were followed by the five ambassadors who made it equally clear to the King that their respective governments would support only Suvanna and his Provisional Government of National Union. The situation nevertheless remained tense. Suvanna was still under virtual house arrest. Kônglae at Vang Viang was threatening to march on Viang Chan with 7000 men, while Radio Pathēt Lao warned Suvanna not to give in to any demands of the Revolutionary Committee. Under such concerted pressure, the coup quickly collapsed.

Why it had been mounted in the first place was not entirely clear. Anger had been growing on the right over Suvanna's attempts to restore the coalition government. The right, by contrast, wanted to do away with the facade of the Provisional Government of National Union and fill the cabinet posts that Suvanna insisted on holding open for the Pathēt Lao. Another target, however, was Phūmī Nôsavan, for now that he was vulnerable, envious eyes coveted his illegal wealth (from gambling, opium, and gold smuggling). In the event, Phūmī hung on and within a few days Suvanna was back as prime minister. But a clear shift of power and allegiance had occurred.[79] Both Phumi and Suvanna saw their political influence eroded. Suvanna attempted to regain the initiative by announcing the merger of neutralist and rightist armed forces under his direction as Defence Minister. This was in accordance with the terms of the Geneva Agreements, Suvanna declared, and he invited the Pathēt Lao to take part. Few were convinced, however, that the army answered to Suvanna.

For its part, the Pathēt Lao denounced the move. In its view, Suvanna had lost all independence of action. At its Second Congress in April 1964, the LPF sought to consolidate the revolutionary movement for what it saw as the struggle ahead. An action program was adopted, comprising 'ten policies and five concrete tasks'. Pathēt Lao ministers refused to return to Viang Chan to take up their ministerial duties while the city remained under the control of the Coordination. As for the neutralists, imminent amalgamation with the right was enough further to divide their dwindling forces and 'several hundred' more troops defected to join Colonel Deuan's 'Patriotic Neutralists'.[80]

The Pathēt Lao capitalized on these defections in mid-May by launching what Suvanna described as a 'general offensive' to drive remaining neutralists from the Plain of Jars – with the overt assistance of Vietnamese forces.[81] Within days, almost the entire plain had been overrun. Only Meuang Suy on its western edge remained in neutralist hands. Subsequently the Pathēt Lao seized upon a reshuffle of neutralist cabinet positions, even though this did not conflict with the agreed division of portfolios, to denounce Suvanna and demand the return of its two deputy ministers still in Viang Chan. Both left for Khang Khai via Hanoi, leaving only a token Pathēt Lao representation in Viang Chan. Desperate diplomatic attempts to revive the coalition by bringing the three princes together again in Paris collapsed in mutual recrimination. In October 1964, a 'National Political Conference' brought about the formal alliance of the LPF with the 'Patriotic Neutralists'. As a political force, the divided neutralists had been reduced to mere appendages of the left and right.

The destruction of the Second Coalition was complete, but where did the blame lie? At one level it had been sabotaged by the activities of General Sīhō's police and undermined by intransigence of rightist military leaders intent on their own power play. At another level it had succumbed to the progressive polarization of political forces and the determination of both left and right to eliminate the neutralist centre. This was a political goal single-mindedly pursued by both, with the active encouragement of their respective backers. At the international level, both the United States and North Vietnam had hoped that Lao neutrality would secure them a strategic edge. When that proved a delusion, neither was prepared to abide by the strict terms of the Geneva Agreements if that meant surrendering any military advantage. Both therefore subverted Lao neutrality for their own ends – the United States rather more obviously than the DRV, although perhaps in response to DRV moves.[82] In the last analysis, the Second Coalition was the victim of the escalating contest of will and weaponry developing between North Vietnam and the United States to decide the future not only of Vietnam, but of all Indochina.

# CHAPTER 5

# WAR AND REVOLUTION, 1964–1975

Within a year of the signing of the 1962 Geneva Agreements, neutrality for Laos was no longer an option. As fighting in Vietnam escalated, Laos was increasingly drawn into the Second Indochina War – a war that spilled over the borders of South and North Vietnam to consume, and all but destroy, both Laos and Cambodia. If the suffering of Laos was less extreme in the end than that inflicted on Cambodia by civil war and the Khmer Rouge, it was more protracted and almost as damaging in its impact on the fragile social structure and economy of the country. More even than Cambodia, Laos was used by both principal protagonists with a callous disregard for those caught up in the fighting. The country's territorial integrity was violated with impunity by both North Vietnam and the United States, in the name of revolution or freedom, neither of which had much meaning for the great majority of the Lao people. What was portrayed by opposing sides as a heroic struggle against imperialism or communism was a drawn-out misery both for those directly involved, and for those whose only escape was to become refugees. As for those Lao Lum of the Mekong towns who were relatively untouched by the war, their suffering lay ahead.

Throughout these years of war, Laos was effectively divided into three regions of *de facto* foreign control: Vietnamese in the east, including the vital Ho Chi Minh trail; US and Thai in the west, the length of the Mekong valley; and Chinese in the north, where road construction gangs were at work. In both Royal Lao government and Pathēt Lao areas, Lao leaders were forced to come to an accommodation with their foreign patrons. Thus on both sides, Lao leaders became the tools, willing or not, of powerful outside forces whose use of Lao territory as an extension of their own conflict showed little concern for its impact on the Lao people.

In the zone controlled by the Royal Lao government, Suvanna Phūmā remained a forlorn figurehead, rejected by the right and kept in power only because the Americans needed him. All but alone in keeping the vision alive of a neutral and independent Laos, he was ultimately powerless to limit US involvement in and direction of the war, matters which were decided not by himself as nominal Defence Minister, but by the US administration and its embassy in Viang Chan.[1] In the face of American monopolization of both economic and military power, Suvanna was left with virtually no political leverage, apart from threatening his own resignation. That he remained prime minister was due largely to his own conviction, bolstered by US urging, that he was indispensable. Yet even Suvanna must have known that, were he to protest against US actions, he could always be replaced by a more pliable figure. In the Pathēt Lao zone the situation was little different. Decisions on the war in Laos were taken in North Vietnam by the Vietnamese supreme military command.[2] The leaders of the Pathēt Lao, equally dependent as they were both economically and militarily, were no more in a position to protest over the presence of Vietnamese forces in Laos and their use of Lao territory, had they wanted to, than was the Royal Lao government with respect to the Americans.

So for a decade from 1964 to 1973 Laos was subjected to the most savage warfare in the nation's history. Throughout this period, the vital tasks of economic development and construction of a modern nation state were overshadowed by the division and destruction of war. The bitterness that this engendered, not least among those minorities most deeply affected, left a lasting legacy. By the time the United States began disengaging from Indochina, the Pathēt Lao with massive Vietnamese communist support had greatly strengthened its position. Formal establishment of a Third Coalition government merely froze the administrative division of the country, and briefly postponed eventual Pathēt Lao seizure of power. It was only through the revolutionary replacement of the Kingdom of Laos by a communist regime that national unity was finally re-established, at the further cost of social and economic disruption and a prolonged haemorrhage of population.

## THE WAR IN LAOS

It is not the purpose of this history to delve into the origins of the Second Indochina War, nor to enquire into how it was fought by its principal protagonists. Nor is it to examine the strategic moves of either side, or explain their outcomes. Our concern, rather, is with the effect the war had on Laos, how the Lao themselves responded; and what the longer-term impact and implications were. For most of the decade from the renewed outbreak of fighting in 1964 to the cease-fire of 1973, the true extent of the the war in Laos remained largely hidden from the outside world by deliberate American deception. This was necessary from Washington's perspective to preserve the pretence of Lao neutrality, but it was possible only because for the United States the war in Laos was always of secondary importance. In a memorable phrase of Secretary of State Dean Rusk: 'After 1963 Laos was only the wart on the hog of Vietnam.'[3] So the 'tacit understanding' between the United States and North Vietnam was maintained, if only because the lifeless facade of the Geneva Agreements still acted as a convenient cover behind which both sides fought out their clandestine war in Laos.

May 1964 marked the beginning of the US air war over Laos. By then Suvanna had become increasingly disillusioned over mounting evidence, provided for him by the US Embassy, both of the extent of Pathēt Lao reliance on North Vietnam and of the increasing number

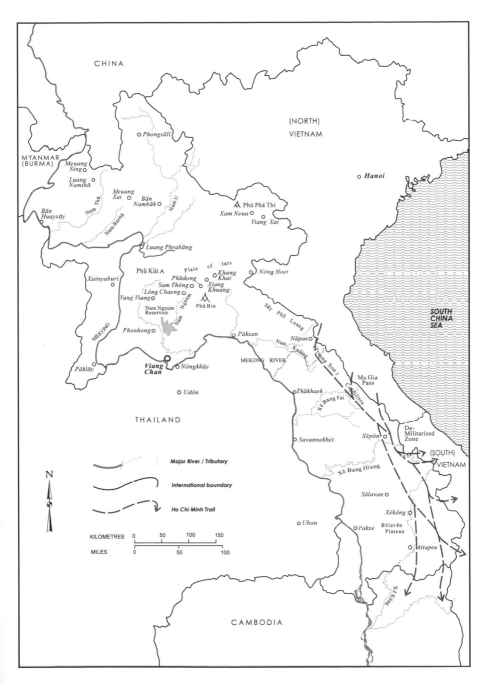

**Map 4** Laos in the Second Indochina War

of Vietnamese troops in Laos. Many of the contortions of the Pathēt Lao in refusing to cooperate with the ICSC had been due, Suvanna recognized, to the need to camouflage the extent to which they depended on their Vietnamese mentors. Suvanna's sense of betrayal in being deceived by the Pathēt Lao, and his desire to protect his country from communism, predisposed him to accept American arguments for the need to fight Vietnamese communism on its own terms. It was in this context that under pressure he agreed that American reconnaissance flights over the Plain of Jars should be protected by armed escort jets with the right to return anti-aircraft fire.

In a further escalation, Royal Lao Air Force T-28s, propeller-driven ground support fighter-bombers, began bombing Pathēt Lao and North Vietnamese targets. When a combined force of 'Patriotic Neutralists', Pathēt Lao and North Vietnamese mounted an offensive to drive Kônglae's neutralists from the Plain of Jars, the air force was reinforced by T-28s with Lao markings flown out of Thai bases by American and Thai pilots. The communists' goal was to recover the maximum extent of territory held jointly by Pathēt Lao and neutralist forces two years before, and in this they were almost entirely successful. Despite air support, Kônglae was forced to abandon his headquarters and retreat west. Renewed fighting provoked a renewed flurry of diplomatic activity. France and China both called for reconvening of the Geneva Conference, while Poland with Soviet blessing suggested as a first step a conference of only six states – Laos, the Soviet Union, Britain and the three ICSC member states. Both alternatives were rejected by the United States unless, as Suvanna demanded, there was an immediate cease-fire and Pathēt Lao forces withdrew from all recently captured territory. In reality it was already too late for diplomacy. Communist forces had no intention of surrendering territory won, and the United States preferred to use its military power.

A new escalation of the air war followed. US jets rocketed Pathēt Lao positions in retaliation for the shooting down of two US aircraft over the Plain of Jars, while Lao T-28 fighter-bombers attacked Pathēt Lao headquarters at Khang Khai, killing one Chinese diplomat and badly damaging the Chinese mission.[4] Annoyed that no Lao permission had been sought for the US retaliation, Suvanna responded to protests from Beijing and Hanoi by threatening resignation unless all such missions were terminated. The US Embassy went into damage control. Within two days Suvanna had agreed to resumption of what were euphemistically called 'armed reconnaissance' flights. Thereafter, from 1964 to 1970, all offensive action in the US air war over Laos was so described in order to maintain the facade of US adherence to the Geneva Agreements.

As fighting seesawed along the western and southern edges of the Plain of Jars, the United States went ahead with plans for the aerial interdiction of Vietnamese supply routes into and through Laos using US navy and air force jets rather than T-28s. To this Suvanna also gave his assent, providing there was no public announcement.[5] Operation Barrel Roll against targets in northern Laos officially began in December

1964, followed by regular bombardment of the Ho Chi Minh trail under the code name Operation Steel Tiger. Within a year, B-52 bombers flying out of Guam were regularly unloading their bombs against the trail, though not until February 1970 were B-52s deployed in the northern theatre.

The air war in Laos was not officially revealed to the American people or Congress for the best part of five years, despite being meticulously reported by both Pathēt Lao and North Vietnamese radio. The full extent of American bombing became public knowledge only after the findings of secret 1969 Congressional hearings by the US Senate Foreign Relations Committee were made public.[6] By the time the air war finally came to an end with the conclusion of a cease-fire agreement early in 1973, Laos had been subjected to some of the heaviest aerial bombardment in the history of warfare.

The ground war in Laos was conducted on two different levels. One was a war along a relatively well-defined line separating the two zones of control throughout most of the country. It was fought between regular Royal Lao Army and Pathēt Lao units, which in places contested strategic locations, but in others came to their own accommodation with each other. The other was the 'secret war', a more implacable and ruthless conflict fought without quarter, mainly in the mountains of northern Laos and often behind Pathēt Lao lines, by the 'Secret Army' (Armée clandestine) funded and directed by the CIA, though from 1965 on secret ground probes were also mounted against the Ho Chi Minh trail. Both the air and ground wars were not just authorized, but coordinated and directed, by the US ambassador in Viang Chan, free of any but the most minimal constraints to consult, or even inform, the Lao government or its military commanders.

For the United States, the importance of the war in Laos related directly to US involvement in Vietnam. What this meant in practice was that strategy in Laos was determined not by what might be required to bring a conclusion to the conflict there, but by what might contribute to an American victory in Vietnam. And the same was essentially true for the (North) Vietnamese. For both the United States and the DRV, two parts of Laos were of essential strategic importance: the Ho Chi Minh trail, providing multiple infiltration routes into South Vietnam; and the Plain of Jars, which Hanoi was determined to prevent the United States using as a staging area from which to threaten northern Vietnam. The air war was directed in support of both these principal theatres of conflict, while the ground war, but for relatively ineffective guerrilla activity against the Ho Chi Minh trail, was concentrated in the northern theatre.

Those who suffered most from the escalating conflict were populations living in the east of the country: overwhelmingly the highland minorities, Lao Thoeng and particularly Lao Sūng (Mien as well as Hmong), but also upland Tai, the Phuan of Xiang Khuang and the Phū-Tai of east central Laos. CIA attempts to recruit Lao Thoeng of the Bôlavēn, first as trail watchers, then as strike teams, resulted only in high casualties and loss of support for the Royal Lao government. As bombing intensified the length of the Ho Chi Minh trail, whole villages sought refuge deeper in the jungle. In the north, tens of thousands fled the fighting. The Plain of Jars was as thoroughly depopulated as it had been by Siamese depredations almost a century before. While the Pathēt Lao recruited and trained its guerrilla forces, much of the heaviest fighting on the communist side was borne by Vietnamese troops. The United States, by contrast, paid mercenaries to do the fighting. The greatest impact fell on the Hmong. In time the whole fabric of Hmong society began to unravel. Displaced villages on remote hilltops came to depend entirely on Air America for essential food supplies. With boys as young as fourteen recruited for war, women were left to bring up children as best they could – children who believed that rice came from the sky, and whose only future was to fight.

During the first four years of renewed warfare, a pattern of annual engagement developed. Communist gains made during the dry season (November to July) were won back by Royal Lao forces during the wet season when they enjoyed an advantage in mobility. Each side nevertheless attempted to gain strategic advantage. Thus in 1966 the two principal theatres of action were at Phū Kūt, a hill commanding the western approaches to the Plain of Jars which fell to communist attack in March, and the Nam Bāk valley some 80 kilometres northeast of Luang Phrabāng, which was occupied by the Royal Lao Army later in the year. Most fighting was, however, more indecisive, as neither side was eager to provoke the other unnecessarily. Only around the Plain of Jars had Hmong guerrillas by the end of 1967 begun to get the upper hand in their 'secret war'.

The year 1968 marked a turning point in the war in Laos, as it did for different reasons in Vietnam. The US response to the communist Viet Cong Tet Offensive in South Vietnam was to initiate protracted negotiations for an eventual end to the war. The only effect this had on the war in Laos, however, was to intensify fighting as both sides attempted to gain military advantage in the two strategic theatres that mattered – the Ho Chi Minh trail and the Plain of Jars. As increasing numbers of DRV replacements moved south to make up for losses suffered by Viet Cong forces during the Tet Offensive, so more were needed in Laos to defend and expand the Ho Chi Minh trail. Vietnamese forces were also increasingly involved in fighting on the side of the Pathēt Lao, notably in inflicting a major defeat on the Royal Lao Army by retaking the strategic valley of the Nam Bāk,[7] and on the Plain of Jars. The US response was to obliterate the towns of Xam Neua, Xiang Khuang and Khang Khai, until then off-limits as targets for US jets.[8] Each action served as a warning to the other side not to transgress their 'tacit understanding'. The Nam Bāk valley remained in Pathēt Lao hands, but fears that communist forces would advance on Luang Phrabāng proved as groundless as they had in 1953.

Instead Vietnamese and Pathēt Lao commanders turned their attention to Vang Pao's 'Secret Army'. One after another, Hmong villages serving as guerrilla bases in Huaphan province were overrun. The most serious loss was Phū Phā Thī, an almost vertical 2000-metre mountain peak less than 30 kilometres from the North Vietnamese border, atop which the US Air Force had built a radar guidance facility. For the few months it was operational, Phū Phā Thī was the most important US forward base directing both the bombing of North Vietnam, and the extraction by helicopter of downed US airmen. Several attempts had been made to destroy the facility, including one bombing raid by two antiquated North Vietnamese biplanes, the only time any US troops were subjected to air attack during the Second Indochina War. Finally, in March 1968, Vietnamese commandos succeeded in scaling the peak, killing several Hmong defenders and US technicians. US air strikes had to be called in to blow up the equipment.[9]

It has been argued that the decision to establish such a vital military facility at Phū Phā Thī marked a change of policy on the part of both CIA and US military planners which had such disastrous consequences for their Hmong allies that it amounted to betrayal. Initially US assistance had been given to help the Hmong protect their mountains from communist infiltration by the Pathēt Lao, backed by a vague promise of self-rule. Phū Phā Thī, as a fixed installation, convinced the North Vietnamese of the strategic need to occupy all northeastern Laos, at whatever cost. Thereafter the mountains of northeastern Laos became just another theatre of the war in Vietnam, in which the Hmong were increasingly used to mount set-piece operations designed to expose Vietnamese forces to massive US aerial bombardment. The result was greatly to increase Hmong casualties, while the original justification for their involvement in the war was forgotten.[10] All attempts to retake Phū Phā Thī failed, and other important Hmong bases were also lost. As morale wavered, some Hmong leaders even began planning escape routes west to Xainyaburī.

Three weeks after the fall of Phū Phā Thī, President Lyndon Johnson announced a partial halt to bombing over the northern part of North Vietnam. Its immediate effect was to escalate bombing in Laos, as aircraft that previously had flown hundreds of sorties daily over North Vietnam were directed against Lao targets instead. Interdiction of the Ho Chi Minh trail was stepped up, coordinated from a control centre at Udôn in Thailand.[11] In the north, Pathēt Lao targets in Huaphan and Xiang Khuang provinces were heavily bombed to relieve pressure on Hmong guerrilla bases. So intensive did the bombing become that Pathēt Lao leaders were forced to seek shelter deep inside the limestone grottoes of Viang Xai. From there they continued to direct, if not the ground war then under Vietnamese command, then at least their own political organization.[12] Recruitment and training of cadres remained a priority. Printing presses and even a few small factories producing such basic necessities as cloth and iron implements were relocated underground. As every village became a target, villagers throughout the Plain of Jars abandoned their homes and took refuge in the forest, where they lived as best they could literally in caves and holes in the ground. Health services and education, both assiduously promoted by the Pathēt Lao, inevitably suffered. Farming could only be carried on at night, in constant fear of triggering unexploded bombs.[13] Thousands fled the war zone, increasing the numbers of internal refugees to over 200,000, a large percentage of whom had to be supplied by the CIA's own airline – Air America.[14] The only area under communist control that was out of bounds to US jets was where Chinese army engineers were building a road network south from the Chinese border into northern Laos. Construction was in accordance with an agreement signed between the Lao and Chinese governments in January 1962, and a political decision was taken in Washington not to provoke China.[15]

As of 1969, the United States waged what the Pathēt Lao labelled as incoming US President Richard M. Nixon's 'intensified special war'. In Viang Chan the hawkish G. McMurtrie Godley took over as ambassador and enthusiastic director of the air war.[16] 'Secret Army' forces were built up in both northern and southern Laos, and the bombing intensified. In response, Pathēt Lao and North Vietnamese forces followed up their earlier victories at Nam Bāk and Phū Phā Thī with successful actions in the south where both the provincial capitals of Sālavan and Attapeu were surrounded and isolated. Thanks to a tacit understanding with the Military Region IV commander, General Phāsuk Rāxaphak, however, neither was overrun.[17] On the Plain of Jars no such accommodation was possible, and savage fighting continued at terrible cost to the Hmong, who were increasingly used not in the small-scale guerrilla operations at which they excelled, but in bloody battles for territory.[18] By 1969, virtually all of eastern Laos had become a free fire zone where US pilots could choose whatever targets they wished to unload their surplus bombs.

In the face of continuing US escalation, the DRV increased its own military intervention alongside the Pathēt Lao. More Vietnamese 'volunteer' forces entered Laos and more Vietnamese 'advisers' were assigned to reinforce Pathēt Lao units. Estimates placed the number of North Vietnamese troops operating in Laos at around 40,000, not including those in transit down the Ho Chi Minh trail.[19] Of this number, some 25,000 were assigned to maintain the trail itself, constructing roads and bridges, repairing bomb damage, running supply depots and field hospitals. The remaining 15,000 were assigned to the northeast. Pathēt Lao and 'Patriotic Neutralist' forces were estimated at 35,000, while the Royal Lao Army and Kônglae's neutralists numbered around 60,000 and 10,000 respectively.[20] Vang Pao commanded perhaps 40,000 in his 'Secret Army', scattered throughout Military Region II.[21] (In the far north, up to 10,000 Chinese troops were involved in road construction, though as noted these were never a target for US bombing, for fear of Chinese retaliation.)[22]

In mid-September 1969, as communist forces reeled under ferocious US bombing, Vang Pao's forces mounted a lightning offensive to reoccupy most of the Plain of Jars. Large quantities of weapons, equipment and ammunition were captured, but the victory was short-lived. With the end of the rainy season, as communist forces prepared for a new offensive, the remaining 30,000 Tai-Phuan who had not already fled the fighting were assembled and flown out to refugee centres near Viang Chan.

The Plain of Jars was too strategically important to North Vietnam to be left in Vang Pao's hands. Early in 1970 a combined force mainly consisting of DRV troops recaptured the entire plain, despite the first use of B-52 bombers. As 'Secret Army' forces withdrew, communist units pressed their attack. By mid-March they controlled the heights ('Skyline Ridge') overlooking Vang Pao's military headquarters at Long Chaeng and the principal Hmong refugee and administrative centre at Sam Thông. This was a veritable town whose population, including satellite settlements, then numbered around 40,000. As thousands of families evacuated Sam Thông, Vang Pao, with the aid of Thai artillery batteries, rallied his exhausted forces to save Lông Chaeng. Under intense aerial and artillery bombardment, Pathēt Lao and Vietnamese troops pulled back, but the cost had been appallingly high for Hmong units. They had fought to save their families, but were exhausted after years of war. Increasingly the 'Secret Army' was forced to rely on Thai army 'volunteers' to meet its manpower requirements.[23]

Military operations also escalated in southern Laos. On 18 March 1970 Prince Norodom Sihanouk was deposed as chief of state of Cambodia. Under agreements concluded in 1963 and 1964, Sihanouk had permitted Vietnamese communist forces to make use of Cambodian territory bordering South Vietnam, and had allowed war materials to be landed at the port of Kompong Som (Sihanoukville) for delivery to the National Liberation Front (Viet Cong).[24] Under Sihanouk's successor, General Lon Nol, both rights were withdrawn. Sihanouk's left-leaning neutrality, designed to keep Cambodia out of the Second Indochina War, was replaced by an alliance with the United States and the Republic of (South) Vietnam which drew Cambodia into the conflict. In April some 70,000 US and South Vietnamese troops drove into Cambodia. The same month Sihanouk, Suphānuvong, DRV prime minister Pham van Dong, and Nguyen Huu Tho, President of the South Vietnamese National Liberation Front, met together at a Summit Conference of Indochinese Peoples, where all pledged 'fraternal friendship' and 'mutual support in the struggle against the common enemy'.[25] Despite a growing desire on the part of the United States to extricate its forces from Vietnam, the Second Indochina War, like the First, had engulfed all Indochina.

The invasion of Cambodia forced Vietnamese communist units to withdraw either deeper into Cambodia or back up the Ho Chi Minh trail into southern Laos. More significantly for Laos, the change of regime in Cambodia increased the importance of the Ho Chi Minh trail as the sole remaining supply route for communist forces in South Vietnam. The decision was therefore taken to consolidate communist control of southern Laos. Pathēt Lao forces seized the long-isolated and indefensible provincial capitals of Attapeu (April), and Sālavan (June). As the DRV tried to compensate for the loss of supply routes in Cambodia by sending ever greater quantities through Laos once the monsoon season was over, fighting over the trail intensified. The number of sorties flown against targets in southern Laos increased to an average of 200 a day, often including round-the-clock bombing by B-52s. Their effectiveness, however, despite the electronic gadgetry used to locate well-camouflaged communist units, was less than claimed. So early in 1971 ground forces for the first and last time attempted to cut the trail.[26]

Operation Lam Son 719 was launched on 31 January, when 20,000 South Vietnamese troops struck west along Route 9 from Khe San towards Xēpōn. It was a target they never reached. Suvanna, who had been notified in advance, issued a *pro forma* condemnation demanding withdrawal of all foreign troops and respect for the Geneva Agreements, and declared a nationwide state of emergency. No forces of the Royal Lao Army were involved, though the army mounted a diversionary thrust further west.[27] The invasion was aptly described as 'a classic military failure: poorly planned, poorly executed, and based on poor intelligence'.[28] By mid-March, after suffering heavy casualties, the South Vietnamese were forced rather precipitously to withdraw, leaving DRV units still in control of the trail. In a booklet that convinced no-one, the Pathēt Lao claimed credit for the victory.[29] By mid-June communist troops had consolidated their 'Route 9–Southern Laos victory' by seizing the entire Bôlavēn region.

In the north, the pattern of seesaw fighting was repeated. 'Secret Army' forces backed by Thai mercenaries again seized parts of the Plain of Jars in a wet-season offensive, only to lose all by the year's end. As the Vietnamese brought up tanks and new heavy artillery, Hmong and Thai defenders at Lông Chaeng again fought off sustained attack. By this time US supply flights were dropping food to 170,000 refugees in northern Laos alone, 80 per cent of them Hmong.[30] Thousands more had moved to areas controlled by the Royal Lao government, leaving forever their beloved mountains, while others had gone over to the Pathēt Lao. By 1972 the war in northern Laos had become increasingly internationalized through the expanding role of Thai 'special guerrilla units' to make up the terrible losses suffered by the 'Secret Army'. An estimated 30,000 Hmong had died, more than 10 per cent of the Lao Hmong population.[31] Despite peace negotiations in Paris, more were still dying in the mountains skirting the Plain of Jars, by then a bombed-out moonscape of craters strewn with unexploded cluster bomblets. In the south, the Bôlavēn plateau remained in Pathēt Lao hands.

By the time a cease-fire was declared early in 1973, over two million tonnes of bombs had been dropped on the Pathēt Lao zone, or more than two tonnes for every inhabitant.[32] The destruction was horrific. Almost all the 3500 villages under Pathēt Lao control had been partly or wholly destroyed. Loss of life on both sides can only be guessed at, but 200,000 dead and twice that number of wounded would be a conservative estimate. At one time or another as many as three-quarters of a million people, a quarter of the entire population, had been driven from their homes to become refugees in their own country.[33] These were the bare statistics, but the impact was also deeply damaging in less tangible ways, in the terror and trauma that scarred individual lives, in families uprooted and torn apart, in social disintegration. The war placed intolerable strains on upland Lao society, weakened the Lao state, corrupted the morality of public life, and set back the cause of national unity and reconciliation. So what, if anything, did it achieve?

US bombing never stemmed the flow of men and matériel down the Ho Chi Minh trail. Nor, despite its sacrifice and heroism, did the 'Secret Army' succeed in holding the Plain of Jars for more than a few months or prevent vital targeting and rescue facilities from eventually being overrun. Vietnamese forces were forced to pay a terrible price for their use of Lao territory, yet nothing that happened in Laos proved to be decisive for the war in Vietnam – unless it was the defeat of Lam Son 719 foreshadowing, as it did, the climactic defeat of the South Vietnamese army four years later.

## THE LAO PREDICAMENT

War tests the cohesion of any society, but civil war exerts far greater strains. Whatever it was for the Americans and Vietnamese, for the Lao the conflict in Laos was a civil war, in which both sides were manipulated by far more powerful forces in conflict for altogether different reasons. This disparity of power between allies on both sides reduced the Lao to a debilitating level of dependency. Decisions were taken out of Lao hands, and Lao leaders were forced to watch helplessly as events unrolled. But whereas on the side of the Pathēt Lao war reinforced the relationship between army and Party (through recruitment, organization and propaganda), on the Royal Lao government side political contradictions and the regional command structure of the armed forces weakened the centralizing structures of an already weak state.

The role of the respective armies differed on each side during this decade of war. Whereas for the Pathēt Lao the Lao People's Liberation Army[34] acted as a closely integrated arm of the Party, on the government side the Royal Lao Army both challenged, and was virtually independent of, political control. In the Pathēt Lao zone the Lao People's Liberation Army mobilized and trained tribal youths in the name of the Party, nationalism and revolution. It thus acted as a force for both social integration and organization, while offering opportunities for individual advancement. Rewards lay in the conviction that the cause was just, and in the promise of future rewards. The Royal Lao Army also offered social mobility. Young officers, many from rural backgrounds, chose the army as a career promising power and status. But there the similarity ended. Except for the organizationally separate 'Secret Army', recruitment into the Royal Lao Army was confined to Lao Lum and so did nothing to advance the cause of ethnic integration. And for too many motivation lay not in patriotic duty, but in desire for personal gain.

Where the two armies differed most was in their relation to political authority. Whereas the Lao People's Liberation Army reinforced the authority of the Party acting through the LPF, the Royal Lao Army consistently undermined the authority of the Royal Lao government and weakened the Lao state. The eclipse of General Phūmī Nôsavan, and the US decision to back Suvanna rather than an alternative military strongman, left the Royal Lao Army without a powerful commander. Army Chief of Staff Uan Rāttikun was more interested in his business dealings than in running the army. Taking their lead from General Vang

Pao in Military Region II and General Phāsuk Rāxaphak in Military Region IV, commanders of the five military regions became virtual warlords in their respective fiefdoms.[35] Down to the district level, army officers usurped authority from civilian bureaucrats. If not deliberately encouraged by the United States, this 'warlordism' was promoted by direct supply and advice to regional commands. Local alliances with regional clans opposed to Suvanna (General Phāsuk was known as Bunūm's man) further undermined central state power.

Not only were the command structure and discipline weaker in the Royal Lao Army than in the Lao People's Liberation Army, and its relationship to civilian authority much more problematical, but it developed its own demoralizing culture of corruption. With the Hmong and Kônglae's neutralists bearing the brunt of the serious fighting, senior officers of the Royal Lao Army found time to pursue their own contest for power and profit. The focus of contention was General Phūmī Nôsavan, but behind the antagonism that pitted officers loyal to Phūmī against those who opposed him lay regional and family rivalries, and competition for the spoils of office. Dissension also arose over the merger of rightist and neutralist armed forces, particularly appointments to the reorganized high command. These strains lay behind an incident in January 1965, when a small group of rightist officers briefly seized the radio station in Viang Chan, demanding an end to corruption and politicking in the army and improved conditions for soldiers and civil servants. Although Suvanna tried desperately to defuse the crisis, the incident was enough to bring tensions within the armed forces to a head. Fighting erupted between police of Sīhō's National Directorate for Coordination loyal to Phūmī, and troops from Military Region V base camp at Chīnāymō on the outskirts of Viang Chan under the command of General Kupasit Aphai. As the latter gained the upper hand, Phūmī and Sīhō fled to Thailand, leaving Kupasit in control of the capital.[36] Minor mutinies in Phūmī's name broke out subsequently in Thākhaek and Pākxan, but were easily contained. Sīhō's power was finally broken when the hated Coordination was disbanded and a Lao National Police force established under the Ministry of the Interior.

The fall of General Phūmī Nôsavan owed much to loss of US and Thai backing. The death of the Thai dictator Marshal Sarit had deprived Phūmī of an important source of financial and military support. Also Suvanna's assumption of the Defence portfolio meant that Phūmī could no longer dispense the patronage he once had in the Royal Lao Army. Jealous officers had cast envious eyes on his business dealings. When he fled, they were only too ready to carve up his empire of drugs, prostitution, gambling and gold smuggling. Thus General Ūan took control of the opium trade and heroin manufacture just as the influx of US troops into South Vietnam provided a ready and expanding market for drugs. Lao and South Vietnamese army officers worked closely to smuggle drugs and gold from Laos into South Vietnam. Other officers smuggled timber to Thailand, or put the squeeze on the Chinese business community. Some rightist officers even sold military equipment to the Pathēt Lao. The example provided to junior officers of greed and corruption at the highest levels in the officer corps did much to impair the quality of military leadership by increasing cynicism and undermining morale. As the spoils of office took precedence over the war effort, discipline suffered. In October 1966, following a disagreement over opium shipments, the Lao Air Force bombed army headquarters on the outskirts of Viang Chan; while a power struggle among neutralist officers forced Kônglae into exile in France.

Nothing could better illustrate the priorities of senior officers of the Royal Lao Army, however, than the military engagement fought in 1967 that became known as the 'opium war'. In Al McCoy's account, based on interviews with General Uan Rāttikun and several others involved in or knowledgeable about opium trafficking, fighting erupted when a Shan warlord from Burma attempted to break the stranglehold that Nationalist Chinese army units based in northern Thailand had on the heroin trade in the so-called Golden Triangle. An attempt was made to drive a pack-horse caravan laden with raw opium from Burma into Laos to supply General Uan's opium refineries near Bān Huayxāy. When former Nationalist Chinese soldiers crossed into Laos in an attempt to head off the caravan and seize the merchandise, Uan bombed both sides and sent in his own troops. Quick victory guaranteed him a regular supply of Burmese opium thereafter. It was added to that grown in northern Laos to meet the growing demand from US troops in South Vietnam for refined heroin.[37]

On the political front, despite the war, it was politics as usual. Though fighting prevented the holding of overdue elections, constitutional amendments permitted an interim National Assembly to be elected on restricted suffrage in July 1965, a compromise measure that seemed to indicate growing political maturity. Political debate continued to be lively, fanned by four daily newspapers of varying anti-communist complexions. But the impression of a healthy political culture was misleading. The structure of the Second Coalition and the need to prop up its lifeless shell imposed a strait-jacket on Lao politics. Suvanna himself was a political prisoner who owed his position not to the support of an organized party, nor to his own uncharismatic personality, but to a decision by the United States, backed by other Western powers, that he had to remain prime minister in order to preserve the pretence of Lao neutrality. This might have protected Suvanna from the machinations of his right-wing opponents, who were united only in their desire to get rid of him, but it left him powerless to play any decisive role in extricating his country from its agony. All Suvanna could do was to reiterate what he stood for, namely Lao independence and neutrality, while waiting for the balance of opportunity to shift in his favour. In the meantime, nothing that either the National Assembly or the government decided could make any difference to the conduct of the war. By 1966, therefore, the United States was as fully in control of the political agenda in Laos as it had been in 1959–60.

Why for a decade did Suvanna play the US game? After all, he could easily have retired in despair or disgust to a comfortable bourgeois existence in France. That he stayed was partly because he genuinely believed in Lao neutrality and the need to keep the idea alive, and partly because he was convinced that he alone had the vision and capacity to lead his country. Suvanna knew better than anyone that for a small, weak, strategically situated country like Laos, neutrality was the only rational foreign policy to pursue, 'imposed on us', as he pointed out, 'by the existence of a thousand kilometres of common borders with countries of the socialist camp'.[38] Even the threadbare pretence of Lao neutrality was preferable to its total abandonment. Besides, he had become deeply concerned about Vietnamese intentions and influence. No longer did he believe the Pathēt Lao were primarily nationalists. Rather they were dupes and puppets of the Vietnamese, whose forces had to be resisted: Suvanna sanctioned American bombing in Laos against *Vietnamese* targets. Once foreign forces withdrew he was determined that the bombing would stop, and political accommodation sought with the Pathēt Lao.[39]

Suvanna's relationship with the United States during this decade of war was never one of subservience. His prickly pride led him to threaten resignation more than once, and he attempted to keep some distance between himself and the US Embassy. He rejected any suggestion that US ground forces might be committed in Laos, and denounced the South Vietnamese attempt to cut the Ho Chi Minh trail. Never did he close off relations with either China or North Vietnam, and the door was always open for renewed talks with the Pathēt Lao. As for the Americans, they not only needed him but recognized his qualities. Suvanna was attracted by neither power nor the spoils of office. He was a patriot and, that rare occurrence in US-dependent regimes, a statesman of personal probity.

If US intervention in Laos failed to undermine the integrity of Suvanna, it had a corrosive effect on Lao political culture. US direction of the war meant that Lao politicians were no longer in a position to decide those matters of greatest national concern. In their place was left only the politics of personal gain, for wealth or status, in a capital strangely insulated from the reality of war.[40] Failure to face up to the political responsibilities of a country at war was evident in the response of the National Assembly to government attempts to limit the growing budget deficit. Moves to increase revenue by raising taxes and import duties on luxury goods were angrily denounced. When in September 1966, the Assembly rejected the budget for the coming year, Suvanna took this as a vote of no confidence, and called for new elections. These were held in January 1967, despite the war, only to be denounced by the Pathēt Lao as 'illegal, secessionist and reactionary'.[41] But at least the result reflected more closely than the previous Assembly the regional power balance and the influence of powerful families. Their influence on national policy was, however, limited. Deputies were well aware of the determination of the United States both to maintain Suvanna as prime minister and to retain the facade of Lao neutrality. Since these were not matters for debate, they tended to go along with the government while devoting most of their energies to feathering their own nests through the usual means of graft and tax evasion.

By the late 1960s, corruption permeated all levels of Lao society. The war brought with it a misleading air of prosperity to the Mekong towns: misleading because it depended almost entirely on US military spending, a substantial portion of which found its way into private pockets. While military expenditure made up much of the Lao budget, some resources were channelled into urban improvement, rural extension programs, infrastructure development, and health and education as part of an interim two-year economic development program. In Viang Chan roads were surfaced, drains dug, and the first traffic lights installed, such projects providing welcome opportunities for commissions and kickbacks. The increased level of affluence due to US aid was evident in the number of motor cycles on the streets, and general consumer spending. A telephone link was established between Viang Chan and Luang Phrabāng, and work commenced on the Nam Ngeum dam under the auspices of the Mekong Development Committee. More new villas were built for rent to foreigners at exorbitant rates. Some private investment in industry also occurred, mainly by Chinese, with new factories established for food processing, metal working, and the manufacture of basic chemicals.[42] In 1969, the government unveiled a new five-year plan which concentrated investment in a number of large-scale projects (including work on the Nam Ngeum dam and two other small hydroelectric projects). The plan also envisaged an increase in the public service (to 16,000), and increased expenditure on education (to 15 per cent of the total budget) and health (to 5 per cent). Despite its optimistic assessments and forecast, however, the real state of the economy and the degree of its dependency on foreign aid were indicated by the continuing disparities between revenue and expenditure and between exports and imports.[43] The dependency of the Royal Lao regime on the United States was economic as well as military and political.

Except for the influx of impoverished refugees who sought employment and accommodation, the war left the Mekong towns virtually unscathed. Thākhaek was threatened and the airport at Luang Phrabāng mortared, but the Pathēt Lao never mounted an urban terror campaign. The destruction wrought by the war was concentrated almost entirely in areas controlled by the Pathēt Lao. Despite the constant bombing and general level of poverty, however, the Pathēt Lao continued to exercise effective administration of its zone. Programs dating from before the beginning of the air war included partial collectivization of agriculture, a literacy campaign, and an educational program providing four years of primary schooling and training for teachers, administrative cadres and health workers. Political education was, of course, given high priority and villagers were inducted into 'associations' according to either age and gender (women, youth) or employment (agriculture, education, administration).[44] Regular meetings were held to denounce the United States and the government in Viang Chan. A revolutionary historiography gave shape and meaning to the Pathēt Lao as a movement of resistance of all ethnic groups, while revolutionary political literature told how heroic partisans of the Lao Patriotic Front triumphed in love and war over those who had sold their country to the Americans.

Recapture of the Plain of Jars in September 1969 and questioning of the displaced population allowed a rare insight into Pathēt Lao methods of administration and the changes they had introduced. Two changes in particular were notable. To the usual administrative hierarchy of village and district chiefs had been added a political hierarchy of representatives of the LPF. These were elected according to criteria that included both local popularity and influence, and political commitment and activism. This political hierarchy had the dual role of propagating the official line of the Lao People's Party and of informing the Party centre of local conditions. A second development entailed use of traditional forms of cooperation, sharpened by the extremes of adversity experienced by most communities, to develop a sense of solidarity and commitment to the revolutionary cause. Even the rice tax functioned to the same end. Contributions of around 15 per cent of the crop were put aside to feed the soldiers of the Lao People's Liberation Army, who in turn were recruited from each village.

As the bombing in the Pathēt Lao zone intensified, however, in places the social fabric began to disintegrate. As villages throughout the zone became targets for US jets with nothing else to bomb, thousands fled deeper into the mountains, or swelled the numbers of refugees. Those who remained led a precarious existence in constant fear of the rain of death from the skies. What is remarkable, in retrospect and given these circumstances, is how effective Pathēt Lao organization and propaganda were in generating and maintaining a sense of revolutionary solidarity and anti-imperialist nationalism. For the first time in Lao history, all ethnic groups were drawn together in a national struggle for independence whose roots lay in the series of ethnic-based revolts against French colonialism. The Vietnamese, fighting and dying alongside their Lao comrades, were successfully portrayed as friends and protectors. America was the demonic adversary.

## THE PATH TO PEACE

The Pathēt Lao reaction to intensified military pressure was defiant. At the end of October 1968, the Lao Patriotic Front held its Third National Congress. A twelve-point political program was announced, the thrust of which was to call for national unity in the face of 'US imperialist aggression', for formation of a 'Government of National Union', and the holding of general elections.[45] The moderate tone of the document, which included respect for the monarchy and Buddhism, coinciding as it did with a complete halt to US bombing of North Vietnam and commitment to a negotiated end to the Vietnam War, seemed designed to provide the basis for a similar settlement in Laos. Suvanna responded by again calling for talks between the government and the Pathēt Lao, but the initiative died in the face of Nixon's 'intensified special war'.

Suvanna had never abandoned his belief that, left to themselves, the Lao could work out a solution to their own problems, if only the DRV would withdraw its forces from Laos.[46] But 1969 was not an auspicious time. The Pathēt Lao denounced Suvanna as a 'traitor, capitulationist, and a follower of the US aggressors'. A suggestion that the Plain of Jars be neutralized was rejected. Settlement of the conflict, in the view of the Pathēt Lao, required prior cessation of all US military activity, followed by US withdrawal from Laos. Only then could a new government be formed on the basis of the 1962 Geneva Agreements, taking account of 'the reality of the present situation'.[47] In other words, negotiations between the two sides ('tripartite' talks were suggested) should lead to reconstitution of the coalition government with additional representation for the Pathēt Lao and 'Patriotic Neutralists' to reflect their enhanced military position – but only after the United States was out of the picture. From this precondition the Pathēt Lao never retreated. In March 1970, the Central Committee of the LPF summed up its demands in its 'five-point peace program' for a political settlement 'based on the principle of equality and national concord'. Suvanna responded with his own proposal for the verified withdrawal of *all* foreign troops, though he did hint that he might accept continued use of the Ho Chi Minh trail by the DRV, provided Vietnamese forces were withdrawn from populated areas.[48]

With the overthrow of Sihanouk in Cambodia, however, the war once again intervened. The military events of 1970 and the first half of 1971 (Pathēt Lao capture of Attapeu and Sālavan; the failure of operation Lam Son 719) brought renewed political pressure to bear on Suvanna. On the right, criticism of his continuing commitment to neutrality and preparedness to negotiate with the Pathēt Lao came especially from the south, orchestrated by Bunūm. Suvanna attempted to counter such criticism by appointing Sīsuk na Champāsak, Bunūm's nephew, as his delegate at the Ministry of Defence in charge of day-to-day direction of the military, and thus effectively his deputy and heir apparent – a move that only provoked more clan jealousy and rivalry, especially from the Xananikôns.[49] Sīsuk used his new powers to reorganize the high command of the Royal Lao Army in order to reduce the autonomy of regional commanders, increase efficiency, and curb corruption in the armed forces. His partial success signalled a net increase in the influence of southerners in the government, which a visit by the King to southern Laos, his first in ten years, seemed to reinforce. Yet even at such a time of national peril any apparent unity of the right was illusory, and the culture of corruption still flourished.

By the early 1970s Laos was a nation deeply weary of war and the corruption it had spawned. The events of the previous decade, in particular the loss of national sovereignty, had led to widespread disillusionment and deeply discredited both politics and politicians. The popular response took two forms: escapism through the pursuit of private pleasure, and anger over what was happening to the country. Both were reflected in a sudden efflorescence of popular writing in the form of sentimental or comic escapism on the one hand, and social criticism on the other. While the former, similar to popular novels and short stories published in Thailand or South Vietnam, told of love unrequited or laughed at plans gone awry, the latter pursued themes of social justice and the corruption of authority, thus contributing to the politicization of Lao youth.[50] Unlike the publications of the Pathēt Lao, neither did anything to strengthen resolve or support the war effort.

Dissatisfaction over the quality of political leadership was widespread, especially among young intellectuals who formed their own political party to contest the National Assembly elections of January 1972. Even though they refused to buy votes (vote-buying had replaced vote-rigging as the preferred way to win elections), their candidates won three out of fifty-nine seats. Only eighteen former sitting members were returned, many others being too corrupt and discredited to stand. But those who replaced them, with a few honourable exceptions, were still nominees either of powerful regional clans or of military leaders. They did not represent organized and disciplined political parties, nor did they offer any vision for the future of the country. Indeed most new deputies were more interested in the perquisites of office than in the parlous state of the nation. Most were men who could be bought and sold, and this the Xananikôns proceeded to do. They stitched together a shaky majority in opposition to Suvanna, which collapsed as soon as it became evident that international support for the prime minister had not wavered.

Though peace talks between North Vietnam and the United States seemed stalled, 1972 was a US presidential election year and some sort of agreement seemed likely, if only to ensure Richard Nixon's re-election. The move against Suvanna should thus be seen as part of the political jockeying for power prior to a peace agreement. Its failure only further divided political opinion and weakened the cohesion of the right. By contrast, in the limestone caves of Viang Xai, the Pathēt Lao were, without publicity, readying themselves for the next stage in the struggle for power. There, in February 1972, the clandestine Lao People's Party held its Second Congress to plan its strategy for the negotiations that lay ahead. Its name was changed to the Lao People's Revolutionary Party; Kaisôn Phomvihān was confirmed as Secretary-General; and a seven-member Political Bureau was elected, along with a 24-member Central Committee. The secret resolution passed by the Congress not only endorsed the LPF five-point peace proposal, but also laid down the political line to be followed once peace had been achieved. For public consumption, the objectives of the LPF – peace, independence, neutrality, democracy, reunification and prosperity – were designed to appeal to people weary of war, while the contrast between the self-serving corruption and division that characterized the political right and the apparent cohesion and commitment of the Pathēt Lao carried its own potent message.

In July 1972 Suvanna formally accepted the five-point proposal that the LPF had put forward two years before as the basis for renewed peace negotiations. It was enough, given the changed circumstances, to bridge the stand-off. A month later the two sides at last met in face-to-face talks in Viang Chan. Immediately differences in the professionalism, efficiency and above all the discipline of the two delegations were evident. As the meetings made little progress, each side accused the

other of failing to negotiate in good faith. Each demanded prior withdrawal of foreign forces supporting the other as a precondition for
substantive negotiations. Though in late September both sides dropped
all preconditions, the shadow boxing continued, for as each side well
knew, no cease-fire in Laos could be concluded prior to a peace settlement in Vietnam. In Paris, North Vietnamese chief negotiator Le Duc
Tho spelled out the link when he assured US Secretary of State Henry
Kissinger that 'Hanoi would bring about a cease-fire in Laos within
thirty days of the cease-fire in Vietnam'.[51]

On 23 January 1973 an agreement was finally announced between the
United States and the DRV, and pressure mounted on both sides in Laos
to conclude their negotiations. As an added incentive, US aircraft continued to bomb communist positions in Laos. Within a month, as Le
Duc Tho had promised, concessions from both sides resulted in signature of the required cease-fire, even if the Agreement on the Restoration
of Peace and National Reconciliation left important political differences
unresolved. It took until mid-year for residual skirmishing to taper off,
but after a decade of the most destructive warfare in the nation's
history, Laos was at last at peace. Bitter enmities remained, even as Thai
forces withdrew and the remnants of the 'Secret Army' were integrated
into the Royal Lao Army.

From 1964 to 1973 the Second Indochina War in all its savagery had
spilled over into Laos. But the burden of war had not been equally
borne. Most affected were the country's ethnic minorities, none more
than the Lao Sūng, the Hmong in particular. The Lao Thoeng also suffered severely, in both northern Laos and the south in the Bôlavēn
region.[52] The lowland Lao suffered least, with many of their leaders
profiting greatly. Sons and fathers went off to war, but life for their
families left behind in the Mekong towns and villages that remained
under government control was otherwise little touched by the war.
Guerrilla raids against military facilities on the outskirts of Viang Chan,
Luang Phrabāng, or Pākxē were infrequent and soon forgotten. Fear of
communist advance on Bān Huayxāy, Thākhaek or Pākxan caused
occasional panic, but even those who fled across the river to Thailand
soon returned.

The war was a tragedy for Laos, not least because it was beyond the
power of any Lao to control. Both sides were reduced to the status of
instruments of more powerful nations whose own interests took precedence over those of Laos and the Lao. Both the United States and the
DRV consistently lied over what each was doing in Laos, and though
few were fooled, least of all the Lao themselves, the very deception
demeaned the nation's independence and international standing. All
the international guarantees of Lao neutrality provided by the 1962
Geneva Agreements did nothing to protect the country, though maintenance of the facade did leave the way open for an eventual political
settlement. At no time did the Pathēt Lao seek to establish a rival
government as in South Vietnam and Cambodia.

War did, as so often, stimulate the economy. Yet the more than
$500 million of US economic assistance that flowed into the country

during this decade did little to promote either private investment or infrastructure development. Most so-called development aid was actually channelled into 'war-related activities', listed by the director of USAID (Laos) as providing medical care and basic subsistence needs for war victims, air support and transportation, and emergency assistance for the flood of refugees.[53] Other aid went to ensure economic stability through contributions to the Foreign Exchange Operations Fund to support the value of the *kip*; to maintain a 'minimum level of government service' by meeting the annual budget deficit; for 'social infrastructure', principally health and education; and, last on the list, to stimulate economic development.[54] Per capita gross national product crept up from about $50 to $70, but it was unevenly distributed: the average for the 'unmonetized village economy' (still 80 per cent of the population) was less than one-third of that of the 'monetized sector'.[55]

The most laudable achievements were in health and education, through hospital construction and the Lao-language Fā Ngum technical schools. Agriculture suffered as a result of the war. The Agricultural Development Organization set up in 1965 failed to achieve its goal of stimulating production of one million tonnes of rice (a one-third increase on 1965 figures), even though new varieties were introduced. Indeed Laos had to import up to $4.5 million worth of rice per annum. Industry remained rudimentary, with local manufacturing producing only a handful of basic items such as soft drinks and cigarettes, plastics and a few chemicals. Everything else had to be imported. Tin mining reached a maximum production of 1500 tonnes of concentrates in 1971, but declined thereafter. The only other significant exports were timber and forest products. Loans to assist private industry amounted to less than half a million dollars for six enterprises; while aid devoted to development projects for the decade 1962–73 was just over $15 million (2.8 per cent of total US aid provided),[56] most of it for the Nam Ngeum dam project. US aid, it is legitimate to conclude, was used not primarily for economic development, but for 'economic, cultural and political domination'.[57]

It was the means by which such domination was achieved that was so damaging. The Americans, like the French before them, found the Lao to be charming, courteous and sensitive, and many an American fell under the Lao spell. But this did not prevent them from treating the Lao much as the French had done, as incompetent, lazy and childlike. So just as the swollen US Embassy usurped political power, so did the parallel organization established by USAID usurp administrative power – in the name of efficiency and necessity. The effect was to undermine and weaken the political and bureaucratic structures of the Lao state. As the United States centralized power in support of its war effort, the Lao government saw its own power fragment. Essential services became the responsibility of USAID departments, whose Lao staff were paid more than even senior Lao civil servants. Aid administered by the United States became, in the words of one report, 'a substitute for national effort'.[58] Far from strengthening the Lao bureaucracy, USAID's parallel administration left it weak and divided, lacking a sense of purpose and responsibility, and ill-equipped to meet the challenges ahead.

The American impact on Lao society was almost as damaging. During two decades of rapid change, Lao society had become more sophisticated, more complex, more modern, but also more morally lax, more materialistic and hedonistic, more corrupt. New avenues for social mobility had opened up through the army, the bureaucracy, business, or in working for the Americans, building on improved opportunities for education and even study abroad. Foundations were thus being laid for development of civil society centred on an expanding, if still small, educated class. Though influence-peddling in business or employment was deeply rooted in Lao culture, talent and skills were beginning to count as well, and this had begun to undermine the status and limit the patronage of the traditional elite. Admittedly such changes were slow and partial, and had little impact on either rural society or gender relations, but some slight effect on the structure of urban Lao society was beginning to be apparent.

Most change happened in and around Viang Chan, where as much as 90 per cent of all industrial investment was concentrated. Urban growth had been rapid: new settlers attracted by the wartime prosperity resulting from US aid came not only from insecure regions, but also from northeastern Thailand. The population of Viang Chan increased from 23,000 in 1943 to 175,000 thirty years later.[59] Population movements also affected rural areas. By the early 1970s several 'migrant' villages had been established in marginal areas of the Viang Chan plain. In 1971 alone, 35,000 additional refugees were relocated in Viang Chan province. Even though new land was opened up, this influx of population placed pressure on land, with two results: limited landlordism appeared as newly wealthy families bought up prime agricultural land; while landless rural labourers were reduced to seasonal work or casual employment in menial capacities in Viang Chan city.[60]

What was of concern to more thoughtful Lao was that the process of modernization brought with it a decline in traditional moral and cultural values, especially among the young. In rural areas, especially the Viang Chan plain, economic competition replaced traditional cooperation, and personal accumulation of wealth took precedence over the making of religious merit. In the towns, self-indulgence and the good life were even more in evidence. More than a dozen nightclubs flourished in Viang Chan to cater not only for the foreign population, but also for the Lao *nouveau riche*. There the sons of the elite would drink imported beer to the value in one night of more than a month's wages for a labourer. Prostitution was also rife, provided by girls from both rural and urban backgrounds, and from northeast Thailand. Gambling was prevalent, not only in the casinos but at temple festivals (*bun*) where the classical slow Lao dance, the *lamvong*, was increasingly supplanted by a quicker Thai or Western beat. As the *bun* became an occasion for vaunting personal wealth, so its religious and communal dimensions were devalued. Drugs too were widely available, despite official restrictions on cultivation and distribution, and numbers of young Lao became addicted,[61] hanging out with the resident Western hippy community in some of the sleazier bars.

For the more sensitive, what was happening was a source of shame and a blow to national honour ('face', *piap*).[62] Buddhist monks implicitly condemned American influence in sermons calling for a return to traditional Lao values. It was a theme reiterated time and again by the Pathēt Lao, whose commitment and discipline stood in stark contrast to the indulgent lifestyle of the young urban elite, and whose revolutionary dedication reflected in a curious way the monastic discipline of the *Sangha*.[63] The monasteries benefited, however, from increased communal wealth to construct new worship halls and dormitories for the monks, and to commission religious images and murals. Yet nothing better illustrated the poverty of Lao artistic and cultural life at this time than the evident crudeness of much of this temple art.

Viang Chan in particular, but other Mekong towns too, witnessed a construction boom as modern concrete villas, schools and businesses extended beyond the old French colonial core of the city. The Chinese commercial area sold an ever-widening selection of consumer goods, from Japanese motor cycles to French cognac and Swiss chocolate. Markets were well stocked with local produce and Thai goods from across the Mekong, including the latest electronic gadgetry. Several theatres showed American, French, Thai and Chinese movies.

With its foreign embassies and diplomatic gatherings, its shady avenues and temples, its busy traffic and commercial life, Viang Chan had the air at least of a national capital. Apart from the number of soldiers in uniform, there was little indication the country was caught up in war. But it was to the war, and particularly to the American presence, that Viang Chan owed its prosperity. As the war came to an end, the bubble economy it stimulated began to collapse, a decline not yet evident to those whose attention was focused on more immediate political developments.

## THE THIRD COALITION AND THE PATHĒT LAO SEIZURE OF POWER

The cease-fire agreement signed in February 1973 stipulated that a Provisional Government of National Union and a National Political Consultative Council should be established within thirty days,[64] and that all foreign military personnel and installations should be withdrawn within sixty days of formation of such a government. Both time limits proved wildly optimistic. A protocol to the agreement had first to be negotiated, which was not signed until September. In the meantime, as agreed, both sides continued to administer their respective zones, thus maintaining *de facto* division of the country until national elections could be held.

Despite international encouragement, negotiations over the protocol were long and difficult. The Pathēt Lao was bargaining from a position of strength, at a time when the United States was only too evidently eager to extricate itself from Indochina.[65] No mention had been made in the cease-fire agreement of the presence of Vietnamese troops, many of whom remained, especially in the south and east of the country. Concern over their presence and an uncertain future led to pointed criticism of Suvanna by the political right, orchestrated by the Xananikôn clan, and by the military. In August former Air Force General Thao Mā slipped back into Viang Chan from exile in Thailand with a small band of supporters, in an attempt to rally officers in the Royal Lao Army opposed to Suvanna's accommodation with the Pathēt Lao. Again the United States threw its support behind Suvanna. Within twenty-four hours the coup had collapsed and its instigator was dead.[66] With this last fiasco, political opposition evaporated, and Suvanna was able to marshal support for the protocol.

The principal provisions of the protocol included, notably, the structure, composition, and function of the Provisional Government and the Consultative Council, neutralization of the cities of Viang Chan and Luang Phrabāng, and formation of a commission to implement these provisions. Suvanna Phūmā remained prime minister, and twelve ministerial portfolios were equally shared between the two sides. Each minister had a deputy from the other side, to ensure that major decisions were unanimous. The Consultative Council comprised forty-two members (sixteen from each side plus ten by common consent), and was equal in standing to the government. The security of Viang Chan and Luang Phrabāng was assured through equal numbers of troops and police from both sides. A Joint Central Commission to Implement the Agreement was established, with seven members from each side, to demarcate opposing zones and supervise withdrawal of foreign forces. Country-wide elections were foreshadowed 'as soon as possible' for a new National Assembly, after which a definitive government would take office.

Formation of the Provisional Government clearly revealed the changes that had occurred in the balance of political forces in Laos. The increased influence of the Pathēt Lao assured it half the seats in cabinet and, thanks to the rule of unanimity, a veto over all government decisions. Moreover the Pathēt Lao had gained an important foothold in both the administrative and royal capitals, while conceding no reciprocal representation to the right in its zone of control. Within days of signature of the protocol, Pathēt Lao security forces and officials began arriving in Viang Chan. The other significant change was the eclipse of the neutralists, who in reality were reduced to the person of Suvanna himself. Secure in his conviction that he was needed by his country, Suvanna presided over a Third Coalition still modelled on the First and Second, but one doomed from the start, as it lacked the centre necessary to hold opposing factions together. Moreover, Suvanna no longer enjoyed his earlier stature. He was an old man, tired and isolated, still doggedly pursuing his vision of national reconciliation in a climate made bitter by war.

Not only was agreement on formation of the Provisional Government a drawn-out process: so too was withdrawal of foreign forces. By the end of 1973, the US military presence had been scaled down and more than half the Thai 'volunteers' had been withdrawn, but there was no indication that the number of DRV forces had been significantly reduced. In fact, work on the Ho Chi Minh trail had progressed steadily since the cease-fire, and the trail itself had been expanded. Infiltration had been stepped up, even as US reconnaissance flights continued. As many as 20,000 Chinese engineering and construction troops remained in northern Laos. When the deadline set for final withdrawal of all foreign forces (4 June 1974) arrived, both Chinese and Vietnamese were still there. American civilians and embassy personnel and Thai military personnel had been withdrawn, though several hundred Americans remained in the country.

It took six months to neutralize the two capitals before the Third Coalition government could be sworn in. Barracks had to be built to house Pathēt Lao contingents, while excess numbers of rightist police and troops had to be relocated.[67] Only when security conditions were considered satisfactory did senior Pathēt Lao leaders fly to Viang Chan. Suphānuvong arrived to a tumultuous popular welcome, and within days composition of the ministry was agreed upon and the Provisional Government and the Consultative Council were sworn in. Suphānuvong, who had been expected to become Pathēt Lao deputy prime minister, left that position to Phūmī Vongvichit (concurrently Foreign Minister), and chose instead to head the Consultative Council. It was a masterly political move. As the Consultative Council enjoyed equal status with the government, Suphānuvong could claim equivalent status to Suvanna. Also, as the Consultative Council met in Luang Phrabāng, Suphānuvong was able to exert all his influence and authority as a royal prince to bend members to his will. The right, seriously underestimating the potential political role of the Consultative Council, appointed to it only a miscellany of second-level officials with no coherent policy and no group discipline. The Pathēt Lao, by contrast, voted as Suphānuvong instructed.

Contrary to all expectations, the government functioned reasonably effectively, despite the unanimity provision. The Pathēt Lao presence was kept small, with only four or five officials attached to each ministry. Phūmī Vongvichit made it clear at the inaugural cabinet meeting that the routine functioning of each ministry would 'proceed as usual'.[68] Joint delegations approached both Western and communist bloc countries for aid. The Pathēt Lao announced support for the Foreign Exchange Operations Fund to stabilize the currency. It was not in the Provisional Government, however, but in the Consultative Council that the Pathēt Lao made the political running.

At the first six-monthly sitting of the Consultative Council in May, Suphānuvong put forward an 'Eighteen-Point Program for the Current Construction of the Fatherland' and a charter of 'Ten Provisional Regulations Guaranteeing Political Freedoms'. Of the eighteen points, twelve concerned internal policies and six foreign policy. As a whole, the document was moderate and liberal-democratic in tone. The monarchy and religion were upheld. Democratic rights and freedoms and a democratic electoral system were proclaimed, along with ethnic and gender equality. Foreign 'cultural vices' were to be eliminated. Economic development was to be based primarily on agriculture and forestry in a mixed economy in which the state would not play an overly prominent role. In the matter of foreign policy, the program stressed respect for Lao independence, unity, neutrality and territorial integrity, and called for assistance without strings from all sources. The regulations were equally uncontroversial, except for allowing a degree of press censorship and restricting some forms of political association. After two weeks of discussion, at the urging of Suphānuvong, both documents were endorsed unanimously by the council.

While establishing the Consultative Council as an influential policy-making body, the Pathēt Lao refused to accord the elected National Assembly any legitimacy. The government agreed that legislation be ratified not by the Assembly as the constitution demanded, but by royal decree. Yet the Pathēt Lao seemed in no hurry to hold elections for a new Assembly. When disgruntled deputies angered by their loss of power and privilege occupied the Assembly building, Suvanna recommended dissolution of the Assembly by the King. A furious debate in cabinet over this, and over Lao recognition of revolutionary governments in South Vietnam and Cambodia, took its toll on Suvanna. The following day he suffered a heart attack, causing consternation not only in the government, but also in the international community. No fewer than seventeen doctors from six nations converged on his sickbed. He recovered, but three months' convalescence in France was recommended.

In Suvanna's absence, the government faced an economic crisis caused by a ballooning budget deficit and rising inflation. The costs of post-war reconstruction and care of refugees were increasing, while revenue was down due largely to collapse of the gold market.[69] Devaluation of the *kip* was resisted, however. Routine administration continued, and the Ministry of Economy and Planning drew up the outline of a 'First Ten Year Plan for Economic Reconstruction and Development 1975–1985', to take place in three stages: two years 'to bind the wounds of war', followed by three years in which to attain agricultural self-sufficiency, demobilize, and develop light industry, and five years to lay the basis for a modern economy exploiting the country's considerable natural resources.[70] Tensions, however, were increasingly evident in some ministries, particularly Defence, and it was with some relief that Suvanna was welcomed home.

Two disquieting developments threatened the authority of the government in the latter part of 1974 and early 1975. In December 'several hundred' rebellious soldiers demobilized from the 'Secret Army' in northern Laos seized the provincial capital of Huayxāy, and demanded repeal of a 1971 law banning opium growing. The rebellion signalled an alarming deterioration in security in an area awash with weapons. A further portent of social unrest was provided by growing student and worker militancy. Formation of the Third Coalition had weakened the bonds of traditional authority and stimulated a number of semi-political organizations and associations. Demonstrations and strikes, both all but unknown in Laos, were held to protest against political corruption and poor working conditions. The National Federation of

Lao Students and the Lao Federation of Trade Unions acted as coordinating bodies for protest action. Faced with the threat of escalating social unrest, Suvanna felt it necessary in January 1975 to ban all public meetings and demonstrations. In the south, however, continuing political agitation prepared the way for 'liberation' of the major Mekong towns.

In mid-April 1975, as communist armies advanced triumphantly in Cambodia and South Vietnam, fighting also broke out in Laos as Pathēt Lao forces seized control of the western edge of the Plain of Jars. As Pathēt Lao units pushed further south down Route 13 towards Viang Chan to take Meuang Kāsī, fear grew that a communist offensive was under way, timed to coincide with events in Cambodia and South Vietnam. Content to have cut the supply route to Vang Pao's headquarters at Lông Chaeng, however, Pathēt Lao forces advanced no further, preferring to remain a threat poised to strike.

The fall of Phnom Penh on 17 April 1975 to the Khmer Rouge, and of Saigon two weeks later to the tanks of the People's Army of Vietnam, caused acute concern among rightist politicians and army officers in Laos. No longer was the United States prepared to intervene militarily to prevent communist victories in Indochina. It had become a matter of *sauve qui peut*. The Pathēt Lao took advantage of what Kaisôn Phomvihān, Secretary-General of the Lao People's Revolutionary Party, referred to as these 'new conditions eminently favourable to the Lao revolution' created by events in Vietnam and Cambodia, and stepped up its political pressure.[71] There were vituperative attacks over Radio Pathēt Lao, and increasingly well-organized demonstrations were coordinated by the newly formed Twenty-one Organizations for Peace, representing students and workers. Their principal targets were the powerful families of the political right – the Xananikôns, the Aphais, the na Champāsaks. At a massive May Day rally, 10,000 demonstrators called for their 'punishment'. Their anxiety was compounded by the apparently non-political assassination five days later of Bunom, brother of Prince Bunūm na Champāsak. It was a situation, as the Pathēt Lao leadership recognized, 'perfectly ripe' for the seizure of administrative power.[72]

Days later, in fear for their lives, and in response to the well-orchestrated mounting wave of protest, three rightist ministers (Sīsuk na Champāsak, Defence; Ngôn Xananikôn, Finance; and Khamphāy Aphai, Public Health) and two deputy ministers resigned and fled the country. They were followed by several generals of the Royal Lao Army, including the Viang Chan region commander Kupasit Aphai. On 14 May, after angrily resigning his command, Vang Pao and his family were flown directly to Thailand from Lông Chaeng aboard an American C-130. Thousands more Hmong were evacuated to makeshift camps at Ubon as the haemorrhage of population began from the Lao Mekong towns. Not only Lao, but many Chinese and Vietnamese began crossing into Thailand. Those with relatives across the Mekong or with foreign passports were free to stay or move on: those without were interned as refugees.

In consultation with the Pathēt Lao, Suvanna moved to stave off the collapse of the Provisional Government and the threat of renewed civil war. Ministers acceptable to the Pathēt Lao were appointed to replace those who had fled. Meanwhile the Defence Ministry was placed under the temporary command of General Khamuan Bubphā, the Pathēt Lao deputy minister, who with Suvanna's agreement, moved quickly to neutralize opposition in the Royal Lao Army to a Pathēt Lao take-over of power. Demoralized army commanders were instructed not to resist the movement of Pathēt Lao troops into their zone of control.[73]

Suvanna has been roundly criticized by those who were initially forced to flee for their lives and by later refugees, for his role in facilitating the Pathēt Lao seizure of power. Certainly his decision not to order his generals to oppose the Pathēt Lao advance, and his appointment of Khamuan Bubphā as acting Minister for Defence, assisted the Pathēt Lao take-over, but by that time Suvanna's priority was to prevent further pointless loss of life. He was well aware, as his generals were too, that no more assistance could be expected from the United States.[74] He was convinced, moreover, of the need for reconciliation above all. His mistake was to believe that his political opponents shared that conviction, and that the Third Coalition would be retained. The Pathēt Lao, by contrast, sought a victory as complete as their ideological comrades in Vietnam and Cambodia, and that meant not just power in their own right, but social revolution. Yet again Suvanna was to discover that his own statesmanlike vision was not shared by those on whom he depended.

The full story of the final victory of the Pathēt Lao in the revolutionary year of 1975 has yet to be told. To focus attention only on what was happening in Viang Chan is to miss the scope of events. Given difficulties of terrain and communications, revolutionary organization was of necessity decentralized, with initiatives left to local commanders. In many regional centres demonstrations denounced rightist officials and the American presence. In Luang Phrabāng and Savannakhēt, USAID offices and facilities were occupied, and American staff placed under house arrest. People's Revolutionary Committees were hastily established to take over local administration and welcome Pathēt Lao forces. By the end of May, almost every town in southern Laos had been peacefully 'liberated', including Pākxē, Savannakhēt, and Thākhaek. The Pathēt Lao entered Luang Phrabāng in early June.

In Viang Chan, with the power of the most influential right-wing families broken and the Royal Lao Army neutralized, attention focused on the symbol of American influence in Laos. On 20 May hundreds of demonstrators, including some of USAID's own Lao employees, seized the USAID compound in Viang Chan, and agreed to leave only after protracted negotiations led to US agreement to withdraw all USAID personnel by the end of June. As some 800 Americans began leaving Laos, the government nevertheless requested continuation of US aid, suggesting that, although the tide of popular protest was clearly being orchestrated by Pathēt Lao activists, those in government recognized the danger posed for the country's fragile finances should all economic assistance be terminated.[75] More occupations of US facilities followed, with demonstrators refusing to permit departing Americans to take personal and household possessions with them. Such events further soured relations, despite attempts by Pathēt Lao ministers to negotiate an end to the occupations, and mend fences. The USAID mission was closed as agreed, and the US Embassy staff reduced to twenty-two. Humiliated, the United States announced it was terminating all aid to Laos, including its contribution to the Foreign Exchange Operations Fund.

The political crisis was immediately reflected in the commercial and financial sectors. Shops closed down and goods disappeared from shelves. As much of the nation's wealth left the country, and people began to hoard gold, the value of the *kip* plummeted. By the end of May it had lost 80 per cent of its value against the US dollar and inflation was continuing to run at 50 per cent.[76] Limited Western aid continued, but most of the shortfall due to termination of US aid had to be made up by assistance from states of the communist bloc. By October there were, by US estimates, as many as 500 Soviet civilian technicians and advisers in the country.

On the political front, the 'quasi-legalism' of the Pathēt Lao road to power continued,[77] even as the Lao People's Revolutionary Party moved to assert control over all aspects of national life. The bureaucracy was subjected to 'purification' by means of popular denunciation of senior officials, some of whom were arraigned before 'people's courts' on charges of corruption while others were forced to undergo self-criticism. Throughout the country, People's Revolutionary Committees decreed new controls and restrictions on prices, property transactions, and personal movement.

Despite the flight of members of leading right-wing families and the predominantly Chinese business community, and disquiet over the future both of themselves and the country, most of the educated middle class that formed the backbone of the bureaucracy preferred to stay and cooperate with the Pathēt Lao. It was generally believed that only a few named rightist politicians and generals were targets for Pathēt Lao vengeance, and that the rest of the population would not face punishment. This idea was reinforced by the show trial of thirty-one prominent rightists, all *in absentia* since they had already fled to Thailand. Six were condemned to death and the rest to long terms of imprisonment.[78] Even so, most Lao who stayed believed that national reconciliation would be achieved in the Lao way, according to the precepts of Buddhism. The war was over: the Pathēt Lao had won. The political order would change, but for the better in that the Pathēt Lao were believed to be less corrupt, more dedicated and hard-working. Greater austerity would be necessary, but this was accepted for it was widely recognized that the nation had been living beyond its means. Most educated Lao were prepared to cooperate in order to build a peaceful and prosperous country along the lines set out in the widely disseminated Eighteen Points. They were, after all, Lao patriots with a deep, if unstated, pride in their history and nation, and a love of their country that overrode ideology.

It was their readiness to cooperate with the Pathēt Lao that partly explains the willingness of so many military and police officers and civil servants to present themselves when instructed to attend political re-education. Another factor was their belief that the process would be of brief duration. Most men, for it was only men who were taken, believed that re-education would last no more than a few weeks. Even when senior officers and officials were flown to Xam Neua in the Pathēt Lao zone, they and their families believed it would only be for a few months at most. Relatively few took the opportunity to escape to Thailand. From July on, more and more were sent off – most junior officers below the rank of major and lower-level civil servants to their own camps segregated from their superiors.

From the Pathēt Lao point of view, the incarceration of senior officials for political re-education was a necessary precondition to eliminate possible opposition to control of the remaining administrative centres of Viang Chan and Luang Phrabāng, for the Pathēt Lao itself could call on very few trained cadres. With the structures of state power thus all but destroyed, political mobilization of the loose coalition calling for political change could be accelerated. On 18 August administration of neutralized Luang Phrabāng was taken over by a People's Revolutionary Committee. The King remained unharmed in his palace. Five days later, a crowd estimated to number 200,000 gathered to listen to Pathēt Lao speeches and welcome a token force of fifty Pathēt Lao women soldiers flown down from Xam Neua to symbolize the 'liberation' of Viang Chan. Speeches took place in a carnival atmosphere, and a coffin containing 'dead American imperialism' was ceremonially burned.[79]

Viang Chan's new municipal authorities began by cleaning up the city. Neighbourhood committees under the direction of the LPF organized associations of women and youth to undertake much of the work. Former soldiers of the Royal Lao Army worked in labour gangs. Offices were whitewashed, homes repaired, streets swept. Pernicious Western influences were denounced. Women were no longer permitted to wear jeans, or youths to grow their hair long. Controls were introduced over personal movement, and the press censored. Political meetings to denounce the former regime and explain the changes became more frequent. On 12 October, the thirtieth anniversary of the declaration of Lao independence by the Lao Issara in 1945 was celebrated with a popular festival at the Thāt Luang in Viang Chan, and by a gathering of communist leaders at Viang Xai, symbolizing conclusion of the 'thirty-year struggle'. Only the final act in the communist seizure of power remained to be performed.

Elections for a new National Assembly were originally scheduled for 1 April 1976, at which time, Suvanna announced, he intended to retire from politics. This suggests that the framework at least of the Third Coalition was to be retained. Within the month, however, it was evident that leaders of the Lao People's Revolutionary Party, meeting in Viang Xai, had had a change of mind. In November, a series of elections was held for the two levels of district (*tāsaeng*) and regional (*meuang*) government. Voting was by secret ballot and compulsory for all over the age of eighteen, and all candidates required endorsement by the

LPF. At the village level, people's committees had already taken over the duties of the village chief. The elections were to replace appointed district chiefs and regional governors by elected people's administrative committees. At each level, an administrative committee made decisions under the close supervision of a parallel Party committee. Indeed in many cases the people's administrative committee chairman and the Party secretary were, then and later, one and the same person. Even at this stage, the impression was given that these were necessary preliminaries for Assembly elections the following April.

In the last week of November an extraordinary joint meeting was called of the Consultative Council and the Provisional Government at Viang Xai. On the 26th, a well-orchestrated rally in the national stadium in Viang Chan demanded formation of 'a new popular and democratic regime'. This was followed two days later by demonstrations denouncing the monarchy and Suvanna Phūmā's government. The situation was discussed by the Consultative Council and the Provisional Government, which endorsed the decision already taken by the leadership of the Party to abolish the monarchy and create an orthodox communist people's republic. Suvanna Phūmā and Suphānuvong flew immediately to Luang Phrabāng, where they presented King Savāngvatthanā with a demand to abdicate his throne. With dignity and resignation, the King accepted the inevitable. In his letter of abdication he handed over the royal lands and palace to the state.[80]

Armed with the King's letter of abdication, Suvanna, Suphānuvong and former Crown Prince Vongsavāng flew next to Viang Chan where they attended a hastily convened secret National Congress of People's Representatives. It was this unconstitutional and unrepresentative body which, on 2 December 1975, officially accepted the King's abdication, ending the six-century-old monarchy, and proclaimed the Lao People's Democratic Republic.

Why was the Lao revolutionary movement victorious? It had not mobilized an exploited peasantry with promises of land reform, for most of the country was under-populated and peasant families generally owned sufficient land for their subsistence needs. The appeal of the Pathēt Lao to their lowland Lao compatriots was in terms of nationalism and independence and the preservation of Lao culture from corrosive American influence; but no urban uprising occurred until the very last minute when effective government had virtually ceased to exist: it did not climax a campaign of civil disobedience. The small Lao intelligentsia, though critical of the Royal Lao government, did not desert it entirely, and their recruitment to the Pathēt Lao was minimal. Neither the monarchy, still less Buddhism, lost legitimacy. To be sure, Pathēt Lao promises to disaffected hill-tribe minorities to include them in a new national political order based on ethnic equality and respect for cultural difference had been effective. But without Vietnamese support, even this degree of revolutionary mobilization and accompanying political violence would probably have been limited. The weakness of the Lao state was certainly a factor, especially in the final seizure of power, as was the unity, discipline and commitment of the Pathēt Lao as a revolutionary movement. But the success of the Lao revolution was ultimately determined by the support of outside powers in the peculiar circumstances of the Second Indochina War. The triumphant entry of communist forces into Saigon was widely seen as an American defeat that implicated all those the United States had supported. War-weariness and the hope of national reconciliation did the rest. In the last analysis, it was foreign intervention, both US and Vietnamese, and the impact of war that created conditions for success of the Lao revolution, an outcome striven for by a tiny ideologically committed elite, but hardly desired by the mass of the Lao people for whom communism was little more than a name.

For the lowland Lao, the war brought with it challenges to traditional values, social dislocation and rapid urbanization. Yet only as the war wound down, and it became clear that US disengagement was imminent, did the need for a solution to civil conflict become urgent. The response was to revert to the previous pattern of coalition government, in the belief, apparently unshaken, that Lao could compromise with Lao if only foreign forces were withdrawn. But this presupposed a commonality of interests and (Buddhist) values, entailing acceptance of a religiously underwritten social, or class, hierarchy. These interests and values were no longer shared. Conflict had sharpened the ideological divide, no matter how skilfully this might be camouflaged. The moderation of the Eighteen Points served only as a screen behind which political mobilization concentrated on destroying the moral standing and thus the social power-base of the leading families. From formation of the Third Coalition this proceeded steadily, but with the events of early 1975 the ideological discourse of revolution gained new momentum and new adherents, and found expression in collective action. Revolution appealed as a metaphor for change that would replace a failed order and offer release from powerlessness, a new solidarity, and quick solutions to political and social problems. The ruling elite, its structures of authority fatally weakened by years of self-serving corruption, was too divided, too irresolute to respond. Defections occurred not only in the bureaucracy, but also in the armed forces which, since their resupply depended on US orders from Thai bases, could offer but limited resistance.

One thing the revolution did achieve, seventeen years after the breakdown of the First Coalition: it restored the unity of the country. If independence was more problematic, unity was still a powerful symbol. The overwhelming hope was for an end to conflict, for many believed that Lao would never have fought Lao had it not been for foreign intervention: the war had been fought not because of Lao intransigence or intractable political hatred, but because external powers had made use of Lao territory for their own ends, and Lao had been forced to choose one side or the other. In the end, however, it was not foreign pressure that prevented compromise, but a foreign ideology (Marxism) espoused by revolutionaries for whom compromise was nothing but tactics in a struggle for power. In the course of those seventeen years the voice of genuine neutrality had been all but silenced, as both right and left exploited rapidly changing circumstances in their own interests – whether personal wealth or the lure of power. And when the war finally came to an end, the divisions that separated individuals, families, and zones of political control were overcome not through a discourse and process of reconciliation, but through the victory of one side over the other. Victory went to the Pathēt Lao, whose revenge took the form of incarcerating their political enemies and establishing a communist regime.

Perhaps it is unrealistic to believe that the leaders of the Lao People's Revolutionary Party should have – or could have – done otherwise, given their commitment to Marxism and the impact of their wartime experience. They had, after all, fought under harrowing conditions for the best part of thirty years for the power that at last was within their grasp. They had accepted a role as part of the First Coalition, blame for the destruction of which lay squarely with the United States and the political right. The breakdown of the Second Coalition and elimination of the neutralists was due to the machinations of both left and right, each manipulated by their powerful patrons. But blame for terminating the Third Coalition rested entirely with the Pathēt Lao, advised by their Vietnamese friends. The result was to destroy both hope and trust, and to open up new divisions just when the country desperately needed both unity and reconciliation.

Participation in all three coalition governments can be interpreted, as Lao communist writers themselves do, as part of a clever overall strategy to gain political power.[81] But the outcome could well have been different. Admittedly the communist leadership of the Pathēt Lao was single-minded in pursuing a clear ideological goal but, had geopolitical conditions been different, any of the three coalition governments might have lasted longer than it did. Indeed, for a few weeks between August and October 1975, the decision as to whether to dispense with the Third Coalition even seems to have hung in the balance.[82] By then the Royal Lao Army had been destroyed as a fighting force, and the entire country was in Pathēt Lao hands. So were the organs of administration and government. Select figures had been tried and sentenced, and a few others could have been singled out. Members of the ruling elite had either fled, or were undergoing re-education. The Lao People's Revolutionary Party had already effectively seized power. If the Party had been content to preside over even the semblance of a continuing coalition, had followed its own Eighteen Points, and had kept its word over the period of re-education at least for more junior officers and civil servants, reconciliation might have been possible. As it was, the Party, fearful of losing its grip on power and ideologically committed to carrying out a Marxist revolution modelled on that of Vietnam, achieved the territorial reunification of the country but closed off the possibility of national reconciliation that so many desired. The resulting haemorrhage of confidence on the part of the educated class that had served the former regime, and the consequent loss of population as most crossed to Thailand, were so serious as to compromise not just the country's capacity to undertake its own reconstruction, but even its very independence. In retrospect, the decision to dispense with the Third Coalition marks not so much the triumph of the Lao revolution, as the self-inflicted final blow in the most tragic period of contemporary Lao history.

# 6

# THE LAO PEOPLE'S DEMOCRATIC REPUBLIC

The National Congress of People's Representatives that met in Viang Chan in December 1975 both marked the change of regime from constitutional monarchy to communist people's republic, and set the direction of future political, social and economic development. For the Lao People's Revolutionary Party, the Congress confirmed the 'far-sighted' leadership of the Party in bringing the Lao 'thirty-year struggle' for political power to a successful conclusion. It also marked the end of the 'national democratic' phase of the revolution, and the beginning of the 'dictatorship of the proletariat' which would bring about the 'transition to socialism'.[1] It was thus an occasion both for self-congratulation on the part of Party leaders and Congress delegates, and of dedication to the tasks that lay ahead.

The new regime gained widespread international recognition, not only from communist bloc states, but also from the United States and its allies. US representation in Viang Chan was reduced to the level of chargé d'affaires, but relations were never broken completely as in the case of Vietnam and Cambodia. Close relations with Vietnam were underscored by the visit of a high-ranking Lao Party delegation to Hanoi to express effusive thanks for the 'extremely precious contribution made by Vietnamese forces in the noble spirit of proletarian internationalism' to the Lao revolution. Both sides committed themselves to further strengthening 'solidarity and long-term cooperation' in all domains between the two parties and two countries.[2]

The priority for the new Lao regime was to assure the monopolization of political power by the Lao People's Revolutionary Party and to defend it against internal and external threats, both real and exaggerated. Legitimization of the new regime stressed both historical continuity and national unity, but failed to bring about national reconciliation. Largely as a result of government policies, fully 10 per cent of the Lao population eventually sought asylum abroad. Equally damaging were premature moves to nationalize industry and commerce, followed by attempted cooperativization of agriculture. Within four years reduced food production put a halt to the policy of cooperativization, and within a decade the first steps were taken to restore the operation of market forces in the commercial and financial sectors. Both changes were endorsed by the Party and given the force of law in the

1991 constitution. There was, however, no matching political liberalization. Despite the collapse of communism in the former Soviet Union
and Eastern Europe, the Party sought to stave off its own demise by
adopting the Chinese model of single-party government presiding over
a free-market economy – a model whose viability depended both on a
relative absence of internal discontent and continuing external support,
neither of which could be guaranteed indefinitely as Laos became
increasingly integrated into the Southeast Asian region.

## REGIME CHANGE AND LEGITIMATION

Even in the euphoria of victory, the small band of leaders of the Lao
People's Revolutionary Party were not unaware of the magnitude of the
task that lay ahead, and the problems likely to be encountered. Their
goal, as frequently stated, was to 'advance, step by step, to socialism
without going through the stage of capitalist development',[3] a propo-
sition Marx himself would have found difficult to endorse. The Party
believed it would be possible to do this by simultaneously pursuing
'three revolutions', the theoretical exposition of which was taken from
Vietnamese Marxism.[4] As the Party's Secretary-General Kaisôn Phomvihān explained, these consisted of the revolution in the relations of
production, the scientific and technical revolution, and the ideological
and cultural revolution. Of the three, the first was the 'guide', in that it
would form the economic base on which Lao socialism would be
constructed; the second was the 'key' to this transformation, since it
would provide the transfer of technology necessary to by-pass
capitalism and create a modern industrial economy; while the third was
always to be a 'step ahead' of the other two, in forming Lao socialist
men and women ideologically committed to socialism and thus bringing about the desired socialist transformation of Lao society and the Lao
economy.[5]

These were the ideological convictions that animated the Party
leadership. While the full transition to socialism would obviously take
time and encounter difficulties, the necessary means were at hand in the
form of the 'people's democratic dictatorship', to be exercised by the
Party, and the governmental structures of a fully fledged 'people's
democratic republic', the models for both of which were taken from the
Soviet Union.

The Party had already prepared itself to exercise its 'historic role' at
its Second Party Congress in February 1972; the Congress agreed upon
not only tactics that led to formation of the Third Coalition government,
but also the broader strategy by which the transition to socialism was
to be achieved. In organizational terms, the previously rather *ad hoc*
structure was formalized to provide for a Political Bureau, a Secretariat
to handle everyday Party affairs, and a Central Committee, with associated special committees concerned with such matters as propaganda,
inspection and control, and ideological training of cadres. The Party
structure was also formalized at each administrative level (province,

district, village) and in the army and mass organizations (the Lao Patriotic Front, and women's, workers', and youth organizations). Indeed Kaisôn had good reason to characterize the Second Congress as 'one of the most important events' in the country's history, marking 'the political and organizational maturity of our Party'.[6]

Membership of the central organs of the Party was not immediately revealed in 1972, but the structure was in place to seize the advantage offered by the events of 1975. The Political Bureau remained limited to seven members – in order, Kaisôn Phomvihān, Nūhak Phumsavan, Suphānuvong, Phūmī Vongvichit, Khamtai Sīphandôn, Phūn Sīpasoet, and Sīsomphôn Lôvanxai – all but two of whom (Suphānuvong and Phūmī Vongvichit) also served on the Secretariat, while the Central Committee was expanded to comprise twenty-one full and six alternate members. This small leadership group was responsible for organizing the structure of government put into place in December 1975, and duly rubber-stamped by the National Congress of People's Representatives.

In theory, the supreme law-making body in the new Lao People's Democratic Republic was the Supreme People's Assembly; in fact, the Assembly was entirely subservient to the Party. Forty-five members were named by the National Congress to constitute an interim Assembly under the presidency of Suphānuvong until elections could be held.[7] Nominally answerable to the Assembly, but in fact answerable only to the Politburo, was the Council of Ministers. It was presided over by Kaisôn as prime minister, and made up initially of twelve ministers, two chairs of state committees, and the president of the National Bank. Four influential ministers without portfolio were responsible for running the prime minister's office, proof if any were needed of the power concentrated in the hands of Kaisôn.

In the view of the Party, its right to rule was legitimized by its victory in the 'people's war' it had led and fought. Some attempt was made, however, to minimize the abruptness of the transition from monarchy to people's republic by naming former King Savāngvatthanā 'Counsellor to the President' and Suvanna Phūmā 'Counsellor to the Government'. Former Crown Prince Vongsavāng was appointed a member of the Supreme People's Assembly. The leading figures in the former regime were thus coopted into lending their prestige and popularity to the new government. Further continuity was provided by Suphānuvong, a prince of the royal house of Luang Phrabāng, in his position as President of the new republic, and in the decision to adopt the same national anthem, with a few changes to the words, and the former Lao Issara flag in place of the triple-headed elephant of the Royal Lao regime.[8]

In his address to the National Congress, Kaisôn sounded the themes of peace, independence, democracy, unity, prosperity, and social progress, and called upon all sectors of the community – including minorities, monks, intellectuals, and Lao abroad – to give their full support to the new regime. The Action Program also stressed the need for national unity of 'all social strata, all ethnic groups, all citizens', and mobilization of the entire population. Although not expressed in precisely these terms, the twin priorities were already clear: defence of the revolution and construction of a modern socialist economy, themes to be reiterated ceaselessly over the following years.

The National Congress revealed the full leadership of the Party for the first time. Broadly speaking, its lowland Lao membership fell into two groups. The first comprised those who had taken a prominent part in negotiations over the years – men like Suphānuvong, active and arrogant; bespectacled, patrician Phūmī Vongvichit; and lesser figures such as Suk Vongsak. These were men either of aristocratic background or linked by birth to some of the more powerful families of the former regime. They were French-educated, able to converse on equal terms with their interlocutors in the Royal Lao government. The second group was made up of more shadowy figures from both the Party and the army who had directed the guerrilla struggle in close coordination with the Vietnamese. Most were of humbler social background, with less education, who had proved their capabilities throughout years of war. Power rested largely, but not exclusively, with this group, whose leading figures were the Party's Secretary-General Kaisôn Phomvihān, a former law student of quick intellect and strong will, and his rather dour deputy Nūhak Phumsavan, a former trucking contractor of hardy peasant stock. Both came from Savannakhēt in central Laos and both enjoyed close relations with the Vietnamese, Kaisôn by birth (his father was Vietnamese), and Nūhak, like Suphānuvong, by marriage. Other members of this group included the military commander of the Lao People's Liberation Army, Khamtai Sīphandôn, foreign affairs spokesman Phūn Sīpasoet, and Sālī Vongkhamxao, responsible for the organization of the Party.

What was remarkable about this leadership was its longevity and cohesiveness. Purges and demotions had occurred, but without causing irreparable divisions in the Party.[9] More significant than any differences among the leadership was the gap that separated leaders from led, and the dominance of Lao Lum in the upper echelons of the Party and, to a lesser extent, the army. While many lower-level cadres were drawn from minority groups – Lao Sūng or Lao Thoeng – their leaders, such as Faidāng Lôbliayao of the Hmong and the traditional Lao Thoeng chieftain Sīthon Kommadam, figured more prominently in the LPF than in the Party. Though disciplined and courageous, minority cadres lacked education. Their importance for the revolutionary movement and their numerical significance in the army were not therefore reflected in the Party hierarchy.[10]

For thirty years war had been the priority, but in 1975 the Party was faced with the task of governing a modern state, complete with ministries, departments, and technical requirements. This would have posed a challenge for the best-organized and most far-sighted revolutionary movement. As it was, the Pathēt Lao made things more difficult for themselves through a combination of their own ill-conceived policies and ingrained paranoia. Though woefully short of skilled administrators, the Party was impatient to bring about the rapid transformation of Lao society for which it had fought. Most Lao expected change and were prepared for it, but the new regime moved in too authoritarian a way, too fast, and on too many fronts at once. Its understandable desire to take immediate control of both the administration and the economy resulted not in national reconciliation, but in mounting mistrust, paralysis, and economic collapse. Ill-trained cadres were appointed to every ministry and office where, instead of being content as previously during the Third Coalition to work with the existing bureaucracy of the Royal Lao government, they presided over purges of personnel denounced as ideologically unacceptable.

Most senior bureaucrats had already been removed to Viang Xai for political re-education. Lower-level officials who remained were ordered to attend interminable meetings to learn the new political orthodoxy and criticize previous government policy. These quickly became occasions for criticism and self-criticism, at which unscrupulous opportunists could settle old scores and advance their own interests. As senior officers and officials failed to return from what the Party had promised would be relatively short programs of re-education, and others were arrested and sent to join them, a climate of fear and suspicion built up which not only brought work in most ministries almost completely to a standstill, but also convinced many who would otherwise have stayed to serve their country to flee to Thailand instead. The opportunity to harness what was essentially nationalist sentiment among those who had served the former Royal Lao regime in the cause of building a new Laos was thus lost, as the old divisions were perpetuated. Throughout 1976 the steady stream of refugees continued, each family of civil servants or technicians representing a net loss of trained personnel that the country could ill afford.[11]

Other policies also contributed to popular apprehension. Russian aid to the tune of several million roubles filled only a portion of the gap left by termination of Western assistance. In the face of a collapsing economy beset by runaway inflation, the government attempted to control prices and black-market hoarding by fixing the price of rice and other basic commodities, and restricting the movement of food and goods. In June a currency reform demonetized the former *kip* and replaced it by a devalued 'liberation' *kip*, a move that did nothing to curtail inflation, though it did reduce the money in circulation. Controls were also introduced on personal movement. No-one was permitted to leave major towns without a pass, which was checked at road-blocks by often illiterate Pathēt Lao guards. As premises were searched and commerce ground to a halt, most of the remaining Chinese and Vietnamese communities packed up and left. By mid-year half the 20,000 Chinese and 15,000 Vietnamese previously resident in Viang Chan had gone,[12] taking what capital they could with them in the form of gold. The boarded-up shop-fronts left behind lent the business district a dilapidated air of neglect.

In addition to imposing personal and economic restrictions, attempts were made to mobilize the population in ideologically 'progressive' ways. By then all independent publications had closed down and information was tightly controlled by the Party. Villagers and townspeople alike were dragooned into attending public meetings (known as *samanā*, from 'seminar') at which communist accounts of the 'thirty-year struggle' and criticisms of the former regime were endlessly repeated. Public servants were encouraged to join work details to clean up the city, dig drains, and whitewash public buildings, and to grow their own vegetables and raise chickens and ducks on any available land – even the roof tops of apartment blocks. Supposedly this was to alleviate food shortages exacerbated by severe drought, but it also served to generate a sense of solidarity in the face of adversity.

The *samanā* were not popular. Most were held in the evenings after everyone had worked a full day. Participants feared being singled out for criticism over some misdemeanour, or for failing to endorse the new policies with sufficient enthusiasm. At first the regime enlisted the assistance of young monks sympathetic to the Pathēt Lao cause to proclaim supposed similarities between Buddhism and socialism (both have compassion for the poor and exploited; both seek an end to suffering) and to call for a return to traditional values and morality. Increasingly, however, pressure was brought to bear to undermine the prestige of the *Sangha* by subordinating it to the organizational control of the Party, and to discourage attendance at Buddhist ceremonies which only wasted scarce economic resources. Monks were told they should no longer rely on gifts of food from the pious offered during the morning 'begging' round, but instead should work for a living, grow their own food, and provide useful social services in the form of education and traditional medicines. As a consequence, many returned to lay life.[13]

A more popular mass mobilization program was aimed at reducing illiteracy. Students, monks, and anyone who could read and write were sent to teach those who could not. Every village held adult literacy classes, and volunteers went to teach literacy in Lao, the sole official national language, to other ethnic groups. Schools and health clinics (little more than first-aid posts) were constructed of local materials in remote villages to fulfil the Pathēt Lao pledge to improve living standards for those ethnic minorities who had supported the 'thirty-year struggle'. According to government claims, illiteracy was reduced in the first year of the campaign from 60 per cent of the population to 40 per cent.[14] Meanwhile the most politically committed students were sent to study in socialist countries. Those already studying abroad in the West were encouraged to complete their courses and return to serve the new regime. Some of the more idealistic did so.

The major target of criticism in the *samanā* was the United States and everything to do with the decadent and depraved lifestyle its malign influence had encouraged under the former regime. Not only was the library of the US Information Agency closed down, but American books, in fact most books published in English on no matter what subject, were withdrawn from libraries, even at the university college at Dong Dōk. American music, dancing, clothes, hairstyles, and sexual permissiveness were denounced and banned. As many as two thousand of the most 'culturally polluted', including drug addicts and prostitutes, were rounded up and sent for rehabilitation on two islands, one for men, the other for women, in the reservoir of the Nam Ngeum dam. Christianity was denounced as a vehicle for Western influences, and Lao citizens discouraged from having any contact with foreigners. At first a few nightclubs and bars remained open in Viang Chan, perhaps for the entertainment of advisers from the communist bloc, but the only dance permitted was the traditional Lao *lamvong* and no single, available girls were to be seen.

What was to replace the polluted culture of the West was pure Lao socialist culture. Because so much of traditional Lao culture was associated with Buddhism, and because the attitude of the new regime towards the *Sangha* was ambivalent to say the least, there was some doubt about just what Lao socialist culture should be. The preferred art style was socialist realism, which appeared on large billboards exhorting the masses to build the new Lao socialist state. The *bāsī* was permitted as a welcoming ceremony for visiting socialist delegations, while the repertoire of the National School of Dance was extended to include the folk dances of ethnic minorities. Short stories and popular theatre dwelt almost exclusively on the heroic 'thirty-year struggle'.

On the economic front, even though Thailand reopened its border, shortages of goods continued, due mainly to import controls and government moves to nationalize commerce and industry. Most private companies were taken over by the state, though a few whose owners remained in the country were converted to joint state-private enterprises. Transportation and retailing were either nationalized or tightly controlled. The importation of most products became the monopoly of state trading companies. Basic products and subsidized food items were sold in state shops. Foreign oil companies were forced out, and petrol rationed as one of several measures taken to reduce import costs. All such measures contributed to the centralizing policies of the socialist state.

Though by and large, given the size of the former Royal Lao Army and police force and the quantity of arms available, the change of regime had been remarkably peaceful, a number of incidents did occur in the first half of 1976 in which armed bands ambushed vehicles and exchanged fire with Pathēt Lao troops. In southern Laos rebels under the command of a former Pathēt Lao officer took up arms to oppose what they denounced as 'the North Vietnamese annexation of Laos'.[15] In February 1976 an opposition organization was formed calling itself the 'Lao National Revolutionary Front 21/18' and demanding strict adherence to the Viang Chan Agreements of 21 February 1973 and the Eighteen-Point Program agreed upon by the Third Coalition. The 21/18 Front was designed to appeal to disgruntled neutralists and even former Pathēt Lao unhappy over the end of the monarchy and formation of a communist regime, but it clearly had the backing of powerful right-wing figures. Its most spectacular exploits were to blow up a bridge and lob grenades into the Lao National Radio building and the grounds of the Soviet Embassy.

The government response was to tighten security, call upon the people to exercise greater vigilance, and deploy more 'peace-keeping forces'. The population was subjected to frequent identity checks, a curfew was imposed, and the banks of the Mekong regularly patrolled to prevent 'saboteurs and terrorists' infiltrating across from Thailand. By the middle of the year these measures were paying off. Relations between Viang Chan and Bangkok improved with the visit of the Thai Foreign Minister. Lao resistance leaders admitted it was proving difficult to recruit supporters inside Laos, especially after seven men were arrested and tried for a series of grenade attacks and sabotage attempts. After a well-publicized trial, three were condemned to death and the other four received long prison terms. By the year's end the government was boasting it had 'smashed all the designs of the enemy' – at least in the Viang Chan area.[16]

The claim was premature, however. Celebrations marking the first anniversary of the new regime were marred by a plot to assassinate Kaisôn. Senior Party officials retreated to the relative safety of the heavily guarded former US housing compound on the outskirts of Viang Chan, where they lived in seclusion along with a handful of top-level Vietnamese advisers. The isolation of senior Party leaders was symptomatic of the defensiveness and lack of confidence of the regime, and its distrust of its former opponents. Obsessive secrecy and frequent admonitions for people to be on their guard against unnamed 'enemies of socialism' created an atmosphere of fear and suspicion that undermined mutual trust and destroyed personal relationships.

This combination of insecurity and fear was largely responsible for the continuing haemorrhage of refugees. Others left because of discrimination, or to escape deteriorating living standards. Throughout 1976 and into 1977, the families of thousands of former army and police officers and civil servants still undergoing political re-education in remote guarded camps were forced to sell off personal possessions just to survive.[17] As promises of early release remained unfulfilled and public confidence in the government eroded further, those with nothing left to sell gave up hope and sought refugee status in Thailand. In their place settled families of the Pathēt Lao, introducing a more varied ethnic mix into the social structure of the Mekong towns.

Farmers responded to the taxes and marketing controls by withholding produce. Even subsidized food in state shops was in short supply and available only to Party members and government officials. By mid-year the collapsing economy and rising popular dissatisfaction led the government to relax some of its more arbitrary restrictions. Movement of produce to market was made easier. A de facto ban on 'wasteful' festivals (bun) was relaxed. In Viang Chan, some Western clothing was permitted. Even the volume of loudspeakers blasting out revolutionary slogans was reduced. It was not always easy, however, to convince regional and local cadres to adopt less draconian controls. From the beginning local guerrillas eagerly initiated their own 'revolutions' with scant reference to central organs of the Party. Indeed decentralization remained characteristic of the regime as regional officials proved reluctant to compromise their newly acquired authority. Visits by Party leaders were welcomed, but their admonitions were often ignored after they had left.

Desperate to increase revenue, the government in September 1976 introduced an unpopular progressive tax in kind on rice and other crops. It also took the first steps towards the cooperativization of agriculture by encouraging peasants to increase traditional cooperation through labour-exchange arrangements. Agricultural cooperativization was believed essential not only because this would free individual peasants from the vagaries of nature, and raise production by permitting the mechanization of farming, but also out of ideological fear that without it rural capitalism could not be eradicated.[18] It was not only the wealthier farmers, however, who were reluctant to cooperate, for the new measures compromised traditional peasant independence. By the end of 1976, the government reported that only a few thousand families, mainly in the former 'liberated zone', in nine out of thirteen provinces were practising any kind of cooperative agriculture. It was a pace too slow for Party ideologues impatient to implement socialist means of production.

Though 1976 had been, in Kaisôn's words, a year of 'critical tests full of great hardship',[19] the regime could claim some achievements. Tens of thousands of internal refugees had returned home, bringing fallow land under cultivation. Some industries were again producing, if at reduced capacity due to shortages of imported materials. By early 1977 the Party felt confident enough to advance to the next stage in the building of socialism. The fourth plenary session of the Central Committee decided to press ahead with policies designed to 'undertake socialist transformations in all domains', notably by reinforcing the 'directive role' of the Party, strengthening the 'worker–peasant alliance', and reinforcing the 'socialist mode of production'.[20] For the Party leadership, the euphoria that came with the challenge of rapidly building a new socialist Laos was sufficient to override any problems caused by a lack of trained cadres or the parlous state of the economy.

## NATIONAL DEFENCE AND SOCIALIST CONSTRUCTION

Security, both internal and external, continued to be a pressing concern for the new regime. In the south, resistance fighters (kū xāt) still crossed from Thailand to attack vehicles and circulate anti-communist propaganda. The resistance itself was divided, however, with new organizations claiming to speak for Lao exiles in Thailand and in France. In the north, in the mountains around Phū Bia, a far more serious resistance movement gained ground throughout 1976 and 1977, recruited from among the former Hmong members of the CIA 'Secret Army' who had remained in Laos.

The Hmong fought either in the vain hope of establishing an independent Hmong kingdom to be ruled by a divine king, or simply to resist Pathēt Lao administrative control. The former were adherents of a messianic revivalist movement known as the Chau Fā, or God's disciples.[21] Both groups were active in ambushing convoys and attacking Pathēt Lao outposts north of Vang Viang along National Route 13 linking Viang Chan with Luang Phrabāng. In March 1977, rightist rebels captured and briefly held the village of Meuang Nān, some 50 kilometres south of Luang Phrabāng. Fearful that the Lao *kū xāt* would make common cause with the Hmong resistance, seize the ex-King and incite a general revolt, the government took the royal family, including Crown Prince Vongsavāng, into custody and banished them to Viang Xai, near the Vietnamese border.[22] Major operations to destroy the Hmong resistance were not undertaken until after the rainy season in November 1977. Vietnamese troops, withdrawn from Laos following the victory of the Pathēt Lao, returned in force. In the fighting that followed, hundreds, perhaps thousands of Hmong were killed as combined Lao and Vietnamese forces used artillery and air strikes to crush the rebels. Thousands more Hmong refugees made their way to Thailand, suffering horrendous casualties *en route*. Including those who had left in 1975, about one-third of the entire Hmong population eventually fled the country.[23]

Security problems were exacerbated when in October 1976 an army *coup d'état* overthrew the moderate, democratically elected Thai government and replaced it with a strongly anti-communist regime dominated by the military. A spate of minor incidents thereafter raised tensions along the Thai–Lao border, as local Thai military commanders gave renewed support to 'enemy commandos, spies and exiled Lao reactionaries'.[24] While the Thai hinted darkly at communist designs on Thailand, Lao National Radio angrily accused Thailand of 'provocation' aimed at overthrowing the Lao regime.[25]

What had become known as the 'special relationship' with the Socialist Republic of Vietnam was formalized by the signing in July 1977 of a 25-year Treaty of Friendship and Cooperation. Under its terms, both sides pledged to 'carry out a close cooperation aimed at reinforcing the defence capacity' of both nations in opposing imperialism and foreign reactionary forces (Article 2), thereby providing the legal basis for the presence of Vietnamese troops in Laos. Both sides agreed to 'strengthen their relations of socialist cooperation' in a wide variety of fields, including the training of cadres (Article 3). Scientific, technical and cultural exchanges were all to be increased. Three secret protocols to the treaty spelled out joint defence arrangements, an agreement on delineating the Lao–Vietnamese border, and Vietnamese economic assistance to Laos for the years 1978–80, including provision of Vietnamese advisers. Over the next several years, dozens of additional agreements were signed, covering everything from financial assistance, communications and transportation, to agriculture, education and information exchange. The anatomy of the 'special relationship' was thus both extensive and intensive, reaching into all areas of Lao national life.[26]

Relations were almost as close with the Soviet Union. Hundreds of Russian experts replaced American aid workers, while Soviet aid, if not quite as generous as that of the United States, accounted for around two-thirds of all foreign assistance received by the LPDR. As in the case of Vietnam, the Soviet Union and Laos exchanged a regular stream of

Party, state, army and 'friendship' delegations. Lao leaders took every opportunity to express their 'close solidarity and all-round cooperation' with the Soviet Union, which they recognized as undisputed leader of the communist bloc. Soviet aid consisted of both budget support to replace the counterpart funds previously generated by the defunct Foreign Exchange Operations Fund, and project aid to fund construction of telecommunications facilities, infrastructure and a hospital in Viang Chan. Soviet military assistance went especially to the air force, and provided heavy weapons and communications equipment for the army. Soviet pilots flew transport aircraft and helicopters.

Despite aid from the communist bloc, economic conditions failed to improve. Thai trade restrictions prevented a list of 273 so-called 'strategic items', including everything from aviation fuel and cement to bicycles and medicines, from reaching Laos. Alternative routes via Vietnam took much longer and were in poor repair. Malaria again became rife, as previous eradication programs collapsed. A second year of drought devastated crops the length of the country, despite relaxation of the ban, widely blamed for the 1976 drought, on the more overtly sexual fertility symbolism of the Rocket Festival (*bun bang fai*). Inflation ate further into meagre government salaries, while shortages in the 130 state-owned shops only made matters worse. The government was forced to appeal to the United Nations for donations of rice to meet a shortfall of over 100,000 tonnes. Even the parade marking the second anniversary of the regime was cancelled as an austerity measure.

Also of concern to the regime at this time were continuing tensions within the communist bloc – between the Soviet Union and China, and increasingly between the neighbouring states of Vietnam and Cambodia. For the Lao, the balance between China and the Soviet Union was easier to maintain than that between Vietnam and Cambodia. Chinese aid was gratefully accepted, but concentrated in the north and northwest, well away from any Soviet or Vietnamese projects. Construction continued on the northern road network linking Laos with southern China; Beijing provided interest-free loans to ease the demand for imports; and work began on a textile factory in Udomxai, where the Chinese had established a consulate.

Lao attempts to steer a middle course between Vietnam and Cambodia were not made any easier by the treaty with Vietnam. Escalating conflict on the Vietnam–Cambodian border during 1977 led the Khmer Rouge regime in Phnom Penh to break diplomatic relations with Hanoi. A last-ditch attempt by Suphānuvong to mediate during an official visit to Phnom Penh in December 1977 met with little success. Khmer Rouge leaders accused the Lao of permitting their territory to be used by Vietnamese forces and of carrying out hostile acts against Cambodia. The latter charge was denied by Viang Chan, though not the former.[27]

By early 1978, internal security was causing less disquiet. Virtually the entire former officer corps of the Royal Lao Army and senior civil servants still remained in detention camps. Many of those who had fled to Thailand had gone on to third countries, most to the United States, France and Australia. Another change of government in Bangkok had brought a more moderate military regime to power. In March of 1978, Laos and Thailand reaffirmed their August 1976 commitment to improve relations and make the Mekong 'a river of true peace and friendship'. The *kū xāt* were less active, and Hmong resistance had been all but eliminated. Even the loss of most of the urban middle class could be considered an advantage in that it removed a potential source of opposition to the regime. Conditions were thus favourable, so the Party believed, for the next step in the socialist transformation of the Lao economy.

In early March at a joint sitting of the Supreme People's Assembly and the Council of Ministers, Kaisôn presented an interim three-year economic development plan to run until 1981, when the country's first five-year plan would coincide with those of Vietnam and the Soviet Union. The interim plan had 'three fundamental political objectives': to strengthen solidarity, both internally and internationally; to strengthen national defence; and to promote the socialist transformation of the economy by developing 'socialist production relations'. These objectives were to be carried out in the face of 'a very subtle, vicious, counter-revolutionary two-faced campaign' conducted by the United States against the LPDR, which had become, in Kaisôn's words, 'the outpost of socialism in Southeast Asia'.[28] On the success of the three-year plan rested, therefore, not only the future of socialism in Laos, but its extension to the rest of the region.

In pursuit of this heroic vision, agriculture and forestry were to provide the basis for the subsequent development of industry. 'Profound revolutionary changes' would be needed in the countryside, Kaisôn told his audience, but conditions were ripe 'for rapidly diverting individual production to collective production'.[29] The Party believed that collectivization would achieve self-sufficiency in food production, while strengthening Party control in the countryside. It would thus both improve the economy and contribute to the defence of the country.

The cooperativization campaign was launched by Kaisôn himself early in June 1978.[30] In theory, a gradual approach was to be adopted to allow peasants time to become convinced of the benefits of collective production. Membership was to be voluntary, with land and basic means of production (buffaloes, ploughs, etc.) the property of the cooperative, but household goods remaining the property of individual families. In practice, however, enthusiastic cadres pressured families into joining against their will. By October the government was claiming a total of 'more than 800' cooperatives, thereby demonstrating the 'revolutionary enthusiasm' of the people. By December, there were 'over 1600'. A year later, the number had climbed to 2800.[31]

Resentment was immediate and widespread. Though land ownership was not uneven enough to warrant a prior program of redistribution, holdings varied sufficiently to make it unlikely that peasants would be equally motivated to pool their resources. Many feared irretrievable loss of land they had intended to pass on to their children. Others believed that cooperativization was but the first step towards the elimination of all private property. The shortage of qualified cadres meant that such fears were inadequately addressed. Moreover, limited resources prevented the state from providing promised technical and financial assistance.

Peasant opposition took various forms, from passive non-coopera-tion to destruction of crops and slaughter of cattle to prevent them becoming communal property, and even migration to Thailand. By the end of 1978, thousands of peasants had fled southern Laos, where plummeting production had been exacerbated by severe floods. Far from strengthening national defence, cooperativization gave renewed impetus to the resistance movement, which exploited popular discon-tent to undermine government credibility and gain recruits.

Concern over rising resistance to cooperativization was matched during 1978 by concern over deteriorating relations between Vietnam and Cambodia, and the implications this had for relations with China.[32] Early attempts to maintain some measure of neutrality had to be abandoned under intense Vietnamese and Soviet pressure. In July, Laos sided openly with Vietnam when Kaisôn, angered by what he believed were Chinese attempts to divide the Lao People's Revolutionary Party, denounced the Chinese leadership as 'international reactionaries', Viet-nam's term of abuse, and accused China of sowing dissension among ethnic minorities in northern Laos. The Chinese were asked to close their mission at Udomxai, the centre for coordination of their aid pro-gram. Over several weeks, meetings were held for senior cadres to explain and justify the decision to side with Vietnam. That the decision met with less than universal agreement even within the Party was suggested, however, both by some unguarded comments from Suphān-uvong, and by the need for subsequent anti-Chinese propaganda campaigns and the purge of some Party members.[33]

By the end of 1978, both security and the state of the economy had once again deteriorated. Reports that China was secretly assisting anti-government insurgents in northern Laos sufficiently alarmed the government for it to order the relocation of re-education camps in Phongsālī province to the Viang Xai area near the Vietnamese border. In the far south, the Lao–Cambodian border was particularly tense; opposition to cooperativization was increasingly exploited by the Thai-based resistance; and the shortfall in the rice harvest had again come in at over 100,000 tonnes.[34]

On 25 December 1978 Vietnamese forces invaded Cambodia to overthrow the Khmer Rouge government of Pol Pot. Two weeks later Laos was the first country formally to recognize the Vietnamese-backed People's Republic of Kampuchea. In March, Suphānuvong paid a state visit to Phnom Penh, during which a cooperative agreement was concluded with the new Vietnamese-backed Cambodian regime. This, though less comprehensive than the treaties signed by each country with Vietnam, effectively completed the formal basis for a new 'solidarity bloc' linking the three states of Indochina, in which Vietnam clearly was *primus inter pares*.[35]

China's February 1979 incursion into northern Vietnam to 'punish' Hanoi for the invasion of Cambodia did not spill over into Laos, but in the aftermath of the invasion, Lao relations with China came under even greater strain. Viang Chan was slow to condemn Beijing, but Lao authorities did – a little belatedly – echo Soviet and Vietnamese accusations that China was massing troops on the border with Laos, and eventually request suspension of all Chinese aid. Later in the year the Lao government demanded that Chinese diplomatic representation be reduced to twelve, the same level permitted the United States. The Chinese responded by warning Laos against 'unfriendly actions' towards China, and announced they were prepared to resettle 10,000 Lao refugees from camps in Thailand. The prospect of China recruiting young Lao for a northern insurgency caused grave concern in Viang Chan, as did the shadowy existence of a Chinese-backed 'Lao Socialist Party' dedicated to liberating Laos from Vietnamese domination.[36] A subsequent purge of suspected pro-Chinese dissidents within the Lao People's Revolutionary Party led to the defection of a number of officials to China.[37]

The grave deterioration of relations between China and both Laos and Vietnam led both states to seek improved relations with the Association of Southeast Asian Nations (ASEAN). For Laos, previous overtures to Bangkok bore fruit with the visit of Thai Prime Minister Kriangsak Chamanand to Viang Chan in January 1979, just as Vietnamese forces were overrunning Cambodia. A return visit by Kaisôn in April resulted in a communiqué reiterating agreement to create 'a zone of peace' along the Mekong by respecting each other's territorial integrity and sovereignty, suppressing insurgent activity, and encouraging trade. A price was also agreed upon for export of electricity from the recently completed second stage of the Nam Ngeum hydroelectric project. As Thai attitudes to the Vietnamese occupation of Cambodia hardened, however, and ASEAN stepped up its demands for withdrawal of Vietnamese forces, tension along the Mekong increased rather than diminished, and the Lao government found itself ever more isolated and dependent on Vietnam.

## RECONSIDERATIONS

By mid-1979, the difficulties facing the country were all too apparent. Events over the previous two years had favoured neither of the national goals of ensuring the security of the regime and increasing socialist production. Just the opposite, in fact. The Vietnamese occupation of Cambodia had resulted in mounting antagonism on the part of China and Thailand, both of which possessed the means to destabilize the Lao regime by supporting internal insurgencies. Lao security forces were none too efficient, and it was humiliating to have to rely on the presence of some 30,000 Vietnamese troops. It was essential, therefore, to minimize internal discontent – if only to reduce the appeal of *kū xāt* propaganda. In February, the Party launched a new Lao Front for National Construction to replace the former Lao Patriotic Front. Its task was to unify all 'patriotic forces' to create 'national solidarity', mobilize the people's 'collective mastery' to build and defend the country, and carry through the 'three revolutions'.[38] But the principal cause of discontent, at least in the rural areas, was the cooperativization drive, which formation of the Front did nothing to address.

By early 1979 Soviet and Vietnamese advisers, not to mention the International Monetary Fund of which Laos remained a member, were all urging a change of policy. In July the government abruptly announced the immediate suspension of cooperativization. Moreover, anyone who had already joined, presumably under duress, was free to opt out. Blame for shortcomings was placed upon unidentified 'enemies' whose effectiveness was openly admitted:

> the people, including the peasants, have become discouraged and unhappy. Some people have abandoned their farms, turned to other occupations, sold or secretly slaughtered their animals or fled to other countries. This has now become an urgent problem which will create an immediate and long-term danger if it is not quickly, effectively and skilfully resolved. It will become not only an economic danger affecting production and the people's living conditions but also a political danger. The enemy will take advantage of this to create confusion, win the support of the people and create difficulties for us.[39]

Suspension of the cooperativization program was the signal for a serious reconsideration of Party policy. Impetus for change came not only from the Party's own estimation of the state of affairs inside the country, but also from foreign advice and precedent. Soviet doubt over the effectiveness of cooperativization, given the paucity of Lao resources, was reinforced by the decision in September by the Vietnamese Communist Party to introduce more liberal economic reforms in southern Vietnam. The first indication of a change of direction in Laos came in early December when the 'liberation *kip*' was replaced by a new 'National Bank *kip*' at the rate of 100 to 1. The new official exchange rate of 10 NB *kip* to the US dollar effectively devalued the currency by bringing it into line with the free-market rate.

Later in the month, Kaisôn delivered what became known as the Seventh Resolution. In a wide-ranging review, Kaisôn proclaimed that in its present stage of development the Lao economy actually comprised five distinct sectors: the 'individual economy' of small-scale producers (farmers, traders, artisans); the collective economy of agricultural cooperatives; the capitalist economy (the few private enterprises still functioning); the state-capitalist joint-venture economy; and the state economy (nationalized industries and trading companies, state farms). Moreover, there remained a substantial subsistence sector outside the monetary economy. It was no use, Kaisôn argued, setting up the formal structures of socialist production relations if increasing productivity did not result. Laos could not hope to by-pass capitalism in this way, any more than the Soviet Union could in the early 1920s when Lenin had reverted to what became known as the 'new economic policy':

Lenin pointed out that under the conditions in which the economy is still composed of five sections [*sic*] and under the conditions of the beginning step of the bypassing period, it is inappropriate, indeed stupid, for any party to implement a policy of forbidding the people to exchange goods or to carry out trading. The implementation of such a policy by a party is suicidal. It is stupid because this policy cannot be successfully implemented in the economic field, and it is suicidal because any party which tries to implement such a policy will only meet with bankruptcy.[40]

If capitalists were permitted to operate as 'agents' of the state, however, the state could use 'the positive aspects' of the private economy to strengthen productive forces in preparation for a later transition to socialism, Kaisôn declared. By implication, capitalism would in future not simply be permitted: it would be encouraged. Private entrepreneurs would be welcome to invest in joint ventures, in industry, construction, transportation and trade for, as Kaisôn admitted: 'Almost all factory directors appointed by the state have had no management experience.'[41] Lip-service was paid to the need to strengthen agricultural cooperatives, but the real thrust of rural policy was already clear from the 'trading orders' promulgated a week earlier establishing a free market in agricultural products, including rice but excluding commercial export crops. All controls on the free circulation of goods were abolished. The state procurement price for rice was raised to close to market rates to encourage production and reduce smuggling to Thailand, and new, lower agricultural taxes were introduced. The immediate result was to increase rice production in 1980 by 16.5 per cent.[42]

The extent of economic reform was greater than expected. Not only was the market to determine the value of goods, but the whole system of socialist management of the economy put into place over the preceding three years was to be radically revised. A new system of 'balanced and profitable management' was foreshadowed based on 'value and utility', along with decentralization of economic decision-making. The reality of continuing regionalism was recognized by giving provinces the right to trade directly with neighbouring countries, a move which opened the way for creeping corruption. Accompanying administrative and Party reforms attempted to curb the arbitrary authority of Party cadres. Recruitment of new cadres was stepped up, and efforts were made to enforce ideological discipline.

Hopes of improved economic performance were dashed, however, by deteriorating relations with Thailand. Thai sensitivity over the Vietnamese military presence in both Cambodia and Laos meant that the slightest border incident provoked an exaggerated response. In June 1980 Bangkok again unilaterally closed the frontier, accusing Laos of 'dancing the steps dictated by those manipulating it'. The Lao responded by blaming 'Thai reactionaries' for implementing the policies of 'the Beijing reactionary ruling clique'. Eventually two crossing points were reopened, but the government was determined to complete an all-weather truck route from Danang to Savannakhēt, along with an oil pipeline to circumvent future Thai blockades. Both projects were under-funded, however, and suffered construction delays.

The deterioration in Lao–Thai relations reflected heightened tensions over Cambodia. By 1980 the lines had been clearly drawn between the three Indochinese states, supported by the Soviet Union and its allies, on one side, and those countries – ASEAN led by Thailand, China and the United States – backing the Cambodian resistance factions on the other.[43] For the next eight years, until Vietnamese forces eventually withdrew from both Cambodia and Laos, this alignment of powers over Cambodia determined the international environment within which the Lao government was forced to pursue the nation's interests. At half-yearly meetings of the Foreign Ministers of the three Indochinese states, and at the first 'summit conference' of their heads of government held in Viang Chan in February 1983, the Lao dutifully supported the Viet-namese position in defence of the regime in Phnom Penh.

The powerlessness of Viang Chan in the face of this international alignment of powers was so evident, however, that of the three countries of Indochina, Laos suffered least in terms of political and economic repercussions. No state broke diplomatic relations with the LPDR: no embargo was placed on international aid. The United States continued to insist on a full accounting of Americans listed as missing in action in Laos during the Second Indochina War (mostly the crews of aircraft shot down over Lao territory), but did not prevent international lending institutions such as the World Bank and Asian Development Bank making loans to the LPDR. The United States did, however, orchestrate an international outcry over the alleged use of chemical agents against Hmong dissidents in northern Laos in the form of so-called 'yellow rain'. Investigations were inconclusive at the time, and subsequently the United States admitted it lacked any real evidence.[44]

Relations with China remained cool, but as Laos posed no threat to Beijing, the Chinese authorities could afford to be magnanimous. By 1983 Beijing had begun to reconsider its support for a Lao Socialist Party and for the factionalized Lao resistance movement,[45] preferring to bide its time until international pressure on Cambodia forced a loosen-ing of Vietnamese 'hegemony' throughout Indochina.[46] While the Lao media ritually voiced criticism of Chinese policy towards Cambodia and Vietnam, rhetoric denouncing the 'Beijing reactionary clique' was not reflected in reality. Tension diminished along the Lao–Chinese border, where traditional trading relations soon resumed.[47] Only relations with Thailand continued to cause concern.

In 1981 the Lao People's Revolutionary Party launched the country's first five-year economic development plan to coincide with similar plans in Vietnam and the Soviet Union. The economic foundations, however, were far from encouraging. While the interim three-year plan had not been a total disaster – thanks to changes introduced in the Seventh Resolution – it had failed to meet almost all its targets. Government expenditure continued to run at double total revenue, leaving a budget deficit that only underlined the country's high dependency on foreign aid to finance development – especially as exports (mainly electricity and timber to Thailand, with some coffee and opium going to socialist countries) amounted to less than half the value of imports.[48]

The plan called for increases in both agricultural and industrial production; though not on the face of it over-ambitious, these were yet, given the state of the economy, virtually unachievable. That few targets were eventually met was due partly to the plan's heavy reliance on foreign assistance, and partly to the lack of trained personnel. Meanwhile technicians and civil servants continued to seek asylum in Thailand for reasons more economic than political, attracted by stories of relatives already resettled in France, the United States, or Australia. The 'close to 10,000' students and workers sent to study abroad between 1976 and 1981, most in Vietnam, were either ill-trained or yet to return. Moreover decision-making remained centralized, with even the most minor technical matters being referred up the hierarchy to the respective minister. Together lack of skilled personnel and poor administrative structures made it difficult even to absorb the relatively modest levels of international aid received (in the vicinity of $US95 million per annum). So the expected benefits of the first five-year plan failed to materialize.

## PARTY REFORMS

By 1982 the Lao People's Revolutionary Party felt sufficiently secure to hold its Third Congress. The four-day meeting took place in Viang Chan at the end of April, ten years after the secret Second Congress, and was a much more public affair. Strict security, including an 11 p.m. curfew and travel restrictions into and out of Viang Chan, protected the Party leadership and visiting delegations. Eventually 228 delegates (208 men and 20 women, reflecting the continued imbalance of gender and power) assembled from all parts of the country. Sixteen foreign fraternal delegations attended, headed by the Soviet Union and Vietnam. The French Communist Party was the only representative from a Western country. China did not send a delegation.

In his political report to the Congress, Kaisôn recognized shortcomings since 1975 but put them down to 'subjectivism and oversimplification'. Party cadres were called upon firmly to grasp the new Party line and policies. As for the economy, a more gradual approach was endorsed, with priority given to agriculture and forestry to create the 'base' on which industry could later develop. The 'militant solidarity' of the special relationship and the 'all-sided cooperation' between Laos, Vietnam and Cambodia were hailed as the mainstay of Lao foreign policy, along with 'solidarity and all-round cooperation' with the Soviet Union. The words were carefully chosen to reflect the longer-standing relations with Vietnam, as against the relative preponderance of influence exercised by as many as 2000 Soviet and East European advisers and technicians working in Laos and the level of Soviet military and economic assistance. Addressing the Party, Kaisôn stressed the need to improve political and ideological training and 'organizational work'.

Just why was revealed in his call to create more Party cells in those 'newly liberated areas' taken over in 1975, and to purge cadres 'no longer exemplary in their conduct' – oblique references both to continuing unpopularity of the Party among lowland Lao and to growing corruption.[49] For the first time, official figures for Party membership were given – at 35,000, well up on the 21,000 said to have been members at the time of the Second Congress in 1972, but still only around 1 per cent of the population.[50]

The Congress elected the same seven-member Politburo that had led the Party for the previous decade. The Secretariat was increased from six to nine members, while the Central Committee was more than doubled. Minority representation also increased, though to nowhere near their proportion of the population. Of the Lao Lum membership, however, several were hill Tai, Phuan or Leu. Fifteen members were veterans of the Indochina Communist Party, while 90 per cent were reported to have attended intermediate or higher Marxist–Leninist theoretical courses, the latter conducted at the Nguyen Ai Quoc Institute in Vietnam.[51] Those promoted to full membership of the Central Committee included eight provincial Party secretaries, eight generals, and seven ministers or vice-ministers – a nice balance between the provinces, the army, and the government. The remainder held positions in the Party or mass organizations. The number of women increased from one to four.

In September, the structure of government was altered in conformity with decisions taken at the Third Party Congress. The previous twelve ministries and three state committees were increased to fifteen ministries and five state committees. All three new ministries had to do with the economy, a good indication of the importance given to economic development and implementation of the five-year plan. The two new state committees were for Veterans and Social Affairs, and for Propaganda, Press, Radio and Television.

Reorganization of the structure of government resulted in creation of three distinct levels. At the apex was an inner cabinet, comprising the prime minister and five deputy prime ministers with broad responsibility for various ministries. This inner cabinet was to draw up policy guidelines, and to direct respective sectors: Nūhak Phumsavan, economy; Sālī Vongkhamxao, planning; Phūmī Vongvichit, education, culture and information; Khamtai Sīphandôn, defence and internal security; and Phūn Sīpasoet, foreign affairs. At the second level were grouped the nineteen ministers and chairs of state committees responsible for individual ministries, while at the third level some eighty-odd vice-ministers and vice-chairs, many with technical expertise and several Western-trained, handled specific administrative duties and decisions.[52]

From the changes brought about by the Third Party Congress, it was possible to identify certain power relationships within the top leadership. The most significant promotion was of Sālī Vongkhamxao to eighth-ranking member of the Central Committee and deputy prime minister in charge of planning. Many thus saw him as Kaisôn's likely successor, as well he might have been had he not suddenly died of a heart attack in January 1991. Significant gains were made by the military. Four vice-ministers of defence gained full Central Committee membership, while four other ministries in addition to the interior were entrusted to former army officers. Meanwhile the appointment of powerful provincial Party secretaries to full membership of the Central Committee went beyond pragmatic recognition of the reality of regionalism to recognize the need to co-opt regional leaders into the centralized power structure.

Throughout 1983, a major effort was also undertaken to organize and consolidate the Party. Everywhere the masses were encouraged 'positively to take part in the building of the Party'. Every anniversary, including the centenary of the death of Karl Marx, was used to sound the same theme. Courses in Marxism–Leninism were held for teachers, women and other groups. An attempt to make the Party journal, renamed *Paxāxon* (The People), more accessible and to increase its distribution met with only limited success. For despite all the propaganda, Marxism–Leninism held little or no appeal for most Lao. Of greater interest than politics was the monthly cultural magazine *Vannasin*, whose lively pages published contributions from readers in verse and prose.

For the first time in 1983, national congresses were held by the Union of Lao Women and by the Lao People's Revolutionary Youth Union. The women's congress in March elected Khamphaeng Bubphā as president and heard Kaisôn proclaim the importance of women's emancipation for the socialist revolution,[53] a speech that might better have been addressed to his male Party colleagues, for revolutionary Laos continued to be a highly patriarchal, male-dominated society. That the Union of Lao Women seemed hardly likely to bring about radical change was evident from its endorsement of the 'three goods' – that it was the duty of all women 'to be a good wife, good mother, and good citizen'.[54] The youth congress in April provided a forum for Thongvin Phomvihān, Kaisôn's wife. Already a full member of the Party's Central Committee, she was elected first vice-president of the youth union (and president two years later). The union claimed a membership of 115,000, represented by 245 delegates, who were encouraged to see themselves as 'shock troops' in the struggle to carry out the 'three revolutions'.

What undermined the best intentions of the Party to promote internal reform was the resurgence, by the mid-1980s, of the system of patronage so deeply ingrained in Lao political culture. Patronage within the Party took the form of promotion and appointment to office. Nepotism ensured rapid promotion for those closely related to powerful leaders. Middle-level cadres not so closely related also came to be identified as belonging not so much to factions in a political or ideological sense, but to patronage networks identified with senior Party figures. Important patronage networks were especially associated with those able to secure economic advantage – that is, with such powerful economic ministers as Nūhak Phūmsavan and Sālī Vongkhamxao. Contracts, import and export permits and authorization to invest in a new enterprise could all be facilitated through such relationships.[55]

Such patronage networks extended outside the Party. As members of the former Lao elite who had remained in Viang Chan began to take advantage of the more liberal political and economic climate resulting from the policy shift announced in the Seventh Resolution, they naturally sought assurances and assistance in facilitating investment from senior Party officials – preferably from those to whom they were related by blood or marriage or with whom they had previously attended the same school, or shared similar experiences, or who came from the same home province. Those with marketable skills or investment capital developed relationships with Party leaders based on a variety of personal, family, and business contacts. Powerful Party leaders thereby built up networks of influence and obligation that extended beyond the Party itself, and came to mirror the patronage exercised by elite clans under the former regime. Such patronage relationships have enabled certain families who were wealthy or powerful under the former regime to re-establish positions of economic and even political influence.

The new economic climate of the 1980s, together with the developing patronage networks, opened up new opportunities for corruption. It might be argued that facilitating economic investment to assist a relative was for the good of the country, but when 'gifts' were given, or kickbacks paid, it became a matter of bribery or graft. In March 1983, two vice-ministers were arrested on charges that were never made public. Rumour suggested corruption in relation to certain foreign business deals, but a more likely reason is that both had been critical of Party decisions. Both had been civil servants under the former regime, and both had been educated in France. Moreover, their appointment as vice-ministers had been resented. Other arrests of minor officials followed. All were tried and found guilty, but the whole episode seems to have had more to do with intra-Party jealousies than with irregularities in administration or improper conduct. In mid-1984, as a result of political pressure rather than available legal processes, a 'special appeals tribunal' ordered the release of both vice-ministers, along with others arrested. All were restored to their former positions without explanation. Such incidents did little to discourage corruption – and nothing to encourage bureaucratic initiative.[56]

In 1984, four more vice-ministers were arrested on various charges – indulging in anti-Party activities (criticizing government economic policy to foreigners), falsely accusing those arrested earlier, and outright corruption (connivance in accepting reconditioned, rather than new, earth-moving machinery from a Thai dealer). Again a number of minor officials were detained. Trials were held in secret, with sentences depending as much on the influence of family connections and powerful 'patrons' as on the crime committed. If nothing else, these proceedings showed up the inadequacies of the legal system, based as it was on politically influenced 'people's courts' rather than on constitutionally

grounded legal statutes.[57] Even though a 'constitution drafting committee' presided over by Suphānuvong had been established as a special
committee of the Supreme People's Assembly, no report had been
released by 1984, when two sub-committees were appointed to examine
work done and 'study and grasp the social situation'. It was to be
another seven years, however, before the regime at last decided upon a
constitution.

In the meantime, regulations were issued designed both to control
corruption and to stimulate private trade and investment. The government admitted that malpractices were occurring, and listed smuggling,
profiteering, formation of monopolies, failure to conform to the Party
line, stealing of state goods, failure to pay government tax, and pressur-
ing peasants to sell privately instead of to the state as those to be
avoided. Tighter currency controls were introduced on foreign trade,
while a special rate of 108 *kip* to the US dollar was introduced for
private transactions to encourage remittances from Lao abroad. Illegal
gambling was circumvented through an officially approved National
Development Lottery. Meanwhile government propaganda castigated
any return to 'capitalist ways', and condemned copious consumption,
whether on Buddhist feast days or in lavish private parties. Censorship
of news and other publications was enforced and the importation of
videos banned, though little could be done to prevent Lao citizens
receiving Thai television beamed across from towns such as Nôngkhāy,
Nakhôn Phanom and Ubon. In December 1983, Lao national television
began broadcasting three nights weekly, but could hardly compete with
Thai programming. Little wonder Kaisôn warned of the continuing
struggle between socialist and capitalist thinking.

Television was only one complicating factor in relations with Thailand. Of greater concern was Thai support for the disparate resistance
groups gathered under the umbrella of the National United Front for
the Liberation of Laos. In southern Laos attacks were mounted on
government installations and development projects. Vehicles were
ambushed, and a Danish employee of the World Bank killed. But claims
that the number of guerrillas was as high as 9000, with roughly 4000
operating in northern Laos (principally Hmong) and 5000 in the south,
were certainly exaggerated. Overall, however, thanks to the continued
presence in Laos by then of up to 40,000 Vietnamese troops, the resistance presented only a limited challenge to the regime, though its
nuisance value required heightened security measures.

Kaisôn's call at the Third Party Congress for 'relations of friendship
and good neighbourliness' with Thailand seemed at first to have its
desired effect. In 1984, however, tension increased dramatically when
Lao troops prevented construction of a Thai road in the vicinity of three
villages on the border of Xainyaburī province. Unsuccessful Thai
attempts to dislodge the Lao force were followed by a full-scale assault
to seize the villages by 1500 Thai troops. What had been a minor border
dispute was thus transformed into a major diplomatic incident. As the
assault followed a visit to Beijing in mid-May by the supreme commander of the Thai army, Lao authorities justifiably suspected collusion

between China and what they called 'ultra-rightist reactionary elements among the Thai ruling circles'. Both sides claimed the villages – the Lao on the basis of the 1907 French map delineating the frontier; the Thai on the basis of an American aerial survey conducted in 1978 purporting to locate the villages on the Thai side of the watershed which officially constitutes the border. When extended negotiations failed to resolve the matter, Laos took its case to the UN Security Council. Thai troops thereupon withdrew from the villages, though not from all territory claimed by Viang Chan, taking most of the 1800 inhabitants with them.[58]

There the matter rested. Demands by Laos for high-level negotiations to resolve the 'three villages' dispute and other outstanding bilateral problems were rejected by Bangkok. The Viang Chan media unleashed a barrage of criticism of the Thai regime to expose 'the dark side of Thai society'. Thai leaders were accused of being both expansionist and beholden to their 'Chinese masters'.[59] By mid-1985 the tone was less shrill, but relations remained strained. Lao annoyance focused also on the arbitrary list of so-called 273 'strategic goods' for which Thailand still refused to issue transit permits. Another irritant was the refugee problem. In 1984, more Lao fled their homeland, many of them young people lured by persistent rumours that they had to reach Thailand by the end of the year in order to be eligible for resettlement in third countries. At the same time, the UN High Commissioner for Refugees began a small repatriation program. Not until November 1986 did Lao–Thai negotiations address Lao complaints (and reduce the list of strategic items to sixty-one). Not until after Vietnamese troops withdrew from Cambodia did some warmth enter into Lao–Thai relations.

## TAKING STOCK

For the LPDR, 1985 was a year of anniversaries, an occasion to assess the nation's achievements and rethink future directions. On 22 March the Party celebrated thirty years of 'correct and creative' leadership of the Lao revolution. Then on 2 December the regime celebrated completion both of its first decade in power and of the first five-year plan. Both were occasions for self-congratulation, but also for a sober assessment of the results of a decade of socialist development. The inescapable conclusion, whether measured by the socialist transformation of the Lao economy or by the formation of dedicated Lao socialist men and women imbued with the ideals of and a commitment to Marxism–Leninism, was that anticipated changes had been less far-reaching than had been hoped. Laos remained a desperately impoverished country, dependent as ever on foreign aid, with a poorly trained workforce, and for most of the population a subsistence standard of living. The regime put a brave face on things, but the reality could not be hidden. Even a year-long 'emulation campaign' designed 'to score as many achievements as possible in strongly and firmly consolidating and perfecting the system of the dictatorship of the proletariat in the political, ideological, and organizational fields' was not enough to create the desired 'atmosphere of revolutionary enthusiasm'.[60]

The thirtieth anniversary of 'the noble, glorious' Lao People's Revolutionary Party was another occasion to re-emphasize the leading role of the Party. About that at least, there was no debate. The Party's 'wise and clearsighted leadership' and its 'correct and creative line' were proclaimed responsible for every victory achieved. Party membership was up to 43,000, an increase of some 8000 since the Third Party Congress.[61] The Party's monopoly of power was complete. Amidst all the hype, however, there could be discerned a note of disquiet over the motivation, and thus the quality, of these who joined the Party. An internal Party document lamented that 'the intellectual level and sense of discipline of members of the Party are very low'.[62] Commitment to the cause of socialism had begun to give way to greed and nepotism. Party membership too often was seen as a means of pursuing personal ambition for gain or power. Two programs were therefore designed to raise the political consciousness of Party members and the masses: Soviet instructors were invited to conduct courses on Marxist–Leninist theory for middle-level cadres, while troops of the renamed Lao People's Army were sent to work at the grassroots level in the countryside. Neither had much long-term effect.

The enhanced political role of the Lao People's Army did, however, reflect the growing influence of the army within the Party and its importance in the social and economic life of the country. The army was described as acting as 'the shock force of ... the Party and people' in pursuing its assigned tasks.[63] Not only was the army active in 'the implementation of Party work' and in 'logistics and technical work to guarantee an improvement of living conditions', but it was also given a significant role in the economic development of the country. In addition to construction projects and the management of army farms and factories, the army was awarded rights to exploit important timber reserves. As of 1985 it was free to negotiate its own contracts with foreign buyers, with profits going to finance purchase of equipment and development projects assigned to the army under the second five-year plan. The army, like provincial administrations, was thus given the means to become a largely self-sufficient economic unit. It was also provided with new opportunities for smuggling and other forms of corruption – which is perhaps why Kaisôn warned that in exploiting its timber concessions, the army would have to 'respect and correctly implement state regulations and procedures'.[64]

As one of its tasks for the anniversary year of 1985, the government conducted the first complete census since independence in 1953. Total population was put at 3,584,803, made up of 49 per cent males and 51 per cent females. A breakdown of the figures was given for each of the sixteen provinces (three – Bôkaeo, Bôlikhamxai and Xēkông – having been newly created) and for the administratively independent municipality of Viang Chan (consisting of seven former districts carved out of Viang Chan province, taking in the city and surrounding villages). The most populous province was Savannakhēt, while the least was Xēkông. Viang Chan municipality had a population of 377,409, though total urban population amounted to only 15 per cent. The population was young: 47 per cent under the age of fifteen, while only 6 per cent was over sixty. The rate of population increase was put at 2.9 per cent annually. Although questions about ethnicity were not asked, one estimated breakdown put the Lao Lum (all those speaking Tai languages) at 68 per cent of the population; Lao Thoeng, 22 per cent; and Lao Sūng (speaking both Hmong-Mien and Tibeto-Burman languages), 10 per cent.[65]

The tenth anniversary of the founding of the LPDR was celebrated with much pomp and ceremony in December. Crowds gathered before dawn to witness a parade of military hardware and floats from each ministry that was bigger and better even than 1980. The economic and social achievements of the regime over the previous ten years in developing the Lao economy and transforming Lao society were proudly proclaimed, though all the propaganda could hardly hide the equally evident shortcomings. The claim by Kaisôn that gross domestic product had more than doubled, while production per head of population had increased by 60 per cent, was misleading in that, as usual, base figures were not given.[66] Presumably increases were calculated on figures for 1975 or 1976, both years of severe economic disruption and low production. A more accurate estimate was provided by a United Nations Development Program (UNDP) draft report which indicated that gross domestic product had risen only slightly or actually fallen in the years from 1980 to 1983, followed by a reasonable recovery in 1984. Average income per annum was put at $US98, making the LPDR still one of the poorest countries in the world.[67]

In the vital agriculture sector, though self-sufficiency in rice had been achieved, production remained variable and dependent on weather. Moreover, yields remained among the lowest in the world, with production improvements due to an increase in the area under cultivation, only 1.25 per cent of which was irrigated. Other food crops also registered increases in production, though significantly Kaisôn gave no figures for industrial crops, except to say that they had been 'progressively developed'. Timber production too had been disappointing, with many of the country's fifty sawmills and its one plywood factory working at below capacity, due in part to the smuggling of unsawn logs.

Surprisingly, Kaisôn credited the formation of agricultural cooperatives with bringing about the 'socialist transformation of agriculture', claiming that more than 50 per cent of all farming families were grouped in over 3000 functioning 'agri-cooperatives'.[68] This was below the first five-year plan target of 60 to 70 per cent of all farmers in cooperatives by the end of 1985, but even so the figure was grossly inflated. Most cooperatives existed only on paper, or were very loosely organized, with farmers permitted to withdraw their land and farm privately when they wished. In fact the UNDP estimated that as many as 90 per cent of all Lao farmers continued to own their own land, averaging 1.5 hectares, despite the existence of cooperatives.[69]

In industrial production, the target of doubling output during the course of the first five-year plan was nowhere near met. In fact output fell in 1982–83 and failed to recover with agriculture in 1984. Industry accounted for just over 5 per cent of gross domestic product, a figure well below the average even for 'least-developed countries'. Management was generally inefficient, and almost all the eighteen large factories under control of the Ministry of Industry continued to run well below capacity. Nor were targets met in either communications or public works, though improvements were made to the road network, thanks to rural road and bridge construction.

As for social and cultural development, Kaisôn succinctly summed up the central task in his tenth anniversary speech. It was, he said, to build a culture and system of education which would create 'a new, socialist type of person' – the third of the 'three revolutions'.[70] Judged by this criterion, the result of ten years of socialism was not encouraging. The government claimed substantial increases in the number of schools and students attending at every level, but the statistics, even if accurate, masked deeper problems – plummeting standards, a total dearth of textbooks, and a lack of qualified teachers, exacerbated by failure to pay teachers regularly and adequately. Most disappointing was the fact that 80 per cent of all primary school students failed to complete the full five years, and large disparities existed between urban and rural areas, and between lowland Lao and minority groups. Literacy had increased markedly, even if nowhere near the 100 per cent claimed by the government. Yet after years of improvement, illiteracy was again on the rise as older people forgot what they learned through lack of practice. At upper levels the standard of comprehension of the few students completing secondary school was so low that many were unable to follow courses either at the Russian-built Polytechnic Institute in Viang Chan or when sent to study overseas. Students returning from communist bloc countries whose languages they had never fully mastered too often possessed diplomas, but little or no knowledge.[71]

In the field of health, the story was much the same: numbers of medical personnel and dispensaries had increased, according to government figures, but the quality of training and service had declined. First-aid posts in most Lao Thoeng villages existed only on paper. Those that still functioned lacked medicines, and health extension services were hopelessly inadequate. Even in the urban centres, the five-year-plan target for the number of hospital beds had been only half filled. By 1985, even according to government figures, only 18 per cent of Lao villages had supplies of potable water. Malaria, intestinal disorders and various other endemic diseases remained pressing health problems, and the diet, especially of ethnic minorities, was often poor to the point of malnutrition.[72]

Some change in lifestyle had come about, however, over the previous five years through relaxation of political tension, greater personal freedoms, and a resurgence of Buddhist festivities. One or two nightclubs were open, and Lao officials mixed more freely with the foreign community in Viang Chan. Christianity was again officially recognized as an 'acceptable' religion.[73] More significantly, Party leaders had come to acknowledge the close relationship between traditional Lao culture and Buddhism. Major Buddhist ceremonies were attended by Politburo members and their wives, and Party members were even permitted to enter the *Sangha* for limited periods. According to official figures, there were 2812 pagodas in Laos, 373 of which had been renovated or built since 1975. In them lived almost 7000 monks and more than 9000 novices, down on the royal Lao period, but indicative of a resurgence of Buddhism after the repression of the late 1970s.[74] Doctrinally, however, Buddhism had been simplified and rationalised, purged of 'super-stitious' elements. The new Buddhism taught three simple rules of conduct: to abstain from sin; to accumulate merit; and to purify the heart. Monks were also obliged to study Marxism–Leninism, a practice defended as necessary in order to understand government policies.[75]

One matter not mentioned in any government report on the tenth anniversary of the republic was the continued detention, after ten years without trial, of thousands of political prisoners from the former regime. Amnesty International issued two key reports in April 1985 and January 1986 on conditions in camps in northern and southern Laos respectively.[76] At that time, some 6000 to 7000 political detainees were still being 'arbitrarily restricted', though after 1983 many were no longer held in 'heavily-guarded internment camps' subjected to political re-education, but were rather assigned to construction camps performing heavy physical labour, such as road building. Moreover, responsibility for the detainees had been transferred from the Ministry of Defence to the Ministry of the Interior. Amnesty expressed strong concern over the lack of legal safeguards for all Lao citizens, particularly political prisoners; prison conditions, including medical facilities; and the many deaths from malnutrition, disease and attempted escape. Over the next three years, under continuing international pressure, the great majority of these detainees were at last released.

In summary, therefore after ten years of socialism, the goal of carrying forward the 'three revolutions' – in mode of production, science and technology, and culture and ideology – whether through propaganda or re-education, had proved largely unsuccessful. Cooperativization had been patchy and partial, and agriculture had hardly been socialized. While major industries had been nationalized, their performance was abysmal and they employed only a tiny workforce of around 8000. Training in science and application of technology had produced few results since educational levels were so low. As for creating a new generation ideologically committed to building Marxism–Leninism, most Lao had simply learned to live with the new system, and to manipulate it in their own interests through the well-understood means of personal contact and the patronage of power.

## SOCIALISM ABANDONED

In his speech to the Supreme People's Assembly in January 1985, Kaisôn Phomvihān warned darkly that 'the struggle to resolve the problem of who is winning over whom between the two lines in our country – socialism and capitalism – developed to a new phase in a fiercer and more uncompromising manner in the past year'.[77] Four times in his speech Kaisôn returned to this theme of the 'two-line struggle'. Evidently a political struggle was being waged within the Party, but between which factions in pursuit of which policies was unclear. Kaisôn himself had pushed through the reforms of the Seventh Resolution – reforms which arguably undermined socialism and constituted a partial reintroduction of capitalism. Were there those in the Party urging that the process should go further, against whom Kaisôn wanted to hold the line? That seemed at the time a likely conclusion. Yet subsequent events were to show that it was Kaisôn who wanted greater liberalization and who over the following five years forced through policies which effectively led to abandonment of a socialist economy.

In retrospect, the 'two-line struggle' of 1984 and 1985 was not between socialism and capitalism, or even between socialism and pragmatism. It was a struggle between those aligned with Kaisôn who wanted to introduce economic reforms designed to make the economy more efficient and thus more productive, and those aligned with Nūhak who were profiting from the system already in place because it provided them with the power of patronage through waiving controls, setting prices, or issuing permits.[78] What seems to have swung the balance in Kaisôn's favour was the support of the army. Both Khamtai Sīphandôn and General Sīsavāt Kaeobunphan were interested in obtaining more of the economic action. Timber contracts and trading rights may well have been the price demanded by the army for its support.[79]

If ideology was not the principal consideration underlying the bitter 'two-line struggle', it was nevertheless fought out in terms of ideological positions. Those supporting Kaisôn argued that the transition to socialism in Laos was impossible, given the current state of economic development. It would be necessary to take a step back by introducing certain capitalist methods in order later to take two steps forward in building true socialism. Those supporting Nūhak were loath to surrender any state control over economic production or distribution, both of which they argued were essential if Laos was to remain a socialist state. The argument over how and how fast the socialist transformation of the Lao economy and society should proceed raged on into 1986, requiring postponement of the Fourth Party Congress from April to November. It was essential to resolve the matter not only in order for the Party to present an apparently unified front at the Congress, but also because of the need to formulate policy guidelines for the second five-year plan due to run from 1986 to 1990.

That some kind of compromise had been worked out was clear from the Congress itself. While Kaisôn as Party Secretary-General presented the lengthy political report, it was Nūhak, not Sālī Vongkhamxao as Planning Minister, who presented the 1986–90 plan with its policies, priorities and targets. Kaisôn made it clear, however, that pragmatism and further reform had won the day. Policies favouring economic development would be pursued at the expense of socialist ideological rectitude where necessary, even if the transition to true socialism was thereby delayed. Kaisôn also seized the opportunity to castigate his opponents and blame them for the disappointing lack of progress over the previous decade. The main shortcomings, he told the Party Congress, lay

> in early activism and haste, in over inclination to abolish the non-socialist economic sectors promptly. In industry, we rashly nationalized many factories, while the state still lacked sufficient management capacity, resulting in production decrease. Regarding trade, there have been rather widespread cases of hindering the free flow of commodities among localities, thus adversely affecting production and people's lives.[80]

The very intensity of criticism, however, suggested the strength of opposition to the reform platform yet remaining within the Party. Prudently, Kaisôn justified his criticism by reference to Lenin on the importance of identifying 'weak points'. He subsequently received support from similar decisions taken by the Sixth Congress of the Vietnamese Communist Party the following month, though Laos was moving further and faster in its reform agenda.

The second five-year plan, when it was finally revealed, essentially followed the directions taken by the previous plan. Emphasis remained on agriculture, with increases called for in per capita rice and total food production. The largest increases, however, were reserved for cash crops, some of which were to be grown almost exclusively for export to pay for imports from the communist bloc. These included coffee, mung beans, soya beans, peanuts and tobacco. Fully 10 per cent of total government investment over this period was to be devoted to development of forestry and a timber industry producing processed timber products.[81] Agriculture took precedence over industry (with more realistic scaled-down targets compared with the first five-year plan), while one-fifth of all investment was to go to infrastructure development, mainly road construction. Spending on health and education was increased, with emphasis placed on improving teacher training and increasing the number of medical workers.

The most significant decision of the Congress, however, was formally to endorse what was called the New Economic Mechanism. This initiative, announced earlier in the year, purported to be about improving efficiency of management, and hence the productivity of state-owned enterprises, by allowing greater autonomy and demanding greater accountability from managers. The old system, which Kaisôn criticized for its 'bureaucratic centralism' and dependency on state subsidies, was to be replaced by a new system in which enterprises were self-financing from their own profits.[82] In other words, under the New Economic Mechanism market forces were to operate, with the implication that state enterprises incapable of making a profit would go to the wall.

Not surprisingly, Nûhak justified the New Economic Mechanism in more orthodox socialist terms as 'an instrument to enhance the initiative and creativeness of the localities and grass-roots'. He could hardly hide the fact, however, that loosening centralized bureaucratic controls and introducing market forces were radical departures. As early as 1983 controls had been relaxed on more successful state enterprises (more productive, more profitable), which were permitted to use up to 40 per cent of profits for reinvestment and worker bonuses. Pressure for the change came not only from Western donors and international lending institutions, such as the Asian Development Bank and the IMF, but also from the Soviet Union and Vietnam where similar experiments were under way. The new mechanism was accompanied by an unpublicized shake-up of the bureaucracy, especially in the economic ministries, bringing in younger and better-trained personnel. Few, however, were yet prepared to take managerial initiatives, given the ubiquitous presence of the Party and 'the lingering atmosphere of distrust and fear' that pervaded the bureaucracy.[83]

Any positive economic impact of the new management system was slow in coming, therefore. Outright opposition, bureaucratic inertia, and the lack of trained personnel all conspired to reduce any immediate effect. The government began by reducing public-sector employment, increasing procurement prices, and dismantling most fixed food subsidies for public servants. The effects were painful. Prices rose, while salary increases as compensation failed to keep pace. Civil servants found it even more necessary to take on extra employment – to the detriment of their official duties. Inefficiency, unrealistic pricing, poor investment decisions, and over-reliance on the state were major problems encountered as state-owned enterprises adjusted to a decentralized market economy.

The Fourth Party Congress predictably endorsed the political leadership. Kaisôn retained his position as Secretary-General, and the same seven senior members of the Politburo were re-elected in the same order.[84] The Politburo was enlarged, however, with election of four additional full and two alternate members constituting a leadership in waiting. The Secretariat remained the same size, while the Central Committee was expanded by five (two full and three alternate members) and its composition, in contrast to the Third Congress, significantly altered through the addition of thirteen full and nine alternate new younger members to replace those dropped. Composition by ethnicity and gender remained roughly the same.

The Congress was attended by, among others, high-ranking delegations from Vietnam and Cambodia, indicating that Indochinese solidarity was still firmly in place. Earlier Kaisôn had sounded three themes uniting the three countries: recognition of Ho Chi Minh and the role of the Indochinese Communist Party as laying the foundations for the revolutions of all three countries; the continuing role of Vietnam as the 'staunch and unbreakable mainstay for the firm militant solidarity' between the three; and the need to defeat 'the dark designs of the Chinese reactionists', their common enemy whose aim was 'to swallow up the three countries'.[85] Among the innumerable delegations continually exchanged between Vietnam and Laos, those reinforcing military cooperation were of particular note. Though the Soviet Union provided training for the more sophisticated equipment, such as MIG-21 jet fighters, the Vietnamese continued to play an important role in equipping and training the Lao People's Army. Estimates of the number of Vietnamese troops in Laos varied, but never fell below 30,000.

By 1985, however, there were subtle signs that the 'special relationship' with Vietnam might be less firm and long-lasting than 'the Truong Son Mountain Range and the Mekong River'. Some differences had arisen over delineation of their common border. References to the 'special relationship' were made more often by the Vietnamese than by the Lao, although Kaisôn did reassure Hanoi that close relations with Vietnam were 'a sacred sentiment and glorious obligation of the Lao Party, administration and people ... and a criterion for fostering the revolutionary qualities for all party members and cadres'.[86] Yet the Lao government was already seeking greater freedom of action in foreign relations. In February, negotiations between Laos and the United States resulted in the first joint excavation of a crash site to clear up the fate of Americans missing-in-action during the Second Indochina War – at a time when no *rapprochement* had yet occurred between the United States and Vietnam. Though the response of Viang Chan to relaxation of tension on the Lao–Chinese border was at first cautious, by late 1986 relations with China had improved to the point where exchanges of high-ranking delegations could take place again at a time when Chinese–Vietnamese relations still remained tense. Even tensions with Thailand had eased by mid-1986.

The thaw in relations between Bangkok and Viang Chan did not last, however. No resolution of problems concerning trade (particularly electricity sales), refugees, or support for Lao insurgents, let alone the territorial dispute, came from two rounds of negotiations. Then in August 1987 another incident occurred on the border of Xainyaburī province, south of the 'three villages', apparently provoked by illegal teak logging. Heavy fighting broke out in November as Thai forces again attempted without success to dislodge Lao troops. Casualties on both sides were substantial before a cease-fire came into effect on 19 February 1988, brokered by the opposing army commanders. Negotiations made little headway thereafter until a Lao delegation, led by the Chief of General Staff of the Lao People's Army, Sīsavāt Kaeobunphan, visited Bangkok at the invitation of a Thai army commander, General Chavalit Yongchaiyudh. This led to an official visit to Laos by Prime Minister Chatichai Choonhaven and a rapid warming of relations. The two countries agreed to set up a joint Lao–Thai border committee, to bridge the Mekong, and to facilitate trade.

The turn-around in relations in the course of a year, from heavy border fighting to professions of friendship, was, on the face of it, extraordinary. Reasons must be sought in the changing constellation of international and regional forces. That a war was fought over teak smuggling had more to do with internal Thai politics and the economic interests of Thai army commanders than with any non-existent threat from Laos to Thailand's territorial integrity. That it was resolved as

amicably as it was owed more to Thai opportunism than recognition of
the absurdity of fighting in the first place. Sino-Soviet *rapprochement* had
already convinced Hanoi of the need to mend relations with Beijing.
Vietnam had announced it would withdraw all its forces from Cambodia. At the same time, Vietnamese troops quietly withdrew from the
LPDR, a withdrawal which Lao authorities claimed had been completed by the end of 1988. Moreover Laos and China had restored full
diplomatic relations, with an exchange of ambassadors in May. It was
not hard for Bangkok to perceive that more was to be gained in this
changing international environment through diplomacy than use of
force.

The sudden economic downturn of 1987, brought on by drought and
a decrease in electricity production, strengthened the hand of those in
the Party who wanted to accelerate economic reform. The chronic
balance-of-payments deficit led to devaluation of the currency. Meanwhile debt was increasing, and along with it dependency on decreasing
amounts of foreign, still mainly Soviet, aid. Under these circumstances
the government accepted IMF advice to reform the state sector, and
open up the economy to foreign investment. Remaining official prices
and subsidies were abolished and state enterprises allowed to determine the prices of their products. At the same time, trade controls were
further relaxed and provinces permitted even more leeway to conclude
their own trade agreements. Thus were the principal elements of the
centralized socialist economy progressively dismantled, a process accelerated by the collapse of communism in the Soviet Union and Eastern
Europe.

In November 1988, the first elections for thirteen years were held
under new electoral procedures for district, provincial and municipal
representatives. These were followed in March 1989 by elections for the
Supreme People's Assembly to replace the depleted and powerless
body named in December 1975. The role of the new Assembly, as
outlined by the Party, was to promulgate a constitution; debate and pass
legislation; endorse state plans and budgets; name the prime minister;
and scrutinize government activities. The new Assembly met in June,
and elected Nūhak Phumsavan as chair. Even though increasingly
relieved of his former responsibilities in overseeing the economy,
largely because of disagreement over the direction of economic reform,
Nūhak remained a powerful if diminished figure in Lao politics. Under
his direction, the Assembly appointed a Constitution Drafting Committee, and embarked on an active program of legislation. In November
codes of criminal law and criminal procedure, and laws relating to
reform of the judiciary, were approved.[87]

Despite signs that the communist regime was, with foreign advice
and assistance, at last close to laying the constitutional and legal
foundations of a modern state, attention was increasingly focused
during 1989 and 1990 on events in the Soviet Union and Eastern
Europe. Of immediate concern to Laos was the reduction of Soviet aid,
which still accounted for well over half of total foreign economic
assistance, and its growing debt to the communist bloc. Kaisôn was told

in Moscow that the Soviet Union could no longer afford to maintain even its reduced levels of aid, and that henceforth trade between the two countries would be on the basis of real value in hard currency. This prompted an appeal by Viang Chan for assistance from, among others, Japan and France, to make up for reductions in communist bloc aid. Laos also increased its multilateral aid borrowings from the World Bank and Asian Development Bank, while several countries associated with the Interim International Mekong Committee offered more than $US25 million to finance development projects in Laos.

The need to seek alternative sources of aid led the country to adopt a more neutral foreign policy. Economic ties with capitalist states such as Japan and Australia were encouraged through bilateral agreements and earlier passage of a liberal foreign investment law, even as close co-operation continued with Vietnam (especially in the context of tripartite agreements including Cambodia). Relations were further developed with member states of ASEAN, especially Malaysia and Thailand (Bangkok had eliminated bans on all previously restricted items in December 1988). Relations with the United States still had to contend with the issue of servicemen missing in action and American concern over narcotics, though Lao authorities were cooperative on both matters. Another matter of continuing concern was the LPDR's human rights record. While most political prisoners had been progressively released, Amnesty International reported thirty-seven still held.[88] The country was still without a constitution, and the drafting of a civil code had progressed slowly.

It must be said that Laos was remarkably successful in diversifying its sources of foreign assistance. Friendly relations continued to be cultivated with Australia, Sweden, Japan and France, but it was with former enemies that relations developed most rapidly. In October 1989, Kaisôn led a high-ranking Lao delegation to Beijing to cement relations with the People's Republic of China, after previously condemning the international outcry over the Tiananmen massacre – a visit returned in December 1990 when Chinese premier Li Peng arrived in Viang Chan. In August 1990, a trade and border agreement was signed between the two countries. This followed agreement after long-drawn-out negotiations on a series of relatively minor revisions to the frontier between Laos and Vietnam.[89] Relations with Thailand meanwhile were raised to a new level of cordiality by the visit of Princess Maha Chakri Sirindhorn, the first member of the Thai royal family to visit the LPDR. This was followed by more Lao–Thai meetings to discuss such matters as the prevention of crime, smuggling, and resistance activities along their common border, civil aviation, and Mekong river development projects.

The collapse of communism in the Soviet Union and Eastern Europe brought renewed hope to foreign-based resistance movements working to bring down the Lao government. In August 1987, the Lao People's Army destroyed a 200-member Vietnamese resistance force attempting to cross southern Laos and enter Vietnam. All were either captured or killed. Clearly the failure of the Vietnamese operation reflected poorly on the support they had depended upon from the Lao resistance. In December 1989, several resistance organizations in the United States and France formed a 'provisional revolutionary government' in exile. While no foreign government took much notice of this move, fighting did break out soon after in northern Laos, where Hmong guerrillas loyal to Vang Pao and his United Lao National Liberation Front were active. New accusations of 'yellow rain' surfaced, eliciting vehement denial from Viang Chan. Nevertheless the insurgents continued to be an irritant to the Lao authorities, who were able to convince the Thai to close the two Hmong refugee centres in northern Thailand. Other expatriate Lao took heart from the United Nations intervention in Cambodia to demand similar action in the case of Laos. Differences between the two were so conspicuous, however, that hopes of UN intervention were quite unrealistic.

The year 1989 was, as the New Year editorial in the Party journal *Paxāxon* admitted, a 'nightmare year' for socialism. By all accounts, deep depression best describes the reaction of the Lao regime. Nevertheless, by 1990 any forebodings the Party may have had about its own possible demise had been dispelled by encouraging signs of improvement in the Lao economy, the success achieved in obtaining alternative sources of aid, political support received from China and Vietnam, neither of which showed any signs of disintegrating, and realization of just how weak opposition to the regime was. It was with renewed vigour, therefore, that the Party sought to silence its critics and reinforce its monopoly of power through legal and political means.

## THE PARTY HANGS ON

A draft of the new constitution of the LPDR was presented to the Politburo in April 1990, and published for discussion two months later. The intention was to hold nationwide grassroots consultations and make any necessary alterations before the fifteenth anniversary celebrations of the founding of the republic at the end of the year. It was indicative of the internal disarray and confusion within the Party that this schedule could not be kept. Kaisôn's ill-health and his absence in Vietnam for medical treatment did not help. Nor did outspoken opposition to the new constitution by a small group of 'social democrats' emboldened by the collapse of communism in Europe to advocate introduction of a multi-party political system in Laos. Three ringleaders of the movement were arrested in October 1990 and held *incommunicado*. At the same time, tight controls remained in place on all forms of communication and channels of information. The warning was clear: no criticism of, and no opposition to, the Lao People's Revolutionary Party would be tolerated.

Criticism of the draft constitution had focused on Article 1, which defined the LPDR as 'a people's democratic state under the leadership of the Lao People's Revolutionary Party'. The final draft referred to the Party as constituting the 'leading nucleus' of the Lao political system, a change which hardly modified the Party's monopoly hold on political power. Moreover it was evident from reference to 'the principle of democratic centralism' that Laos would remain a 'people's democracy' in the Marxist sense, with the Party exercising a dictatorship on behalf of the 'multi-ethnic Lao people' in order to lead them to a state of 'collective mastery' (Articles 5 and 7). Other changes to the draft constitution strengthened the role of the military (Article 11), and liberalized economic provisions. A small, but highly symbolic, change in the final draft was to replace the gold star at the apex of the national emblem by the silhouette of the Thāt Luang pagoda.

The Lao People's Revolutionary Party held its Fifth Congress at the end of March 1991. Whereas at the previous Congress debate had centred on economic policy, at the Fifth Congress political concerns predominated. The role of the Party, the structure of Lao political institutions, and the constitution had been the principal matters of debate leading up to the Congress. In his address to delegates, Kaisôn made a strong plea for Party unity, a clear sign that deep divisions existed at least at the level of the Central Committee. He also called for better inspection and control by the Party 'to put an end to bureaucratism, abuse of power, parochialism, groupism, dishonesty and wrong behaviour, [including] embezzlement, corruption, bribery and lack of sense of responsibility',[90] a damning indictment of the ills besetting the Party, and the decline in morality evident since liberalization of the economy.

Amendments to the Party statutes passed by the Congress reinforced the 'leading role' of the Party in guiding 'the entire nation' in 'advancing step by step towards socialism' through relying on the 'general tenets of Marxism–Leninism'[91] – a brave statement given the international circumstances, but hardly one likely to convince any but the most ideologically committed. Party organization, recruitment and discipline all came in for special attention. Of particular note were two new chapters added to the statutes, one reinforcing the political role and status of the Party, the other firmly asserting Party control over the armed forces.

Also significant were changes to political institutions agreed upon by the Congress and enshrined in the constitution. The final draft reduced the powers assigned to the Supreme People's Assembly (renamed the National Assembly), and particularly its Standing Committee chaired by the Assembly president. It seems probable that the changes reflected a power struggle between Nūhak, whose power base lay in the National Assembly, and Kaisôn, who was named State President and subsequently President of the Party, following the resignation of Suphānuvong. In any event, the power of State President was greatly enhanced, not just by rights transferred from the Standing Committee of the National Assembly, but also by additional powers written into the final draft of the constitution. These included command of the armed forces, appointment of provincial governors, and the right to preside over meetings of the government 'when necessary'. The final draft also made provision for appointment of a vice-president, though no-one was named, and eliminated any reference to democratic processes at the local government level.

Major changes occurred at the Fifth Congress both to the organization of the Party itself, and to the make-up of the government. The Party Secretariat was abolished, leaving day-to-day direction of the Party in the hands of the President. As President both of the Party and the state, Kaisôn saw his personal power increase. As to membership of the Politburo, five vacancies brought about by resignation (Suphānuvong, Phūmī Vongvichit, Sīsomphôn Lôvanxai), death (Sālī Vongkhamxao) or demotion (Sīsavāt Kaeobunphan) were filled by new faces.[92] The most significant promotion was of the Defence Minister Khamtai Sīphandôn to third position in the Politburo, and heir apparent in the event that either Kaisôn or Nūhak should step down. The Lao People's Army gained three positions on the Politburo and fourteen on the Central Committee of the Party (out of fifty-five full and four alternate members), an indication of its growing influence within the Party.

In August the Supreme People's Assembly formally adopted the constitution, together with an electoral law for the new National Assembly. Phūmī Vongvichit, as his last duty as Acting President, promulgated the constitution before tendering his resignation. The Assembly then unanimously elected Kaisôn as President of the LPDR, in addition to Party President. Khamtai Sīphandôn, as expected, became prime minister. Thus was the transition smoothly and efficiently carried through. In November 1992 when Kaisôn died, his two powerful positions were shared between Nūhak as State President and Khamtai, who assumed the presidency of the Party.

In its political decisions of 1991 taken at the Fifth Party Congress and formally enshrined in the constitution, the Lao People's Revolutionary Party demonstrated its determination to maintain its monopoly of political power. This determination was reinforced in October 1992 when the three leaders of the 'social democracy' movement were sentenced to long prison terms. All political opposition inside Laos was crushed, and the regime proved entirely unresponsive to pressure from even politically moderate expatriate organizations. Encouragement was given to expatriate Lao to return to assist in the economic development of the country – to the point of returning confiscated property – but only on condition that they leave politics to the Party.[93] Taking its lead from China and Vietnam, the Party was prepared to encourage a free-market economy, but not political liberalization. Through its foreign policy, including foreign investment, and its political toughness the Party had positioned itself to hang on to political power. Provided factionalism within the Party, corruption, regionalism, and ethnic unrest could be contained, there was every indication that it would do so.

## TOWARDS REGIONAL INTEGRATION

In April 1994 the first bridge across the Mekong between Thailand and Laos was officially opened. The symbolism was evident to all. Not only had a new era of friendly Lao–Thai relations dawned, but Laos was being drawn into an increasingly integrated region. Thai capital investment in Laos, by then greater than that of any other country, was already bringing with it economic influence to match the political influence still exerted by Vietnam. The opening towards Thailand not only reinforced the move towards a more traditional Lao role of buffer state between more powerful neighbours, but also promised increased trade and tourism with Western and ASEAN states and an influx of new technologies and new ideas that the LPDR would have difficulty assimilating. By the mid-1990s, therefore, the powerful international influences impinging on the LPDR were no longer nations in conflict, but the increasing economic modernization and integration of the region.

The strategic geographic location of Laos made it central to sub-regional economic cooperation between southern China and the states of mainland Southeast Asia, for efficient transportation of both goods and people between Yunnan and northern Thailand, and between northeastern Thailand and central Vietnam, depended on direct routes through Laos. These routes would require stepped-up road construction and more bridges across the Mekong: at least one in the north at Huayxāy; another on the central reach of the river, either at Thākhaek or Savannakhēt; and a third in the south near Pākxē. The road network foreshadowed in the 1990 National Transport Survey provided not only for the transit of goods across the country between neighbouring states, but also for links between provincial capitals and district towns that were more important for national integration.[94] Improvements were also envisaged in river transport from southern China as far south as Luang Phrabāng, and an extension of the Bangkok–Nôngkhāy railway was planned as far as Viang Chan.

If Laos was centrally situated with respect to land transport in the region, as once it had been the crossroads of overland trade routes, so potentially it stood to become the central regional supplier of energy. By the mid-1990s, several massive hydroelectric projects were either under way or well advanced in planning. A Power Development Plan envisaged completion of eight projects at a cost approaching $US3 billion by the year 2000, to generate 2500 more megawatts of power.[95] Whether such an ambitious target would be met by the due date was less significant than that the vast potential generating capacity of the Lao river system was at last being tapped. For Laos, sale of electricity was set to become the country's most valuable export, ahead of agricultural products, timber, minerals, and light manufactured goods, mainly textiles produced in Laos to take advantage of quotas available in European and American markets.

While the prospect of being drawn ever more closely into an increasingly integrated region was welcomed by many Lao as a stimulus to the country's own economic development, others expressed disquiet over the effect this might have on the Lao environment, culture and way of life. In part this disquiet reflected legitimate concerns, over such problems as the impact of heavy tourist traffic on Lao towns and the spread of HIV/AIDS; in part it reflected fear that the sense of Lao national identity was still too weak, and Lao culture insufficiently resilient, to withstand the social and cultural pressures that would inevitably accompany the process.

The environmental impact of rapid economic development was also a matter of real concern. Problems already evident included deforestation, soil erosion, water pollution, ecological degradation, and loss of species diversity. Construction of hydroelectric dams threatened not only to inundate valuable agricultural land and displace vulnerable minority communities, but also to affect water quality and flow. Of greatest threat to the environment, however, was the rate of deforestation due to both timber extraction and slash-and-burn cultivation. Mountain minorities continued to resist resettlement, while attempts by the government to impose export quotas on unsawn timber were frustrated by illegal extraction and smuggling, usually with the connivance of provincial authorities. While as much as half of all remaining Lao forests remained virtually inaccessible, deforestation was already causing erosion and degradation of fragile tropical soils.

Another concern was over threats to the country's wildlife, both as a result of deforestation and through an unsustainable trade in animal products. The former 'Land of a Million Elephants' had but a few hundred left, and these were under threat from poachers. In March 1993, the government moved to protect the country's dwindling wildlife. All species were classified into three categories: prohibited, protected, and 'general' for those not at risk. Fines of up to $US1400 were stipulated for killing the most valuable prohibited species, such as tiger, rhinoceros and elephant. A total ban on hunting was imposed during the three-month Buddhist Lent (from August to October) coinciding with the breeding season for most species.[96] But, given the level of corruption and the demand for rare meats and other animal products to stimulate the jaded palates and boost the declining libidos of wealthy Chinese, even these measures seemed unlikely to be effective.

Threats to the Lao cultural heritage and way of life were seen as coming primarily from Thailand and tourism. As relations, both diplomatic and economic, warmed between Thailand and Laos, so did the LPDR become increasingly porous to the more brash and vulgar elements of Thai popular culture. No longer did political vigilance limit the reception of Thai television and radio. Thai videos, novels, and even newspapers were readily available in Lao Mekong towns. These media brought with them images of the good life in Bangkok, including lavish lifestyles and conspicuous consumption. Nightclubs again flourished, where wealthy young Lao drank and danced to Thai and Western popular music – much to the disgust of veteran revolutionaries who openly proclaimed the need to inculcate traditional Lao (that is, Buddhist) moral values.[97]

Projected increases in tourism also threatened the country's cultural heritage, though tourism did stimulate handicraft production. More than 100,000 tourists, most of them Thai, visited Laos in 1993, with a fivefold increase to half a million projected by 2000. What effect such an influx might have on the fragile beauty and limited facilities of Luang Phrabāng and other Lao cultural centres was already causing concern.

Major cultural and historical sites were declared protected by presidential decree, and the government sought to promote a 'middle way' for Lao tourism between the virtual exclusion that prevailed in the 1980s and mass tourism Thai-style.[98] But whether these measures would be effective seemed doubtful. Thai interests were investing heavily in hotels and resorts, while the number of tour operators seemed only to increase.

Concern over the impact of too many tourists spilled over into fear of 'cultural pollution' in the form mainly of drug addiction, prostitution and HIV/AIDS. Drugs, while illegal, were readily available in a country where production of marijuana and opium, both traditional crops, continued despite programs of resettlement and crop substitution. As social control over prostitution diminished, young Lao girls were lured to work in Thai brothels. On their return, they brought with them HIV/AIDS infection, as did Lao men who had visited Thai prostitutes. By 1995 HIV/AIDS was already a major worry for Lao health authorities, and millions of dollars of foreign aid were being spent on a national awareness campaign.

Despite the possible adverse impact of regional economic integration, however, the Lao leadership faced the future with some confidence. A Public Investment Program to the year 2000, along with associated socio-economic development strategies, was presented to the fifth Round Table Meeting of aid donors in June 1994. These committed the government to continuing its program of economic and legal reform.[99] Foreign investment and labour laws were subsequently passed, reinforcing measures already adopted to improve the legal framework and climate for investment, which was expected to grow steadily to at least $US300 million per annum by the turn of the century. Thus, despite continuing problems with budget and balance-of-payments deficits, economic prospects seemed relatively promising.

Standards of living thus seemed set to rise, provided wealth was relatively evenly distributed. During the first few years of economic liberalization, most of the benefits had flowed to lowland, predominantly Lao Lum, areas, particularly the Mekong towns, at the expense of upland areas inhabited by Lao Sūng and Lao Thoeng. Those who had profited most were the families of powerful political leaders and a new, still small, middle class of managers and entrepreneurs, many linked to foreign investors.

The urge to get rich quick may be the driving force behind the capitalist mode of production, but it confronted the Lao regime with one of its most intractable problems: what to do about corruption. In March 1993 an Anti-Corruption Commission was established, given a substantial support staff, and ordered to report to the prime minister. Some idea of the size of the problem came a year later when it was revealed that embezzlement of state assets since the regime had been in power, largely (though this was not stated) on the part of members of the Party itself, amounted to a massive $US30 million, only half of which investigators had managed to recover.[100] At the same time, greater efforts were made to control illegal logging and smuggling of timber by limiting the right to cut timber, imposing controls on provincial trade, and setting quotas for timber in transit to third countries.[101] But timber was only one profitable commodity smuggled: drugs were another. What made corruption so difficult to control was its very ubiquity. As under the previous regime, a culture of corruption had been fostered by the example of senior officials. As before, the politically powerful avoided paying tax, accepted 'commissions' for facilitating projects or awarding contracts, and pocketed pay-offs for reducing charges, duties or taxes for family and friends – little wonder that those further down the hierarchy seized similar opportunities to boost their meagre salaries. But the culture of corruption so created threatened to corrode both the level of popular trust and the legitimacy accorded the regime. Tax evasion reduced government revenue, while bureaucratic graft diminished popular support for the Party.

Such were some of the pressures and problems facing leaders of the Party when they met for the Sixth Congress of the Party in March 1996. The outcome was a victory for those determined that the pace and benefits of modernization would be controlled. Leading proponents of more rapid liberalization who had taken their lead from deputy prime minister Khamphuy Kaeobualaphā were dropped from the Central Committee (Khamphuy was excluded from both the Politburo and the Central Committee). In their place the army took control of the Party. Of the nine members elected to the Politburo, six were generals and one a former colonel, all members of the Pathēt Lao revolutionary elite, all hard men determined that the Party, through the army, would continue to monopolize power. Immediately below Khamthai Sīphandôn in the Party hierarchy were ranked Generals Samān Vinyakēt and Chummalī Xainyasôn. Nūhak stood down from the Politburo on account of his age, but resolutely hung on to the presidency of the republic. Somewhat surprisingly back in favour was General Sīsavāt Kaeobunphan, whose standing as a member of the Politburo was reinforced by being named Vice-President of the LPDR.

Analysis of the new political line-up revealed a shift in power not just to the army, but through it also to minority ethnicities and to regions outside Viang Chan. Three of the new Politburo members (two of them generals) belonged to ethnic minorities, the highest proportion since formation of the LPDR, while most of the new members of the Central Committee were provincial representatives. One way of reading the army's intentions was as determination to ensure poorer, more disadvantaged parts of the country shared in national development. Another was to see the army's move as securing its own economic interests. Either way, the army, though conservative and authoritarian, was not opposed to economic development *per se*: it merely wished to direct and control it – not least through its own three powerful commercial ventures, located in the north, centre and south of the country.[102] What remained to be seen was whether the army could bring discipline and probity to the Party, or whether its own officers would take advantage of new opportunities for graft and corruption.

As Laos prepared to join ASEAN and enter the twenty-first century, prospects for a more democratic and open system seemed dim. Rather, the LPDR seemed likely to remain an authoritarian single-party state, with power concentrated firmly in the hands of those few individuals constituting the Party (and army) hierarchy. The culture of power, like the culture of corruption which it fostered, owed its ethos to the example and activities of this Party elite. As under the previous regime, family connections and clan patronage often counted for more than merit and ability in appointment to office, whether in the Party, the army, or the bureaucracy. Yet there was growing recognition of the need to replace the exercise of power by right of Party membership by the exercise of power in accordance with law. As a framework of constitutional law began to take shape, however, officials proved reluctant to subordinate themselves, even under the 'all-encompassing' guidance of the Party, to institutional controls and legal processes which limited opportunities for doing personal favours in exchange for some recompense.

In their use of power in pursuit of interests, the Lao ruling elite differed little from political leaders anywhere. In comparison with other Southeast Asian states, however, the educated class was smaller, civil society less developed, the media more tightly controlled. This meant that checks and balances on the arbitrary exercise of power were fewer and less effective. Corruption was hardly greater than in Thailand or Indonesia: the seriousness of its potential impact, however, whether politically in terms of public trust, or economically in terms of plunder of national resources, lay in the threat it posed to the relatively weak sense of Lao national cohesion and identity.

Just as it had been for the royal Lao regime, for the Lao People's Revolutionary Party in the late 1990s a pressing priority remained the need to promote a stronger sense of national unity and identity. Some advance had certainly been made in developing a more inclusive political culture, but regionalism and failure to deliver promised improvements in living standards for the ethnic minorities threatened to undermine what had been achieved. The unwillingness of the regime to face up to the challenge of national reconciliation meant that more educated Lao lived abroad than in Laos, while the country slipped from one dependency to another – from the United States, to the Soviet Union and Vietnam, to Thailand, China and the World Bank. Membership of ASEAN offered both refuge, in the sense of providing Laos with regional support for its separate identity as a member, and threat, in the sense that increasing economic integration might facilitate the absorption of whatever was uniquely Lao into a wider Thai cultural sphere. Yet if Luxembourg could survive as a separate entity in a united Europe, so too presumably could Laos in a united Southeast Asia, in much the same sense of 'survive'. For whether the country was prepared for it or not, its future would inevitably lie in ever closer integration with other states in the region.

# NOTES

## CHAPTER 1    THE KINGDOM OF LĀN XĀNG

1  Thongsā Xainyavongkhamdī et al., *Pavatsāt Lao* (History of Laos), vol. III (Viang Chan, 1989).
2  In accordance with what has become common usage, the term 'Tai' is used in a linguistic and cultural sense to refer to all those related ethnic groups speaking Tai–Daic languages, while 'Thai' is reserved for the citizens and language of the present-day state of Thailand.
3  O. W. Wolters, *History, Culture, and Region in Southeast Asian Perspectives* (Singapore, 1982), pp. 6–8.
4  Adopted by C. Higham in *The Archaeology of Mainland Southeast Asia* (Cambridge, 1989), pp. 239–40.
5  M. Colani, *Mégalithes du Haut-Laos*, vols I and II (Paris, 1935).
6  C. Archaimbault, *Structures Religieuses Lao (Rites et Mythes)* (Vientiane, 1973), p. 100.
7  I owe this terminology to Souneth Phothisane, '*The Nidān Khun Bôrom*: Annotated Translation and Analysis', PhD thesis, University of Queensland, 1997.
8  T. Hoshino, *Pour une Histoire Médiévale du Moyen Mékong* (Bangkok, 1986), pp. 62, 81.
9  For an extended account of early Lao history, see M. Stuart Fox, *The Lao Kingdom of Lān Xāng: Rise and Decline* (Bangkok, 1997).
10  G. F. de Marini, 'Relation nouvelle et curieuse du Royaume de Lao (1660)', reprinted in *Revue Indochinoise* 8 (1910), 158.
11  Annotated translation in J.-C. Le Josne, *Gerritt van Wuysthoff et Ses Assistants: Le Journal de Voyage au Laos (1641–42)* (Metz, 1986), p. 167.
12  De Marini, 'Relation nouvelle', 162.
13  Mayoury and Pheuiphanh Ngaosyvathn, *Chau Ānu, 1767–1829: Paxāxon lao lae āxī ākhanē* (Viang Chan, 1988). I am grateful to the authors for making the manuscript of their extended English version of this work available to me.
14  Mayoury and Pheuiphanh Ngaosyvathn, *Kith and Kin Politics: The Relationship Between Laos and Thailand* (Manila, 1994).
15  F. Garnier, *Voyage d'Exploration en Indochine* (Paris, 1985), p. 104.
16  M. Stuart-Fox, 'On the Writing of Lao History: Continuities and Discontinuities', *Journal of Southeast Asian Studies* 24 (1993), 106–21.

## CHAPTER 2    FRENCH LAOS

1  Examined in M. Stuart-Fox, *Buddhist Kingdom, Marxist State: The Making of Modern Laos* (Bangkok, 1996), Chapter 1.
2  'Exposé des Droits historiques de l'Annam sur le Laos central', 15 June 1893, Archives d'Outre-Mer (AOM), Aix-en-Provence, Fonds des Amiraux, 14488.

3   P. de Sémeril, *En colonne au Laos, 1887–1888* (Paris, 1900), p. 52, quoted in G. Taboulet, *La Geste Française en Indochine*, vol. II (Paris, 1956), p. 889.
4   To use Pavie's own oft-quoted description. A. Pavie, *A La Conquête des Cœurs: Le Pays des Millions d'Eléphants et du Parasol Blanc* (Paris, 1942).
5   P. le Boulanger, *Histoire du Laos Français* (Paris, 1931), p. 277, note 1.
6   Report of M. François Deloncle to the French Ministry of Foreign Affairs, 17 July 1889, quoted in C. H. M. Toye, *Laos: Buffer State or Battleground?* (London, 1968), Appendix 1, p. 211.
7   Le Boulanger, *Histoire du Laos Français*, pp. 290–2.
8   L. de Reinach, *Le Laos* (Paris, 1911), p. 25.
9   De Reinach, *Le Laos*, p. 36.
10  B. Gay, 'La frontière vietnamo-lao de 1893 à nos jours', in P.-B. Lafont, ed., *Les Frontières du Vietnam* (Paris, 1989), pp. 204–32.
11  French Laos had a population which Tournier probably over-estimated at around 800,000, of whom 350,000 were tribal minorities: A. Tournier, 'Note sur les progrès accomplis au Laos de 1897 à 1901', in P. Doumer, *Rapport sur la situation de l'Indochine, 1897–1901* (Hanoi, 1902), p. 449.
12  P. Lévy, *Histoire du Laos* (Paris, 1974), p. 68.
13  The Lao, in the view of J. Taupin, were 'marching rapidly towards decadence', a view he apparently shared with the reverend fathers of the Ubon mission: J. Taupin, 'Rapport à M. le Gouverneur-Général', *BSEI*, Série 1 (1888), 54.
14  Vietnam was divided into separate *pays* of Tonkin, Annam and Cochinchina.
15  These figures are taken from Lao People's Democratic Republic, 'Socio-Economic Development Strategies', report prepared for the fifth Round Table Meeting, Geneva, 21 June 1994, p. 1, and thus presumably reflect the latest border agreements.
16  Chao Nyūy was awarded the exalted Siamese rank of *Rātxathānī* but never received formal investiture as king of Champāsak from the court in Bangkok. The French treated him more shabbily. In 1934 he was compulsorily retired like any other civil servant at the age of sixty and the governorship lapsed: P. Lintingre, *Les Rois de Champassak* (Pākxē, 1972), p. 20.
17  *Journal Officiel de la République Française*, 5 June 1930.
18  By 1904, the Garde Indigène comprised 723 Vietnamese as against 591 Lao, who were reported not to make good soldiers: Conseil Supérieur de l'Indo-Chine, 'Situation politique et économique du Laos', July 1904, AOM Aix, Fonds de la Résidence Supérieur, D3.
19  K. G. Izikowitz, *Lamet: Hill Peasants in French Indo-China* (New York, 1979), p. 346.
20  Cf. G. C. Gunn, *Rebellion in Laos: Peasants and Politics in a Colonial Backwater* (Boulder, 1990), pp. 49–54.
21  De Reinach, *Le Laos*, p. 246.
22  Calculated from figures provided by de Reinach, *Le Laos*, pp. 243–4.
23  B. Gay, 'Les mouvements millénaristes du Centre et du Sud Laos et du Nord-Est du Siam, 1895–1910', PhD thesis, University of Paris (1987), p. 1057. Gunn, *Rebellion in Laos*, pp. 89–90.
24  Two major studies have been undertaken of this revolt. The earlier (1978) is F. Moppert, 'Mouvement de résistance au pouvoir colonial français de la minorité proto-indochinoise du plateau des Bolovens dans le sud du Laos: 1901–1936', PhD thesis, University of Paris (1978); a summary of which is provided in F. Moppert, 'La révolte des Bolovens (1901–1936)' in P. Brocheux, ed., *Histoire de l'Asie du Sud-Est: Révoltes, Réformes, Révolutions* (Lille, 1981), pp. 47–62. Gay's 1987 thesis – 'Les mouvements millénaristes' – includes a thousand pages of documents culled from the French archives.

While Moppert's approach is broadly Marxist and places most of the blame on colonial exactions, Gay is more sympathetic towards the French.

25 Mobilization was through circulation of *lai thaeng*, secret messages written on palm leaves which must be passed on to others if ill is not to befall the reader: Thongsā Xainyavongkhamdī et al., *Pavatsāt Lao*, vol. III, p. 64.

26 Conflicting accounts exist of these events: Gay, 'Les mouvements millénaristes', pp. 1085–9; J. B. Murdoch, 'The 1901–1902 "Holy Man's" rebellion', *Journal of the Siam Society* 62/1 (1974), p. 59; C. F. Keyes, 'Millennialism, Theravada Buddhism and Thai Society', *Journal of Asian Studies* 34 (1977), 298–9.

27 Le Boulanger, *Histoire du Laos Français*, p. 346. Gay, 'Les mouvements millénaristes', p. 1093, gives 130 Thongsā killed and 200 wounded. Lao historians claim 200 died, along with 300 more when Phô Khaduat was hunted down and killed. Thongsā et al., *Pavatsāt Lao*, vol. III, p. 67.

28 Gay, 'Les mouvements millénaristes', p. 1106.

29 Moppert, 'La révolte des Bolovens', pp. 173–4.

30 J.-J. Dauplay, 'Rapport du 24 Octobre 1907', AOM Aix, Fonds de la Résidence Supérieur, F5, p. 11.

31 L. Mogenet, 'Les impôts coloniaux et les incidents du Sud Laos en 1937', *Péninsule* 1 (1980), 78.

32 Quoted in Gunn, *Rebellion in Laos*, p. 120.

33 G. Aymé, *Monographie du 'Ve Territoire Militaire'* (Hanoi, 1930), pp. 113–14.

34 'Ve Territoire Militaire', May 1926, AOM Aix, Fonds de la Résidence Supérieur, Q2.

35 Isabelle Alleton, 'Les Hmong aux confins de la Chine et du Vietnam: la révolte du "Fou" (1918–1922)', in P. Brocheux, ed., *Histoire de l'Asie du Sud Est*, pp. 31–46.

36 F. M. Savina, 'Considérations sur la révolte des Miao (1918–1921)', *L'Eveil Economique de l'Indochine* (3 August 1924), 11.

37 G. Y. Lee, 'Minority Policies and the Hmong', in M. Stuart-Fox, ed., *Contemporary Laos: Studies in the Politics and Society of the Lao People's Democratic Republic* (St Lucia, Qld), 1982, p. 200.

38 Lao Lum too were unhappy over taxation. In 1920 anti-taxation agitation in the Viang Chan area led by a former schoolteacher named Khūkham was crushed when ringleaders were arrested after a brief insurrection. Thongsā et al., *Pavatsāt Lao*, vol. III, pp. 98–101.

39 B. Anderson, *Imagined Communities: Reflections on the Origin and Spread of Nationalism* (London, 1983). Cf. C. J. Christie, 'Marxism and the History of the Nationalist Movements in Laos', *Journal of Southeast Asian Studies* 10 (1979), 146–58.

40 V. Thompson, *French Indochina* (London, 1937), pp. 380–1.

41 Quoted in le Boulanger, *Histoire du Laos Français*, p. 225

42 B. Gay, 'Les relations entre hommes et femmes au Cambodge et au Laos, vues par la littérature coloniale de fiction', unpublished paper, quoting J. Ajalbert, *Raffin Su Su* (Paris, 1911), p. 33.

43 De Reinach, *Le Laos*, p. 386.

44 The figures for 1910 are calculated from de Reinach, *Le Laos*, pp. 256–65; the others are taken from J. M. Halpern, 'Population Statistics and Associated Data', *Laos Project Papers*, no. 3, University of California, March 1961, table 7, and *Annuaire Statistique du Laos, 1951–1952*, pp. 38–9.

45 Discours prononcé par Monsieur le Résident Supérieur au Laos, 30 August 1923, AOM Aix, Fonds de la Résidence Supérieur, F5.

46 B. Clergerie, 'L'œuvre française d'enseignement au Laos', *France-Asie* 125–7 (1956), 368.

47 R. Meyer, *Le Laos* (Hanoi, 1930), p. 52.
48 Lévy, *Histoire du Laos*, p. 82; Clergerie, 'L'œuvre française', 371. By one estimate 68 per cent of all certificates awarded for completion of primary studies in French-language schools in Laos went to Vietnamese (in 1935): Gunn, *Rebellion in Laos*, p. 38.
49 G. Gunn, *Political Struggles in Laos, 1930–1954* (Bangkok, 1988), p. 32.
50 H. Hervey, *Travels in French Indo-China* (London, 1928), p. 214.
51 'La questionne laotienne: opinions du Prince Phetsarath', *France-Indochine* (21 March 1931).
52 Uthin Bunyavong, *Mahā Sīlā Viravong: Xīvit lae Phonngān* (Life and Work) (Viang Chan, 1990), pp. 250–1.
53 For a fuller discussion of French economic policy, see M. Stuart-Fox, 'The French in Laos, 1887–1945', *Modern Asian Studies* 29 (1995), 111–39.
54 De Reinach, *Le Laos*, pp. 386–7.
55 J. Harmand, 'Les Laos et les sauvages de l'Indochine', *Le Tour du Monde* 39/1 (1880), 260.
56 E. Aymonier, *Voyage dans le Laos* (Paris, 1895), pp. 7, 64.
57 G. Taboulet, 'Les origines du chemin de fer de Saigon à My-Tho: Projet Blancsubé d'un chemin de fer de pénétration au Laos et au Yunnan (1880)', *BSEI*, Nouvelle Série 16/3 (1941), 10–14. Other overly ambitious plans were suggested by R. Bartélemy, 'Un chemin de fer au Laos', *Revue Indochinoise* (31 August 1908), 232–42; and G. Aymé-Martin, 'Les chemins de fer au Laos', *Bulletin de la Société de Géographie Commerciale de Paris* 31 (1909), 697–718.
58 For an account of the Lao mining boom and bust, see P. Deloncle, 'La mise en valeur du Laos', in J. Renaud, *Laos: Dieux, Bonzes et Montagnes* (Paris, 1930), pp. 150–4, and C. Robequain, *The Economic Development of French Indochina*, trans. I. A. Ward (London, 1944), p. 265.
59 'Rapports faits à la Conférence des Gouveneurs Généraux à Paris', 3 November 1936, AOM Aix, Fonds de la Résidence Supérieur, D2.
60 Meyer, *Le Laos*, p. 98.
61 E. Pietrantoni, 'Note sur les classes de revenus au Laos et au Tonkin avant 1945', *BSEI*, Nouvelle Série 43/3 (1968), 183–5. Based on revenue for the five income levels for 1943, Pietrantoni concludes that some 40 per cent of the Lao population were 'middle class' (peasants of moderate means) as compared with a mere 7 per cent in this category in Tonkin.
62 The Vietnamese population numbered 20,500 in 1935, but had almost doubled to 39,000 four years later: E. Pietrantoni, 'La population du Laos de 1912 à 1945', *BSEI*, Nouvelle Série 28/1 (1953), 34.
63 E. Pietrantoni, 'La population du Laos en 1943 dans son milieu géographique', *BSEI*, Nouvelle Série 32/3 (1957), 243.
64 Toye, *Laos*, p. 45.
65 Gunn, *Political Struggles*, p. 32.
66 Gunn, *Political Struggles*, pp. 43–5.
67 M. Brown and J. J. Zasloff, *Apprentice Revolutionaries: The Communist Movement in Laos, 1930–1985* (Stanford, 1986), p. 15.
68 In a 1939 article in *La Patrie Annamite*, quoted in P. Gentil, *Sursauts de l'Asie: Remous du Mékong* (Paris, 1950), p. 24.
69 K. D. Sasorith, *Le Laos: son évolution politique, sa place dans l'Union Française* (Paris, 1953), p. 13.
70 C. Rochet, *Pays Lao: Le Laos dans la Tourmente, 1939–1945* (Paris, 1946), p. 43.
71 J. Decoux, *A la Barre de l'Indochine: Histoire de mon Gouvernement-Général, 1940–1945* (Paris, 1952), p. 409.
72 Rochet, *Pays Lao*, pp. 106–8.
73 For the text of de Gaulle's policy declaration on Indochina, see *Journal*

*Officiel de la République Française: Ordonnances et Decréts* (25 March 1945), 1606–7. Lao reservations about being part of a Vietnamese-dominated Indochina had been expressed as early as 1931: C. E. Goscha, *Vietnam or Indochina? Contesting Concepts of Space in Vietnamese Nationalism, 1887–1954* (Copenhagen, 1995), pp. 57–8.

74 Phetxarāt maintained that the French–Japanese conflict had nothing to do with the Lao. D. K. Wyatt, ed., *Iron Man of Laos: Prince Phetsarath Ratana-vongsa*, by '3349', trans. J. B. Murdoch, Cornell Southeast Asia Program Data Paper no. 110 (Ithaca, NY, 1978), p. 23. Care must be exercised with this source, however, for as Arthur Dommen demonstrates in his 'Preface to the 1988 edition', much of it was clearly not written by Phetxarāt himself.

75 C. Norindr, *Histoire Contemporaine du Laos, 1860–1975* ([Bangkok], 1992), p. 239.

76 Un's memoirs provide the best account of the movement. D. K. Wyatt, ed., *Lao Issara: The Memoirs of Oun Sananikone*, trans. J. B. Murdoch, Cornell Southeast Asia Program Data Paper no. 100 (Ithaca, NY, 1975).

77 Cf. Mongkhol Sasorith, 'Les forces politiques et la vie politique au Laos', PhD thesis, University of Paris (1973), p. 196.

78 Rochet, *Pays Lao*, p. 5.


## CHAPTER 3   INDEPENDENCE AND UNITY

1 J. B. de Crèvecœur, *La Libération du Laos, 1945–1946* (Chateau de Vincennes, 1985), pp. 17–18.

2 Wyatt, ed., *Iron Man of Laos*, p. 36.

3 For the text of Phetxarāt's proclamation of Lao unity, see J. Deuve, *Le Laos 1945–1949: Contribution à l'histoire du mouvement Lao Issala* (Montpellier, n.d.), pp. 295–7.

4 De Crèvecœur, *La Libération du Laos*, p. 51.

5 Neither was then a member of the ICP. Kaisôn joined in 1949: Sīxana Sīsān, ed., *Kaisôn Phomvihān: Lūk Không Paxāxon* (Son of the People) (Viang Chan, 1991), p. 16.

6 Tran Van Dinh, 'The Birth of the Pathet Lao Army', in N. S. Adams and A. W McCoy, eds, *Laos: War and Revolution* (New York, 1970), p. 430.

7 Uthit Pasakhom, 'Beyond a Soviet–Vietnamese Condominium', *Indochina Report* 1 (1985), p. 3.

8 Gunn, *Political Struggles*, p. 168.

9 Of whom 12 dead and 17 wounded were Europeans and the rest Lao: de Crèvecœur, *La Libération du Laos*, p. 144. For Un Xananikôn's account, see *Lao Issara*, pp. 42–4. Cf. also Sīxana Sīsān, 'The Battle of Thākhaek', in Anon., ed., *Autobiography of Prince Souphanouvong* (Viang Chan, 1990), pp. 12–24. Some sources put Lao and Vietnamese casualties even higher: Norindr, *Histoire Contemporaine du Laos*, p. 343.

10 Brown and Zasloff, *Apprentice Revolutionaries*, p. 34.

11 R. Lévy, *Indochine et ses Traités* (Paris, 1947), pp. 55–69.

12 Anon., *Le Royaume du Laos: ses institutions et son organisation générale* (Vientiane, 1950), p. 76.

13 Preamble to the constitution; *La Documentation Française, Notes et Etudes Documentaires*, no. 725.

14 J. M. Halpern, 'Observations on the Social Structure of the Lao Elite', *Asian Survey* 1/5 (1961), 26.

15 J. M. Halpern, *Government, Politics, and Social Structure in Laos: A Study in Tradition and Innovation* (New Haven, 1964), pp. 102–4; J. Deuve, *Le Royaume*

*du Laos, 1949–1965: Histoire événementielle de l'indépendance à la guerre américaine* (Paris, 1984), pp. 3–6.

16  Anon., *Le Royaume du Laos*, p. 92. The increase was from 187 schools in 1945 to 545 in 1949 catering for more than 36,000 pupils: Halpern, *Government, Politics, and Social Structure*, p. 189, table 6.

17  Deuve, *Le Royaume du Laos, 1949–1965*, p. 5.

18  V. Thompson and R. Adloff, *Minority Problems in Southeast Asia* (Stanford, 1955), p. 202. Others maintain that he had only twelve wives and twenty-four children.

19  Particularly effective were the polemical writings of Katāy. Cf. *Une Amnistie? Fi Donc!* (Bangkok, 1948).

20  G. Taboulet, *La Geste Française en Indochine*, vol. II (Paris, 1956), pp. 923–4.

21  Boun Oum, 'Allocution à l'occasion de la signature des Conventions Franco-Laotiennes', *France-Asie* 119 (1945–50), 630.

22  Wyatt, ed., *Lao Issara*, pp. 51–2; Deuve, *Le Laos 1945–1949*, p. 217.

23  Brown and Zasloff, *Apprentice Revolutionaries*, p. 38. In the north were Phūmī Vongvichit and Uan Rāttikun; in the centre Un Xananikôn, Phūmī Nôsavan and Sing Rattanasamai; and in the south Khamtai Sīphandôn and Phūn Sīpasoet.

24  Even in setting up a guerrilla base in Xainyaburī, Phūmī Vongvichit depended heavily on Vietnamese help: Phūmī Vongvichit, *Khuam Thongcham nai Xīvit Khong Thaphachau* (Memoirs of My Life) (Viang Chan, 1987), pp. 58–60.

25  According to Vietnamese sources, 500 to 700 political and military agents were sent into Laos in late 1946 and early 1947, rising to as many as 7000 by early 1951, and 17,000 in 1953: Motoo Furuta, 'The Indochinese Communist Party's Division into Three Parties: Vietnamese Communist Policy Towards Cambodia and Laos, 1948–1951', in T. Shiraishi and M. Furuta, eds, *Indochina in the 1940s and 1950s* (Ithaca, NY, 1992), p. 161, note 81.

26  The name refers to *Rāxavong* Ngau, hero of the 1827–28 war against the Siamese. Credit is claimed by Kaisôn in *La Révolution Lao*, p. 14, but as Lao guerrilla units had already been fighting the French for more than three years, to take this as the founding of the Lao People's Liberation Army has more to do with glorification of Kaisôn as first Secretary-General of the Lao People's Revolutionary Party than with any actual historical event.

27  Arsène Lapin in French. Katāy means 'rabbit' in Lao. Cf. Katāy, *L'Amitié ou la Haine* (Bangkok, 1949).

28  Translations of this correspondence are in Brown and Zasloff, *Apprentice Revolutionaries*, pp. 338–61; see also pp. 42–5.

29  Even the CIA acknowledged that Phetxarāt 'sought the unity and independence of Laos throughout his life': 'Prince Phetsarath Returns to Laos', Intelligence Report no. 7479, compiled by the Office of Intelligence Research, Department of State, Washington, 9 April 1957, p. 4.

30  About 9000 Vietnamese remained in Laos in 1958 out of an estimated 50,000 in 1940: Toye, *Laos*, p. 73, note 54.

31  Cf. M. J. P. Barber, 'Migrants and Modernisation: A Study of Change in Lao Society', PhD thesis, University of Hull (1979); and E. Braunstein, 'Urbanisation et transition à socialism au Laos', PhD thesis, University of Paris (1978), chapter III.

32  Of a total of $1200 million provided by the United States towards the military cost of the First Indochina War, France is estimated to have spent $30 million in Laos, including budgetary support: M. E. Goldstein, *American Policy Towards Laos* (Rutherford, NJ, 1973), pp. 62, 127.

33  Deuve, *Le Royaume du Laos 1949–1965*, p. 25.

34  In 1959, after a reign of fifty-six years, the king was known by name to only

34 per cent of people in Viang Chan and 19 per cent of all villagers surveyed: Halpern, *Government, Politics, and Social Structure*, pp. 43–4.

35 For this the French were partly to blame: as one French advisor later admitted: 'We built the body ... but we were not concerned with the soul.' Deuve, *Le Royaume du Laos 1949–1965*, p. 25.

36 The surname Phomvihān was an adopted one, and is the Lao term for the series of four Buddhist heavens known as the Brahmavihāra (Rod Bucknell, personal communication). As this is not a Lao surname, the choice is significant.

37 *20 Years of Lao People's Revolutionary Struggles* (n.p., 1966), pp. 19–20.

38 Tuan Viet, 'The Laotian Revolution', *Hoc Tap* 10 (1965), 31–41, trans. Joint Publications Research Service, 1965.

39 P.-B. Lafont, 'Images laotiennes', *Revue de Psychologie des Peuples* 21 (1966), 472–88, and 22 (1967), 216–26.

40 According to two different Vietnamese documents, there were 31 or 140 Lao members of the ICP. At a time when the ICP claimed only 2091 members, the former figure seems more likely: Furuta, 'The Indochinese Communist Party's Division into Three Parties', pp. 145, 162, note 85. Claims that there were 600 Lao members in the ICP must therefore include Vietnamese resident in Laos. Cf. J. M. Halpern and W. S. Turley, eds, *The Training of Vietnamese Communist Cadres in Laos* (Brussels, 1977), p. 3. Brown and Zasloff, *Apprentice Revolutionaries*, appendix C2, list only fifteen former ICP members in the Central Committee of the Lao People's Revolutionary Party.

41 Brown and Zasloff, *Apprentice Revolutionaries*, p. 47.

42 G. Modelski, 'The Viet Minh Complex', in C. E. Black and T. P. Thornton, eds, *Communism and Revolution: The Strategic Uses of Political Violence* (Princeton, NJ, 1964), p. 197, note 31.

43 Its existence was not formally acknowledged until October 1966 when Kaisôn signed himself Secretary-General: P. F. Langer, 'Comments on Bernard Fall's "The Pathēt Lao: A 'Liberation' Party"', Rand Report P-3751 (Santa Monica, January 1968), p. 4.

44 Interview with Sīxana Sīsān, Viang Chan, 3 November 1990; Sīsān, ed., *Kaisôn Phomvihān*, pp 17–18.

45 This was denied by Sīxana Sīsān in an interview with the author, Viang Chan, 3 November 1990. Yet if Brown and Zasloff are correct in reporting (*Apprentice Revolutionaries*, p. 58) that only 25 delegates founded the Phak Paxāxon Lao (Lao People's Party) in 1955, all former members of the ICP, it is difficult to see why the process took four years. Existence of a separate Lao Workers' Party (Phak Khon Ngān) was claimed in B. Fall, 'The Pathēt Lao – "Liberation" Party', in R. A. Scalapino, ed., *The Communist Revolution in Asia: Tactics, Goals and Achievements* (Englewood Cliffs, NJ, 1965), but this was disproved by Zasloff, *The Pathet Lao*, p. 13. Thompson and Adloff's Resistance Party (Cu Xat, *kū xāt*), was equally illusionary: *Minority Problems*, p. 208.

46 M. Caply, 'L'action politico-militaire du Pathet-Lao contre un poste isolé', *Revue Militaire Générale* 3 (1973), 393–411.

47 B. Fall, *Anatomy of a Crisis: The Laotian Crisis of 1960–1961* (Garden City, NY, 1969), p. 49.

48 Dommen, *Conflict in Laos*, p. 41.

49 H. Deydier, *Lokapala: Génies, Totems et Sorciers du Nord Laos* (Paris, 1954), pp. 164–83.

50 Phūmī Vongvichit, *Le Laos et la Lutte Victorieuse du Peuple Lao contre le Néo-colonialisme Américain* (n.p., 1968), p. 55.

51 Deuve, *Le Royaume du Laos 1949–1965*, p. 47.

52 *Documents Relating to the Discussion of Korea and Indo-China at the Geneva Conference, April 27–June 15, 1954* (London, 1954), p. 116.
53 *Documents*, pp. 154, 155.
54 *Further Documents Relating to the Discussion of Indo-China at the Geneva Conference, June 16–July 21, 1954* (London, 1954), p. 41.
55 Final Declaration of the Geneva Conference, in *Further Documents*, paragraph 3.
56 The account that follows draws heavily on J. Deuve, *Le Complot de Chinaimo, 1954–1955* (Paris, 1986).
57 *First Interim Report of the International Commission for Supervision and Control in Laos* (London, 1955), p. 16.
58 P. F. Langer and J. J. Zasloff, *North Vietnam and the Pathet Lao: Partners in the Struggle for Laos* (Cambridge, Mass., 1970), p. 63 and organizational chart, p. 64. In August 1955, Pathēt Lao forces stood at 6000, according to US National Intelligence Estimate 63.3–55, in E. C. Keefer and D. W. Mabon, eds, *Foreign Relations of the United States, 1955–1957*, vol. XXI: *East Asian Security; Cambodia; Laos* (hereafter *FRUS, 1955–1957*) (Washington, 1990), p. 674.
59 *Second Interim Report of the International Commission for Supervision and Control in Laos, January 1–June 30, 1955* (London, 1955), p. 9.
60 Phuy's Independent Party won ten, the Democratic Party four, the National Union Party two, and non-affiliated four. Post-election manoeuvring increased the Progressive tally by at least three: F. M. LeBar and A. Suddard, eds, *Laos: Its People, Its Society, Its Culture* (New Haven, 1960), p. 106.
61 *Third Interim Report of the International Commission for Supervision and Control in Laos, July 1, 1955–May 16, 1957* (London, 1957), pp. 52–3.
62 Toye, *Laos*, pp. 95–6.
63 Cited in Goldstein, *American Policy Toward Laos*, p. 89.
64 Goldstein, *American Policy Toward Laos*, p. 97. Katāy actually attended the inaugural meeting of SEATO as an observer.
65 At the time the Royal Lao Army numbered about 17,000, as against 5000 to 6000 Pathēt Lao guerrillas. Cf. Oudone Sananikone, *The Royal Lao Army and United States Army Advice and Support* (Washington, DC, 1981), p. 26. Suvanna as Defence Minister quoted a round figure of 30,000, including the National Guard, and suggested reduction to 25,000: Telegram Legation (Yost) to State Department, 25 May 1955, *FRUS, 1955–1957*, p. 650.
66 The police numbered eventually some 4000 men. The CIA also assisted development of military intelligence, counter-propaganda, and counter-subversion operations for the Lao army: Fred Branfman, 'The President's Secret Army: A Case Study – The CIA in Laos, 1962–1972', in R. L. Borosage and J. D. Marks, eds, *The CIA File* (New York, 1976), pp. 46–78.
67 Halpern, *Government, Politics, and Social Structure*, pp. 47–9. At the time, few Lao read either newspapers (three published with total circulation of 3000) or books (18 library books per 1000 people), but all could listen to the radio. Both Pathēt Lao radio and the government's radio Lao Sērī (Free Laos) broadcast in several minority languages.
68 Figures from Goldstein, *American Policy Toward Laos*, pp. 135–7.
69 US Congress, House of Representatives, *US Aid Operations in Laos: Seventh Report by the Committee on Government Operations* (Washington, DC, 1959), p. 13.
70 Dommen, *Conflict in Laos*, p. 106, table 3.
71 C. Stevenson, *The End of Nowhere: American Policy Toward Laos Since 1954* (Boston, 1972), p. 49. According to some estimates, in 1958 the Royal Lao Army actually numbered only around 15,000 at a time when 25,000 were on

the US payroll: R. Gilkey, 'Laos: Politics, Elections and Foreign Aid', *Far Eastern Survey* 27 (June 1958), 93.

72 Dommen, *Conflict in Laos*, p. 105, table 2.
73 Stevenson, *The End of Nowhere*, p. 37.
74 LeBar and Suddard, eds, *Laos*, p. 33.
75 R. Gauthereau, 'L'aide économique et technique française au Laos', *Coopération Technique* 13 (1959), 9–17.
76 *New York Times*, 25 February 1958; M. Field, *The Prevailing Wind: Witness in Indo-China* (London, 1965), p. 51. Suvanna was not entirely naïve, however. A new secret intelligence organization was set up to engage in a propaganda struggle with the Pathēt Lao: Jean Deuve, *La Guerre Secrète au Laos contre les Communistes, 1955–1964* (Paris, 1995), pp. 55–76.
77 Deuve, *Le Royaume du Laos 1949–1965*, p. 75.
78 Kaisôn Phomvihān, Speech marking 25th anniversary of the Lao People's Revolutionary Party, 22 March 1980.
79 Deuve, *Le Royaume du Laos 1949–1965*, pp. 75–6; and for the 'Action Program' of the Front, Annex 5 (272–4).
80 *Third Interim Report*, pp. 54–7.
81 *Lao Presse*, 8 August 1956, cited in Deuve, *Le Royaume du Laos 1949–1965*, p. 92.
82 Dulles cabled the Embassy in Laos (7 August 1956), 'we do not like statement neutrality made with Communist leader or mention coalition government': *FRUS, 1955–1957*, p. 788.
83 Souvanna Phouma, 'Le Laos: avant-garde du monde libre', *France-Asie* 164 (1960), 1431.
84 Even the US Embassy was forced to admit that Suvanna had maintained Lao neutrality, and that 'nothing happened at Peking or Hanoi': Telegram Embassy (Parsons) to State Department, 7 September 1956, *FRUS, 1955–1957*, p. 811.
85 US Congress, House of Representatives, *US Aid Operations in Laos: Hearings Before the Foreign Operations and Monetary Affairs Subcommittee, March 11–June 1, 1959* (Washington, DC, 1959), p. 195. Parsons continued his pressure on Suvanna, including threats to cut off US aid, until the last moment before final agreement with the Pathēt Lao: Telegrams Embassy (Parsons) to State Department, 24 October 1957, 1 November 1957: *FRUS, 1955–1957*, pp. 1003, 1012.
86 The United States had come to a secret understanding with Suvanna that the Provisional Government would not establish diplomatic relations with either China or North Vietnam: Telegram 706 Embassy to State Department, Department of State Central Files, National Archives, Washington, DC. (I am grateful to Arthur Dommen for bringing this reference to my attention.)
87 *Fourth Interim Report of the International Commission for Supervision and Control in Laos, May 17, 1957 to May 31, 1958* (London, 1958), pp. 44–51.

## CHAPTER 4   NEUTRALITY SUBVERTED

1 Quoted in Deuve, *Le Royaume du Laos 1949–1965*, p. 102.
2 Suphānuvong acknowledged that American aid would be needed 'not for several years but for several decades': Toye, *Laos*, p. 113.
3 W. Haney, 'The Pentagon Papers and the United States Involvement in Laos', in N. Chomsky and H. Zinn, eds, *The Pentagon Papers: Critical Essays*, vol 5 (Boston, 1972), p. 252.
4 *US Aid Operations in Laos: Seventh Report*, p. 2.

5 J.-P. Barbier, 'Dix-sept ans d'aide économique au Laos: un pays malade de l'aide étrangère', PhD thesis, University of Paris (1973), especially pp. 492–7 on corruption and ostentatious expenditure.

6 F. M. LeBar and A. Suddard, eds, *Laos: Its People, Its Society, Its Culture* (New Haven, 1960), pp. 77–8.

7 LeBar and Suddard, eds, *Laos*, p. 215.

8 Deuve, *Le Royaume du Laos 1949–1965*, p. 157, note 42.

9 Madame Khamphaeng Bubphā, the first woman elected to the National Assembly. See Mayoury Ngaosyvathn, *Remembrances of a Lao Woman Devoted to the National Liberation Struggle: Khampheng Boupha* (Vientiane, 1993), especially pp. 40–2.

10 Deuve, *Le Royaume du Laos 1949–1965*, p. 112.

11 US Secretary of State Dulles had urged the Embassy in Viang Chan to encourage such a group of 'new faces' a month before: Telegram Department of State to Embassy Laos, in E. C. Keefer and D. W. Mabon, eds, *Foreign Relations of the United States, 1958–1960*, vol. XVI: *East Asia–Pacific Region; Cambodia; Laos* (Washington, DC, 1992), p. 440 (hereafter *FRUS, 1958–1960*).

12 Opposed by the Polish delegation *(Fourth Interim Report*, pp. 13–17), the Pathēt Lao and North Vietnam: J. M. Halpern and H. B. Fredman, *Communist Strategy in Laos*, Rand Report RM–2561 (Santa Monica, 14 June 1960), pp. 16–17.

13 Pegged at 35 to the dollar, as against around three times that amount on the black market: H. Muller, 'A Bulwark Built on Sand', *The Reporter* (13 November 1958), 13.

14 The United States wanted Suvanna replaced as prime minister by a 'strong' (i.e. right-wing) government by royal decree: Telegrams State to Embassy, 27 May 1958, and Embassy (Smith) to State, 20 July 1958, *FRUS, 1958–1960*, pp. 449, 465.

15 *People's Daily*, 26 March 1956, quoted in G. M. Chittenden, 'Laos and the Powers, 1954–1962', PhD thesis, University of London (1969), p. 54.

16 War Experiences Recapitulation Committee of the High-Level Military Institute, *The Anti-US Resistance War for National Salvation, 1954–1975: Military Events* (Hanoi, 1980), trans. Joint Publications Research Service, 3 June 1982, pp. 30–2 (hereafter *Anti-US War*).

17 *Lao Presse*, 11 December 1958, quoted in Halpern and Fredman, *Communist Strategy in Laos*, pp. 13–14.

18 Sisouk na Champassak, *Storm Over Laos: A Contemporary History* (New York, 1961), p. 67.

19 Dommen examines this question at some length in *Conflict in Laos*, pp. 336–54, including a detailed map of the region (p. 339). He concludes that the disputed territory was Lao.

20 Deuve, *Le Royaume du Laos 1949–1965*, p. 120, note 64; and *Anti-US War*, p. 37.

21 Deuve, *Le Royaume du Laos 1949–1965*, p. 121.

22 Vongvichit, *Le Laos et la Lutte Victorieuse*, p. 127.

23 Halpern and Fredman, *Communist Strategy in Laos*, p. 44.

24 Toye, *Laos*, p. 147.

25 The Pathēt Lao seems to have been in two minds, with Suphānuvong in Viang Chan accepting integration (cf. Dommen, *Conflict in Laos*, p. 118), and 'the Party' in Viang Xai opposed (Phomvihane, *La Révolution Lao*, p. 21). See also note 28 below.

26 J. M. Halpern, *Government, Politics, and Social Structure*, pp. 56–60, 161–4; M. Stuart-Fox and R. Bucknell, 'Politicization of the Buddhist Sangha in Laos', *Journal of Southeast Asian Studies* 13 (1982), 63–5.

27 *New York Times,* 28 August 1959; it also reported an increase in the Programs Evaluation Office by 100 (who were in fact Special Forces advisors). Village militia forces were increased from 16,000 to 20,000. According to American intelligence, the Pathēt Lao had 'probably 1500 to 2000 at most' with 'considerable additional potential strength' – presumably by reactivating up to 5000 former guerrillas: US Department of Defense, *United States–Vietnam Relations, 1945–1967* (Washington, DC, 1971), Bk 10, p. 1246. Cf. Bk 2, IVA5, p. 61.

28 Amphay Doré argues that this was the point at which Suphānuvong and those who supported his policy of accommodation leading to the First Coalition lost out to the more radical faction led by Kaisôn: *Le Partage du Mékong* (Paris, 1980), pp. 59–60. That this policy in force from 1954 to 1959 might not have had the full approval of the DRV is indicated by a captured Vietnamese document referring to the Vietnam Workers' Party *'re-establishing* close relations with the Lao People's Party in May 1959': Smith, *An International History of the Vietnam War,* vol. 1, p. 82. Kaisôn's own reservations are suggested by his later comment that the 'political behaviour' of those who participated in coalition governments had to be monitored to combat the 'illusion' of national concord: *La Révolution Lao,* p. 117. It would seem that the decision to resume armed struggle was taken without consultation with Pathēt Lao leaders then in Viang Chan, probably on Vietnamese advice.

29 The only 'evidence' was that the Pathēt Lao did not have the capacity to launch such a series of coordinated attacks: Sisouk, *Storm Over Laos,* pp. 91–2. Even the US did not believe that North Vietnamese Army units were involved, though it did not say so publicly: Telegram Embassy (Smith) to State Department, 9 August 1959, *FRUS, 1958–1960,* pp. 555–6.

30 Neither the French nor the British believed any invasion had occurred. The role of the international, especially the American, press in exaggerating this crisis is castigated by Fall in *Anatomy of a Crisis,* pp. 126–40.

31 Dommen, *Conflict in Laos,* p. 124.

32 Cf. C. J. Christie, 'Marxism and the History of the Nationalist Movements in Laos', *Journal of Southeast Asian Studies* 10 (1980), 153–8.

33 Deuve, *Le Royaume du Laos 1949–1965,* p. 139. American opinion was divided, however, with the Programs Evaluation Office and the CIA favouring General Phūmī, and both intriguing behind the back of Ambassador Horace Smith, much to Smith's annoyance: Telegram Embassy (Smith) to State, 30 November 1959, and Smith's personal letter to the Assistant Secretary of State for Far Eastern Affairs (Parsons), 15 December 1959, *FRUS, 1958–1960,* pp. 680–3, 690–5.

34 Yet on Suphānuvong's instructions, nine LPF candidates did stand: Dommen, *Conflict in Laos,* p. 129. Five Santhiphāp candidates also stood.

35 Deuve, *Le Royaume du Laos 1949–1965,* p. 145, gives fractional estimates for every province.

36 Goldstein, *American Policy Toward Laos,* p. 157. The CIA was implicated in election rigging: Dommen, *Conflict in Laos,* p. 133.

37 Dommen, *Conflict in Laos,* p. 132.

38 Quoted in Halpern, *Government, Politics and Social Structure,* p. 40.

39 Toye, *Laos,* pp. 148–9. Cf. Dommen, *Conflict in Laos,* p. 150, and Field, *The Prevailing Wind,* p. 87, who blame Kônglae's broadcast opposing Phūmī's inclusion in the new government for his change of mind.

40 In fact the British and French, in the US view, displayed 'disturbing complacency': Memorandum of Discussion, 455th Meeting of the National Security Council, Washington, 12 August 1960, *FRUS, 1958–1960,* pp. 787–9.

41  A. M. Schlesinger, Jr, *A Thousand Days: John F. Kennedy in the White House* (London, 1965), p. 297.
42  Toye, *Laos*, p. 150. The Vietnamese subsequently revealed that the liberation of Huaphan province was carried out 'in coordination with the Vietnamese volunteer troops': *Anti-US War*, p. 44.
43  *New York Times*, 20 January 1961.
44  Schlesinger, *A Thousand Days*, p. 298.
45  Deuve, *Le Royaume du Laos 1949–1965*, p. 177. Deuve, a close advisor to Suvanna, reveals how Suvanna's options were progressively reduced, as the United States schemed to get rid of him. Cf. telegrams State (Herter) to Embassy, *FRUS, 1958–1960*, pp. 953–4, 963–5.
46  The US Embassy paid deputies 'considerable sums money' to defect, and flew them to Savannakhēt: Telegrams Embassy (Brown) to State, 17 November, 9 December 1960, *FRUS, 1958–1960*, pp. 966–9, 1001–2.
47  Fall, *Anatomy of a Crisis*, p. 196; Toye, *Laos*, p. 158, note 48; Field, *The Prevailing Wind*, pp. 104–7. Among the dead was the commander of a contingent of Pathēt Lao troops which a later Party history claims went to the aid of Kônglae: MS produced under the direction of Sīxana Sīsān but criticized by the Party, and never published, entitled 'Pavatsāt Phak Paxāxon Pativat Lao' (History of the Lao People's Revolutionary Party), pp. 84–6. (I was only able to obtain photocopies of a few pages of this MS.)
48  By mid-January 1961, according to US intelligence, the plain was held by 2600 Pathēt Lao and 500 neutralist troops: Brown and Zasloff, *Apprentice Revolutionaries*, p. 77.
49  Dommen, *Conflict in Laos*, p. 184.
50  *Documents relating to British Involvement in the Indo-China Conflict 1945–1965*, Miscellaneous series no 25 (Cmd 2834), pp. 166–8.
51  *New York Times*, 24 March 1961. For the full text, see US Department of State, *Bulletin*, 17 April, 1961, pp. 543–4.
52  Chairman Nikita Khrushchev was cavalier about Laos, while Soviet Foreign Minister Andrei Gromyko told US Secretary of State Dean Rusk that the Soviet Union wanted 'nothing' there: Telegram Embassy Moscow to State, 10 March 1961; Notes by Secretary of State Rusk, 18 March 1961; and Memorandum for the Record, 30 April 1963, in E. C. Keefer, ed., *Foreign Relations of the United States, 1961–1963*, vol. XXIV, *Laos Crisis* (Washington, 1994) (hereafter *FRUS, 1961–1963*), p. 47, note 1, pp. 82, 94, 1006. Despite this lack of interest, by early March the Soviet airlift had flown 2000 sorties to bring in 2400 tons of supplies: Memorandum of Conference with President Kennedy, Washington, 9 March 1961, p. 74.
53  'Joint Communiqué Issued After Talks in Vienna', Australian Department of External Affairs, *Select Documents on International Affairs: Laos*, no. 16, Canberra, April 1970, p. 96. Also Memorandum of Conversation (between President Kennedy and Chairman Khrushchev), Vienna, 4 June 1961, *FRUS, 1961–1963*, pp. 231–6; and Anon., *Laos in the Mirror of Geneva* (Peking, 1961), pp. 27–30.
54  Blaufarb, *The Counterinsurgency Era*, p. 147. At the time the United States was providing 'arms, ammunition, and other support' to 7700 Hmong fighters: Memorandum from Assistant Secretary of State for Far Eastern Affairs (McConaughy) to Under-Secretary of State (Bowles), 26 June 1961, *FRUS, 1961–1963*, p. 263.
55  The comparative importance is obvious from Secretary of State Dean Rusk's preparedness to divide Laos if that would ensure that South Vietnam and Thailand were 'insulated': Telegram from Secretary of State Rusk to State, Paris, 2 June 1961, *FRUS, 1961–1963*, pp. 222–3; and from the Memorandum

from the President's Deputy Special Assistant for National Security Affairs (Rostow) to President Kennedy, 17 August 1961 (pp. 371–4).

56 Plans for intervention continued to be canvassed up to the eve of the Geneva Agreements: Analysis of the Situation for Military Planning Re Laos, 1 June 1962; Memorandum of Conversation, 2 June 1962; and Memorandum from the President's Military Representative (Taylor) to President Kennedy, 4 June 1962, *FRUS, 1961–1963*, pp. 806–12, 817–23.

57 By 1961, the US view of Suvanna was that he was a sincere patriot, and 'basically anti-Communist', but suffered from 'an infinite capacity for self-deception' with respect both to his own abilities and to the intentions of the Pathēt Lao: Memorandum of Conversation [between Brown and President Kennedy], Washington, 3 February 1961, *FRUS, 1961–1963*, p. 47.

58 McCoy, *The Politics of Heroin*, pp. 259–60.

59 The degree of American responsibility for the fiasco is unclear, for Phūmī seems once again to have received conflicting signals. Toye, *Laos*, p. 184, and Deuve, *Le Royaume du Laos 1949–1965*, p. 221, both well in a position to know, assert that Phūmī received American encouragement. Dommen, *Conflict in Laos*, p. 214, maintains that Phūmī went against American advice, a position that receives support from a Special National Intelligence Estimate dated 9 May 1962, *FRUS, 1961–1963*, p. 727. The Vietnamese later claimed to have 'coordinated' this 'rather large-scale operation': *Anti-US War*, p. 52.

60 Telegrams from State to Embassy in Laos, 13, 19 May 1962, and Message to Director of Central Intelligence McCone, Vientiane, 13 May 1961, *FRUS, 1961–1963*, pp. 765–6, 781–3 and 762–4.

61 Officially the ICSC verified that 666 US personnel left Laos, plus Thais and Filipinos, but only 40 Vietnamese. Covert operations continued in association with the Hmong, while as many as 6000 Vietnamese remained, many integrated into Pathēt Lao units: Stevenson, *The End of Nowhere*, pp. 186–7.

62 US Department of State, *A Threat to the Peace* (Washington, DC, December 1961).

63 Toye, *Laos*, pp. 188–9.

64 M. Taylor, *Swords and Plowshares* (New York, 1972), p. 218.

65 Memorandum from the President's Special Assistant for National Security Affairs (Bundy) to President Kennedy, 1 April 1961, *FRUS, 1961–1963*, p. 115.

66 Deuve, *Le Royaume du Laos 1949–1965*, p. 231.

67 Personally authorized by Suvanna in Washington, but not by the Provisional Government: Memorandum for the Record, 28 July 1962, *FRUS, 1961–1963*, p. 880.

68 Jean Deuve places the blame squarely on General Kupasit Aphai, commander of Military Region V: *La Guerre Secrète*, p. 144.

69 Memorandum Prepared in the Central Intelligence Agency, 29 March 1963, *FRUS, 1961–1963*, pp. 948–52.

70 Deuve, *Le Royaume du Laos 1949–1965*, p. 240.

71 Quoted in Deuve, *Le Royaume du Laos 1949–1965*, p. 228.

72 Attachment to the Summary Record of the 513th National Security Council Meeting, Washington, 22 April 1963, *FRUS, 1961–1963*, pp. 995–7.

73 Deuve, *Le Royaume du Laos 1949–1965*, p. 242.

74 Soutchay Vongsavanh, *RLG Military Operations and Activities in the Laotian Panhandle* (Washington, DC, 1981), pp. 37–40.

75 Taillard sets out his arguments in 'Le village lao de la région de Vientiane: un pouvoir local face au pouvoir étatique', *L'Homme* 17/2–3 (1977), 71–100; and 'Le dualisme urbain-rural au Laos et la récupération de l'idéologie traditionelle', *Asie du Sud-est et Monde Insulindien* 10/1 (1979), 41–56.

76 J. M. Halpern, *Economy and Society of Laos: A Brief Survey* (New Haven, 1964), pp. 125–6.

77 Reports of Suvanna's visit to China and archival sources in Washington suggest that Suphānuvong may have sabotaged these talks deliberately at the behest of the Vietnamese, who feared that China was prepared to back the genuine neutralization of Laos. (Arthur Dommen, personal communication.)

78 Deuve, *Le Royaume du Laos 1949–1965*, p. 249. That the coup aimed at eliminating General Phūmī was obvious: he was the only general (out of eighteen) *not* named a member of the 'Revolutionary Committee'.

79 The new general staff of the Royal Lao Army consisted of nine rightist generals and only one neutralist: P. D. Scott, 'Laos: The Story Nixon Won't Tell', in M. Gettleman et al., eds, *Conflict in Indo-China: A Reader on the Widening War in Laos and Cambodia* (New York, 1970), p. 282.

80 Stevenson, *The End of Nowhere*, p. 119.

81 The Vietnamese later described this engagement as 'the battlefield which determined the victory of the revolutionary war in Laos': *Anti-US War*, p. 59.

82 Norman Hannah argues that the 'tacit understanding' between the United States and the communist bloc to put Laos 'on the back burner' and accept the *de facto* division of the country effectively prevented the United States from recognizing all Indochina as a single theatre of war, thus leading to the 'loss' of South Vietnam: N. B. Hannah, *The Key to Failure: Laos and the Vietnam War* (Boston, 1987), pp. 56–73, 297–306.

## CHAPTER 5   WAR AND REVOLUTION

1 Stevenson, *The End of Nowhere*, pp. 192, 199, 201, 208, 210.

2 M. Maneli, *War of the Vanquished* (New York, 1971), p. 185.

3 Quoted in Stevenson, *The End of Nowhere*, p. 180.

4 Five more Chinese were wounded. The Chinese response was angry, but restrained, with Beijing calling again for a reconvening of the Geneva Conference: C.-J. Lee, *Communist China's Policy Toward Laos: A Case Study* (Lawrence, Kans., 1970), p. 116.

5 Suvanna was not informed in any detail about much the United States was doing: Haney, 'The Pentagon Papers', pp. 270–2.

6 Known as the Symington Hearings: US Senate, Committee on Foreign Relations, *United States Security Agreements and Commitments Abroad: Kingdom of Laos, Hearings before the Subcommittee on United States Security Agreements and Commitments Abroad*, 91st Congress, 1st session, 1970.

7 *Anti-US War*, pp. 102–3. Casualties were put at around 1000, with another 2000 captured.

8 As one US air force officer remembered, 'After the two days, you could say that ... as little cities, little towns, for all practical purposes, [they] really didn't exist any longer': *New York Times*, 29 October 1972.

9 A graphic account of the fall of this key installation can be found in J. Hamilton-Merritt, *Tragic Mountains: The Hmong, the Americans, and the Secret Wars for Laos, 1942–1992* (Bloomington, 1993), pp. 171–87.

10 R. Warner, *Back Fire: The CIA's Secret War in Laos and Its Link to the War in Vietnam* (New York, 1995), pp. 236–42.

11 G. Gurney, *Vietnam: The War in the Air* (New York, 1985), p. 217: S. M. Hersh, 'How We Ran the Secret Air War in Laos', *New York Times Magazine*, 29 October 1972.

12 E. T. McKeithen, *Life Under the PL in the Xieng Khouang ville area* (Vientiane, 1969), pp. 4–10, 26–7.

13 T. Decornoy, 'Guerre oubliée au Laos', *Le Monde*, 3–8 July 1968.
14 The United States claimed refugees fled the Pathēt Lao zone to escape 'the rice tax, porterage, and the draft': *Facts on Foreign Aid to Laos*, p. 105. That they were in fact fleeing the bombing is clear from refugees' reports: Fred Branfman, *Voices from the Plain of Jars: Life under an Air War* (New York, 1972); and also from the correlation evident between increased bombing and the increased flow of refugees: Embassy of the United States of America USAID Mission to Laos, *US Economic Assistance to the Royal Lao Government 1962–1972* (Vientiane, December, 1972), p. 2, which shows that from 1963 to 1968 refugees averaged around 115,000, but that from 1969 to 1972 this figure more than doubled to over 300,000.
15 For the debate over whether to bomb the Chinese road network, see G. M. Godley and J. St Goar, 'The Chinese Road in Northwest Laos 1961–73: An American Perspective', in J. J. Zasloff and L. Unger, eds, *Laos: Beyond the Revolution* (London, 1991), pp. 285–314.
16 For a devastating criticism of Godley and his behaviour, see C. Mullin, 'The Secret Bombing of Laos: The Story Behind Nine Years of US Attacks', *The Asia Magazine* 14/19 (12 May 1974), 6.
17 Lao army officers were trading rice and other commodities to the North Vietnamese: Soutchay Vongsavanh, *RLG Military Operations*, p. 54.
18 An estimated quarter of all Hmong troops taking part in this offensive lost their lives: *New York Times*, 13 November 1968.
19 Ministry of Foreign Affairs, Royal Lao Government, *White Book on the Violations of the 1962 Geneva Accords by the Government of North Vietnam* (Vientiane, 1969), p. 58. Another estimate placed the number of Vietnamese at 45,000, as against 1750 US civilian and military personnel: *New York Times*, 14 April 1968. To the American figure should be added personnel involved in the 'secret war' but based outside Laos, and those conducting the air war, a figure as high as 50,000, according to Branfman ('The President's Secret Army', p. 78).
20 Department of State, 'Kingdom of Laos', Appendix 5, pp. 358–9.
21 *New York Times*, 26 October 1969. Of these 15,000 were 'regulars' while the remaining 25,000 were part-time fighters. R. Shaplen, 'Our Involvement in Laos', *Foreign Affairs* 48 (1970), 492. Army units were seldom at full strength because when desertions occurred, a fictitious name would be inserted in the lists, payment for whom would go to senior officers. Cf. Houy Pholsena, 'L'Armée Nationale du Laos', PhD thesis, University of Aix-en-Provence (1971), p. 59.
22 Of these an estimated 7000 were engineering troops, while 3000 were there in a protective capacity (including manning anti-aircraft batteries).
23 Thai 'volunteers' increased from around 10,000 costing the United States $100 million per annum, according to hearings before the Senate Foreign Relations Committee (*New York Times*, 8 May 1972) to double that within a year: US Senate, Committee on Foreign Relations, *Thailand, Laos, Cambodia, and Vietnam: April 1973: A Staff Report Prepared for the Use of the Subcommittee on US Security Agreements and Commitments Abroad*, 93rd Congress, 1st session (Washington, DC, 1973), p. 15.
24 Chandler, *The Tragedy of Cambodian History*, p. 140.
25 Phomvihane, *La Révolution Lao*, p. 31.
26 South Vietnamese forces had already been crossing into Laos in hot pursuit for 'several years', though only in limited numbers: *New York Times*, 19 May 1970.
27 The Lao resented not even being kept informed of the progress of the operation: Soutchay Vongsavanh, *RLG Military Operations*, pp. 61, 107.

28 S. M. Hersh, *The Price of Power: Kissinger in the White House* (New York, 1983), p. 307. For a less damning appraisal, see K. W. Nolan, *Into Laos: The Story of Dewey Canyon/Lam Son 719; Vietnam 1971* (Novato, Calif., 1986), pp. 359–62.

29 *A Historic Victory of the Lao Patriotic Forces* (n.p., 1971). For their part, the Vietnamese do acknowledge some Pathēt Lao contribution: *Anti-US War*, pp. 134–6.

30 *New York Times*, 16 March 1971.

31 Warner, *Back Fire*, p. 350.

32 By official count, 2,093,100 tons, at an estimated total cost of $US7200 million: M. Stuart-Fox and M. Kooyman, *Historical Dictionary of Laos* (Metuchen, NY, 1992), pp. 2–3.

33 Some estimates were even higher: *New York Times*, 15 March 1971, quoting Senate sub-committee figures of 750,000 to one million.

34 The Lao People's Liberation Army was formed following the 'marriage' of Pathēt Lao and 'Patriotic Neutralist' forces after a joint conference in October 1965: Brown and Zasloff, *Apprentice Revolutionaries*, p. 94. It was commanded by Khamtai Sīphandôn, who had replaced Singkapō Sīkhôt-chunnamālī as commander of the Pathēt Lao armed forces after the latter was demoted in 1963 for being too closely identified with the neutralists on the Supreme Mixed Military Committee. For this 'ideological rectification campaign', see Chou Norindr, 'Le Néolaohakxat ou le Front Patriotique Lao et la révolution laotienne', doctoral dissertation, University of Paris, 1980, pp. 501–3.

35 Cf. F. Branfman, 'Presidential War in Laos, 1964–1970', in Adams and McCoy, eds, *Laos: War and Revolution*, pp. 223–5. The power of regional commanders was not broken until the military reorganization of July 1971.

36 Phūmī retired to southern Thailand. He briefly lent his name to anti-communist resistance organizations in the early 1980s, and died in 1985. Sīhō returned to Laos in June 1966, was arrested, and shot – allegedly while attempting to escape custody.

37 McCoy, *The Politics of Heroin*, pp. 296–308. Casualties from the fighting were around 200.

38 Souvanna Phouma, 'Laos: le fond du problème', *France-Asie* 166 (March–April 1961), 1825.

39 Cited in Perry Stieglitz, *In a Little Kingdom* (Armonk, NY, 1990), p. 168.

40 A somewhat cynical defence of this position was argued by Nyūy Aphai: Stieglitz, *In a Little Kingdom*, pp. 78–80.

41 *New York Times*, 28 November 1966. The LPF took every opportunity to demand a return to the Geneva Agreements. Cf. *Impérialism Américain: Saboteur des Accords de Genève de 1962 sur le Laos* (Zone libérée Lao, 1967).

42 J. Lejars, 'Situation industrielle du Laos et rôle des forces externes', *Tiers Monde* 13 (1972), 624–9. Of 19 new factories established between 1967 and 1969, 17 were Chinese-owned (p. 629).

43 Commissariat Général au Plan, *Plan Cadre 1969–1974: Programme Annuel de Réalisation 1970–1971* (Vientiane, 1970).

44 G. Chapelier and J. van Malderghem, 'Plain of Jars: Social Change under Five Years of Pathet-Lao Administration', *Asia Quarterly* 1 (1971), 61–89.

45 'Political Program of the Neo Lao Haksat', in Brown and Zasloff, *Apprentice Revolutionaries*, Appendix A3, pp. 291–6.

46 Prior withdrawal of Vietnamese forces was for Suvanna the *sine qua non* for a settlement in Laos. The Vietnamese, by contrast, were prepared as late as 1969 to back a settlement, provided Suvanna withdrew permission for the United States to bomb the Ho Chi Minh trail: Shaplen, 'Our Involvement in Laos', p. 486.

47 Broadcast over Pathēt Lao Radio, 10 July 1969, cited in Brown and Zasloff, *Apprentice Revolutionaries*, p. 95.
48 This claim is made by Chao Sopsaisana, 'Laos After Viet Nam', *Pacific Community* 1/4 (1970), 712.
49 A. J. Dommen, 'Lao Politics under Prince Suvanna Phouma', in J. J. Zasloff and A. E. Goodman, eds, *Indochina in Conflict: A Political Assessment* (Lexington, Mass., 1972), pp. 84–7.
50 Cf. Saveng Phinith, 'La littérature lao contemporaine' in P.-B. Lafont and D. Lombard, eds, *Littératures contemporaines de l'Asie du Sud-est* (Paris, 1974), pp. 35–7.
51 H. Kissinger, *Years of Upheaval* (London, 1982), p. 10.
52 At least one in ten Hmong died (T. N. Castle, 'Alliance in a Secret War: The United States and the Hmong in Northeastern Laos', MA thesis, San Diego State University, 1979, p. 91), but no estimates are available for other ethnic groups.
53 US Embassy, *Facts on Foreign Aid to Laos*, pp. 121–4.
54 Memo of 3 March, 1970, quoted in Branfman, 'Presidential War in Laos, 1964–1970', p. 259.
55 At $55 per annum compared with $180: *Facts on Foreign Aid to Laos*, pp. 73–4.
56 For 1970, for example, development aid amounted to $2.8 million out of a total of $52.5 million: *Facts on Foreign Aid to Laos*, p. 151.
57 J.-P. Barbier, 'Objectifs et résultats de l'aide économique au Laos: une évalua-tion difficile', *Tiers Monde* 16 (1975), 352.
58 Quoted in Barbier, 'Objectifs et résultats de l'aide économique', p. 336.
59 Barber, *Migrants and Modernisation*, p. 398.
60 Grant Evans, 'Land Reform in the Lao Revolution', in A. Butler, ed., *Proceedings of the International Conference on Thai Studies* (Canberra, 1987), vol. 3, part 2, pp. 461–2.
61 Heroin in particular was readily available after 1972: J. Westermeyer, *Poppies, Pipes, and People: Opium and Its Use in Laos* (Berkeley, 1982), pp. 156–63.
62 Amphay Doré, *Le Partage du Mékong* (Paris, 1980), p. 67.
63 David Chandler makes a similar point about the Khmer Rouge in Cambodia, and Pol Pot in particular. Cf. *Brother Number One: A Political Biography of Pol Pot* (Boulder, 1992), pp. 80, 182.
64 No mention was made of the existing National Assembly, which was not recognized by the Pathēt Lao.
65 The United States was mainly interested in prisoners held by the Pathēt Lao (6) and servicemen listed as missing in action in Laos (311): *New York Times*, 1 January 1973. A total of 81 US servicemen had died in Laos by the time the cease-fire was declared, not including members of the CIA: *New York Times*, 25 July 1973.
66 After his aircraft was hit and crash landed, Thao Mā was apprehended and executed on the orders of General Kupasit Aphai. His co-conspirator, Bunloet Saisôn, escaped to Thailand: Norindr, *Histoire Contemporaine du Laos*, pp. 529–31; N. Peagam, 'Laos Shrugs off a Five Dollar Putsch', *Far Eastern Economic Review*, 27 August 1973.
67 Under the terms of the agreement, security in Viang Chan was to be assured by 1000 police and 1200 troops from each side, with half those numbers for Luang Phrabāng: 'Laos: Protocol Agreement to the Ceasefire', *Australian Foreign Affairs Record* 44/10 (October 1973), 674–87.
68 M. Brown and J. J. Zasloff, 'The Pathēt Lao and the Politics of Reconciliation in Laos, 1973–1974', in J. J. Zasloff and M. Brown, eds, *Communism in Indochina: New Perspectives* (Lexington, Mass., 1975), p. 265.

69 By 1967, Laos was importing 72 tons of gold, on which an 8.5 per cent duty provided the government with more than 40 per cent of its total tax revenues. Most found its way onto the Saigon black market: McCoy, *The Politics of Heroin*, p. 250.

70 'The First 10 Year Plan for Economic Reconstruction and Development 1975–1985', roneoed copy.

71 Phomvihane, *La Révolution Lao*, p. 39.

72 *Documents sur le 25e anniversaire de la fondation du Parti Populaire Révolutionnaire Lao* (Vientiane, 1980), p. 9.

73 Cf. Oudone Sananikone, *The Royal Lao Army and US Army Advice and Support* (Washington, DC, 1983), p. 168. The Pathēt Lao had already provoked mutinies in several Royal Lao Army garrisons: A. Dommen, 'Communist Strategy in Laos', *Problems of Communism* 24 (1975), 62.

74 Clearly stated in conversation with his son-in-law: Stieglitz, *In a Little Kingdom*, p. 211.

75 US aid amounted to $32 million in economic aid in fiscal 1975, together with $30 million in military aid: *New York Times*, 26 May 1975.

76 *New York Times*, 26 May 1975, by which time an estimated 25 per cent of the nation's entire wealth had been converted to gold.

77 The term is McAlister Brown's in 'The Communist Seizure of Power in Laos', in Stuart-Fox, ed., *Contemporary Laos*, p. 32. Brown argues that the communist seizure of power in Laos most resembles that in Czechoslovakia, a comparison made as early as 1957 by American officials opposed to the First Coalition. Cf. McAlister Brown, 'Communists in Coalition Government: Lessons from Laos', p. 41; and A. Dommen, 'Lao Nationalism and American Policy, 1954–9', p. 257; both in Zasloff and Unger, eds, *Laos: Beyond the Revolution*.

78 J. Everingham, 'Vientiane's Trial of the "Traitors"', *Far Eastern Economic Review*, 3 October 1975.

79 J. Everingham, 'The Pathēt Lao Make It Official', *Far Eastern Economic Review*, 5 September 1975.

80 *New York Times*, 2, 3 and 4 December 1975.

81 Cf. Phomvihane, *La Révolution Lao*, pp. 99–102, 116. That this was a deliberate tactic was confirmed by the Polish diplomat Mieczyslaw Maneli, *War of the Vanquished* (New York, 1971), p. 190.

82 Suphānuvong is reported to have remarked to French teachers that victory had come a few years too early. And Kaisôn himself admitted, 'Our preparations were not complete ...': *La Révolution Lao*, p. 129. For further discussion of the Lao revolution, see M. Stuart-Fox, 'The Lao Revolution: Errors and Achievements', *World Review* 16 (1977), 3–15; and 'Reflections on the Lao Revolution', *Contemporary Southeast Asia* 3 (1981), 41–57.

## CHAPTER 6   THE LAO PEOPLE'S DEMOCRATIC REPUBLIC

1 *Documents du Congrès national des Représentants du peuple* (Vientiane, 1976), an English translation of which appeared as *Documents of National Congress of the People's Representatives of Laos* (New Delhi, n.d. [1976]). The best summary of the role of the Lao People's Revolutionary Party in directing the Lao revolution is in *Documents sur le 25è anniversaire de la fondation du Parti Populaire Révolutionnaire Lao*, especially pp. 13–14.

2 Département de Presse, Ministère des Affaires Étrangères, 'Documents de la politique extérieure', *Bulletin de Nouvelles*, 26 April 1983, pp. 1–12, especially p. 9.

3 See, for example, Foreign Broadcasts Information Service, *Daily Report: East Asia* (hereafter FBIS), 24 March 1976.

4  A. Doré, 'The Three Revolutions in Laos', in Stuart-Fox, ed., *Contemporary Laos*, pp. 101–15.

5  Phomvihane, *La Révolution Lao*, pp. 200–10.

6  Phomvihane, *La Révolution Lao*, p. 36.

7  Vice-presidents were Sīsomphôn Lôvanxai, Sīthon Kommadam, Faidāng Lôbliayao and Khamsuk Kaeolā, not incidentally representing upland Tai, Lao Thoeng, Lao Sūng and Lao Lum ethnic groups: *Documents of the National Congress*, pp. 27–9.

8  A more detailed examination of the legitimation of Pathēt Lao political authority is provided in M. Stuart-Fox, 'Marxism and Theravāda Buddhism: The Legitimation of Political Authority in Laos', *Pacific Affairs* 56 (1983), 428–54. This and other articles on which this chapter draws can be found in M. Stuart-Fox, *Buddhist Kingdom, Marxist State: The Making of Modern Laos* (Bangkok, 1996).

9  For example, see Chou Norindr, 'Le Néolaohakxat', pp. 501–5.

10  Neither Faidāng nor Sīthon ever won a place on the Party Central Committee, though both were subsequently named, along with Kaisôn and Suphānuvong, among the four 'heroes of the revolution'.

11  According to figures from the UN, almost 20,000 lowland Lao arrived as refugees in Thailand during 1976, a figure that more than doubled again in 1978: UN High Commissioner for Refugees, 'Indo-Chinese Refugees and Asylum Seekers in Thailand: As of 31 May 1991' (Bangkok, 1991), p. 1.

12  R. Shaplen, 'Letter From Laos', *New Yorker*, 2 August 1976, p. 73.

13  M. Stuart-Fox and R. S. Bucknell, 'Politicization of the Buddhist Sangha in Laos', *Journal of Southeast Asian Studies* 13 (1982), 60–80. Lay people were unhappy over these restrictions since they curtailed opportunities to 'make merit'.

14  M. Brown and J. J. Zasloff, 'Laos 1976: Faltering First Steps Towards Socialism', *Asian Survey* 17 (1977), 110.

15  Agence France Presse, Bangkok, 2 February 1976 (FBIS, 3 February 1976).

16  Radio Viang Chan, 15 November 1976 (FBIS, 16 November 1976).

17  Reports of 40,000 to 50,000 detainees in re-education camps were probably exaggerated. Cf. *New York Times*, 11 November 1976, 3 May 1977. The number of those held in five camps in the Viang Xai area was less than 1500. If a similar number was held in the south, this would make 3000, including almost all senior police and army officers above the rank of major. A full list of names is given in Joanna C. Scott: *Indo-China's Refugees: Oral Histories from Laos, Cambodia and Vietnam* (Jefferson, NC, 1988), pp. 269–305. As many as ten times the number of lower-ranking officers and civilians were probably also held for greater or lesser periods, so a figure of 30,000 for much of 1976 and 1977 is probably nearer the mark.

18  Cf. G. Evans, *Lao Peasants under Socialism and Post-Socialism* (Chiang Mai, 1995), pp. 17–19.

19  Cited in N. Peagam, 'Kaysone's Critical Year', *Far Eastern Economic Review*, 17 December 1976.

20  Y. Mikhéev, *Les débuts du socialisme au Laos* (Moscow, 1985), pp. 44–5.

21  G. Y. Lee, 'Minority Policies and the Hmong', in Stuart-Fox, ed., *Contemporary Laos*, pp. 212–15.

22  J. Everingham, 'Royalists rankle the regime', *Far Eastern Economic Review*, 25 March 1977. Though the regime issued no official statement, both the King and Crown Prince apparently died in detention in 1978, while Queen Khamphuy lived on until December 1981. Cf. P. Delorme, 'Le destin tragique du dernier roi du Laos', *Historia* 497 (May 1988), 94–101.

23  W. C. Robinson, 'Laotian Refugees in Thailand: The Thai and US Response, 1975 to 1988', in Zasloff and Unger, eds, *Laos: Beyond the Revolution*, table 9.1,

p. 236. Of one group of 8000 Hmong that fled the Phū Bia region, only 2500 reached Thailand: Lee, 'Minority Policies and the Hmong', p. 214.

24 In the words of Radio Viang Chan, 11 January 1978 (FBIS, 12 January 1978).

25 The Thai were undoubtedly aware of loose talk in Laos about 'recuperating' the Isān region of northeastern Thailand. Indeed, this intention was used to justify the 'special relationship' with Vietnam: Doré, *Le Partage du Mékong*, p. 216.

26 Cf. Martin Stuart-Fox, *Vietnam in Laos: Hanoi's Model for Kampuchea* (Claremont, Calif., 1987). The Lao were always aware of a degree of Vietnamese condescension in their relationship, no matter how hard the Vietnamese tried to avoid showing it: personal interviews with several senior Lao officials.

27 A Lao spokesman later admitted that Vietnamese troops in Laos had been used in the 1979 invasion of Cambodia: *New York Times*, 23 March 1979.

28 Kaisôn Phomvihān, Report to the Joint Session of the Supreme People's Assembly and Council of Ministers, 2 March 1978, broadcast over Radio Viang Chan, 6 March 1978 (FBIS, 17 March 1978), pp. 22, 6.

29 Kaisôn, Report, 2 March 1978, p. 31.

30 Grant Evans argues that the timing was dictated by the 'ever-tighter interlocking of international developments with domestic decisions': Evans, *Lao Peasants*, p. 49.

31 Cf. *Khaosān Pathēt Lao, Bulletin Quotidien*, 28 November 1978; Kaisôn, Sixth Resolution, p. 1, February 1979 (Joint Publications Research Service, South and East Asia, 808 of 19 March 1979); Kaisôn, Seventh Resolution, 26 December 1979 (FBIS, 18 January 1980).

32 Kaysone Phomvihane, *Selected Speeches and Articles* (New Delhi, 1978), p. 61.

33 See M. Stuart-Fox, 'Laos: The Vietnamese Connection', in L. Suryadinata, ed., *Southeast Asian Affairs 1980* (Singapore, 1980), pp. 191–209.

34 Nayan Chanda, 'Laos: Back to the Drawing Board', *Far Eastern Economic Review*, 8 September 1978.

35 No formal treaty of friendship and cooperation was signed between Laos and Cambodia of the kind that bound both countries to Vietnam, though an economic, cultural, scientific and technological cooperation agreement was signed: FBIS, 26 March 1979.

36 On Chinese intentions, to the extent these could be then discerned, see M. Stuart-Fox, 'Laos in China's Anti-Vietnam Strategy', *Asia Pacific Community* 11 (1981), 83–104.

37 A pro-Chinese 'plot' allegedly uncovered in mid-1980 led to the arrest of as many as 500 civil servants and Party members: *New York Times*, 21, 22 October 1980. Though most were subsequently released after undergoing political re-education, the Party leadership were deeply angered by what they regarded as Chinese attempts to split the Party: interviews with Party officials.

38 *Les principaux documents importants du Congrès du Front* (Vientiane, 1980), pp. 34–45.

39 Cited in N. Chanda, 'Economic Changes in Laos, 1975–1980', in Stuart-Fox, ed. *Contemporary Laos*, p. 124.

40 Kaisôn Phomvihān, Seventh Resolution, 26 December 1979 (FBIS, 18 January 1980), p. I/30.

41 Kaisôn Phomvihān, Seventh Resolution, FBIS Supplement, 8 February 1980, p. 12.

42 G. Evans, 'Planning Problems in Peripheral Socialism: The Case of Laos', in Zasloff and Unger, eds, *Laos: Beyond the Revolution*, p. 102.

43  The three factions were the Khmer Rouge, armed and supplied by China via Thailand; the followers of Prince Sihanouk; and the rightist Khmer People's National Liberation Front, led by former prime minister Son Sann – the last two drawing their support from ASEAN and the United States

44  J. Guillemi and M. Meselson, 'Yellow Rain: The Story Collapses', *Foreign Policy* 86 (1987), 100–17. The best study is G. Evans, *The Yellow Rainmakers: Are Chemical Weapons Being Used in Southeast Asia?* (London, 1983).

45  The Chinese were disillusioned by the factionalism and lack of discipline in the Lao resistance: interview with General Kônglae, Paris, November 1985.

46  As was made clear to the author by the Chinese *chargé d'affaires* in an interview in Viang Chan, 24 August 1985.

47  M. Stuart-Fox, 'Laos in 1983: A Time of Consolidation', in P. Thambipillai, ed., *Southeast Asian Affairs 1984* (Singapore, 1984), pp. 188–9.

48  International Monetary Fund, *Lao People's Democratic Republic – Recent Economic Developments*, SM/80/174, 22 July 1980.

49  Ministry of Foreign Affairs, LPDR, 'Political Reporting [*sic*] of the Central Committee of the Lao People's Revolutionary Party presented at its Third Party Congress by Comrade Kaysone Phomvihane, General Secretary, Vientiane, 27–30 April 1982' (Viang Chan, n.d.).

50  'Rapport sur les amendements à apporter aux statuts du Parti Populaire Révolutionnaire Lao', *Khaosān Pathēt Lao, Bulletin Quotidien*, 1 May 1982, p. 1.

51  'Résultats des élections aux organismes de direction suprême du parti', *Khaosān Pathēt Lao, Bulletin Quotidien*, 1 May 1982, pp. 17–19.

52  For a full analysis of these important changes, see M. Stuart-Fox, *Laos: Politics, Economics and Society* (London, 1986), pp. 62–3, 72–8.

53  'Allocution du Camarade Secretaire General Kaysone Phomvihane au 1er Congrès National de l'Union des Femmes Lao', *Bulletin de Nouvelles* (Viang Chan), no. 45, 24 April 1984. In the first decade of communist government in Laos, only four women gained places on the Party Central Committee, while not one was appointed to a ministerial or vice-ministerial position in government.

54  Mayoury Ngaosyvathn, *Lao Women Yesterday and Today* (Vientiane, 1993), p. 105. The Union of Lao Women also endorsed the Party's ban on contraception, designed to increase population.

55  Cf. M. Stuart-Fox, 'Politics and Patronage in Laos', *Indochina Issues* 70 (October 1986), 2–4. So annoyed were Party officials over this publication that the author was denied a visa to visit Laos for two years.

56  This account was pieced together from interviews with Lao informants.

57  Cf. the criticisms of Amnesty International, 'Background paper on the Democratic People's Republic of Laos describing current Amnesty International Concerns', ASA 26/04/85 (April 1985), p. 13.

58  Joseph J. Zasloff, 'The Three-Village Dispute between Laos and Thailand', *University Field Staff International Reports*, no. 23 (1985).

59  *Khaosān Pathēt Lao, News Bulletin*, 28 March 1985.

60  FBIS, 11 February 1985.

61  Mikhéev, *Les débuts du socialisme au Laos*, p. 58.

62  *Le Monde*, 3 December 1985.

63  FBIS, 14 January 1985.

64  FBIS, 29 January 1985.

65  State Statistical Centre, Ministry of Economy, Planning and Finance, *Population of the Lao PDR* (Viang Chan, 1992); UNICEF, *Children and Women in the Lao People's Democratic Republic* (Viang Chan, 1992), p. 9.

66  Kaisôn Phomvihān, 'Speech at the Grand Rally in Celebration of the 10th anniversary of the Lao People's Democratic Republic' in *Khaosān Pathēt*

*Lao, News Bulletin*, 3 December 1985, p. 4. The government gave its own accounting in State Planning Committee, State Statistical Centre, *10 Years of Socio-Economic Development in the Lao People's Democratic Republic* (Viang Chan, 1985), though the statistics therein should be treated with some caution.

67 UNDP, 'Draft Report submitted to the government of the LPDR', August 1985.

68 Kaisôn, 'Speech at the Grand Rally', p. 4. More precise figures were given in *Nouvelles du Laos*, December 1985, as 3184 cooperatives grouping 61.5 per cent of farming families and 58 per cent of agricultural land.

69 UNDP, 'Draft Report', August 1985.

70 Kaisôn, 'Speech at the Grand Rally', p. 5.

71 The author was a member of an Asian Development Bank consultancy group investigating the state of Lao education in November–December 1990, which revealed shockingly low standards.

72 Interview with Health Minister Khamliang Phonsēnā, Viang Chan, 14 August 1985.

73 Linda and Titus Peachey, 'Religion in Socialist Laos', *Southeast Asia Chronicle* 91 (1983), 18. By 1988, there were reported to be 45,000 Christians in the LPDR (30,000 Catholics and 15,000 Protestants), down from an estimated 70,000 in 1975: FBIS, 12 July 1988.

74 Interview with head of the Lao *Sangha*, Thongkhūn Anantasunthôn, Viang Chan, 8 August 1985.

75 Interviews with several monks, Viang Chan, July and August 1985. The regime made some effort to eliminate the 'superstitious' worship of *phī*, but without success. Cf. *Viang Chan Mai*, 14 May 1983.

76 Amnesty International, 'Background paper on the Democratic People's Republic of Laos' (April 1985); and Amnesty International ' "Re-education" in Attapeu province, the People's Democratic Republic of Laos', ASA 26/01/86, January 1986.

77 Broadcast over Radio Viang Chan and translated in FBIS, 29 January 1985.

78 Cf. Kaisôn's reference to the primary 'battlefront' in the struggle as that of 'circulation and distribution and economic relations with foreign countries': FBIS, 29 January 1985.

79 This account is necessarily speculative. No Lao Party or government records are available (if any were ever kept) of the horse-trading that must have gone on. I am grateful to Lao sources who must remain anonymous for assisting in reconstructing this struggle for power.

80 Kaisôn Phomvihān, 'Political Report of the Central Committee of the Lao People's Revolutionary Party presented at its Fourth Party Congress', roneoed English translation, p. 12.

81 'Guidelines and Tasks of the Second Five-Year Plan (1986–90) for Economic and Social Development of the Lao People's Democratic Republic', roneoed English translation.

82 Kaisôn, 'Political Report to the Fourth Party Congress', p. 68.

83 Ng Shui Meng, 'Laos in 1986: Into the Second Decade of National Reconstruction', in *Southeast Asian Affairs 1987* (Singapore, 1987), pp. 186–7.

84 Even though Suphānuvong had been forced to step down from the presidency of the republic in October 1986 (at the age of 77) due to ill-health, he still retained his position on the Politburo. Phūmī Vongvichit became acting president. In September 1987, Phūmī also replaced Suphānuvong as acting president of the Lao Front for National Construction. Suphānuvong formally resigned in October 1988 as president of the Front, but remained president of the republic until March 1991.

85 FBIS, 24 February 1983.

86 FBIS, 27 March 1985.

87 Elements of the criminal code dealing with matters such as treason, organization of protests, and slander of the state were so broad, however, as to cause concern both to expatriate Lao and to human rights organizations. Cf. Amnesty International, 'Freedom of Expression Still Denied', ASA 26/03/93, July 1993.

88 Amnesty International, 'Laos', ASA 26/01/89, March 1989.

89 B. Gay, *La nouvelle frontière lao-vietnamienne: Les accords de 1977–1990* (Paris, 1995).

90 Kaisôn Phomvihān, 'Political Report of the Executive Committee of the Central Committee of the Lao People's Revolutionary Party presented at the Vth Party Congress', roneoed English translation distributed to embassies and foreign delegations (of which there were only four in attendance – the Soviet Union, China, Vietnam and Cambodia).

91 'Report of the Executive Committee of the Party Central Committee on amendments to the Statute of the Lao People's Revolutionary Party at its Vth Congress' read by Udom Khattinya, Chair of the Party's Propaganda and Training Committee, roneoed English translation.

92 Additions included Udom Khattinya, Chummalī Xainyasôn, Somlat Chanthamāt, Khamphuy Kaeobualaphā, and Thongsing Thammavong.

93 All expatriate Lao who left the country illegally were deemed to have renounced their Lao citizenship. To regain it they had to renounce any other citizenship and make applications which were assessed primarily on political criteria. None of this was spelled out in the citizenship law, except for the provision denying dual citizenship (Article 2): Law on Lao Nationality, adopted by the Supreme People's Assembly, 29 November 1990.

94 Ministry of Transport, PDR, 'National Transport Survey Plan to the Year 2000' (Viang Chan, 1990).

95 Ministry of Industry, PDR, 'Power Development Plan, 1991–2010' (Viang Chan, 1991).

96 *Khaosān Pathēt Lao, News Bulletin*, 29 March, 8 August 1993.

97 Interview with Phūmī Vongvichit, Viang Chan, 8 December 1993. Phūmī died on 7 January 1994.

98 Boun Nhang Sengchandavong, 'An Agenda for Promoting Tourism', *Dok Champa* 2/1 (January–March 1994), 22–5.

99 Lao People's Democratic Republic, 'Outline Public Investment Program 1994–2000', and 'Socio-Economic Development Strategies', both presented to the fifth Round Table Meeting, Geneva, 21 June 1994.

100 The Economist Intelligence Unit, *Country Report: Indochina* 2 (1994), p. 34.

101 *Khaosān Pathēt Lao, News Bulletin*, 27 May 1994. Imposition of quotas on timber in transit was a vain attempt to prevent Lao logs being passed off as imported timber in transit, which attracted a much lower tariff.

102 The Ministry of National Defence runs three important corporations, of which the largest and most profitable is the Mountain Area Development Company, with timber and other interests in central Laos.

# SELECT BIBLIOGRAPHY

Following usual practice, Lao and Thai authors have been listed by their first names.

## CONTENTS

Bibliographies
Government Documents
    Australia
    France
    Laos
      Royal Lao Government
      Pathēt Lao
      Lao People's Democratic Republic
    United Nations
    United Kingdom
    United States of America
    Vietnam
Books
Articles
Unpublished Theses
Journals and Newspapers

## BIBLIOGRAPHIES

Cordell, H., *Laos*, World Bibliographic Series no. 133, Oxford, 1991.
Lafont, P.-B., *Bibliographie du Laos*, vols I and II, Paris, 1968, 1978.
Lafont, P.-B. (ed.), *Les Recherches en Sciences Humaines sur le Laos*, Paris, 1994.
Sage, W. W., and Henchy, J. A. N., *Laos: A Bibliography*, Singapore, 1986.

## GOVERNMENT DOCUMENTS

### *Australia*

*Australian Foreign Affairs Record.*
Department of External Affairs, *Laos*, Select Documents on International Affairs no. 16, Canberra, April 1970.

*France*

Archives de France, Section Outre-Mer, Aix-en-Provence.
Archives Nationales, Section Outre-Mer, Paris.
Conventions et Traités entre la France et le Siam rélatifs au Laos (1893–1947), *Péninsule* nos. 16–17 (1988).
La Documentation Française, *Journal Officiel de la République Française, Notes et Etudes Documentaires.*

*Laos*

**Royal Lao Government**
*Accord sur la cessation de tous actes hostiles dans les provinces de Sam Neua et Phong Saly*, Vientiane, 1955.
*Agreement on Restoring Peace and Achieving National Concord in Laos*, n.p., 1973.
*Annuaire statistique du Laos*, Vientiane, 1951–74.
*Le Royaume du Laos: ses institutions et son organisation générale*, Vientiane, 1950.
*Livre blanc sur les violations des Accords de Genève de 1962 par le Gouvernement du Nord Vietnam*, Vientiane, 1965.

**Pathēt Lao**
*Crimes des aggresseurs américains au Laos*, n.p., 1968.
*Douze années d'intervention et d'aggression*, n.p., 1966.
*A Historic Victory of the Lao Patriotic Forces on Highway 9 – Southern Laos*, n.p., n.d. [1972].
*Nixon's Intensified Special War in Laos: A Criminal War Doomed to Fail*, n.p., 1972.
*Pages historiques de la lutte héroïque du peuple lao*, Vientiane, 1980.
*Phoukout Stronghold*, n.p., 1967.
*Program of Action of the Neo Lao Haksat*, n.p., 1964.
*A Quarter Century of Grim and Victorious Struggle*, n.p., n.d. [1971].
*Twelve Years of American Intervention and Aggression in Laos*, n.p., 1966.
*20 Years of the Lao People's Revolutionary Struggle*, n.p., 1966.
*Worthy Sons and Daughters of the Lao People*, n.p., 1966.

**Lao People's Democratic Republic**
*Basic Data About the Social and Economic Development of Lao People's Democratic Republic*, Vientiane, 1990.
*Documents of National Congress of the People's Representatives of Laos*, Delhi, n.d. [1976].
*Documents sur le 25e anniversaire de la fondation du Parti Populaire Révolutionnaire Lao*, Vientiane, 1980.
*Front Lao d'Edification Nationale (F.L.E.N.): Les principaux documents importants du Congrès du Front*, Vientiane, 1990.
'Guidelines and Task of the Second Five-Year Plan (1986–1990) for Economic and Social Development of the Lao People's Democratic Republic', roneoed, Viang Chan, 1986.
Ministry of Foreign Affairs, *Report on the Economic and Social Situation Development Strategy and Assistance Requirements*, Vientiane, 1983.
Ministry of Industry, 'Power Development Plan, 1991–2010', roneoed, Viang Chan, 1991.

Ministry of Planning, 'Outline Public Investment Program, 1994–2000', roneoed, Viang Chan, 1994.

Ministry of Transport, 'National Transport Survey Plan to the Year 2000', roneoed, Viang Chan, 1992.

National Statistical Centre, *Basic Statistics about the Socio-economic Development in the Lao P.D.R., 1992* and *1995*, Vientiane.

National Statistical Centre, *Lao Census 1995*, Preliminary Reports 1 and 2.

'Political Report of the Central Committee of the Lao People's Revolutionary Party at its Fourth Party Congress', roneoed, Viang Chan, November 1986.

'Political Report of the Executive Committee of the Party Central Committee of the Lao People's Revolutionary Party presented at the Vth Party Congress', roneoed, Viang Chan, March 1991.

*Population Census of 1985*, Vientiane, 1986.

*Report on the Economic and Social Situation, Development Strategy, and Assistance Requirements*, Geneva, 1983.

*Socio-Economic Development Strategies*, Report prepared for the fifth Round Table Meeting, Geneva, 21 June 1994.

*10 Years of Socio-Economic Development of the Lao People's Democratic Republic*, Viang Chan, 1985.

*Third Congress of the Lao People's Revolutionary Party: Documents and Materials, April 27–30, 1982*, Moscow, 1984.

*White Book: The Truth about Thai–Lao Relations*, Vientiane, 1984.

**United Nations**

UN Children's Fund, *Children and Women in the Lao People's Democratic Republic*, Vientiane, 1992.

UN Development Program, *Development Cooperation: Lao People's Democratic Republic, 1991 Report*, Vientiane, 1992.

UN High Commissioner for Refugees, 'Indo-Chinese Refugees and Asylum Seekers in Thailand: As of 31 May 1991', roneoed, Bangkok, 1991.

**United Kingdom**

British Information Services, *Laos*, R5498/70, London, 1970.

*Declaration and Protocol on the Neutrality of Laos, July 23, 1962*, Treaty Series no. 27, Cmnd 2025, 1962.

*Documents Relating to Discussion of Korea and Indochina at the Geneva Conference, April 27–June 15, 1954*, Miscellaneous no. 16, Cmd 9186, 1954.

*First Interim Report of the International Commission for Supervision and Control in Laos, August 11–December 31, 1954*, Cmd 9445, 1955.

*Fourth Interim Report of the International Commission for Supervision and Control in Laos, May 17, 1957–May 31, 1958*, Cmnd 541, 1958.

*International Conference on the Settlement of the Laotian Question, May 12, 1961– July 23, 1962*, Cmnd 1828, October 1962.

*Laos: Political Developments 1958–1960*, R-3706, London, February 1958.

*Second Interim Report of the International Commission for Supervision and Control in Laos, January 1–June 30, 1955*, Cmd 9360, 1955.

*Third Interim Report of the International Commission for Supervision and Control in Laos, July 1, 1955–May 16, 1957*, Cmnd 541, 1957.

**United States of America**

Department of Defense, *Laos: Country Study and Station Report*, Washington, DC, 1959.

Department of State, *The Situation in Laos*, Washington, DC, 1959.

Department of State, *Background Notes: Kingdom of Laos*, Washington, DC, 1970.

Embassy in Vientiane, *Facts on Foreign Aid to Laos*, Vientiane, August 1971.
Embassy in Vientiane, *US Economic Assistance to the Royal Lao Government 1962–1972*, Vientiane, December 1972.
*Foreign Relations of the United States, 1955–1957*, vol. XXIV: *East Asian Security; Cambodia; Laos*, ed. E. C. Keefer and D. W. Mabon, Washington, DC, 1990.
*Foreign Relations of the United States, 1958–1960*, vol. XVI: *East Asia–Pacific Region; Cambodia, Laos*, ed. by E. C. Keefer and D. W. Mabon, Washington, DC, 1992.
*Foreign Relations of the United States, 1961–1963*, vol. XXIV: *Laos Crisis*, ed. E. C. Keefer, Washington, DC, 1994.
House of Representatives, *United States Aid Operations in Laos: Seventh Report by the Committee on Government Operations*, Washington, DC, 1959.
Senate Committee on Foreign Relations, *United States Security Agreements and Commitments Abroad, Kingdom of Laos, Part 2*, 91st Congress, 1st session, 20–22 and 28 October 1969.
Senate Committee on Foreign Relations, *United States Security Agreements and Commitments Abroad, Kingdom of Laos*, 91st Congress, 2nd session, 20–22 and 28 October 1970.
Senate Committee on Foreign Relations, *Laos: April 1971 – A Staff Report*, 92nd Congress, 1st session, 3 August 1971.
Senate Committee on the Judiciary, *War-Related Civilian Problems in Indochina, Part I: Laos and Cambodia*, 92nd Congress, 1st session, 22 April 1971.
'US Involvement in Laos', *Congressional Record*, 92nd Congress, 1st session, 3 August 1971, vol. 117, no. 124, S12930–S12966.

**Vietnam**
*The Anti-US Resistance War for National Salvation, 1954–1975: Military Events*, Hanoi, 1980, trans. Joint Publications Research Service, 3 June 1982.
*Cambodia and Laos Fight Hand in Hand with Vietnam for Freedom*, n.p., April 1951.
*In the Liberated Zone of Laos*, Hanoi, 1968.
*The Indochinese People Will Win*, Hanoi, 1970.


BOOKS


Adams, N. S., and McCoy, A. W. (eds), *Laos: War and Revolution*, New York, 1970.
Anon. (ed.), *Autobiography of Prince Souphanouvong* Viang Chan, 1990.
Archaimbault, C., *Structures Religieuses Lao (Rites et Mythes)*, Vientiane, 1973.
Aymé, G., *Monographie du Territoire Militaire*, Hanoi, 1930.
Blaufarb, D. S., *The Counter-Insurgency Era: US Doctrine and Performance*, New York, 1977.
Branfman, F., *Voices from the Plain of Jars: Life Under an Air War*, New York, 1972.
Brocheux, P. (ed.), *Histoire de l'Asie du Sud-est: Révoltes, Réformes, Révolutions*, Lille, 1981.
Brown, McA., and Zasloff, J. J., *Apprentice Revolutionaries: The Communist Movement in Laos, 1930–1985*, Stanford, 1986.
Burchett, W. G., *Mekong Upstream*, East Berlin, 1959.
Burchett, W. G., *The Second Indochina War: Cambodia and Laos*, New York, 1970.
Cable, J., *The Geneva Conference of 1954 on Indochina*, New York, 1986.
Caply, M. [J. Deuve], *Guerilla au Laos*, Paris, 1966.
Castle, T. N., *At War in the Shadow of Vietnam: US Military Aid to the Royal Lao Government, 1955–1975*, New York, 1993.
Chandler, D. P., *A History of Cambodia*, 2nd edn, St Leonards, NSW, 1993.
Chazee, L., *Atlas des Ethnies et des Sous-Ethnies du Laos*, Bangkok, 1995.
Chen Yi et al., *Concerning the Situation in Laos*, Peking, 1959.

Chi Do Pham (ed.), *Economic Development in Lao P.D.R.: Horizon 2000*, Vientiane, 1994.

Chomsky, N., and Zinn, H. (eds), *The Pentagon Papers: Critical Essays*, vol. 5, Boston, 1972.

Chou Norindr, *Histoire Contemporaine du Laos, 1860–1975*, Bangkok, 1992.

Coedès, G., *The Indianized States of Southeast Asia*, trans. S. B. Cowing, Canberra, 1989.

Damrong Tayanin, *Being Kammu: My Village, My Life*, Ithaca, NY, 1992.

de Berval, R. (ed.), *Kingdom of Laos: The Land of the Million Elephants and the White Parasol*, Saigon, 1959.

de Crèvecœur, J., *La Libération du Laos, 1945–1946*, Chateau de Vincennes, 1985.

de Reinach, L., *Le Laos Français*, Paris, 1911.

Decoux, J., *A la Barre de l'Indochine: Histoire de mon Gouvernement Général, 1940–1945*, Paris, 1949.

Deschamps, J. M., *Tam-tam sur le Mékong*, Saigon, 1948.

Deuve, J., *Le Laos, 1945–1949: Contribution à l'histoire du mouvement Lao Issala*, Montpellier, n.d..

Deuve, J., *Le Royaume du Laos, 1949–1965: Histoire événementielle de l'indépendance à la guerre américaine*, Paris, 1985.

Deuve, J., *Un épisode oublié de l'histoire du Laos: Le complot de Chinaimo*, Paris, 1986.

Deuve, J., *La Guerre Secrète au Laos contre les Communistes, 1955–1964*, Paris, 1995.

Deydier, H., *Introduction à la Connaissance du Laos*, Saigon, 1952.

Deydier, H., *Lokapala: Génies, Totems et Sorciers du Nord Laos*, Paris, 1954.

Dommen, A. J., *Conflict in Laos: The Politics of Neutralization*, rev. edn, New York, 1971.

Dommen, A. J., *Laos: Keystone of Indochina*, Boulder, 1985.

Doré, A., *Le Partage du Mékong*, Paris, 1980.

Doré, A., *Aux Sources de la Civilisation Lao*, Metz, 1987.

Doumer, P., *Rapport sur la situation de l'Indochine, 1897–1901*, Hanoi, 1902.

Evans, G., *The Yellow Rainmakers: Are Chemical Weapons Being Used in Southeast Asia?*, London, 1983.

Evans, G., *Agrarian Change in Communist Laos*, Occasional Paper no. 85, Singapore, 1988.

Evans, G., *Lao Peasants under Socialism and Post-Socialism*, Chiang Mai, 1995.

Evans, G., and Rowley, K., *Red Brotherhood at War: Vietnam, Cambodia and Laos since 1975*, 2nd edn, London, 1990.

Fall, B. B., *Anatomy of a Crisis: The Laotian Crisis of 1960–1961*, New York, 1969.

Fforde, A., *From Plan to Market in Laos, 1975–95: A Study of Transition and its Aftermath*, Canberra, 1995.

Field, M., *The Prevailing Wind: Witness in Indo-China*, London, 1965.

Fredman, M. B., *Laos in Strategic Perspective*, Rand P-2330, Santa Monica, 7 June 1961.

Gay, B., *La Nouvelle Frontière Lao–Vietnamienne*, Paris, 1995.

Gentil, P., *Sursauts de l'Asie: Remous du Mékong*, Paris, 1950.

Ginsberg, N. S., *Area Handbook on Laos*, Chicago, 1955.

Goldstein, M. E., *American Policy Toward Laos*, Teaneck, NJ, 1973.

Goscha, C. E., *Vietnam or Indochina? Contesting Concepts of Space in Vietnamese Nationalism, 1887–1954*, NIAS Report no. 28, Copenhagen, 1995.

Gunn, G. C., *Political Struggles in Laos, 1930–1954*, Bangkok, 1988.

Gunn, G. C., *Rebellion in Laos: Peasant and Politics in a Colonial Backwater*, Boulder, 1990.

Halpern, J. M., *The Role of the Chinese in Lao Society*, Rand P-2161, Santa Monica, 1 March 1961.

Halpern, J. M., *Economy and Society of Laos: A Brief Survey*, New Haven, 1964.
Halpern, J. M., *Government, Politics and Social Structure in Laos: A Study of Tradition and Innovation*, New Haven, 1964.
Halpern, J. M., and Fredman, H. B., *Communist Strategy in Laos*, Rand RM-2561 Santa Monica, 14 June 1960.
Halpern, J. M., and Turley, W. S. (eds), *The Training of Vietnamese Communist Cadres in Laos*, Brussels, 1977.
Hamel, B., *Résistance en Indochine, 1975–1980*, Paris, 1980.
Hamilton-Merritt, J., *Tragic Mountains: The Hmong, the Americans, and the Secret Wars for Laos, 1942–1992*, Bloomington, Ind., 1993.
Hammer, E. J., *The Struggle for Indochina*, Stanford, 1954.
Hannah, N., *The Key to Failure: Laos and the Vietnam War*, Boston, 1987.
Hersh, S. M., *The Price of Power: Kissinger in the White House*, New York, 1983.
Hervey, H., *Travels in French Indochina*, London, 1928.
Higham, C., *The Archaeology of Mainland Southeast Asia*, Cambridge, 1989.
Hilsman, R., *To Move a Nation: The Politics of Foreign Policy in the Administration of John F. Kennedy*, Garden City, NY, 1967.
Hoshino, T., *Pour une Histoire Médiévale du Moyen Mékong*, Bangkok, 1986.
Iché, F., *Le Statut Politique et International du Laos Français: sa condition juridique dans la communauté du droit des gens*, Toulouse, 1935.
Ivarsson, S., Svensson, T., and Tønnesson, S., *The Quest for Balance in a Changing Laos: A Political Analysis*, NIAS Report no. 25, Copenhagen, 1995.
Izikowitz, K. W., *Lamet: Hill Peasants in French Indochina*, New York, 1979.
Kaisôn Phomvihān, *Lūk không paxāxon* [Son of the People], Viang Chan, 1991.
Kaisôn Phomvihān, *see also* Kaysone Phomvihane.
Katay Don Sasorith, *Le Laos: son évolution politique, sa place dans l'union française*, Paris, 1953.
Kaysone Phomvihan, *Selected Speeches and Articles*, New Delhi, 1978.
Kaysone Phomvihane, *La Révolution Lao*, Moscow, 1981.
Kemp, P., *Alms for Oblivion*, London, 1961.
Khan, A. R., and Lee, E., *Employment and Development in Laos: Some Problems and Policies*, Bangkok, 1980.
Kunstadter, P. (ed.), *Southeast Asian Tribes, Minorities, and Nations*, 2 vols, Princeton, 1967.
Lafont, P.-B., and Lombard, D. (eds), *Littératures contemporaines de l'Asie du Sudest*, Paris, 1974.
Langer, P. F., *The Soviet Union, China and the Pathēt Lao*, Rand P-4765, Santa Monica, January 1972.
Langer, P. F., and Zasloff, J. J., *The North Vietnamese Military Adviser in Laos: A First Hand Account*, Rand RM-5388-ARPA, Santa Monica, July 1968.
Langer, P. F., and Zasloff, J. J., *North Vietnam and the Pathet Lao: Partners in the Struggle for Laos*, Cambridge, Mass., 1970.
*Laos: An Outline of Ancient and Contemporary History*, Hanoi, 1982.
Larteguy, J., and Dao, Y., *La Fabuleuse Aventure du Peuple de l'Opium*, Paris, 1979.
Le Boulanger, P., *Histoire du Laos Français: Essai d'une étude chronologique des principautés laotiennes*, Paris, 1931.
Le Josne, J.-C., *Gerritt van Wuysthoff et ses Assistants: Le Journal de Voyage au Laos (1641–42)*, Metz, 1986.
LeBar, F. M., Hickey, G. C., and Musgrave, J. K., *Ethnic Groups of Mainland Southeast Asia*, New Haven, 1964.
LeBar, F. M., and Suddard, A. (eds), *Laos: Its People, Its Society, Its Culture*, New Haven, 1960.
Lee, C.-J., *Communist China's Policy Toward Laos: A Case Study, 1954–1967*, Lawrence, Kans., 1970.

Lévy, P., *Histoire du Laos*, Paris, 1974.
Lévy, R., *Indochine et ses Traités*, Paris, 1947.
Lintingre, P., *Les Rois du Champassak*, Paksé, 1972.
Luther, H. V., *Socialism in a Subsistence Economy: The Laotian Way*, Bangkok, 1983.
Maneli, M., *War of the Vanquished*, New York, 1971.
Mangra Souvannaphouma, *L'Agonie du Laos*, Paris, 1976.
Mayoury Ngaosyvathn, *Lao Women Yesterday and Today*, Vientiane, 1993.
Mayoury Ngaosyvathn, *Remembrances of a Lao Woman Devoted to the National Liberation Struggle: Khampheng Boupha*, Viang Chan, 1993.
Mayoury and Pheuiphanh Ngaosyvathn, *Kith and Kin Politics: The Relationship between Laos and Thailand*, Manila, 1994.
McCoy, A. W., et al., *The Politics of Heroin in Southeast Asia*, New York, 1972.
McKeithen, E. T., *Life under the Pathet Lao in the Xieng Khuang ville Area*, Vientiane, 1969.
Meyer, R., *Le Laos*, Hanoi, 1930.
Mikhéev, Y., *Les Débuts du Socialisme au Laos*, Moscow, 1985.
Ng Shui Meng, *The Population of Indochina*, Singapore, 1974.
Nolan, K. W., *Into Laos: The Story of Dewey Canyon II/Lam Son 719; Vietnam 1971*, Novato, Calif., 1986.
Oudone Sananikone, *The Royal Lao Army and US Army Advice and Support*, Washington, DC, 1983.
Pavie, A., *Mission Pavie: Indochine, 1879–1895*, 10 vols, Paris, 1898–1919.
Pavie, A., *A la Conquête des Cœurs: Le pays des Millions d'Eléphants et du Parasol Blanc*, Paris, 1942.
Phoumi Vongvichit, *Laos and the Victorious Struggle of the Lao People against US Neo-Colonialism*, n.p., 1969.
Phūmī Vongvichit, *Khuam Thongcham nai Xīvit Khong Thāphachau* (Memories of My Life), Viang Chan, 1987.
Quincey, K., *The Hmong: History of a People*, Cheney, Wash., 1987.
Ratnam, P., *Laos and the Superpowers*, New Delhi, 1980.
Robequain, C., *The Economic Development of French Indochina*, trans. I. A. Ward, London, 1944.
Rochet, C., *Pays Lao: Le Laos dans la tourmente*, Paris, 1946.
Savada, A. M. (ed.), *Laos: A Country Study*, 3rd edn, Washington, DC, 1995.
Schlesinger, A. M., *A Thousand Days: John F. Kennedy in the White House*, London, 1965.
Scott, J. C., *Indochina's Refugees: Oral Histories from Laos, Cambodia and Vietnam*, Jefferson, NC, 1989.
Shiraishi, M., and Furuta, M. (eds), *Indochina in the 1940s and 1950s*, Ithaca, NY, 1992.
Sila Viravong, *History of Laos*, trans. Joint Publications Research Service, New York, 1964.
Sisouk na Champassak, *Storm over Laos: A Contemporary History*, New York, 1961.
Sīxana Sīsān, ed., *Kaisôn Phomvihān: Lūk Không Paxāxon* (Son of the People), Viang Chan, 1991.
Smuckarn, S., and Breazeale, K., *A Culture in Search of Survival: The Phuan of Thailand and Laos*, New Haven, 1988.
Soutchay Vongsavanh, *RLG Military Operations and Activities in the Laotian Panhandle*, Washington, DC, 1981.
Stevenson, C. A., *The End of Nowhere: American Policy Towards Laos Since 1954*, Boston, 1972.
Stieglitz, P., *In a Little Kingdom*, Armonk, NY, 1990.
Strong, A. L., *Cash and Violence in Laos*, Peking, 1961.

Stuart-Fox, M. (ed.), *Contemporary Laos: Studies in the Politics and Society of the Lao People's Democratic Republic*, St Lucia, Qld, 1982.

Stuart-Fox, M., *Laos: Politics, Economics and Society*, London, 1986.

Stuart-Fox, M., *Vietnam in Laos: Hanoi's Model for Kampuchea*, Claremont, Calif., 1987.

Stuart-Fox, M., *Buddhist Kingdom, Marxist State: The Making of Modern Laos*, Bangkok, 1996.

Stuart-Fox, M., and Kooyman, M., *Historical Dictionary of Laos*, Metuchen, NJ, 1992.

Taboulet, G. (ed.), *La geste française en Indochine: Histoire par les textes de la France en Indochine*, 2 vols, Paris, 1955.

Taillard, C., *Le Laos: Stratégies d'un Etat-tampon*, Montpellier, 1989.

Taylor, M., *Swords and Plowshares*, New York, 1972.

Thee, M., *Notes of a Witness: Laos and the Second Indochina War*, New York, 1973.

Thompson, V., *French Indo-China*, London, 1973.

Thongsā Xainyvongkhamdī et al., *Pavatsāt Lao* (History of Laos), vol. III, Viang Chan, 1989.

Toye, C. H. M., *Laos: Buffer State or Battleground?*, London, 1968.

Uthin Bunyavong, ed., *Mahā Sīlā Viravong: Xīvit lae Phonngān* (Life and Work), Viang Chan, 1990.

Warner, R., *Back Fire: The CIA's Secret War in Laos and Its Link to the War in Vietnam*, New York, 1995.

Westermeyer, J., *Poppies, Pipes, and People: Opium and Its Use in Laos*, Berkeley, 1982.

Whitaker, D. P., et al., *Laos: A Country Study*, 2nd edn, Washington, DC, 1971.

Wolters, O. W., *History, Culture and Region in Southeast Asian Perspectives*, Singapore, 1982.

Wyatt, D. K., *Thailand: A Short History*, New Haven, 1984.

Wyatt, D. K. (ed.), *Lao Issara: The Memoirs of Oun Sananikone*, trans. J. B. Murdoch, Cornell Southeast Asia Program Data Paper no. 100, Ithaca, NY, 1975.

Wyatt, D. K. (ed.), *Iron Man Of Laos: Prince Phetsarath Ratanavongsa*, by '3349', trans. J. B. Murdoch and '3264', Cornell Southeast Asia Program Data Paper no. 110, Ithaca, NY, 1978.

Zago, M., *Rites et Ceremonies en Milieu Bouddhiste Lao*, Rome, 1972.

Zasloff, J. J., *The Pathet Lao: Leadership and Organization*, Lexington, Mass., 1973.

Zasloff, J. J. (ed.), *Postwar Indochina: Old Enemies and New Allies*, Washington, DC, 1988.

Zasloff, J. J., and Brown, McA. (eds), *Communism in Indochina: New Perspectives*, Lexington, Mass., 1975.

Zasloff, J. J., and Goodman, A. E. (eds), *Indochina in Conflict: A Political Assessment*, Lexington, Mass., 1972.

Zasloff, J. J., and Unger, L. (eds), *Laos: Beyond the Revolution*, London, 1991.

## ARTICLES

Amnesty International, *Political Prisoners in the People's Democratic Republic of Laos*, ASA 26/02/80, London, March 1980.

Amnesty International, 'Background Paper on the Democratic People's Republic of Laos Describing Current Amnesty International Concerns', ASA 26/04/85, London, April 1985.

Amnesty International, 'Re-education in Attopeu Province, The People's Democratic Republic of Laos', ASA 26/01/86, London, January 1986.

Barbier, J. P., 'Dix-sept ans de l'aide économique au Laos: un pays malade de l'aide étrangère', *Asie du Sud-est et Monde Insulindien* 5/1 (1974), 202–5.

Barbier, J. P., 'Objectifs et résultats de l'aide économique au Laos: une évaluation difficile', *Tiers Monde* 16 (1975), 333–53.

Bourdet, Y., 'Reforming Laos' Economic System', *Economic Systems* 16 (1992), 63–88.

Branfman, F., 'No Place to Hide', *Bulletin of Concerned Asian Scholars* 2/4 (1970), 14–46.

Brown, McA., 'Anatomy of a Border Dispute: Laos and Thailand', *Pacific Focus* 11/2 (1987), 5–30.

Brown, McA., and Zasloff, J. J., 'Laos 1974: Coalition Government Shoots the Rapids', *Asian Survey* 15 (1975), 174–83.

Brown, McA., and Zasloff, J. J., 'Laos 1975: People's Democratic Revolution – Lao Style', *Asian Survey* 16 (1976), 193–9.

Caply, M. [J. Deuve], 'Le Japon et l'indépendance du Laos (1945)', *Revue d'Histoire de la Deuxième Guerre Mondiale* 86 (1972), 67–82.

Caply, M. [J. Deuve], 'L'action politico-militaire du Pathet Lao contre US poste isolé', *Revue Militaire Générale* 3 (1973), 393–411.

Chapelier, G., and van Malderghem, J., 'Plain of Jars, Social Changes under Five Years of Pathet-Lao Administration', *Asia Quarterly* 1 (1971), 61–89.

Christie, C. J., 'Marxism and the History of the Nationalist Movements in Laos', *Journal of Southeast Asian Studies* 10 (1979), 146–58.

Condominas, G., 'Notes sur le bouddhisme populaire en milieu rural lao' (parts I and II), *Archives de Sociologie des Réligions*, 25, 26 (1968), 81–110, 111–50.

Crozier, B., 'Peking and the Laotian Crisis: An Interim Appraisal', *China Quarterly* 7 (1961), 128–37.

Crozier, B., 'Peking and the Laotian Crisis: A Further Appraisal', *China Quarterly* 11 (1962), 116–23.

de Marini, G. F., 'Relation nouvelle et curieuse du Royaume de Lao', *Revue Indochinoise* 8 (1910), 151–81, 257–71, 358–65.

Delorme, P., 'Le destin tragique du dernier roi du Laos', *Historia* 497 (May 1988), 94–101.

Dommen, A., 'Laos: the Troubled "Neutral"', *Asian Survey* 7 (1967), 74–80.

Dommen, A., 'Communist Strategy in Laos', *Problems of Communism* 24/4 (1975), 53–66.

Evans, G., 'Rich Peasants and Cooperatives in Socialist Laos', *Journal of Anthropological Research* 44 (1988), 229–50.

Fall, B. B., 'The International Relations of Laos', *Pacific Affairs* 30 (1957), 22–34.

Fall, B. B., 'The Laos Tangle', *International Journal* 16/2 (1961), 138–57.

Fall, B., 'The Pathet Lao: A "Liberation" Party', in R. A. Scalapino (ed.), *The Communist Revolution in Asia: Tactics, Goals, and Achievements*, Englewood Cliffs, NJ, 1965, pp. 173–97.

Gay, B., 'La perception des mouvements millénaristes du Sud et Centre Laos (fin du XIXe siècle au XXe siècle) depuis la décolonisation', in R. V. Pogner and O. V. Rybina (eds), *Premier Symposium Franco-Soviétique sur l'Asie du Sud-Est*, Moscow, 1989, pp. 229–40.

Gilkey, R., 'Laos: Politics, Elections and Foreign Aid', *Far Eastern Survey* 27/6 (June 1958), 80–94.

Girling, J. L. S., 'Laos: Falling Domino', *Pacific Affairs* 43 (1970), 370–83.

Gunn, G. C., 'Resistance Coalitions in Laos', *Asian Survey* 23 (1983), 316–40.

Halpern, J. M., 'Observations on the Social Structure of the Lao Elite', *Asian Survey* 1/5 (1961), 25–32.

Halpern, J. M., 'The Role of the Chinese in Lao Society', *Journal of the Siam Society* 49/1 (1961), 21–46.

Hiebert, L., and Hiebert, M., 'Laos: A New Beginning', *Indochina Chronicle* 46 (1976), 1–19.

Hill, K. L., 'Laos: The Vientiane Agreement', *Journal of Southeast Asian Studies* 8 (1967), 257–67.

Ireson, C. J., and Ireson, W. R., 'Ethnicity and Development in Laos', *Asian Survey* 31 (1991), 920–37.

Ireson, W. R., and Ireson, C. J., 'Laos: Marxism in a Subsistence Rural Economy', *Bulletin of Concerned Asian Scholars* 21/2-4 (1989), 59–75.

Kerr, A. D., 'Municipal Government in Laos', *Asian Survey* 12 (1972), 510–17.

Ky Son, 'The Special Vietnam–Laos Relationship Under Various Monarchies and During the Anti-French Resistance', *Vietnam Courier* 16/7 (July 1980), 10–13.

Lafont, P.-B., 'Images laotiennes', *Revue de Psychologie des Peuples* 21 (1966), 472–88; 22 (1967), 216–26.

Langer, P. F., 'The Soviet Union, China and the Revolutionary Movement in Laos', *Studies in Comparative Communism* (Spring–Summer 1973), 66–98.

Lejars, J., 'Situation industrielle du Laos et rôle des forces externes', *Tiers Monde* 13 (1972), 621–32.

Lintingre, P.,'Permanence d'une structure monarchique en Asia: Le Royaume de Champassak', *Revue Française d'Histoire d'Outre-Mer* 59 (1972), 411–31.

Luce, E. P., 'Les structure administratives locales du Laos', *Revue Juridique et Politique* 28 (1974), 463–94.

Mahajani, U., 'President Kennedy and the United States Policy in Laos, 1961–1963', *Journal of Southeast Asian Studies* 2 (1971), 87–99.

Mayoury and Pheuiphanh Ngaosyvathn, 'Lao Historiography and Historians: Case Study of the War Between Bangkok and the Lao in 1827', *Journal of Southeast Asian Studies* 20 (1989), 55–69.

Mirsky, J., and Stonefield, S. E., 'The United States in Laos, 1945–1962', in E. Friedman and M. Selden (eds), *America's Asia: Dissenting Essays on Asian–American Relations*, New York, 1971, pp. 253–323.

Modelski, G., 'The Viet Minh Complex', in C. E. Black and T. P. Thornton (eds), *Communism and Revolution: The Strategic Uses of Political Violence*, Princeton, NJ, 1964, pp. 185–214.

Mogenet, L., 'Les impôts coloniaux et les incidents du sud Laos en 1937', *Péninsule* 1 (1980), 73–93.

Mullin, C., 'The Secret Bombing of Laos: The Story Behind Nine Years of US Attacks', *Asia Magazine* 14/19 (12 May 1974), 3–8.

Murdoch, B., 'The 1901–1902 "Holy Man's" Rebellion', *Journal of the Siam Society* 62/1 (1974), 47–66.

Patrick, R., 'Presidential Leadership in Foreign Affairs Reexamined – Kennedy and Laos Without Radical Revisionism', *World Affairs* 140 (1978), 245–58.

Paul, R. A., 'Laos: Anatomy of an American Involvement', *Foreign Affairs* 49 (1971), 533–47.

Pheuiphanh Ngaosyvathn, 'Thai–Lao Relations: A Lao View', *Asian Survey* 25 (1985), 1242–59.

Pietrantoni, E., 'La population du Laos de 1912 à 1945', *BSEI* 28/1 (1953), 25–38.

Pietrantoni, E., 'La population du Laos en 1943 dans son milieu géographique', *BSEI* 32/3 (1957), 223–43.

Pietrantoni, E., 'Note sur les classes de revenue au Laos et au Tonkin avant 1945', *BSEI* 43/3 (1968), 179–96.

Randle, R., 'Peace in Vietnam and Laos: 1954, 1962, 1973', *Orbis* 18 (1974), 868–87.

Robinson, J., Guillemin, J., and Meselson, M., 'Yellow Rain: The Story Collapses', *Foreign Policy* 68 (1987), 100–17.

Scott, P. D., 'Laos: The Story Nixon Won't Tell', *New York Review of Books* 14/7 (9 April 1970), 35–41.

Shaplen, R., 'Letter from Laos', *New Yorker*, 20 October 1962, 197–212.

Shaplen, R., 'Letter from Laos', *New Yorker*, 4 May 1968, 136–62.

Shaplen, R., 'Our Involvement in Laos', *Foreign Affairs* 48/3 (1970), 478–93.

Shaplen, R., 'Letter from Laos', *New Yorker*, 2 August 1976, 64–76.

Simmonds, E. H. S., 'Independence and Political Rivalry in Laos, 1945–1961', in S. Rose (ed.), *Politics in Southern Asia*, London, 1963, pp. 164–99.

Simmonds, E. H. S., 'The Evolution of Foreign Policy in Laos since Independence', *Modern Asian Studies*, 2 (1968), 1–30.

Smith, R. M., 'Cambodia's Neutrality and the Laotian Crisis', *Asian Survey* 1/5 (1961), 17–24.

Smith, R. M., 'Laos', in G. McT. Kahin (ed.), *Government and Politics of Southeast Asia*, 2nd edn, Ithaca, NY, 1964, pp. 408–74.

Somlith Pathammavong, 'Compulsory Education in Laos', in *Compulsory Education in Cambodia, Laos, and Vietnam*, Paris, 1955, pp. 69–111.

Stanton, T. H., 'Conflict in Laos: The Village Point of View', *Asian Survey* 8 (1968), 887–900.

Stuart-Fox, M., 'The Lao Revolution: Leadership and Policy Differences', *Australian Outlook* 31 (1977), 279–88.

Stuart-Fox, M., 'The Lao Revolution: Errors and Achievements', *World Review* 16/2 (1977), 3–15.

Stuart-Fox, M., 'The Initial Failure of Agricultural Cooperativization in Laos', *Asia Quarterly* 4 (1980), 273–99.

Stuart-Fox, M., 'Socialist Construction and National Security in Laos', *Bulletin of Concerned Asian Scholars* 13/1 (1981), 61–71.

Stuart-Fox, M., 'Reflections of the Lao Revolution', *Contemporary Southeast Asia* 3 (1981), 42–57.

Stuart-Fox, M., 'Marxism and Theravada Buddhism: The Legitimation of Political Authority in Laos', *Pacific Affairs* 56 (1983), 428–54.

Stuart-Fox, M., 'The First Ten Years of Communist Rule in Laos: An Overview', *Asia Pacific Community* 31 (1986), 55–81.

Stuart-Fox, M., 'Politics and Patronage in Laos', *Indochina Issues* 70 (1986), 1–7.

Stuart-Fox, M., 'Lao Foreign Policy', in D. Wurfel and B. Burton (eds), *The Political Economy of Foreign Policy in Southeast Asia*, London, 1990, pp. 273–87.

Stuart-Fox, M., 'The Constitution of the Lao People's Democratic Republic', *Review of Socialist Law* 17 (1991), 299–317.

Stuart-Fox, M., 'On the Writing of Lao History: Continuities and Discontinuities', *Journal of Southeast Asian Studies* 24 (1993), 106–21.

Stuart-Fox, M., 'The French in Laos, 1887–1945', *Modern Asian Studies* 29 (1995), 111–39.

Stuart-Fox, M., and Bucknell, R. S., 'Politicization of the Buddhist Sangha in Laos', *Journal of Southeast Asian Studies* 13 (1982), 60–80.

Souvanna Phouma, 'Le Laos, avant-garde du monde libre', *France-Asie* 164 (November–December, 1960), 1427–34.

Souvanna Phouma, 'Le Laos: Le fond du problème', *France-Asie* 166 (March–April 1961), pp. 1824–26.

Taillard, C., 'Le village lao de la région de Vientiane: Un pouvoir local face au pouvoir étatique', *L'Homme* 17/2–3 (1977), 71–100.

Taillard, C., 'Le dualisme urbain-rural au Laos et la récupération de l'idéologie traditionnelle', *Asie du Sud-est et Monde Insulindien* 10/2–4 (1979), 91–108.

Taupin, J., 'Rapport à M. le Gouverneur-Général', *BSEI*, I/4 (1888), 23–82.

Taylor, S. C., 'Laos: Escalation of a Secret War', in E. J. Errington and B. J. C. McKercher (eds), *The Vietnam War as History*, New York, 1990, pp. 73–90.

Westermeyer, J. J., 'Traditional and Constitutional Law: A Study of Change in Laos', *Asian Survey* 11 (1971), 562–9.

Worner, W., 'Economic Reform and Structural Change in Laos', *Southeast Asian Affairs 1989*, Singapore, 1989, pp. 187–208.

Wyatt, D. K., 'Siam and Laos, 1767–1827', *Journal of Southeast Asian Studies* (1963), 13–32.

Young, K. R., 'The United States and Laos: The Kong Le Debacle', *Asian Forum* 4/1 (1972), 22–40.

Zasloff, J. J., 'Laos 1972: The War, Politics, and Peace Negotiations', *Asian Survey* 13 (1973), 60–75.

Zasloff, J. J., 'The Three-Village Dispute Between Laos and Thailand', *University Field Staff International Reports*, no. 23 (1985).

## UNPUBLISHED THESES

Barber, M. J. P., 'Migrants and Modernization: A Study of Change in Lao Society', PhD thesis, University of Hull, 1979.

Brailey, N. J., 'The Origin of the Siamese Forward Movement in Western Laos, 1850–1892', PhD thesis, University of London, 1968.

Castle, T. N., 'Alliance in a Secret War: The United States and the Hmong in Northeastern Laos', MA thesis, San Diego State University, 1979.

Chittenden, G. M., 'Laos and the Powers, 1954–1962', PhD thesis, University of London, 1969.

Chou Norindr, 'Le Néolaohakxat ou le Front Patriotique Lao et la révolution laotienne', thesis, Doctorat en Etudes Orientales, University of Paris, 1980.

Gay, B., 'Les mouvements millénaristes du Centre et du Sud Laos et du Nord-Est du Siam, 1895–1910', thesis, Doctorat du 3e Cycle, University of Paris, 1987.

Houy Pholsena, 'L'Armée Nationale du Laos', thesis, Doctorat du 3e Cycle, University of Aix-Marseille, 1971.

Mongkhol Katay Sasorith, 'Les forces politiques et la vie politique au Laos', thesis, Doctorat du 3e Cycle, University of Paris, 1973.

Moppert, F., 'Les mouvements de résistance au pouvoir colonial français de la minorité protoindochinoise du plateau des Bolovens dans le sud Laos, 1901–1936', thesis, Doctorat du 3e Cycle, University of Paris, 1978.

Pornsak Phongphaew, 'The Political Culture and Personality of the Laotian Political-Bureaucratic Elite', PhD thesis, University of Oklahoma, 1976.

Souneth Phothisane, 'The *Nidān Khun Bôrom*: Annotated Translation and Analysis', PhD thesis, University of Queensland, 1997.

Vistarini, W. J. E., 'Representations of Laos: Late Nineteenth Century French and Lao Constructs', PhD thesis, La Trobe University, Melbourne, 1994.

## JOURNALS AND NEWSPAPERS

*Asiaweek*
*Bangkok Post*
*Beijing Review*
*Bulletin des Nouvelles* (Viang Chan)
Economist Intelligence Unit, *Country Report: Indochina: Vietnam, Laos, Cambodia*
*Far Eastern Economic Review*
FBIS, *Daily Report: East Asia*
*Indochina Chronicle*
*Indochina Chronology*

*Indochina Issues*
Khaosān Pathēt Lao, *Bulletin Quotidien*
Khaosān Pathēt Lao, *News Bulletin*
*Lao Presse*
*Le Monde*
*New York Times*
*Southeast Asian Affairs*
*The Times* (London)
*Vietnam Courier*
*Washington Post*

# INDEX

administration: French, 29–33, 42, 43, 44, 46, 50, 52, 57, 60, 66–7; Lao Issara, 63, 64; Pathēt Lao, 150; Royal Lao government, 74, 76, 77, 84, 88, 94, 96

agriculture, 42, 44, 50, 66, 75, 77, 91, 101, 130, 158, 179, 185, 193, 196; cooperativization, 168, 176, 179–80, 182; crops, 50, 183, 185, 193, 196

Air America, 114, 127, 130, 142

air war over Laos, 136, 138–9, 141, 143–4, 224 n.32; casualties, 144, 150

Ānuvong, 14–15

arrest of officials, 188–9, 201; *see also* purges

art, 45, 77–8, 131, 156

Asian Development Bank, 184, 197, 200

Association of Southeast Asian Nations, 4, 181, 184, 200, 204, 208

Australia, 132, 178, 185, 200

Bak Mī, 34

Bôlavēn plateau, 9, 33, 34, 35, 36, 40, 47, 50, 51, 71, 72, 73, 102, 139, 144, 153

Bong Suvannavong, 67, 86, 87, 102

Bosc, Jules, 36, 43

Britain, 15, 22, 24–8, 59, 60, 62, 65, 75, 85, 95, 106, 119, 132, 138; co-chairs Geneva conferences, 86, 96, 110, 119, 128

Brown, Winthrop G., 113, 114

Buddhism, 6, 7, 9, 10, 11, 13, 19, 35, 43, 77, 100, 150, 162, 164, 173, 174, 193–4, 205; Pathēt Lao policies towards, 83; Royal Lao government control, 107–8; similarities with socialism, 173; *see also* Sangha

budget: federal Indochina, 32, 51; LPDR, 178, 184, 206; Royal Lao government, 43, 51, 76, 77, 96, 148, 149, 154, 159

Bundy, McGeorge, 125

Bunkhong, Chau, *uparāt*, 30, 45

Bunūm na Champāsak, 60, 61, 66, 70, 102, 110, 113, 115, 116, 118, 123, 130, 146, 151, 160; government of, 76, 116, 119, 121

bureaucracy, 45, 77, 155, 162, 172, 197, 208; *see also* civil service

Burma, 7, 9, 12, 13, 24, 25, 27, 43, 68, 147

cadres of LPRP: calibre, 172, 191; recruitment, 183; shortage, 163, 176, 179

Cambodia, 9, 11, 12, 13, 16, 21, 23, 26, 27, 28, 50, 52, 54, 57, 78, 85, 89, 116, 135, 153, 159, 161, 168, 178, 197, 200, 201, 229 n.43; anti-French resistance, 79, 80, 81, 83; in Second Indochina War, 143, 151, 160; neutrality, 104, 124; relations with LPDR, 185, 228 n.35; Vietnamese occupation, 180, 181, 183, 184, 199; *see also* Khmer Rouge; Sihanouk

cease-fires: (1954), 84, 86, 87; (1957), 95; (1973), 136, 139, 153, 156, 225 n.67

censorship, 106, 163, 189

Central Intelligence Agency, 57, 90, 91, 130, 214 n.29, 225 n.65; and the Secret Army, 117, 119, 121, 139, 176; support for CDNI, 103, 219 n.36; support for Phūmī Nôsavan, 114–15, 219 n.33

Champāsak, Kingdom/royal family, 1, 14, 15, 16, 29, 60, 66, 67, 97

Chatichai Choonhaven, Thai prime minister, 198

China, 6, 8, 10, 16, 20, 23, 25, 26, 37, 38, 79, 101, 119, 138, 222 n.4; at Geneva conferences, 85, 106; attitude towards Lao neutrality, 104, 132; economic aid to LPDR, 178, 181; military aid to Pathēt Lao, 117; Nationalist forces in Laos, 59, 62, 63, 64, 65, 147; numbers of communist Chinese troops in Laos, 142; People's Republic of, 75, 80, 123; relations with LPDR, 178, 180, 181, 184, 185, 190, 198, 199, 200; relations with Royal Lao regime, 93, 105, 148, 217 n.86; relations with Vietnam, 178, 180–1, 184; road construction in Laos, 136, 142, 158, 178, 223 n.22; support for anti-LPDR resistance, 180, 184

Chinese in Laos, 32, 38, 39, 42, 44, 46, 47, 75, 92, 130, 146, 162; Lao attitudes towards, 80; numbers, 51, 172;
Christianity, 13, 33, 174, 193, 230 n.73
Chummalī Xainyasôn, General, 204, 231 n.92
civil service, 31, 52, 69, 154, 197; *see also* bureaucracy
civil war, 99, 104, 108, 111, 112, 113, 115, 117, 118, 145
clan rivalry, 67–8, 75, 77, 86, 87, 102, 103, 151, 152
class structure, 10, 52, 60, 67–8, 97, 130
coalition government, 79, 94, 95, 96, 124; First Coalition, 59, 93–8, 99, 104, 109, 114, 157, 165, 166; Second Coalition, 99, 117, 121, 128, 129, 134, 147, 157, 166; Third Coalition, 136, 157, 159, 165, 166, 167, 169, 172, 174
Cold War, 68, 72, 74, 76, 94, 96, 100, 121, 124, 125
Committee for Lao Resistance in the East, 71–2, 79
Committee for the Defence of the National Interest, 103, 105–6, 110–12, 118
Committee for the Organization of the Party, 81, 94
communications, 30, 37, 42, 44, 69, 90, 91, 101, 127, 149
communism, 6, 52–3, 72, 74, 76, 80, 89, 94, 97, 104, 105, 116, 135, 138, 165, 169
Congress of People's Representatives, 78–9
constitution: of the Kingdom of Laos, 66–7, 119, 159; of the LPDR, 169, 188–9, 200, 201–2, 203
cooperatives, 179, 192, 194
corruption 4, 31, 56; under LPDR, 183, 186, 188, 189, 191, 203, 206–7, 208; under Royal Lao regime, 77, 91, 92, 100–1, 102, 103, 105, 111, 129–30, 146, 149, 151, 152, 155, 159, 218 n.5
corvée labour, 31, 32, 33, 34, 37, 44, 49, 51, 79
*coup d'état* (1960), 112–14, 117; attempts, 110, 132
culture: traditional, 19, 45, 55, 155, 156, 164; preservation, 45, 164; rehabilitation, 173–4
currency, 76, 82, 91, 103–4, 105, 131, 154, 159, 162, 172, 182, 189, 218 n.13; *see also* Foreign Exchange Operations Fund; inflation

Dauplay, J.-J., 36

de Gaulle, Charles, 56, 60, 62
de Lagrée, Doudart, 20
de Lanessan, Jean, 23, 24
de Reinach, Lucien, 26, 46
Decoux, Jean, 54, 55, 56
defence: of the Lao state, 75, 83, 84, 85–6; of the Lao revolution, 171
Democratic Party, 102, 103, 216 n.60
Democratic Republic of (North) Vietnam, 4, 75, 83, 85, 106, 108, 119, 120, 125, 126, 128, 139, 143, 151, 153, 217 n.86, 219 n.29; as threat to Laos, 105, 122; forces in Laos after 1954, 99, 109, 117, 129, 132, 136, 138, 140, 141, 142, 144, 148, 150, 156, 157, 168, 220 n.42, 221 n.61, 222 n.81, (numbers) 142, 214 n.25; intervention in Laos, 129, 136, 165; military assistance (to Pathēt Lao), 88, 93, 104, 117, 127, 128–9, (to LPDR) 177, 181, 189, 198; policies towards Laos, 93, 95, 104, 124, 134, 219 n.28, 223 n.26; relations with Royal Lao government, 123, 148; *see also* Ho Chi Minh trail
demonstrations, 159–60, 161–2
Deuan Sunnarāt, 127, 128, 133
Deuve, Jean, 127, 220 n.45, 221 n.68
development, economic, 46–52, 154, 159; plans, 77, 96, 105, 179, 184–5, 196
Doumer, Paul, 30, 49
drugs, 155, 206; *see also*, heroin; opium
Dulles, John Foster, 89, 90, 94, 217 n.82, 218 n.11

Economic Commission for Asia and the Far East, 75, 96
economy, 14, 33; reform, 182–3, 184, 199; sectors, 182; socialist transformation, 169, 171, 174, 179, 182, 195, (abandonment) 195–6; subsistence, 50, 100, 101, 182; under the French, 49–51; under the LPDR, 182–3, 184, 185, 192–3, 197, 199, 201; under the Royal Lao regime, 100, 149, 153–4, 156
education, 43–4, 52, 55, 66, 69, 75, 77, 83, 100, 141, 149, 154, 173, 193, 194, 196, 212 n.48, 214 n.16
Eighteen-Point Program, 158, 162, 165, 166, 174
Eisenhower, Dwight D., 89
elections, 62, 86, 93, 94, 95, 106, 124, 150, 156, 159, 163, (1947) 66, 67, (1951) 76, (1955) 88–9, 216 n.60, (1958 – supplementary) 101–2, (1960) 110–1, (1965 – restricted suffrage) 147, (1967) 148, (1972) 152, (1975 – local and regional) 163–4, (1988–89) 199

elite, social and political: traditional, 3, 4, 10, 18, 19; under the French, 20, 32, 34, 37, 40, 42, 43, 51, 52; under Royal Lao regime, 60, 66, 67–8, 77, 91, 92, 97, 100, 155, 165, 166, 188
ethnic minorities, 2, 77, 79, 80, 84, 100, 101–2, 109, 153, 164; policy towards (Royal Lao regime), 68, 109, (Pathēt Lao) 79–80, 208; relations between, 31, 39, 68, 79; see also Hmong; Khamu; Lao Sūng; Lao Thoeng; Mien

Fā Ngum, 9–10, 11, 18
Faidāng Lôbliayao, 40, 71, 72, 73, 78, 79, 80, 94, 102, 109, 171, 227 n.7, 227 n.10
First Indochina War, 4, 59, 68, 72, 80, 81, 83, 84
foreign aid: amount, 185; dependency, 149, 184, 200, 201, 208
Foreign Exchange Operations Fund, 130, 154, 158, 162, 178
forest products, 11, 16, 50, 63, 154
forestry, 50, 75, 158, 179, 185, 196, 205; see also timber
France, 2, 6, 18, 19, 63, 72, 80, 83, 85, 92, 96, 119, 120, 124, 132, 138, 147, 159, 176, 185, 188, 201; aid to LPDR, 200; aid to Royal Lao regime, 92, 100; attitudes towards Lao, 41–2; colonial administration, 29–34, 37, 42, 44, 52, 60, (impact on traditional relationships) 34, 36–7, 40; policy towards colonial Laos, 3, 28–9, 41, (ambiguity) 41, 51–2; reconquest of Laos, 60, 65, 71; relations with Royal Lao regime, 69, 70, 74, 75, 76, 93, 97, 112; responsibility for defence of Laos, 61, 83, 84
Franco-Lao modus vivendi (1946), 30, 66, 67, 68, 70
Franco-Lao General Convention (1949), 70, 74
Free Laos Front (Naeo Lao Issara), 78, 80, 94
French Military Mission, 75, 85, 90
French Union, 56, 59, 66, 67, 70, 75, 83, 85
French Union Army, 75, 82
frontiers, 9, 10, 11, 18, 24, 26–7, 28, 84, 148

Garde Indigène, 30, 31, 35, 39, 44, 51, 56, 66, 210 n.18
Garnier, Francis, 20
gender relations, 155, 158, 187; sexual attitudes, 41–2; see also women
Geneva Agreements: 1954, 59, 81, 84–7, 88, 89, 90, 93, 103, 106, 110, 119; 1962, 119–24, 125, 126, 127, 129, 133, 134, 135, 136, 138, 144, 151, 153

Geneva conferences, 3, 89, 104, 110, 117, 120, 121, 138, 222 n.4
Godley, G. McMurtrie, 142
gold, 133, 146, 159, 172, 226 n.69, 226 n.76
Government of National Union, 94, 125, 150; Provisional, 96, 121, 123, 128, 132, 133, 156, 157, 158, 161, 164

Harmand, Jules, 47
Harriman, W. Averell, 121, 122
health, 44, 66, 69, 75, 77, 83, 100–1, 141, 154, 178, 193, 196
heroin, 146, 147, 225 n.61; see also drugs; opium
HIV/AIDS, 204, 206
historiography, 1–3, 4, 6, 15, 18–19, 40–1, 45–6, 149
history, 18–19, 45, 55, 77, 80, 117, 150, 167
Hmong, 16, 38, 39–40, 56, 65, 68, 71, 88, 120, 153, 160, 171, 221 n.61; and Pathēt Lao, 73, 79, 109; in 'secret army', 117, 119, 121, 127, 128, 131, 139–40, 141, 142, 144, 146, (casualties) 144, 223 n.18, 225 n.52, 227 n.23; resist LPDR, 176–7, 179, 184, 201; US support for, 121, 127, 129, 220 n.54; see also 'yellow rain'
Ho Chi Minh, 52, 61, 63, 65, 71, 75, 85, 197
Ho Chi Minh trail, 125, 129, 135, 139, 140, 141, 142, 143, 145, 148, 151, 158, 224 n.46
'Holy Man's revolt', see phū mī bun revolt

Imfeld, Hans, 60, 62, 64
income per capita, 100, 154, 192
Independent Party, 76, 102, 103, 216 n.60
Indigenous Consultative Assembly, 42, 43
India, 86, 92, 93, 119
Indochina, 2, 18, 20, 21, 23, 24, 32, 33, 41, 43, 52, 70, 81, 84, 134, 143, 160, 222 n.82; Federation, 56; 'solidarity bloc', 180, 197
Indochinese Communist Party, 52–3, 57, 71, 72, 78, 79, 81, 94, 186, 197, 213 n.5, 215 n.40, 215 n.45
Indonesia, 72, 78, 91, 93
industry, 75, 101, 154, 176, 179, 183, 192–3, 196, 224 n.42; nationalization, 168
inflation, 82, 100, 104, 159, 162, 172, 178
International Commission for Supervision and Control, 86, 88, 96, 103, 106, 108, 119, 120, 121 123, 124, 128, 132, 138, 221 n.61
International Monetary Fund, 182, 197
International Mekong Commission, 200

Japan, 54, 125, 200; coup de force (1945), 56, 58, 59; in Laos, 51, 56–8, 61

Kaisôn Phomvihān, 63, 102, 111, 176, 179, 180, 181, 187, 189, 191, 192, 198, 200, 201, 203, 213 n.5, 215 n.36, 226 n.82, 227 n.10, 230 n.78; and economic reform, 182–3; and the Lao revolutionary movement, 72, 78, 79, 81, 93, 94, 99, 108, 219 n.28; and the 'two-line struggle', 194–6; as Secretary-General of the LPRP, 152, 160, 169, 170, 171, 185, 197, 202, 214 n.26; plot to assassinate, 175

Katāy Don Sasorit, 55, 63, 71, 73, 74, 86, 87, 88, 89, 92, 96, 102, 105, 216 n.64

Kennedy, John F., 119, 121, 123; administration, 122

Ketsanā Vongsuvan, 127, 128

Khamhum (Deo Van Tri), 22

Khammao Vilai, 63, 71, 74, 76

Khamphan Panyā, 111

Khamphāy Aphai, 160

Khamphaeng Bubphā, 187, 218 n.9

Khamphuy Kaeobualaphā, 207, 231 n.92

Khamsaen, 53

Khamtai Sīphandôn, 73, 79, 170, 171, 186, 195, 203, 207, 214 n.23, 224 n.34

Khamu, 7, 9, 16, 38, 39, 129

Khamuan Bubphā, 114, 161

Khmer Rouge, 135, 160, 178, 180, 225 n.63, 229 n.43

Khrushchev, Nikita, 120, 220 n.52

Khun Bôrom 1, 7, 8, 11, 12

Kindāvong, Prince, 65, 67

Kinim Phonsēnā, 102, 113, 115, 116, 118, 123, 126, 127, 128

King's Council, 54, 67

Kissinger, Henry, 153

Kommadam, see Ong Kommadam

Kônglae, 112–16, 117, 118, 126, 127, 128, 133, 138, 146, 147, 219 n.39, 220 n.47

Koret, Peter, 4, 5

Korean War, 76, 80, 83

Kriangsak Chamanand, 181

Ku Aphai, 67

Ku Vôravong, 67, 87, 128

Kupasit Aphai, 132, 146, 160, 221 n.68, 225 n.66

Lān Xāng, Kingdom of, 1, 2, 3, 6–19, 24, 27, 43, 46, 77, 80

Lao Air Force, 117, 147

Lao Federation of Trade Unions, 160

Lao Front for National Construction, 181–2, 230 n.84

Lao Issara, 30, 40, 57–8, 59–65, 66, 69, 70–4, 78, 88, 110, 163, 170; and Vietminh, 64, 70–4; cooperation with local Vietnamese, 60, 61, 63, 65; government-in-exile, 70–4; provisional government, 62–5; Thai support, 65, 70–2

Lao Lum, 8, 18, 32, 33, 34, 35, 36, 37, 50, 68, 77, 109, 112, 135, 145, 171, 186, 192, 206, 227 n.7

Lao National Revolutionary Front 21/18, 174

Lao National Union Party, 67, 86, 216 n.60

Lao Patriotic Front, 94, 101, 102, 103, 104, 106, 107, 108, 110, 111, 126, 133, 149, 151, 171, 181, 219 n.34; congresses, 94, 133, 150; peace proposals, 151, 224 n.41; political program, 94

Lao Pen Kāng (Neutral Laos) Party, 126

Lao Pen Lao (Laos for the Lao), 55, 57, 61, 63, 87

Lao People's Army, 191, 198, 200 203, 207

Lao People's Democratic Republic, 3, 4, 62, 74, 79, 164, 168–208

Lao People's Liberation Army, 72, 81, 83, 145, 150, 171, 214 n.26, 224 n.34

Lao People's Party, 81, 94, 150, 215 n.43, 215 n.45

Lao People's Revolutionary Party, 73, 152, 160, 166, 168, 169, 170, 176, 179, 180, 181, 182, 184, 190–1, 193, 196, 201–3, 207, 208, 226 n.1; Central Committee, 152, 169, 170, 176, 186, 187, 197, 202, 203, 207, 208, 227 n.10, 229 n.53; composition, 186, 197; congresses, (Second) 152, (Third) 185–6, 189, 191, 197, (Fourth) 195–6, 197, (Fifth) 203, (Sixth) 207; leadership, 171; membership, 186, 191; policy errors, 171–2, 175; presidency, 202, 203; reforms, 183, 185–7; Secretariat, 169, 170, 186, 197, 203

Lao People's Revolutionary Youth Union, 187

Lao Sērī, 57, 61, 63

Lao Socialist Party, 181, 184

Lao Sūng, 16, 18, 31, 32, 33, 37, 40, 50, 52, 109, 117, 139, 153, 171, 192, 206, 227 n.7; see also Hmong; Mien

Lao Thoeng, 7, 8, 10, 18, 31, 32, 33, 34, 35, 36, 37, 39, 40, 50, 51, 52, 68, 79, 102, 109, 112, 139, 153, 171, 192, 206, 227 n.7; see also Khamu

law, 10, 194, 199, 200, 231 n.87, 231 n.93; legal system, 188, 208; see also people's courts

Le Duc Tho, 153

Lenin, V. I., 182–3, 196

Leria, Giovanni-Maria, 13

Leuam Insīxiangmai, 67, 102

liberated zone, *see* Pathēt Lao, zone controlled by
Līfung, 40
Li Peng, 200
literature: French on Laos, 42; Lao, 45, 55, 77, 149, 151–2
literacy, 43, 90, 173, 193, 216 n.67
Lôbliayao, 40
Luang Phrabāng, Kingdom of, 15, 16, 22, 29, 30; legal status, 29–30

Mao Zedong, 75
Marxism, 2, 53, 57, 81, 100, 126 129, 165, 166, 169
Marxism–Leninism, 187, 190, 191, 194, 202
McCoy, Al, 147
merit (*bun*), 11, 14, 19, 155, 227 n.13
*meuang*, 8–11, 14, 16, 18–19, 21, 23, 29, 31, 37, 38, 60, 163
Mien, 16, 130, 139
Military Assistance Advisory Group, 90
Military Territory V, 30, 38
monarchy, 66, 68, 110, 158, 168; as unifying force, 69
Mouhot, Henri, 16
Movement for National Renovation, 54–5, 58, 61, 63, 67

Naeo Lao Issara, *see* Free Laos Front
Nam Ngeum dam, 149, 154, 174, 181
Nanthasēn, 14
Navarre, General Henri, 84
National Assembly, 67, 76, 87, 89, 95, 96, 102, 103, 104, 105, 124, 126, 131, 147, 148, 152, 157, 159, 163, 202, 203, 225 n.64; *see also* elections
National Congress of People's Representatives, 164, 168, 170, 171
National Directorate for Coordination, 118, 126, 127, 129, 132, 133, 146
National Federation of Lao Students, 159–60
National Political Consultative Council, 156, 157, 158, 159, 164
National Progressive Party, 76, 86, 89, 102, 103
National United Front for the Liberation of Laos, 189
nationalism, 2, 3, 20, 40–1, 45, 52–8, 59–6, 68, 74, 76, 77, 79, 81, 97, 109, 150; Pathēt Lao develops, 79–80, 81
New Economic Mechanism, 196–7
newspapers, 55, 106, 163, 187, 201, 216 n.62
neutralists, 116, 118, 120, 122, 124 146, 157; alliance with Pathēt Lao, 116, 117, 118,

120, 126; armed forces, 114, 117, (size) 142, 220 n.48; divisions between, 126–8; pressures on, 128–9, 134
neutrality/neutralization of Laos, 93, 94, 95, 97, 99, 100, 104, 108, 110, 112, 117, 119, 124–6, 129, 134, 135, 136, 147, 148, 165, 217 n.84
Ngo Dinh Diem, 122
Ngōn Xananikôn, 160
Nixon, Richard M., 142, 150, 152
Nūhak Phumsavan, 63, 72, 78, 79, 85, 94, 170, 171, 186, 188, 199, 202, 203, 207; and the 'two-line struggle', 195–7
Nyūy Aphai, 55, 63
Nyūy, Chau, 29, 210 n.16

Ō Anurak, 72
Office of Strategic Services, 57, 60, 70
Ong Kaeo, 34–6
Ong Kham, 37
Ong Kommadam, 35–6, 42, 51
Ong Man, 35
Operation Lam Son 719, 144, 145, 151, 223 n.27, 224 n.29
opium, 16, 32, 34, 38, 50, 56, 63, 122, 130, 133, 146, 147, 185, 206  224 n.37

Pāchai, 39–40
Parsons, J. Graham, 95, 114–15, 217 n.85
Pathēt Lao, 2, 4, 5, 40, 59, 62, 89, 106, 112, 123, 124, 129, 132, 141, 152, 158, 159, 172, 176; alliance with neutralists, 116, 117, 118, 120, 126; armed forces, 84, 94, 107, 117, 119, 122, 128, 131, 133, 138, 140, 141, 144, 148, 220 n.47, 224 n.34, (size) 93, 94, 96, 99, 142, 216 n.58, 216 n.65, 219 n.27, 220 n.48; election campaign, 102–3; leadership, 78–9, 207; methods, 81–2, 93–4, 101, 111, 115; military alliance with Vietminh, 78–82, 88; military support from (North) Vietnam, 91, 93, 99, 104, 120, 127, 136, 142; negotiations with Royal Lao government, 88–9, 93–6, 114, 148, 156, (preconditions) 151, 153; policies, 94, 110–11, 114, 133, 151; Resistance government, 78, 83, 85; seizes power, 159–67, ('quasi-legalism') 162; zone controlled by, 83, 85, 87–8, 111, 135, 145, 150, 157, 176
Patriotic Neutralists, 128, 133, 138, 142, 224 n.34
patronage: in LPDR, 187–8, 194; under Royal Lao regime, 60, 67, 69, 92, 97, 102, 146
Pavie, Auguste, 21–4, 29, 41

Paxā Sangkhom (Social Democratic Party), 111
people's courts, 162, 188; *see also* law
People's Revolutionary Committees, 161, 162, 163
Pham Van Dong, 85, 143
Phāsuk Rāxaphak, 142, 146
Pheng Phongsavan, 123, 126
Phetxarāt Rattanavongsā, Prince, 2, 3, 45, 52, 54, 55–8, 78, 87, 93, 95, 97, 109, 213 n.74, 214 n.29; as leader of Lao Issara, 61–3, 65, 66, 71, 73, 74
Phibunsongkhram, 54, 72
Phô Kaduat, 35
Phôthisālarāt, 12
Phra Sāthôn, 82
*phū mī* bun rebellion, 34–6, 40, 210 n.24, 211 n.25, 211 n.27
Phū Phā Thī, battle for, 140–1, 142
Phuan, 11, 16, 27, 39, 139, 142, 186
Phūmī Nôsavan, 63, 68, 105, 107, 111, 112, 118, 119, 121, 123, 128, 129, 130, 132, 133, 145, 146, 214 n.23, 222 n.78, 224 n.36; and aftermath of 1960 *coup d'état*, 113, 115–16, 219 n.33, 219 n.39, 221 n.59; attempted *coup d'état* (1959), 109–10
Phūmī Vongvichit, 5, 73, 78, 79, 96, 99, 101, 102, 123, 128, 129, 158, 170, 171, 186, 203, 214 n.23, 214 n.24, 230 n.84
Phūn Sīpasoet, 79, 170, 171, 186, 214 n.23
Phuy Xanaikôn, 67, 76, 85, 86, 87, 102, 104, 105, 106, 107; government, 76, 104, 108, 118
Plain of Jars: strategic importance, 140–1, 145; battle, 134, 142–3, 144, 160
police, 44, 66, 69, 76, 90, 106, 110, 118, 126, 132, 134, 146, 213 n.36, 225 n.67; secret, 31, 53, 75; *see also* National Directorate for Coordination
political culture, 60, 68, 77, 104, 147, 148, 208
political crises, 87–9, 103–4, 105, 109–10, 129, 162
population, 28, 46, 111, 131, 136; census, 10, 190–2; composition, 191–2, 212 n.61; forced relocation, 14, 15, 27; foreign, in Laos, 51, 62, 92; movements, 8, 62, 75, 140, 155, 172, 175; size, 42, 155, 210 n.11, 212 n.62
prices, 51, 82, 130, 162, 172, 195, 197, 199
Pridi Phanomyong, 70
Programs Evaluation Office, 90, 218 n.27, 219 n.33
prostitution, 92, 131, 146, 155, 206

purges: by rightists, 105, 118; of Royal Lao civil servants, 172; within the LPRP, 171, 180, 181, 186

Rally of the Lao People (Lao Huam Lao), 103, 105, 111, 112
rebellions: anti-French, 20, 34–41; millenarial and messianic character, 35, 39, 40, 51; 'proto-nationalist' interpretation, 40
reconciliation, national, 76, 89, 95, 104, 106, 108, 110, 144, 165, 166, 168, 208
re-education, 163, 166, 172, 178, 180, 194; numbers, 227 n.17
refugees, 3, 4, 52, 223 n.14; from the LPDR, 172, 175, 185, 190; from the war zone, 131, 142, 149, 150, 154, 155, 160, 166, (numbers) 144, 223 n.14, 224 n.33, 227 n.11
regionalism, 60, 61, 67–8, 69, 75, 78, 103, 175, 187, 203
Republic of (South) Vietnam, 89, 91, 104, 108, 126, 140, 143, 146, 159; relations with Royal Lao government, 105, 114; troops in Laos, 131, 144, 223 n.26
resistance: to Siam, 15–16; to the French, 33, 34, 40, 59, (by the Lao Issara) 65, 70–3, (by the Pathēt Lao) 78–81; to the LPDR, 174–5, 176–7, 179, 181, 184, 189, 200–1, (Thai support) 177, 189
revenue: under the French, 20, 32, 44, 47, 51; under Lao Issara, 63; under LPDR, 176, 184, 207; under Royal Lao government, 69, 130, 148, 149, 159, 226 n.69
revolutionary movement, 41, 78, 79, 80, 81, 97, 133, 190; reasons for success, 164–7; *see also* Pathēt Lao
rice, 19, 50; imports, 154; price, 183; production, 154, 183; shortfall, 178, 180
rightists, 99, 102, 113, 114, 115, 116, 127, 160, 162; relations with neutralists, 126, 131, 132, 133
roads, 33, 44, 47–9, 91, 193; Chinese constructed, 135, 142, 158, 178
Rochet, Charles, 55
Royal Lao Army, 84, 85, 90, 92, 94, 96, 99, 103, 105, 107, 108, 111, 113, 129, 144, 153, 157, 160, 161, 163, 166, 174, 178, 222 n.79; calibre, 119, 122, 140; composition, 109; corruption, 145, 146–7, 223 n.17; cost, 91, 100, 219 n.27; relation to civil authority, 145; reorganization, 151; size, 90, 108, 142, 146, 216 n.65, 216 n.71, 223 n.21
Rusk, Dean, 136

Sālī Vongkhamxao, 171, 186–7, 188, 195, 203
Samān Vinyakēt, 207
Sāmsaenthai, 10
Sangha, 11, 13, 14, 15, 43, 106, 156; Royal Lao government control, 107–8; LPRP control, 173–4; see also Buddhism
Santhiphāp Pen Kāng (Party of Peace through Neutrality), 102, 104, 110, 113, 126, 219 n.34
Sarit Thanarat, 121, 122, 132, 146
Savāngvatthanā, 56, 61, 69, 96, 97, 103, 109, 110, 112, 115, 116, 119, 121, 127, 132, 151, 159, 163, 170, 177; abdication, 164
Second Indochina War, 4, 83, 97, 99, 121, 141, 143, 153, 165, 184, 198; impact on Laos, 136–7, 144–5
Secret Army, 117, 121, 139, 140, 142, 143, 144, 145, 153, 159, 176; size, 142
secret war, 117, 129, 139
Seventh Resolution, 184, 188, 195; see also economy, reform
Siam, Kingdom of, 2, 6, 13, 14, 15, 16, 18, 19, 20, 22, 23, 24, 25, 26, 28, 29, 34, 50, 51, 52, 53, 54, 140; see also Thailand
Sihanouk, 78, 83, 104, 116, 118, 121, 124, 143, 151
Sīhō Lānphutthakun, 118, 129, 132, 134, 146, 224 n.36
Silā Vīravong, 2, 45
Sing Rattanasamai, 63, 64, 214 n.23
Singkapō Sīkhōtchunnamālī, 224 n.34
Siribunyasān, 14
Sirindhorn, Maha Chakri, 200
Sīsavāngvong, 5, 59, 60, 61, 62, 64, 65, 69, 74, 78, 82, 95, 109, 112, 120, 214 n.18, 214 n.34, 227 n.22
Sīsavāt Kaeobunphan, 195, 198, 203, 207
Sīsomphôn Lôvanxai, 170, 203, 227 n.7
Sīsuk na Champāsak, 151, 160
Sīthon Kommadam, 72, 73, 78, 79, 80, 94, 102, 109, 171, 227 n.7, 227 n.10
smuggling, 50, 133, 146, 183, 189, 191, 192, 198, 200, 205, 206
socialism, transition to, 168, 169, 183, 196, 202
Somsanit Vongkotrattana, 63, 111, 113
Southeast Asia Treaty Organization, 90, 121, 122, 123, 216 n.64
Soviet Union, 4, 75, 85, 105, 106, 115, 121, 132, 138, 169, 178, 182, 184, 185, 199; advisers in Laos, 162, 177, 182, 185, (numbers) 162, 185; co-chairs Geneva conferences, 86, 96, 104, 110, 119, 128; economic aid to LPDR, 172, 177, 200;

military aid to LPDR, 178, 197–8; military aid to neutralists, 116, 117, 127, 220 n.52; relations with LPDR, 177–8, 185
Special Forces, US, 115, 117, 122, 219 n.27
'special relationship' (Laos–Vietnam), 177, 198, 228 n.25
Suk Vongsak, 78, 79, 171
Sukarno, 78
Sunthôn Pathammavong, 76
Suphānuvong, Prince, later President, 63, 65, 72, 79, 85, 88, 93, 94, 95, 102, 106, 115, 118, 119, 129, 132, 143, 164, 170, 171, 180, 189, 202, 203, 217 n.2, 218 n.25, 219 n.34, 226 n.82, 227 n.10, 230 n.84; and Lao Issara, 63–4, 73–4; and Vietminh, 71, 78; arrest and imprisonment, 107, 108, 219 n.28; escape from prison, 111–12; in coalition government, 96, 99, 100, 101, 123, 128, 158, 159
Supreme People's Assembly, 170, 179, 189, 194, 199, 202, 203
Sûreté Général de l'Indochine, 31, 53
Surinyavongsā, 12–13
Suvanna Phūmā, 3, 5, 63, 76, 100, 102, 103, 104, 110, 112, 116, 118, 121, 131, 138, 145, 146, 164, 170, 217 n.76, 217 n.86, 220 n.45, 221 n.57, 221 n.67, 222 n.5, 224 n.46; and Lao Issara, 64, 71, 74; and Pathēt Lao seizure of power, 161; as prime minister, 76, 87, 89, 104, 123, 133, 135–6; government, 76, 87, 114, 116, 119, 164; in First Coalition, 93–7; in Second Coalition, 125–30, 134; in Third Coalition, 157, 160; in negotiations with Pathēt Lao, 88, 152; in negotiations with the right, 113–15; policies, 93–6, 104, 147–8; propped up by the West, 147–8
Suvannarāt, Prince, 66, 67

'tacit understanding' (US–North Vietnam), 125, 136, 140
Tai, hill/upland, 27, 38, 39, 109, 139, 186, 227 n.7
Taillard, Christian, 130
taxation, 10, 11, 14, 16, 31, 32–3, 34, 37, 44, 50, 51, 76, 148, 211 n.38; agricultural tax, 183; head tax, 32; land tax, 31, 130; rice tax, 176, 223 n.14
Taylor, Maxwell, 126
Thailand, 2, 6, 8, 15, 54, 57, 65, 77, 82, 87, 88, 91, 92, 114, 122, 141, 146, 160, 162, 172, 176, 208; enforces blockade, trade embargo, 114, 178, 183–4, 190; military assistance to Laos, 111, 119, 137, 143, 144; military volunteers in Laos, 129,

Thailand, *contd*
143, 144, 153, 157, 221 n.61, 223 n.23;
relations with Lao regimes, 15, 75, 89,
108, 111, 135, 175, 177, 179, 181, 183–4,
189–90, 198–9, 200, 203–4, (with Lao
Issara) 70–2; security of, 90, 120, 125
Thao Ma, 157, 225 n.66
'thirty-year struggle', 62, 163, 168, 173, 174
Thompson, Virginia, 41
Thongvin Phomvihān, 187
'three revolutions', 169, 182, 187, 194
timber, 50, 154, 185, 192, 196, 204, 206–7,
231 n.101, 231 n.102; *see also* forestry
tin mining, 20, 49–50, 53, 154
tourism, 205–6
Toye, Hugh, 107, 113, 114, 125
trade, 10, 11, 13, 16, 46, 74, 196, 198; terms,
185, 200
transport, 47–9, 50, 91, 101, 154, 183, 204
Treaty of Friendship and Association
(Laos–France), 83
Treaty of Friendship and Cooperation
(Laos–Vietnam), 177
Truman, Harry, 60, 76
Tūbī Līfung, 40, 56, 71

Uan Rāttikun, 145, 147, 214 n.23
Un Xananikôn, 57, 61, 63, 65, 214 n.23
Union of Lao Women, 187, 229 n.54
United Nations, 70, 75, 86, 108, 109, 201;
General Assembly, 130; Security
Council, 190
United Nations Development Program,
192
United Nations High Commissioner for
Refugees, 190
United States, 4, 60, 69, 71, 72, 75, 76, 88,
89–93, 99, 106, 109, 118, 124, 132, 134,
135, 152, 153, 156, 178, 185, 217 n.86, 219
n.29, 222 n.82; advisers in Laos, 106,
108, 111 (*see also* Special Forces, US); aid
to Laos, 68, 90–2, 100–1, 109, 128, 131,
(amount) 109, 153–54, 225 n.56, 226
n.75, (suspension) 103–4, 162, 217 n.85;
and Geneva conferences, 84–5, 89–90,
120, 123; bombing of Laos, 138–42, 222
n.8; citizens in Laos, 92, 158, 161, 223
n.19; controls political agenda in Laos,
92, 147; criticized by Pathēt Lao, 173–4;
Embassy in Laos, 96, 97, 101, 104, 105,
126, 135 136, 138, 154, 162, 220 n.46;
impact on Laos, 154–5, 165; military
assistance: (during First Indochina War)
76, 80, 84, 214 n.32, (to Royal Lao
government) 90, 100, 130, (to neutralists) 127, 129, 131, (suspension)

103–4, 114, 161; missing-in-action, 184,
198; opinion of Suvanna, 115, 121, 220
n.45, 221 n.57; plans for military
intervention in Laos, 121, 221 n.56;
policy towards Laos, 93, 94–5, 96, 97,
119, 120–1, 125, 136, 139; relations with
LPDR, 184, 198, 201; relations with
Royal Lao government, 111, 116;
response to Laos crisis, 119, 122;
support for rightists, 106–7, 110, 113–15,
117, 218 n.14, (withdrawal) 123–4, 146
(*see also* Hmong; Secret Army)
United States Agency for International
Development, 92, 101, 130, 154, 161, 162;
as parallel administration, 154;
demonstrations against, 161–2
United States Congress, Hearing on Laos,
91, 95, 139
United States Information Agency, 90,
173
United States Operations Mission, 90, 91
unity, national, 68, 69, 76, 78, 79, 88, 97, 99,
100, 136, 144, 150, 164, 166, 168
Unkham, 22
urbanization, 75, 155, 165
Ūthong Suvannavong, 67

van Wuysthoff, Gerritt, 13
Vang Pao, 117, 121, 130, 132, 142, 143, 145,
160, 201
Vannaphūm, 37
Viang Chan Agreements, 96, 106, 107, 110,
174
Viang Chan: Kingdom of, 14, 15, 27; city,
battle for, 116–17, 118, 126; character, 44,
132, 156
Vietminh, 57, 60, 61, 62, 63, 64, 65, 68, 70,
71, 72, 74, 75, 80, 85; Lao Issara Military
Convention with, 64; invasions of Laos,
82–4; relations with Pathēt Lao, 78–82
Vietnam, 4, 8, 9, 11, 15, 20, 23, 27, 57, 58,
59, 69, 78, 79, 80, 97, 101, 139, 161, 166,
168, 178, 181, 197, 210 n.14; ambitions in
Laos, 56–7, 148; assistance to Lao Issara,
63–4, 71–3, (to Lao revolution) 78, 81,
83, 99, 160, 171, 175; numbers of troops
in LPDR, 181, 189, 198, 228 n.27;
People's Army, 160; 'People's
Volunteers', 88, 120; relations with
LPDR, 168, 177, 180, 184, 185; *see also*
'special relationship' (Laos–Vietnam)
Vietnam War, *see* Second Indochina War
Vietnam Workers' Party, 81, 104, 219
n.28
Vietnamese Communist Party, 81, 182,
196

Vietnamese in Laos, 29, 46, 47, 50, 53, 57; in French administration, 31, 42, 43, 44; in Garde Indigène (q.v), 29, 31, 44, 210 n.18, 212 n.62; migration to Laos, 45, 51; numbers, 51, 52, 92, 172, 214 n.30, 223 n.19

villages, 31, 46, 75, 77, 81, 100, 131, 132, 141, 155; number, 69

Vixun, 10, 11

Vo Nguyen Giap, 82, 84

Vongsavāng, 164, 170, 177, 227 n.22

women, 41–2, 55, 163, 170, 186, 187, 229 n.53; *see also* gender relations

workers, 94, 100, 106, 130, 194; numbers, 194

World Bank, 184, 189, 208

Xēnō military base, 84, 124, 129

Xētthāthirāt, 12

'yellow rain', 184, 201

Zhou Enlai, 85